BROKEN
GOVERNMENT

Also by John W. Dean

Conservatives Without Conscience

Worse Than Watergate: The Secret Presidency of George W. Bush

Warren G. Harding

Unmasking Deep Throat—History's Most Elusive News Source

The Rehnquist Choice: The Untold Story of the Nixon Appointment
That Redefined the Supreme Court

Lost Honor

Blind Ambition—The White House Years

BROKEN GOVERNMENT

How Republican Rule
Destroyed the Legislative, Executive,
and Judicial Branches

John W. Dean

VIKING

VIKING
Published by the Penguin Group
Penguin Group (USA) Inc., 375 Hudson Street,
New York, New York 10014, U.S.A.
Penguin Group (Canada), 90 Eglinton Avenue East, Suite 700,
Toronto, Ontario, Canada M4P 2Y3 (a division of Pearson Penguin Canada Inc.)
Penguin Books Ltd, 80 Strand, London WC2R 0RL, England
Penguin Ireland, 25 St Stephen's Green, Dublin 2, Ireland
(a division of Penguin Books Ltd)
Penguin Books Australia Ltd, 250 Camberwell Road, Camberwell,
Victoria 3124, Australia (a division of Pearson Australia Group Pty Ltd)
Penguin Books India Pvt Ltd, 11 Community Centre,
Panchsheel Park, New Delhi–110 017, India
Penguin Group (NZ), 67 Apollo Drive, Rosedale, North Shore 0745,
Auckland, New Zealand (a division of Pearson New Zealand Ltd)
Penguin Books (South Africa) (Pty) Ltd, 24 Sturdee Avenue,
Rosebank, Johannesburg 2196, South Africa

Penguin Books Ltd, Registered Offices: 80 Strand, London WC2R 0RL, England

First published in 2007 by Viking Penguin, a member of Penguin Group (USA) Inc.

1 3 5 7 9 10 8 6 4 2

LIBRARY OF CONGRESS CATALOGING-IN-PUBLICATION DATA
Dean, John W. (John Wesley), 1938–
Broken Government: how Republican rule destroyed the legislative,
executive, and judicial branches / John W. Dean
p.   cm.
Includes bibliographical references and index.
ISBN 978-0-670-01820-8
1. United States—Politics and government—2001– 2. Public administration—
United States. 3. Federal government—United States. 4. Conservatism—United States.
5. Republican Party (U.S. : 1854–) I. Title.
JK275.D43 2007
973.931—dc22   2007023127

Printed in the United States of America
Set in Adobe Garamond
Designed by Francesca Belanger

For Franny, Sally, and Molly

*... with the wish that you inherit a nation that is everything
our founders hoped and dreamed it could be ...*

It has been frequently remarked that it seems to have been reserved to the people of this country, by their conduct and example, to decide the important question, whether societies of men are really capable or not of establishing good government from reflection and choice, or whether they are forever destined to depend for their political constitutions on accident and force.

—Alexander Hamilton, *Federalist No. 1*

CONTENTS

PREFACE   xi

INTRODUCTION: **Process Matters**   1

CHAPTER ONE: **First Branch: Broken but Under Repair**   25

CHAPTER TWO: **Second Branch:
   Broken and in Need of Repair**   71

CHAPTER THREE: **Third Branch: Toward the Breaking Point**   119

CHAPTER FOUR: **Repairing Government:
   Restoring the Proper Processes**   175

ACKNOWLEDGMENTS   203

APPENDICES   205

NOTES   253

INDEX   317

PREFACE

This book completes an unplanned trilogy addressing post-Watergate Republican rule in Washington. When I first started to write about problems with the Bush administration I had no idea they would keep growing. As they continued, so has my writing. While working on the prior two books, *Worse Than Watergate: The Secret Presidency of George W. Bush* (2004) and *Conservatives Without Conscience* (2006), it became clear, at least to me, that Republicans had learned little about abusing power in the ways that ultimately destroyed the Nixon presidency. Given my familiarity with that now mostly forgotten history, I find it astonishing that the Republican party has actively incorporated such an undemocratic mentality into its governing philosophy, and in the process turned once conventional conservative thinking about congressional, presidential, and judicial powers upside down, and then sideways. More strikingly, it has gotten away with it, although it seems a reckoning may finally have come.

In the pages that follow, drawing on findings of my earlier works but viewing their subject matter in a far broader context, I examine the troubling consequences of this new "Republican" way of thinking. It has been new on Capitol Hill since about 1997, about three years after the GOP regained control of the House; it has been new to the White House since 2001, with the arrival of George W. Bush and Richard B.

Cheney, although its roots first emerged during the Nixon presidency and began blossoming in the Reagan and Bush Senior years. This is not a how-to book, nor is it prescriptive, but rather a heads-up account about the way Republicans behave when in power. Rational-thinking Americans should hope that the 2008 presidential election confronts the need to repair the government, rather than adopts agendas or selects candidates bound to produce more damage. It is that hope that prompted my writing this book at this time, and I plan to do as much as I can to raise awareness of these issues with voters and candidates, for they simply cannot be ignored.

In *Worse Than Watergate* I pointed out striking parallels between Bush's governing style and Nixon's, focusing particularly on the use of excessive and unnecessary secrecy by both presidencies, along with the resulting consequences. Given my involvement in Nixon's presidency, not to mention its undoing with Watergate, I recognized early in the Bush administration exactly the same mind-set that had caused such havoc thirty years earlier. I had no doubt that this mentality would result in a calamity of some sort—which, in fact, it has done. Asserting then that Bush's presidency was *worse* than Nixon's has proven, in any case, to be an understatement, for in fact it has proven to be *much, much worse.* Suffice it to say that no one died, nor was anyone tortured, because of Nixon's so-called Watergate abuses of power.

In *Conservatives Without Conscience* I sought to explain the reasons why conservatives govern as they do—callously and ruthlessly—and why loyal conservative followers are so compliant with the wishes of their leaders. I focused my study on the conservative disposition in the Republican-controlled Congress, along with that in the conservative rank and file of the Grand Old Party, all of whom acquiesced in Bush and Cheney's actions, regardless of how offensive they were to their own core beliefs. Social scientists, I discovered, have been studying such compliant followers (as well as aggressive and dominating leaders) for decades, whom they call "authoritarians." Surprisingly, studies of authoritarianism, which are based on a half century of empirical testing, had not been presented for general readers. Accordingly, with the assistance of Bob Altemeyer, one of the leading researchers in the field, I explored this research in *Conservatives Without Conscience*—delving into the dark side of conservatism. For example, social scientists have found, based on anonymous responses from tens of thousands of people, that authoritarians are "enemies of freedom, antidemocratic, anti-equality, highly prejudiced, mean-spirited, power hungry, Machiavellian, and amoral"—to mention only a few of their troubling traits, all of which are contributing to the breakdown of our democratic system.

This book completes the analysis I began in those previous works by examining the operations of all branches of the federal government, as set forth in the Constitution: legislative, executive, and judicial, which are commonly referred to by their placement in Articles I through III as the first through third branches. More to the point, I wish to argue that they have failed to function properly under the control of the Republican Party's current governing philosophy. I have also sought to answer several basic questions that have been asked repeatedly by my readers—questions that I could not, at the time, satisfactorily answer.* Many wanted to know specifically what damage, if any, Bush, Cheney, and the Republican Congress—and other "conservatives without conscience"—have done to our government. Have they broken the system? Others asked what, if anything, they could do. Where should they focus their attention? Could an average citizen make a difference? To find reliable answers, I again searched for the best scholarly and professional political advice, and I've reported what I found in the following pages.

While *Broken Government* draws on my earlier works, it is not necessary to have read them to understand the argument I present here. For example, the excessive secrecy of the Bush administration, and the

---

*Some questions were posed during question-and-answer sessions during which I had the opportunity to visit with readers; others were raised in letters. Regrettably, I am unable to respond to all the mail I receive—it is actually overwhelming at times. While I do read it all, there are not enough hours in each day to answer it personally, nor do I have the staff to handle it. I feel considerable guilt in not being able to reply to many of the thoughtful letters, but I hope this book answers many of the recurring questions.

fact that Congress and the federal courts have tolerated it, is compelling evidence of broken government, but because this information is featured in *Worse Than Watergate* I have not repeated here, although I have occasionally incorporated it by reference. Throughout the following pages I refer to "authoritarian conservatives" —the focus of *Conservatives Without Conscience*—but I have done so in a way that the use of the term is self-explanatory.

I described *Worse Than Watergate* as a polemic, for it was precisely that in the tone of its arguments against the Bush II administration. When it became apparent how Republicans ruled when they controlled all three branches of the federal government, I wrote *Conservatives Without Conscience*—this time, not as a polemic, but as an analysis of what had become of modern conservatism since authoritarianism had come to dominate the conservative movement. *Broken Government* is both a polemic and an analysis, for I believe something must be done about the negative impact that Republican control has had on the federal government. Although I will be accused by my former compatriots of having become a partisan for their enemies, that is not the case. Those who will attack me have a vested interest in Republicans remaining in power. I have no such interest, for either party. My only concern is about the well-being of our government, which actually performs best when it is employed on behalf of the public. Today, any objective observer must conclude that it is the Democrats who—while they certainly enjoy power—have the needs of the public at the top of their agenda. Republicans, on the other hand, have become the party of special interests. Republicans seem to think that if their desires are satisfied, everyone will benefit. Unfortunately, it does not work that way. Republicans have sought to reshape the federal government in a manner that best suits them, and in so doing they appear determined to destroy it branch by branch.

In the chapters that follow I have made no effort to collect, and catalog, everything that has gone wrong under Republican rule, for to do so would require many volumes. Instead I have elected to examine vital fault lines underlying each branch in order to gauge where government operations have slipped from their constitutional foundations, to determine what (and who) caused it, and to determine if there has been structural damage. As I explain in the introduction, I have further narrowed my examination to those breakdowns in the system that significantly affect the lives of all Americans. Chapter 1 collects a broad cross section of well-informed views about the legislative branch under GOP rule; Chapter 2 explores how post-Watergate Republican rule has culminated in the Bush White House, hell-bent on expanding presidential power endlessly; and Chapter 3 explores the concerted efforts by Republicans to accomplish their goals through the judicial branch, working from the Supreme Court down, because they cannot achieve their aims democratically. Their actions have brought the federal judiciary to its tipping point. Finally, in Chapter 4, I set forth what should and can be done to fix the damage and restore the government. Because not everything I felt needed to be known or said about the operations of Congress and the particular abuse of power that has become the favorite of Republican presidents—the power of war and peace—fit into their respective chapters, so I have also included several appendices, where I have outlined in nontechnical and broad terms information about the separation of powers, the appropriation process, and the dubious legal legerdemain being relied upon by contemporary conservative Republicans to take the American presidency far beyond Nixon's "imperial presidency," a concept that was rejected by Americans long ago.

This is not a book about policy; rather, it is a book about the often ignored processes of the federal government. Candidates for federal office almost never discuss process, under the mistaken belief that no one much cares about it. In the pages that follow I will show that we ignore process at our peril and will advocate far more attention to be paid to government process, for the simple reason that good policy follows from well-functioning processes. In fact, given the Republicans' efforts to redesign the federal system, if process is ignored much longer the government our Founders established—a system built on separations of powers, with checks and balances—will vanish, and in its place will be the modern Republican conservative philosophy that can be described as autocratic presidentialism—although the Republicans themselves use much more innocuous terms, like "unilateralism" and "unitary executive theory."

Political pundits and commentators dismiss "process issues" by claiming they are of no interest to Americans. They are wrong, as I will show. Today, in Washington, process is the name of the game, and those who do not understand this fact are operating in ignorance. Political observers who disregard process are missing the real action, and voters who do not make an effort to understand process matters will remain uninformed.

Myriad operational problems are apparent to anyone who follows government in Washington as closely as I have for years. Rather than merely collecting everything I believe to be amiss, however, I have also sought to gather the thinking of others who study government. I have examined the work of countless political scientists, economists, lawyers, psychologists, sociologists, and other specialists and experts, men and women of all political persuasions, who have studied the institutions of our government and analyzed its workings. In addition, I have spoken with a number of old pros who have been observing the workings of the government as long as I, and far more closely the branch or branches of government that are of professional interest to them. Finally, I have examined the work of experienced journalists who know their way around Washington and have attempted to call attention to many problems as well.

As I suggested, it is not happenstance that I am publishing this book before the 2008 presidential election. Regardless of whom the Democrats and Republicans select as their nominees, or if a viable third-party candidate emerges, I do not believe the problems created by a broken government can be overlooked, although it has become the new norm to do just that. Fixing the compromised processes should be a priority. If this book is hard on Republicans, it is because they have demonstrated during the past several decades a remarkable incapacity to govern at the national level and should accordingly be held responsible for the damage they have done to democracy. In fact, as currently constituted, I do not believe the Republican Party can be trusted with control of the national government, not because of its policies (many of which I confess to favoring) but rather because of its philosophical disposition toward the processes of government, which they so easily abuse in their pursuit and exercise of power. Their thinking has proven ruinous.

It is good form for an author to state his or her biases and disposition, and those who have read *Conservatives Without Conscience* know that I consider myself a Goldwater conservative on many issues, but I have rejected the authoritarianism of contemporary conservatism. As a California voter, I have not registered as affiliated with any political party and, when voting, pay little attention to party labels. For polling purposes I respond that I am an independent. By nature, I am optimistic. Not of the Pollyanna school, but hopeful that humankind can learn to use its powers of reasoning. To temper my glass-half-full view, however, I try to regularly take doses of reality, and no one dispenses that medicine better than MIT linguistics professor and philosopher Noam Chomsky, who has recently reminded us that the survival of our species is no sure thing.

Biology teaches that we are the only species with the intelligence essential to establishing civilization (which, of course, is evidenced by a high level of cultural and social organization, accompanied by sophisticated systems of government) as Chomsky wrote in *Hegemony or Survival: America's Quest for Global Dominance* (2003). He explained that biologists estimate that about fifty billion life-forms have existed on our planet, and an "average life expectancy of a species is about 100,000 years." He posed the rather fundamental question of whether our intelligence will distinguish our species, or are we mere "biological errors" that can think and use our allotted 100,000 years to destroy our species as well as much else.[1]

There is not the slightest doubt that our species, if not our planet, will only survive if we use the gift of our intelligence wisely. Modern civilization, of which government is such an integral element, can be maintained only when those governments further the well-being of our species as a whole, and not merely individual nations, states, and tribes. My bias and my interest are tied to a belief that no people yet has conceived of a fundamentally better national system of government than that which our Founders bequeathed Americans (and the world). While it is not perfect, it is doubtful that perfection exists. There is no certain method to guarantee the survival of our species, but there are many ways to hasten its demise, and high on that list is selfish, self-righteous, and self-interested government promoted by the authoritarian conservatives who now control the Grand Old Party, and have given us broken government.

BROKEN GOVERNMENT

INTRODUCTION

Process Matters

Overwhelming numbers of Americans—three out of every four—believe that their government in Washington is broken. Poll data revealing this fact was published by CNN shortly before the 2006 midterm elections. Quite likely, this information helped the Democrats, since at that time the Republicans controlled all three branches of the federal government. In the coming chapters, I'll provide support to show that the American people are absolutely correct in their conclusion, although with all due respect to the wisdom of crowds, I am not sure many of them can explain precisely how the system got broken, which parts are not working, and why. The situation is one, rather, that they sense and intuitively understand. Most Americans, in fact, do not pay close attention to government and politics.*

My former tribe—the Republican Party—has its fingerprints all over the rubble and wreckage scattered about the federal landscape, not to mention the failed, flawed, and deeply dysfunctional efforts to govern

---

*For example, "[L]ess than a third of Americans know that a member of the House serves for two years or that a senator serves for six. In 2000, only 55 percent knew the Republicans were the majority party in the House. Just two years after he had presided at the Clinton impeachment trial in the Senate, only 11 percent could identify William Rehnquist as Chief Justice of the United States." Jacob S. Hacker and Paul Pierson, *Off Center: The Republican Revolution and the Erosion of American Democracy* (New Haven, Conn.: Yale University Press, 2005), 164.

that produced the mess. Republicans do not actually govern but rule the various branches of government when they control them. They soon will have controlled the executive branch for all but twelve of the last forty years. During these four decades Republican presidents have appointed some of their most conservative supporters, increasingly those at the hard right-wing of the party, to the majority of the judgeships of the federal judiciary, working assiduously to tilt the federal judiciary to the right, and bringing it to a dangerous point. When conservative Republicans have controlled part, or all, of Capitol Hill, they have consistently demonstrated that they seek to run the government only for those who share their beliefs, not for all Americans.

All these years of Republican rule have had a profoundly negative impact on the federal system, literally destroying many of the government's operations. Although voters did deny them control of Congress in 2006, Democrats have not really pressed the case against them that should be made, and based on recent history, they may never do so. (It seems more likely that responsible and disgusted Republicans— or former Republicans who now call themselves independents—will be the ones to start calling their former compatriots to task. But the expatriated Republicans are few in number, although their ranks are growing.)

Despite being the majority party, Democrats have become afflicted with what one Washington reporter (CNN's Candy Crowley) calls "the wuss factor"—meaning the lack of intestinal fortitude needed to go toe-to-toe, nose-to-nose with Republican miscreants, most of whom are well known for their nastiness and unwillingness to take responsibility for anything. Too many Democrats have avoided matters relating to Republicans' bending or manipulating government processes until they are broken. It is not that they are not deeply troubled by what they see the GOP doing, but they have dismissed these activities as "process issues." Conventional wisdom within the Washington Beltway supports their thinking. It is said that no one cares about process issues, so they have become unpopular with the Washington press corps;

political consultants, who now run most campaigns; and ultimately candidates.

Such received attitudes about process are, in fact, dead wrong. Hard data shows that people do care about process, and they are particularly interested in processes relating to the fundamental operations of their system of government. It is past time to set the record straight on the topic, because broken government is just such a process issue, and it is a serious problem that it would be foolhardy, irresponsible, and wrong to ignore.

News Media Aversion to Political Process Issues

What exactly is process in the context of government and politics? *Safire's New Political Dictionary* defined it as "the majesty of the machinery; the inexorable procedures of government; more broadly, the American way of self-government."* Safire reported that the term came into vogue in the mid-1970s as a short form of both "the democratic process" and the "decision-making process," and he provided examples of its use. "Now that he has had a year's experience," Vice President Mondale said of President Jimmy Carter's first year in office, "he has seen how the process works first hand." Safire also quoted an aide to then California governor Jerry Brown as saying the governor drove people nuts when he quoted Gandhi on the subject: "The means are the ends in process."[1] Governor Brown, however, makes a good point.

Democracy is a process whose unique, fundamental elements are set forth in our Constitution: representative government, co-equal branches, bicameralism, separations of powers, checks and balances, and

---

*The *American Heritage Dictionary* more broadly defines process as "a system of operations in the production of something," and "a series of actions, changes, or functions that bring about an end or result." Synonyms for process include: procedure, method, practice, actions, proceedings, and means.

the sharing of power among and between the government's branches as well as state governments. Rules that regulate the proceedings of the U.S. House of Representatives and the U.S. Senate relate to process. Lobbying is a process. Broadly speaking, process is also what produces policy. The line between process and policy can, at times, be fuzzy and indistinct. While "reforming" government programs like taxes, social security, and health care have process implications, at heart they are matters of policy. To make matters even more confusing, a given position on a particular process can become a policy. For example, it was the policy of the House Republicans when they controlled Congress to be in session only two days a week. It is now the policy of the Democrats to meet five days a week. Issues like term limits and campaign finance reform and presidential nominations subject to the "advice and consent" of the Senate are considered process, but the position that the Republicans or Democrats may take on these processes can make them represent policy. While bright line distinctions are difficult to draw, for the purposes of this discussion no such effort is necessary.

Process is important, however, and too often it is used as a reason to dispose of the underlying issues relating to government operations and political activities. Politicians, pundits, and other political players now more than ever regularly dismiss process matters, like those associated with broken government, as irrelevant. Within the Washington news media community there has been a growing distaste for process, which may explain why political consultants, and in turn candidates, now reject process topics as valid campaign issues.[2] David Corn, the Washington editor of *The Nation,* explained the typical reaction in a column discussing Senate Democrats' charging Senate Republicans with "unfairly rigging the game" on judicial nominations. Although Senate Republicans had regularly blocked nominees sent to the Senate by Democratic president Bill Clinton (often not even giving them a hearing), these same Senate Republicans attacked Democrats for blocking President Bush's nominees. This process issue, which at the time threatened a near procedural meltdown of the U.S. Senate over the uses and abuses of the filibuster in response to judicial nominations, was, however, considered of little general interest. As Corn reported, the matter raised "what political consultants call a 'process issue,' and the conventional rule in politics is that 'process issues' rarely resonate with large blocs of voters beyond those base-voters already engaged in such things."[3] Another example of this attitude was expressed by Washington political analyst and senior writer for *U.S. News & World Report*, Michael Barone, who, when commenting on the procedural battles between Senate Republicans and Democrats over judicial nominees, dismissed them as "process issues," adding, "One of my rules of life is that all process arguments are insincere."[4]

Time magazine political columnist Joe Klein similarly slighted process, describing then ABC News anchor Ted Koppel's questions during a 2004 New Hampshire debate among Democratic presidential contenders as "kind of silly" because "there were all these questions about process."[5] A few months later, on NBC's *Meet the Press*, Klein observed, "I think that Howard Dean's campaign started drifting down a little bit when he began to emphasize the kind of process issues."[6] In his book *Politics Lost: How American Democracy Was Trivialized by People Who Think You're Stupid* (2006), Klein lamented news coverage relating to the "process of politics," particularly when it involves "horse-race" coverage of matters like "the cross-tabs, the buys, the ground war, the weird fetish of numeric expectations ('If Edwards can stay within ten points of Kerry, he will blah-blah-blah') ... , as opposed to the qualities of candidates."[7]

Fred Barnes, executive editor of the *Weekly Standard*, the Washington-based neoconservative journal of opinion and a regular on Fox News, frequently discusses process, a topic he, too, usually slights. When Vice President Dick Cheney refused to provide what was then known as the General Accounting Office with information about his secret meetings with energy executives to formulate the nation's energy policy, a number of pundits criticized Cheney's intransigence "as the biggest political blunder of the year." Barnes, however, minimized it as a process issue: "People don't care about process issues. That's why they never cared about the deficit, even during the Reagan years, when the deficits were actually very large."[8] When President Bush refused to permit his newly appointed assistant for Homeland Security, Tom Ridge, to testify before Congress because he was then on the White House staff, many in Washington thought it unwise politics. For Barnes, again, it was merely "a pure process issue that really excites people in Washington, but nowhere else."[9] Barnes likewise considered Howard Dean's lack of experience in foreign affairs "a process issue," and dismissed it;[10] after being shown a clip of Howard Dean saying in 2000 that the Iowa presidential caucus system was "dominated by the special interests on both sides," and then a clip of Dean claiming in early 2004, when running for president, that he had changed his mind about Iowa, Barnes characterized the flip-flop as merely "a process issue."[11]

Not all process issues are dismissed so cavalierly by the Beltway Boys. David Carney, a political consultant and longtime Republican operative who works both inside the Beltway and out, has observed that "only Washington insiders care ... deeply about 'process issues' like campaign-finance reform."[12] Fred Barnes would agree, but the subject of campaign finance may be an exception. When Senator Mitch Mc-Connell (R-KY) announced that he would go to court—and he did go all the way to the Supreme Court—to contest the constitutionality of the McCain-Feingold campaign finance reform law, saying that he had hired former solicitor general, federal judge, and independent counsel Ken Starr to represent him, Barnes was thrilled. "I usually dump on process issues, and this is a process issue, but this is an important one," Barnes declared.[13] Typically, though, contemporary political journalism's aversion to reporting about process matters—which thankfully is not shared by all political journalists*—runs right to the top of the journalism establishment, where there is a great aversion to reporting

---

*Some of the best political journalists today address the workings of government: Thomas Ricks (*Fiasco: The American Military Adventure in Iraq*), James Risen (*State of War: The Secret History of the CIA and the Bush Administration*), Ron Suskind (*The Price of Loyalty* and *The One Percent Doctrine*), and Bob Woodward (*Bush at War* and *State of Denial*).

inside baseball–type stories. (*Safire's Political Dictionary* defines "inside baseball" coverage as relating to "specialized or private knowledge; the minute political details savored by those in-the-know, found boring by most others.") A study by the Pew Research Center for the People and the Press found that most Americans were more interested in a presidential candidate's character qualities than positions on issues.[14] Based on this influential report (which did not examine whether Americans were interested in process versus policy), journalists were advised by the Project for Excellence in Journalism (PEJ) to steer clear of "inside baseball" and "tactical" coverage of politics.[15] What is ironic about the Beltway insiders' avoidance of process reporting, and the advice of PEJ, is that it seems to have fallen on deaf ears. While politicians and pundits may try to steer clear of the subject, process remains; in fact, it is the mainstay of political reporting.

There are few empirical studies of news media that analyze process versus policy coverage of government and politics, but one recent investigation examined such coverage of Congress. Political scientists Jonathan Morris and Rosalee Clawson surveyed over twenty-six hundred congressional news stories from the *New York Times* and *CBS Evening News* for the period 1990 through 1998. They found that 95 percent of the *New York Times* stories, and 87 percent of the *Evening News* stories, "mentioned one or more aspects of the legislative process." In particular, this journalism, while often arising in relation to policy matters, focused on legislative maneuvering, conflicts between the Republicans and Democrats, and conflicts between Congress and the president, as well as on compromises made and accommodations reached. Stories of "scandal and personality [were] comparatively infrequent."[16] Based on my own crude content analysis (the study of news coverage of politics based on over a hundred LexisNexis transcripts for the week following the November 4, 2006, elections, and then for the first week that the 110th Congress was convened in January 2007), it appears that newspapers like the *New York Times,* the *Los Angeles Times,* and the *Washington Post* (which supply most of the grist for the political blogs) provide a steady stream of process-related stories with enough internal tactical information to clog the Project for Excellence in Journalism's content-coding system perpetually. The ratings of network television news, however, have been steadily decreasing, and those shows reach a larger audience than the lead newspapers. Cable news, however—when not infatuated with a missing white female child, Anna Nicole Smith, Paris Hilton, or a gruesome crime of the moment—will address process issues. Bloggers, too, love process.

Given that there is no shortage of attention to process in the media, why have candidates for national office, particularly Democrats, avoided this issue in recent campaigns?

Candidate Rejection of Process Issues

When writing about the excessive secrecy of the Bush administration in *Worse Than Watergate,* I believed I was discussing a subject that would prove to be a serious issue in the upcoming 2004 presidential campaign. I was confident that President Bush's Democratic opponent would seek to hold him accountable for his baseless and troubling behavior. Admittedly, I had not taken into consideration the increasing distaste for process in the Washington press crops, but rather based my thinking on the fact that process had been an important topic in past presidential races, and had been spelled out in great detail in both Democratic and Republican party platforms.

Inexplicably, in 2004, the Democratic Party at the national level chose to totally ignore process matters. For the first time ever it did not mention a single process matter in its platform, which is quite remarkable given the fact the Bush/Cheney administration had provided them a long list of activities that should have been called to the attention of voters.* Like his party, or because he so instructed them, Senator

*Throughout this book (as with my prior books) I refer to the "Bush/Cheney" administration or presidency because after six-plus years of studying this presidency, I cannot determine any significant break between the two men on this issue, and

John Kerry was silent on process as well; its absence was stunning and conspicuous. The day before the nation went to the polls, a member of the *New York Times* editorial board expressed her personal dismay that Kerry had given Bush a pass on his secrecy. In her bylined editorial, "Psst. President Bush Is Hard at Work Expanding Government Secrecy," Dorothy Samuels confessed "to feeling disappointed over Senator John Kerry's failure to home in hard on one of the more worrisome domestic policy developments of the past four years—namely the Bush administration's drastic expansion of needless government secrecy."[17]

When writing a postelection chapter for the paperback edition of *Worse Than Watergate,* I specifically asked a number of Democrats, as well as individuals who headed Kerry's presidential campaign, about their silence on this matter. I received the same answer from everyone: Secrecy is "a process issue," which they were convinced interests no voters. A year later, when researching *Conservatives Without Conscience,* I discovered that the editor of *The American Prospect,* Robert Kuttner, had been told by Democrats that they were reluctant to criticize the Republicans' stunningly antidemocratic behavior in operating the House of Representatives. "Democrats are ambivalent about taking this issue to the country or to the press because many are convinced that nobody cares about 'process' issues," Kuttner reported.[18]

Both Democrats and Republicans once held process matters significant enough to consistently make them major planks in their respective party presidential platforms. Comparing the process language found in their respective platforms from 1960 to 2004 (see word counts in the footnote), we see that Democrats devoted a rough total of 15,104 words in their platform planks to process issues; over the same period Republicans devoted almost double that amount; or, 24,056 words.* These planks dealt with every conceivable aspect of government operations.[19] Although the degree of attention to this area fluctuated, never before 2004 had one

---

they have operated since before the 2000 campaign as a partnership and team. Given Cheney's influence, it is the most accurate way to characterize this presidency.

*Words counts devoted to process issues in the parties' platforms by year. See p. 10.

party given, without explanation, the other a complete pass on process-related matters. If this was inadvertent, which is doubtful, it can be corrected; if someone has specifically advised the Democratic Party to avoid process issues, as the quotes above indicate, this was bad guidance.

Thankfully, not all Democratic candidates ignore process. For example, Congresswoman Jan Schakowsky, who represents Evanston, Illinois, publicly criticized the GOP for running an undemocratic House, addressing the subject early in the 2004 campaign. "The process," she told a reporter, "particularly in the House, has been one of systematically shutting out debate and democratic procedures" and, by extension, shutting out the voices of millions of Americans.[20] When interviewed on a Chicago radio show in November 2005, the congresswoman told the host, "You know, this is a story where, you know—*we don't gripe that much about process questions*" (emphasis added), a statement that no doubt reflected the official position of the House Democratic leadership. But having made the point that she was not griping, she proceeded to lodge a very legitimate complaint: "You have to understand that the democratic processes in the House of Representatives have literally been shut down. We have closed rules where we can't offer amendments. People are indeed locked out of conference committees.

YEAR	DEMOCRATS	REPUBLICANS
1960	731	566
1964	285	405
1968	630	672
1972	2,665	1,057
1976	3,591	2,395
1980	2,631	3,994
1984	850	1990
1988	190	2,514
1992	847	2,887
1996	1,396	3,924
2000	1,288	2,449
2004	None	1,203
Total	15,104	24,056

Debate is limited to be very brief on either side. A fifteen-minute vote becomes a three-hour vote while they persuade people, or bribe people, and there was the allegation of having offered a bribe on the floor of the House." Unfortunately, the host cut her off before she laid out a complete list of abuses of process that Republicans had inflicted on the House Democrats.[21] Ms. Schakowsky, now a member of the House Democratic leadership, has not forgotten that "under the Republican House leadership, the reality was that Democrats were shut out of the process." On November 13, 2006, she assured her constituents that it would be different under the control of the Democrats. "Nancy Pelosi has pledged not only a new direction for our country, but a new way of doing business in the Congress. The American people want us to actually get things done and work together. That is our intention and, hopefully, that of the Republican minority."[22] Democrats have since gone about the job of repairing the damage done by twelve years of ruthlessly partisan Republican rule of the House.

Events can occasionally force process issues to the attention of the voters—typically, when they have become problems that are so serious that they cannot be ignored. This occurred in a number of the 2006 midterm elections campaigns, which raised process matters such as fiscal deficits; two-day workweeks for Congress; failure to protect underage congressional pages from the sexual advances of Florida Republican representative Mark Foley; corruption and influence peddling by GOP lobbyist Jack Abramoff; as well as the Bush administration's use of fear politics, incompetence in handling the Iraq war and the disaster accompanying Hurricane Katrina, gratuitous expansion of presidential powers, electronic spying on Americans without warrants, and special legislation to force the federal courts into the private family tragedy of Terri Schiavo (even though Florida courts had determined she was in a persistent vegetative state) and then attacking federal judges when they failed to reverse the Florida court's handling of it, and the like. In fact, these very issues were used by CNN to introduce an investigative report on broken government.

CNN Presented Broken Government as a Process Issue

Leading up to the November 7, 2006, midterm election, CNN broad-cast a multipart series entitled "Broken Government." On a Web site devoted to the series the network described it as an examination of "all branches of government" to explore "how much of the system may be broken beyond repair."* These programs initially struck me as being about as blunt, and negative, as it gets in the mainstream news media. As the series progressed, however, I realized CNN was not offering its own assessment based on independent inquiry, but rather was reporting Americans' beliefs about the situation. The hard news of the series was the fact that overwhelming numbers of the country's citizens acknowl-edged that Washington was out of order.

CNN's growling curmudgeon-in-residence, Jack Cafferty, opened the series on October 19 by pulling no punches. "It's my fervent hope that every single incumbent on the ballot will lose. It's time to start over," he declared. To justify his fervent hope Cafferty cited poll num-bers: 68 percent of the nation said the country was going in the wrong direction; 64 percent opposed the war in Iraq; 61 percent disapproved of the job President Bush was doing. "And then there's Congress," he sneered, "a joke." And he added, "Seventy-one percent disapprove of the job Congress is doing. The other, what is it, twenty-nine percent, they just haven't read the paper. Our government is broken, and Con-gress has failed to do anything meaningful." All this data did not neces-sarily mean, however, that the government was broken beyond repair. To get more specific, Cafferty explained: "We sent crews around the country to find out what you think about all this, and here's some of what's on your mind."

These "people on the street" interviews were revealing, even though they, too, were quite general. The first video clip featured a man who

*See "Broken Government" at www.cnn.com/CNN/Programs/broken.govern ment/.

said that "our elected officials act like a bunch of second-graders; and that's not even fair, second-graders have better discourse in the class-room than our representatives do." Next a woman questioned the usefulness of Congress "when they can't do anything, . . . you know, bipartisanship." Then came two more interviews with men, one say-ing that if the political parties were not broken, "they're in bad shape," and the other adding, "I don't think [government officials are] doing a good job [because] they're not listening to people, they have their own agenda; and they're not working as hard as they should be." Not one person complained about policy; rather, they all focused on various processes of government, the way it was failing to work.

Most Americans, CNN reported, have concluded that our system of government is broken. It posted two polls to support that conten-tion. The first—which was completely unscientific but informative—reflected an ongoing vote by people who visited CNN's Web site. By a steady 9 to 1 ratio, respondents agreed with the statement "the po-litical system is broken," with almost twenty thousand people voting. Far more devastating, CNN published a national poll conducted by the Opinion Research Corporation between October 13 and 15 that asked Americans whether they agreed or disagreed with the statement: "Our system of government is broken *and cannot be fixed.*" (Emphasis added.) A startling 71 percent agreed, another 7 percent felt that, while the government was "seriously flawed," it could be fixed.[23] These num-bers are alarming for several reasons. First, they are so much worse than the data regarding lack of trust in government by Americans, which were bad enough.* Second, aside from CNN's raising the subject, and reporting its data, there has been virtually no media attention what-

---

*Data that has been collected over the course of several years generally dem-onstrates that a majority of Americans have either "a great deal" or at least "some" trust in the federal government. For example, a Gallup poll in September 2006 showed 15 percent had a "great deal" and 31 percent had a "fair amount" of trust and confidence in the president and executive branch; 15 percent had a "great deal" and 54 percent had a "fair amount" of trust and confidence in the judicial branch and Supreme Court; and 6 percent had a "great deal" and 50 percent had a

soever calling attention to the fact that (or claiming that) the federal government is broken—ever.* This lack of confidence did not develop suddenly. As is often the case Americans were and are far ahead of their leaders, and instinctively understand when their national government is not functioning.

The CNN series garnered solid audiences.[24] It was a gutsy effort, one that required considerable corporate fortitude by TimeWarner to broadcast, not to mention their aggressive promotion of the series, with its blunt title. Most of the negative reaction, as it happened, came from the right side of the blogosphere.[25] The only comment from the mainstream news media occurred in response to the dustup that occurred when Dick Cheney's wife took CNN to task for the series. Second Lady Lynne Cheney thought the programs biased, beginning with the title. She also claimed that CNN was "following a Democratic Party line." (Democrats, as noted, did not raise the issue of "broken government" during the 2006 midterm campaigns.) Mrs. Cheney insisted that the reporting included "terrible distortions of the president's and vice president's positions on many issues."[26] (She was vague about these distortions, and showed remarkable denial, or blind hubris, by asserting that the CNN series was off base for being critical of the administration's response to Hurricane Katrina.)

The information assembled by the CNN series did not, in fact, support the conclusion that our system of government is broken beyond repair. But CNN did not structure the programs to prove that point,

---

"fair amount" of trust and confidence in the legislative branch. See "Major Institution," PollingReport.com at www.pollingreport.com/institut.htm.

*A check of the record for the past ten years in LexisNexis and several other databases with national archives of news media coverage revealed only one commentator writing about "broken government" at the federal level: Harlan Ullman, a former naval officer, a senior associate at the Center for Strategic and International Studies, and a columnist for the *Washington Times*. Mr. Ullman also published a book that makes broad charges about dysfunctional government. The author is also unhappy with the structure of the Constitution itself, not to mention operations under it.

for they were not intended as a polemic. By and large viewers were left to draw their own conclusions regarding the functioning of the national government. The network provided information voters wanted, even when candidates ignored it.

Why Political Process Matters

In groundbreaking studies little noticed outside the political science academic community, University of Nebraska (Lincoln) political scientists John R. Hibbing and Elizabeth Theiss-Morse have examined the question of how Americans feel about process. In doing so, they challenged accepted truths about process, although that was not the reason for their research. Nonetheless, they found that for a significant percentage of Americans process is more important than any other factor in their consideration of government and politics. In their books *Congress as Public Enemy: Public Attitudes Toward American Political Institutions* (1995) and *Stealth Democracy: Americans' Beliefs about How Government Should Work* (2002), and in a number of related papers presented at scholarly conferences and published in professional journals, they have demonstrated the significance of process to Americans.[27] "Political scientists have all but ignored the study of process," Hibbing and Theiss-Morse wrote, explaining that their professional peers, when studying voting and why people vote as they do, or not vote at all, they have focused on "candidate image, issue, and party."[28] Their research was not directed at establishing the concept of a broken government, yet their findings about process help understand it, as well as what can and cannot be done to fix it.

In their research on public attitudes of Americans toward government institutions (like the Congress, the presidency, and the Supreme Court), Hibbing and Theiss-Morse gathered information from "more than 1,400 thirty-minute telephone interviews with a nationwide sample of voting-age residents," plus "eight two-hour focus-group sessions conducted at locales across the country and consisting of approximately ten participants each."[29] They were taken aback by what they discovered. They had assumed, as do most political scientists, that Americans are "confused by governmental processes while retaining at least a few clear policy desires."[30] In fact, they had it backward: People do not find process complicated, but rather find policy to be so. Their research revealed that Americans are "influenced at least as much by the processes employed in the political system as by the particular outputs emanating from the process." They offered a striking example in public disgust with Congress after the Anita Hill–Clarence Thomas hearings. While very few Americans cared whether or not Thomas was confirmed for the Supreme Court, they did have very clear negative feelings about "the process leading to that decision: the way things looked; the way the hearings were run and how they unfolded; and the institution's [referring to the Senate's] structure, rules, and norms."[31] In short, Hibbing and Theiss-Morse discovered that average Americans have no trouble whatsoever judging institutions of government by how their key processes are carried out.[32] Process "is what they relate to," because most people "have understandable difficulties comprehending the substantive complexities of [policy] issues," while they "often have a gut reaction to process."[33]

Needless to say, these studies also found that process is not for everyone. For example, Hibbing and Theiss-Morse found that of the 1,433 people in their survey just over half, 53 percent, were inclined to view politics and government through one of three well-known political propensities (or inclination by which the public perceives these activities in the public square): people, party affiliation, policy, or process. More specifically, within the 53 percent they found the following breakdown of propensities: 10 percent viewed politics primarily by the people or person involved; 5 percent looked first at the party involved; 25 percent were primarily interested in policy; and 14 percent viewed politics and government by looking first at process.* Within the group that

---

*This subject is addressed in greater detail in chapter 4 at pages 179–89. I make the point here merely to note that significant numbers of people are primarily if not exclusively interested in process.

had a process propensity, which is of particular interest to me, they reported that 31 percent of their respondents interested in process were Democrats, 43 percent were independents, and 27 percent were Republicans.* Most important, 74 percent of the process-oriented group was politically active.[34] Not only are these the people that candidates should want to reach, but they are also news and information consumers whom journalists should not ignore, as well as a ready audience for bloggers who will give them what the mainstream news will not. By my reading of this data, process issues are important to not less than 20 million voters. As I will explain, such issues should be important to all voters.

It is difficult to imagine a more cricital process issue than whether our system of government is broken beyond repair. By way of further introduction, however, a brief note about the outlook of contemporary conservative Republicans may help set the stage to view what they have done to the processes of the three branches.

Republican Governing Philosophy

Leaders of the current Republican Party have shown that they have mastered the art of winning elections, notwithstanding a few miscalculations about 2006. Democrats did not exactly beat Republicans that year, but instead did a superb job of running aggressive campaigns, which placed them in a perfect position once Republicans began imploding. Republicans are also very good at raising money, not to mention the fact that those in the rank and file were until recently far more affluent than the Democrats; while their ranks have recently thinned, the GOP remains well-heeled.** Republican corporate connections have given the

---

*John Hibbing advised me that these numbers exceed 100 percent because of rounding up, which was done rather than having a string of decimals.

**The Pew Research Center reports that the "Republican Party has traditionally garnered its strongest backing among wealthier voters. But the recent overall decline

party cutting-edge marketing and advertising skills in local, state, and national campaigns. The party's highly committed core membership is willing to undertake the thankless tasks of elective politics, grunt work they perform with a zeal that cannot be bought. Once elected, Republicans are extremely inclined toward opposing Democratic programs, not only because their philosophy is inherently antigovernment but because they are instinctively contrarian to anything and everything liberal or progressive. When campaigning or when opposing Democrats, Republicans are unmatched in modern politics for their willingness to play dirty, to go negative and nasty, and to play hardball, a ruthlessness well matched to their uncompromising competitiveness.

Today's conservative-based Republican Party in fact excels at everything in modern politics except governing the nation. Given conservatism's fundamentally antigovernment attitude, the inability of Republicans to govern successfully is to be expected. Conservatives have few guiding principles relating to effective governance. Just as conservatism itself defies definition by conservatives, so does its governing philosophy. Nonetheless, conservatives clearly believe that Ronald Reagan's statements about government in his first inaugural address on January 20, 1981, are gospel: "[G]overnment is not the solution to our problem; government is the problem. From time to time we've been tempted to believe that society has become too complex to be managed by self-rule, that government by an elite group is superior to government for, by, and of the people. Well, if no one among us is capable of governing himself, then who among us has the capacity to govern someone else?" He provided the answer to that question himself, and it was not the federal government: "It is my intention to curb the size and influence of the federal establishment and to demand recognition of the distinc-

---

in Republican Party affiliation nationwide has taken a toll even on GOP support among affluent voters. The latest Pew surveys find Democrats pulling even with Republicans among registered voters with annual family incomes in excess of roughly $135,000 per annum." Pew Research Center, "Money Walks" (April 12, 2007) at pewresearch.org/pubs/451/money-walks.

tion between the powers granted to the federal government and those reserved to the states or to the people. All of us need to be reminded that the federal government did not create the states; the states created the federal government."[35]

Former Reagan aide Michael Deaver later assembled a collection of brief essays from prominent contemporary conservatives entitled *Why I Am a Reagan Conservative.* A notable recurring theme runs through these pieces, as shown by a few typical examples:

- Robert D. Novak (columnist): "What really makes a conservative is whether you think the government always is the problem rather than the solution. I became a conservative in 1976 when I came to the conclusion—based on close observation as a reporter of how Washington worked—that it was the problem."
- Trent Lott (U.S. senator from Mississippi): "I am a conservative because I feel as Thomas Jefferson did, that the best government is the government closest to the people and that the federal government should be held in check whenever possible. ... I believe in a strong national defense because all our other freedoms and liberties could be lost without that."
- Edwin Meese III (Reagan's attorney general): "The characteristics of a conservative society include individual liberty, limited government, and free-market economics."
- Grover Norquist (conservative activist): "The sole legitimate function of government is to create and protect liberty. That is why we have courts, police, and a national army. To keep out, stop, or punish those who would infringe on our liberty. ... [T]he center-right coalition is a coalition of groups and individuals that—on the issues that moves them to vote—wish to be left alone by the central government. Gun owners do not want their Second Amendment rights infringed upon. Property owners do not want their property rights interfered with.... Businessmen and -women do not want their businesses taxed and regulated. Homeschoolers want to raise their own children. And all communities of faith—evangelical

Protestants, conservative Catholics, Orthodox Jews, Muslims, Mormons—all want to be able to practice their faith free of government coercion."

- Edwin J. Feulner (president, Heritage Foundation): "A philosophy that believes that, while government is necessary, it should be limited.... Conservatives believe that individual liberty is protected by the preservation of national sovereignty, making national defense a high moral duty."
- Chuck Hagel (U.S. senator from Nebraska): "Individual rights, limited government, free trade, fiscal responsibility, balanced budget, and limited foreign entanglements make up my philosophy of governance."
- Katherine Harris (former U.S. representative from Florida): "I am conservative because I believe in the fundamental values of limited government and unlimited prosperity through lower taxes, less regulation, and responsible stewardship of the public purse."
- Orrin Hatch (U.S. senator from Utah): "We believe the answer lay in lower taxes, less government, fewer regulations, less centralized power, and a wiser use of the power that must be exercised on behalf of the people."[36]

Democrats would no doubt agree with some of these general statements, but I doubt they would subscribe to the near universal assumption by conservatives that government is a burden. The negativity toward government in contemporary conservative thinking raises the question of why these people ever enter public service at the national level, other than to dismantle the federal government by lowering taxes and abolishing programs and agencies. It should come as no surprise that Republicans have twisted and distorted government processes to their breaking points, given this mind-set. Of course, Republicans proudly proclaim that they love their country; they love their flag; they love their automatic weapons; they love their Constitution; and they love their democracy, given the alternatives. But where the federal government is concerned: It is too big, too powerful, too expensive, too lax in demanding morality, and too invasive with all its health and safety requirements to be able to run a really profitable business. Republicans want to starve the federal government and shrink it in Grover Norquist's infamous formulation, so they can "drown it in a bathtub."

Out of curiosity, I have from time to time checked to see what people do when they leave high-level government service, in particular the subcabinet-level appointmentees and members of the White House staff. There is a rather consistent pattern of those who work in Republican administrations going on to join businesses, and profiting from their government experience, while those from Democratic administrations continue with some form of public service, whether returning to academic life, affiliation with nonprofit and charitable foundations, and even further government service. Of course there are many exceptions to these patterns, but what I did discover confirmed what I had come to realize when I was active in the inner circles of my old party: Republicans seek federal power because it can help them achieve *their* agenda, and it also helps them in *their* careers. Few are driven to assist their fellow citizens, or to serve their country. It is power that attracts them; it is a tropism for authoritarian personalities, like the moth to the candle. Where power is concerned, Republicans consistently confirm Lord Acton's aphorism that absolute power corrupts absolutely.

As I explained in *Conservatives Without Conscience,* inconsistent thinking has become common in Republicans, which is apparent in brief statements I have quoted from Mike Deaver's book about conservative beliefs. All conservatives hold dear the principles of a limited federal government and correspondingly lower federal taxes, and the decentralization of power. Yet, as will be discussed in the following pages, contemporary conservatives have abandoned the long-held concern of conservatism about the dangers inherent in aggregations of power. Post-Watergate conservative Republicans now embrace the notion of a neo-Nixonian presidency, one that calls for a chief executive to be always wearing his commander-in-chief uniform, constantly strutting about flexing his muscles, and beating the other branches of government into less than constitutionally coequal status. Nixon's GOP successors have picked up where he left off in expanding presidential powers, focusing in particular on dominating national security and ideologically transforming the federal judiciary.

Each of the three coordinate branches of government is addressed in the following three chapters, with an unavoidable overlap in the discussions because of the inherent overlap in the system. I have not sought to prepare laundry lists of all the broken processes that affect each branch of the federal government; instead, I have identified what I believe to be the major breakdowns in areas where I have personal knowledge, and also have consulted the expertise of others who have concluded that the process is not working as it was designed. For example, the growth of special-interest lobbying that has occurred in Washington when Republicans controlled Congress is startling. Former majority leader Tom DeLay (R-TX), who resigned from Congress when he was indicted for money laundering in Texas, proudly admitted in his autobiography *No Retreat, No Surrender* that he allowed lobbyists to draft legislation. "With the start of the Republican revolution I was trying to deregulate everything I could to get government off the backs of people, as Ronald Reagan said, and liberate the private sector to achieve its best," DeLay explains. "If you want to get government regulations off the backs of energy producers, for example, talk to the energy producers about how government gets in their way. Then get their government affairs people to help you draft legislation. You'll certainly get better results than you would by talking to the Environmental Protection Agency or the energy experts at Harvard."[37] This, of course, is the type of conduct that offends most Americans, for it benefits special interests rather than the regulating businesses in a manner that protects national health and welfare. While energy lobbyists have had a bonanza with Republicans controlling government, lobbying itself is not unconstitutional. To the contrary, the Constitution assures Americans that they can petition their government, so I have not raised it as a point of discussion. Likewise, because I have written previously about the dysfunctions of the legislative and executive branches, and because they are thoroughly covered by the mainstream media, I have provided only a brief history or background when examining the damage Republican rule has done to them. For most Americans the federal judiciary is the least known branch. Few people are aware how Republican presidents have spent the last four decades remaking the judiciary in their own image, and in so doing have politicized—and diminished—the nonpolitical branch.

If I could turn on a blicking red light to catch a reader's attention, to give him a heads-up to alert him to pay attention, I would place it next to the following observations of political scientist Alan Wolfe:* "Political parties expend the time and grueling energy to control government for different reasons," he explained, viewing politics with his wide-angle lens.

Liberals, while enjoying the perquisites of office, also want to be in a position to use government to solve problems. But conservatives have different motives for wanting power. One is to prevent liberals from doing so; if government cannot be made to disappear, at least it can be prevented from doing any good. The other is to build a political machine in which business and the Republican Party can exchange mutual favors; business will lavish cash on politicians (called campaign contributions) while politicians will throw the money back at business (called public policy). Conservatism will always attract its share of young idealists. And young idealists will always be disillusioned by the sheer amount of corruption that people like Gingrich and DeLay generate. If yesterday's conservative was a liberal mugged by reality, today's is a free-marketer fattened by pork.[38]

If you understand these observations of Alan Wolfe you have grasped the essence of Republican rule. If not, reread this passage, for

*Alan Wolfe, a Ph.D. from the University of Pennsylvania, is a professor of political science and director of the Boisi Center for Religion and American Public Life at Boston College, and a prolific author.

you will never find a more succinct explanation of the quintessence of modern Republicanism.

I have taken little joy in writing this book. Frankly, I once believed Republicans would be good at governing. But I was wrong: They have demonstrated that they can only rule for limited periods. As used in the pages that follow, "governing" is a craft, a skill, even an art; it is an effort to find common rules under which all can pursue happiness; "ruling," in contrast, is merely reigning and exercising power.

*All legislative powers herein granted shall be vested
in a Congress of the United States, which shall consist of
a Senate and House of Representatives.*

—Article I, Section 1, U.S. Constitution

CHAPTER ONE

First Branch:
Broken but Under Repair

On January 4, 2007, congressional Democrats assumed control of both the U.S. House of Representatives and the U.S. Senate. The margin in the House has some cushion, but there was none in the Senate.* The change of leadership came none too soon, because the mess in Congress was growing worse by the week. Republican rule had been ruinous to Congress's institutional processes, including one of its primary constitutional responsibilities and functions: providing funding to operations of government. Under GOP control Congress has demonstrated a conspicuous inability, unwillingness, or incompetence to operate according to "regular order"—which means by long-established traditions, norms, rules, and laws—not to mention the Constitution itself. As a nominally co-equal branch, with the powers to check and balance the presidency, Congress instead:

- condoned (if not encouraged) excessive secrecy by the Bush and Cheney administration;

---

*A majority in the House is 218 votes, and in the Senate, 51 votes. The House has 233 Democrats versus 202 Republicans, and the Senate has 49 Democrats versus 49 Republicans with two independents (Joe Lieberman of Connecticut and Bernie Saunders of Vermont, who are caucusing with the Democrats).

- refused to stand behind their own accounting and investigative arm, the General Accountability Office, when Vice President Cheney declined to provide the sort of basic information that has always been made available to Congress;
- provided the vice president—who is the president of the Senate, not to mention part of the executive branch—with a luxurious Capitol Building office in the House wing (which complements his luxurious office as president of the Senate in the Senate wing) so he could more easily lobby for White House activities in both chambers;
- effectively became a mere extension of the White House, abandoning all responsibility for conducting oversight of the executive branch; thus it neither said nor did anything when it became apparent that Bush and Cheney had deceived Congress to justify going to war in Iraq (clearly an impeachable offense);
- tolerated and supported Bush/Cheney policies that have made the United States despised around the world for its preemptive war in Iraq, and its uses of torture in defiance of the nation's treaty obligations, not to mention the badly botched war against terrorists; and
- fostered an atmosphere of hostility, utterly lacking the collegiality and civility that had made it a great deliberative body.

Fortunately, as the 2006 midterm election approached, increasing numbers of knowledgeable people began speaking out about this state of affairs. Much of the concern was about process, but the mainstream news media largely ignored the growing criticism. Some of this commentary was politically motivated, but much of it took the form of nonpartisan reports by professionals who care about Congress and are not inclined to see the system fall apart. But even more casual observers recognized that as the midterm elections approached the weight of the evidence, available to anyone inclined to examine it, established beyond any doubt that Congress was seriously out of order.

Consensus Analysis of Failed Republican Congressional Rule

Thomas E. Mann, who is affiliated with the center-left Brookings Institution, and Norman J. Ornstein, who is with the center-right American Enterprise Institute, published their book, *The Broken Branch: How Congress Is Failing America and How to Get It Back on Track*, at the height of the 2006 campaign. Those unfamiliar with the informal protocols of Washington would not appreciate the significance of this publication. Its authors, both University of Michigan Ph.D.s who have devoted much of their professional careers to the study of Congress, are not bomb throwers, not typical political activists with a specific agenda. While they've been critical of Democrats in the past (and they remain critical of Democrats in their book), they had not previously thrust themselves directly into a general election campaign as they did in 2006—repeatedly firing high-power warning flares that could only help the Democrats regain control of Congress.* They were campaigning on behalf of Congress, the institution, and whatever their political affiliations, both men are clearly establishmentarians.[1] As such, their indictment of the Republican Congress seemed to be a last resort: They were worried that Congress was imploding under Republican rule, and if control was not taken from the GOP, the institution might well not survive. Regardless of their motives, however, both men are owed a sincere debt of gratitude for speaking out, for their book reached many opinion leaders, people whose views provided cues for countless less informed newspeople and voters. It is difficult to believe that they did not have an impact on the 2006 elections and help save Congress from further savaging at the hands of the GOP.[2]

---

*For example, on July 12, 2006, they participated, with former speakers Foley and Gingrich, in an American Enterprise Institute conference on their work (www.aei.org/events/filter.all,eventID.1357/event_detail.asp). Norman Ornstein, in particular, appeared regularly on national television programs discussing the book right up to (and after) the election.

Washington Post Capitol Hill reporter Juliet Eilperin titled her book about the House, quite appropriately, *Fight Club Politics: How Partisanship Is Poisoning the House of Representatives.* Eilperin, who had covered the House for a decade, published her book shortly before the 2006 election, and while she did not have the impact of Mann and Ornstein, she, too, helped educate voters—but not as Republicans might like them educated. Eilperin was watching as Newt Gingrich "remade the House of Representatives."[3] She was there when Gingrich and his Republican colleagues discredited and literally sought to destroy Congress in the 1980s and early 1990s, "so they could rebuild it in their own image."[4] As Eilperin described it, before gaining control in 1994, the GOP "launched a sustained attack, questioning [Democratic] House leaders' ethics, and focused on crafting an alternative policy agenda rather than on pursuing legislative compromises with the majority." They literally ousted Democratic speaker Jim Wright, "portraying the House as an evil institution." Typical of the Republican shenanigans was how Jim Nussle (R-IA) "demonstrated his outrage on national television by appearing on the House floor with a paper bag over his head, declaring he was ashamed to be a member of the House."[5] These gambits worked, and Eilperin, dismayed, witnessed firsthand the conservative GOP leaders "dismantle" the House, and then take control, claiming they would institute reform, but they utterly failed to come close to meeting that promise.

North Carolina Democratic representative David E. Price's concern about the abuses of power by House Republicans was clear when he assembled 132 Democratic members of the House (including Democratic minority leader, now Speaker, Nancy Pelosi) to join him in introducing a resolution to amend the rules of the House "to protect the integrity of the institution."* Needless to say, the proposal went nowhere—that

---

*Representative David E. Price has a Ph.D. from Yale and is a former political science professor at Duke University; he has represented the Fourth District of North Carolina for twenty years. The proposal he and his colleagues introduced

is, until the Democrats took control on January 4, 2007, when they embraced these and other measures to start the process of repairing the House. Price made a special effort to reveal the dysfunctional operations of the House of Representatives under GOP control to his professional peers in an article in the professional journal *PS: Political Science & Politics* (April 2006).[6]

Writing in the *Washington Monthly* (July/August 2006), Alan Wolfe explained in an article entitled "Why Conservatives Can't Govern" that, in general, as "a way of governing, conservatism is another name for disaster. And the disasters will continue, year after year, as long as conservatives, whose political tactics are frequently as brilliant as their policy-making is inept, find ways to perpetuate their power." Antigovernment conservatives are bad at governing, Wolfe explained, for "the same reason that vegetarians cannot prepare a world-class boeuf bourguignon: If you believe that what you are called upon to do is wrong, you are not likely to do it very well."[7]

Mann, Ornstein, Eilperin, Price, and Wolfe are all members of the Washington cognoscenti. *Rolling Stone* contributing editor Matt Taibbi, who attended Bard College and Leningrad State Technical University, worked as a sports editor for the *Moscow Times* and a correspondent for the Mongolian National News Agency before distinguishing himself in the United States with a remarkably tasteless piece about the death of the pope, is not. He is, however, an obviously intelligent, wicked-witted outsider who paused long enough to study the GOP Congress to write a Gonzoesque piece for *Rolling Stone* headlined "The Worse

---

sought to make congressional travel off-limits to lobbyists; strengthen fiscal responsibility; curb abuses of power; prevent the use of earmarks to buy votes; end the two-day congressional workweek; prohibit legislation from being voted on without members having time to familiarize themselves with it; and prevent legislative items from being slipped into conference reports without a vote of the conference committee—all favorite tactics of Republicans. See "Cleaning (the) House," at price.house.gov/News/DocumentSingle.aspx?DocumentID=37512.

Congress Ever: How Our National Legislature Has Become a Stable of Thieves and Perverts—in Five Easy Steps." Taibbi's no-holds-barred report, which also appeared shortly before the GOP lost control of Capitol Hill in the midterm election, is enlightening precisely because he has *not* made a career of studying Congress. Even so, his analysis of the GOP-controlled Congress provides a convenient touchstone for a consensus, as his five-point analysis, blunt but colorful, reached the same basic conclusions as Mann, Ornstein, Eilperin, Wolfe, Price, and others. While their observations slightly overlap, their distinct points of view do not. Distilling their perspectives offers a realistic portrait of the Congress under Republican control. These perspectives are not featured in an effort to pile it on, but rather to suggest the strength of the accumulated evidence.

"Step One: Rule by Cabal"

Matt Taibbi's assertions that the GOP "ruled by cabal" is appropriately descriptive of the secretive and manipulative style of the House and Senate leadership under the Republicans, particularly since cabals by definition serve private interests rather than the public interest. The GOP congressional cabal has destroyed the ability of the House to function in the deliberative fashion contemplated by the nation's founders. Its relentless rule was certainly obvious to Taibbi's untrained eye. A political reality of Capitol Hill is that the party in control has always taken care of its own and, as the minority sees it, gives them "the shaft." Taibbi pointed out, however, that there was "a marked difference in the size and the length of the shaft" the Republicans gave Democrats during the years they controlled Congress.[8] For Republicans literally cut the Democrats out of the legislative process altogether and legislated only for other Republicans, particularly their special corporate interests.

Tom Mann and Norm Ornstein reported that "adherence to regular order—the rules, precedents, and norms guaranteeing opportunities for genuine debate and deliberation in the House—was trumped by the overriding desire of the new [Republican] majority to produce legislative results."[9] Initially, when Republicans gained control of the House in 1995, they were uncertain of their capacity to maintain their control, so they moved cautiously. After the 1996 election, however, when Bill Clinton held the presidency and the GOP held the House, they became confident, and began changing the way they did business. By the time Taibbi began looking at Congress a decade later, Republican rule on Capitol Hill was nothing short of brutal. "The GOP's 'take that, bitch' approach to governing has been taken to the greatest heights by the House Judiciary Committee," Taibbi wrote. "The committee [was] chaired by the legendary Republican monster James Sensenbrenner Jr., an ever-sweating, fat-fingered beast who wields his gavel in a way that makes you think he might have used one before in some other arena, perhaps to beat prostitutes to death."[10]

Even before taking control of Congress in 1995, Republicans were changing the atmosphere on Capitol Hill. Juliet Eilperin reported how Newt Gingrich organized the Republicans into a hostile and warring band of political vipers—my summary description, not hers—by changing the way of life in Congress. "Gingrich and his deputies," she noted, transformed "the Hill's social network by urging junior members to keep their families at home in their districts rather than bring them to Washington."[11] In earlier years, she explained, "families often socialized with each other regardless of party, and these personal ties curbed members' tendency to demonize each other.... This sort of lifestyle disappeared in the late 1980s and early 1990s when GOP firebrands ... declared themselves members of the 'Tuesday to Thursday Club' and spent as little time as possible in Washington.... At the same time members started rushing to catch their Thursday flights back home, they began shunning congressional trips abroad that have traditionally provided another avenue for bipartisan bonding."[12] To those unfamiliar with Congress, it might seem that, the fewer the foreign travel junkets, the better, and this is exactly what many Republicans claimed as they cut back on overseas travel with colleagues. But this parochial view, often embraced by contemporary conservatism, ignores the fact that some, if not most, members of Congress become better representatives and senators because of such travel, which is often both hard work and highly educational. Our world is too small to believe we can survive being ignorant of our neighbors. There are many examples of members of the House and Senate developing important friendship while traveling with members of the opposition party.*

Taibbi had it right when he explained that pre-GOP Washington was "once a chummy fraternity in which members of both parties golfed together, played in the same pickup basketball games, probably even shared the same mistresses." But when Gingrich and colleagues took charge, they made it "a one-party town—and congressional business [was] conducted accordingly, as though the half of the country that the Democrats represent simply [did] not exist."[13] Republican leaders frowned on rank-and-file members fraternizing and socializing with Democrats. In the House and Senate dining rooms Republicans and Democrats had always lunched together at the same tables, but that conviviality largely ended when the GOP took control. Attitudes of members of the House and Senate were shared by their staffs, who were even more hostile toward one another than the members themselves.

When members of the Congress and their staffs do not know one another personally it affects the functioning of government negatively. Proceedings of the House under GOP control revealed such consequences in the breakdown of civility. As Eilperin reported, "Members not only stopped sharing free time together over the past decade [of Republican control], they found themselves debating each other less often

---

*A revealing case of this occurred when Senators Hillary Clinton (D-NY) and John McCain (R-AZ) traveled to Estonia during the summer of 2004, where they engaged in a vodka drinking contest. McCain decided Hillary was "one of the guys," and they bonded. Both serve on the Senate Armed Services Committee, and ever since that trip they have been known for working closely and well across party lines. See Anne E. Kornblut, "2008 May Test Clinton's Bond With McCain," *New York Times,* July 29, 2006, at query.nytimes.com/gst/fullpage.html?res=9C04E0DE 133FF93AA15754C0A9609C8B63.

on the House floor.... By limiting lawmakers to two-minute speeches, leaders stifled opportunities for real debate and encouraged pithy, partisan attacks." Or as one member rhetorically told Eilperin, "What can you do in two minutes? Insult the other guy."[14]

Representative David Price, wearing his political scientist's hat, explained the impact of Republican control of Congress to his professional peers, and noted that Republicans had gone "far beyond what we Democrats aspired to, much less achieved." Price reported that Gingrich had ended the seniority system and appointed committee chairs so that he could control the agenda of both committees and the House. Notwithstanding Speaker Dennis Hastert's (R-IL) professed desire to abolish this system and return to "regular order," he never did, but rather continued with the Gingrich system. Price said Gingrich and Hastert exerted a level of control over the House the likes of which had not existed "since the days of [Republican Speakers] Thomas B. Reed [1889–1891, 1895–1899] and Joseph G. Cannon [1903–1911]." Operating the House so autocratically naturally gave reason for concern. "First, there [were] legitimate issues of fairness and institutional openness—to the participation and contributions of Democratic members and to the interests of the districts (almost half of the country) that we represent." Price noted that such GOP-efficient structures were "no substitute for responsible leadership, and they may [have] enable[d] irresponsible or inept leaders to do far more damage. It is therefore important to temper party efficiency and discipline with processes that foster diverse input, due deliberation, and the building of consensus." Or, as I might restate it, the fact that the Republicans made the trains run on time did not necessarily mean they had them going to the right places. Last, Price explained that the "sharply partisan approach of President Bush and congressional leaders arguably ... decreased rather than increased their ability to handle [complex] areas."[15] In short, running the House for the benefit of the Republicans was not only undemocratic, it did not prove to be particularly productive.

Alan Wolfe observed that transformation of the Republican Party into "a highly disciplined organization determined to get its way without cooperation from the Democrats" did little more that substitute "British-style party discipline and ideological extremism for bipartisan cooperation and moderation in the U.S. House of Representatives." Wolfe noted that Gingrich and then majority leader Tom DeLay (R-TX) sought to institutionalize Republican rule by "developing redistricting rules to favor Republicans; encouraging House Republicans to vote as a unified bloc; weakening seniority so as to strengthen party leaders; [and] freezing the opposition party out of a role in governance." And within less than a decade of control the GOP leaders were running the U.S. House of Representatives without so much of even "a pretense of valuing fairness and deliberation."[16]

Mann and Orenstein explained that the "virtual collapse of genuine deliberation in the House" and the resulting "bitter and destructive relations between the two parties" was the result of the GOP's anti-Washington attitude. Mann and Orenstein believe that "Gingrich and the new Republican majority were the modern-day Anti-Federalists," given their "pronounced disdain for Washington and its political class" and their "deep suspicion of deliberative processes." In addition, their "strong links to evangelicals and the business community were reminiscent of the democratic forces that gathered in the new republic two centuries earlier [to oppose the Constitution]."[17] This, of course, is consistent with conservatism's antigovernment outlook.

The GOP conservative cabal controlling Congress may have lost in November 2006, but they plan a mighty fight to regain control in the 2008 election. White House political operative Karl Rove has targeted twenty House seats held by Democrats that he believes are vulnerable.[18] Republicans need sixteen additional seats to take control. It is too early to project what is going to happen in the House, for it is likely to be a close race, since many independents who voted for Democrats had an unrealistic hope that they could quickly end the war in Iraq, but that possibility never really existed, given the presence of conservatives in both parties who support the war. As for the Senate, a few pundits believe that the Democrats might be able to reach the magic number of sixty senators, which means they would have sufficient votes to cut off any and all Republican filibusters.[19] This thinking is bolstered by the raw numbers: Thirty-three senators are up for reelection in 2008, of which twelve are Democrats and twenty-one are Republicans. The GOP has a lot more seats to defend, and the Bush/Cheney administration has done great damage to GOP prospects. Still, while the Democrats' gaining sixty seats is possible but not likely, only a disaster could result in their losing control of the Senate. As I see it, they may pick up three to five additional seats.

"Step Two: Work as Little as Possible— and Screw Up What Little You Do"

"It's Thursday evening, September 28th, and the Senate is putting the finishing touches on the Military Commissions Act of 2006, colloquially known as the 'torture bill.' It's a law even Stalin would admire, one that throws habeas corpus in the trash, [and] legalizes a vast array of savage interrogation techniques," Matt Taibbi observed from a seat in the Senate's press galley high above the floor. His bird's-eye view of the GOP-controlled Senate at work continued: "Senator Pat Leahy of Vermont comments on the rush to torture during the final, frenzied debate. 'Over 200 years of jurisprudence in this country,' Leahy pleads, 'and following an hour of debate, we get rid of it?' Yawns, chatter, a few sets of rolling eyes—yeah, whatever, Pat. An hour later, the torture bill is law." Next Taibbi watched

> the diminutive chair of the Defense Appropriations Subcommittee, Sen. Ted Stevens [(R-AK)], read off the summary of the military-spending bill to a mostly empty hall; since the members all need their sleep and most have left early, the "debate" on the biggest spending bill of the year is conducted before a largely phantom audience. "Mr. President," Stevens begins, eyeing the few members present. "There are only four days left in the fiscal year. The 2007 defense appropriations conference report must be signed into law by the president before Saturday at midnight."

Watching Ted Stevens spend half a trillion dollars is like watching a junkie pull a belt around his biceps with his teeth. You get the sense he could do it just as fast in the dark. When he finishes his summary—$436 billion in defense spending, including $70 billion for the Iraq "emergency"—he fucks off and leaves the hall.

Taibbi was surprised that the GOP Congress devoted so little time to appropriations legislation that rolled eight bills "into one giant monstrosity known as an Omnibus bill and pass[ed] it with little or no debate." In fact, this had become standard operating procedure under the Republicans, and its consequences were obvious to him: "Rolling eight-elevenths of all federal spending into a single bill that hits the floor a day or two before the fiscal year ends does not leave much room to check the fine print."[20]

Mann and Ornstein are troubled by the lack of floor debate under GOP control, not to mention the general breakdown of the legislative processes: "[T]he change from the past—and the lack of time spent in meaningful floor debate—has been striking. For 2006, the second session of the [last Republican] Congress, the ... total number of calendar days, even if counted generously, is ninety-seven, the smallest number in sixty years," they noted, and added,

> Beyond the attenuation of meaningful action and debate on the floor, we have seen as well the decline of committees, and not only through the disappearance of oversight. Major bills that in the past would have required weeks of hearings and days of markups are now often reviewed in days of hearings and with little or no visible time spent by the committee on systematic analysis of the legislation line by line and word by word. Much of the action now takes place behind closed doors, with bills ... put together by a small group of leadership staff, committee staff, industry representatives, and a few majority party members and then rammed through subcommittee and committee with minimal debate.[21]

Most of the floor proceedings of the House of Representatives are controlled by the Rules Committee, which writes rules for each bill to determine the length of debate to be allowed and the number of amendments that will be permitted. Such an arrangement is necessary because of the size of the House, for without limits on the proceedings nothing would get accomplished. Juliet Eilperin described the activities of the Rules Committee "as one of the House's least decipherable aspects to outside observers." But, she explained, "it has a huge impact on what kinds of polices emerge from the House." The Rules Committee is controlled by the Speaker of the House, and under GOP speakers, the Rules Committee all but shut off floor debate with "closed rules," which so limited debate as to make it meaningless, prohibited amendments, and effectively shut out the Democrats' ability to alter legislation in any fashion. On most GOP bills, Democrats were left with the choice to either vote for or against them. Closed rules enabled the GOP, with just a bare majority, to muscle legislation through the House with no Democratic support whatsoever. Republican leaders often broke the rule permitting fifteen minutes for voting when they were one or two votes short, because holding the vote open gave them the opportunity to apply the necessary pressure on holdouts. They mastered the art of the one-vote victory, which was all they cared about. Eilperin, who interviewed House GOP leaders, revealed that they claimed, "They have no choice but to adopt a hard line, because of their narrow margin of control. Obtaining the necessary [House majority of] 218 votes, culled almost entirely from within the Republican conference, means striking several complicated deals that a single amendment could derail. That's a risk they're not willing to take."[22] Often legislation is not only made more politically acceptable when amendments are possible, but badly drafted bills can be corrected and improved. That, of course, did not happen in the GOP Congress, where closed rules became the norm, particularly after Bush and Cheney entered the White House.

"With the accession of George W. Bush, a Republican president determined to govern from the 'right-in' rather than the 'center-out,' GOP control [in the House] took on a harder edge in terms of tactics designed to eliminate dependence on or participation by Democrats, while keeping the narrow Republican majority in line," David Price explained to other political scientists. "Most obvious [was] the practice of going to the floor with a narrow whip count [the nose count taken by leaders known as 'the whips' before a vote] and [ignoring the fifteen-minute rule for votes by] holding the vote open as long as necessary to cajole the last few Republican members to vote 'yes.'" Another tactic GOP leaders employed was to exclude Democrats from attending House-Senate conference deliberations, which take place when there are differences between the House- and Senate-passed versions of a particular piece of legislation, with each chamber selecting conferees from both parties; after the differences are sorted out, the conference report is sent back to the respective chambers for approval. Conferences have always been bipartisan gatherings, at least until Republicans changed the process. As Price said, "The poster boy for the practice [was] Ways and Means chairman Bill Thomas (R-CA), who told House Democratic conferees on the Medicare prescription drug bill that sessions would be cancelled if they showed up."[23]

"Step Three: Let the President Do Whatever He Wants"

The entire group of congressional observers I have drawn upon—Mann, Ornstein, Eilperin, Price, Wolfe, and Taibbi—were amazed and troubled by the conspicuous lack of executive branch oversight by the Republican Congress of a Republican president. When Democrats have controlled Congress with a Democrat residing in the White House, they have not abandoned their institutional responsibility of checking and balancing the executive branch. However, as Matt Taibbi observed,

> The Republican-controlled Congress has created a new standard for the use of oversight powers. That standard seems to be that when a Democratic president is in power, there are no matters too stupid or meaningless to be investigated fully—but when George Bush is president, no evidence of corruption or incompetence is shocking

enough to warrant congressional attention. One gets the sense that Bush would have to drink the blood of Christian babies to inspire hearings in [the Republican] Congress—and only then if he did it during a nationally televised State of the Union address and the babies were from Pennsylvania, where Senate Judiciary chairman Arlen Specter was running ten points behind in an election year.*

He also reported how Republican congressional leaders have changed long-standing customs regarding oversight.

From the McCarthy era in the 1950s through the Republican take-over of Congress in 1995, no Democratic committee chairman is-sued a subpoena without either minority consent or a committee vote. In the Clinton years, Republicans chucked that long-standing arrangement and issued more than 1,000 subpoenas to investigate alleged administration and Democratic misconduct, reviewing more than 2 million pages of government documents. Guess how many subpoenas have been issued [by the Republican Congress] to the White House since George Bush took office? Zero—that's right, zero.[24]

During the first six years of the Bush/Cheney administration, Mann and Ornstein found that congressional oversight had "virtually col-lapsed."** To demonstrate that such behavior was aberrant and far from

*Taibbi was off a bit on this observation. Arlen Specter is a moderate. Penn-sylvania's hard-right conservative was former senator Rick Santorum, who would have found that baby in the middle of the state, for James Carville accurately describes Pennsylvania's political landscape as Arkansas between Pittsburgh and Philadelphia.

**In addition to the discussion in their book, they set forth their view on oversight relating to foreign affairs in a lengthy essay, Norman J. Ornstein and Thomas E. Mann, "When Congress Checks Out," *Foreign Affairs* (November/December 2006): 67 at www.foreignaffairs.org/20061101faessay85607/norman-j-ornstein-thomas-e-mann/when-congress-checks-out.html?mode=print. This *Foreign Affairs* essay is the source of the quoted material in this section.

the norms of the Democrats, they provided a number of examples in the field of foreign affairs, one of the most important areas of oversight:

- Representative John Dingell (D-MI) is now the dean of the House, and he conducted oversight through "seven presidents.... Often as the chair of [the] vaunted Oversight and Investigations Subcommittee, Dingell oversaw the executive branch to make sure it acted without bias or malfeasance. He did not shrink from making presidents, Democrat and Republican alike, uncomfortable. At times, even colleagues winced when he grilled bureaucrats. But the result was better execution of policy."

- "In February 1941 then senator Harry Truman (D-MO) proposed the creation of a special committee. Within a few months, the body had begun a long series of hearings.... Truman biographer David McCullough has written, 'any member of the Senate was welcome to ... take part in the hearing.... There was no browbeating of witnesses, no unseemly outbursts tolerated on the part of anybody.' In the weeks after Pearl Harbor, President Franklin Roosevelt was urged to try to disband [Truman's inquiry].... He demurred. The committee produced more than 50 reports, all unanimous, and conducted more than 500 hearings. It is said to have saved the country $15 billion."

- "During the Korean War, a special committee chaired by then senator Lyndon Johnson (D-TX) strongly criticized the Truman administration, [and] ... it also 'reduced waste, improved the efficiency of wartime agencies and reaffirmed the patriotism of administration officials—no trivial matter when [Senator Joseph] McCarthy (R-WI) and his allies saw every small mishap as evidence of disloyalty and subversion."

- "In the 1970s, there were the committee investigations of intelligence failures and secret illegal surveillance [by Democratic senator Frank Church]." His historical digging looked at both Republican and Democratic presidents.

- "In the 1980s, [the Democratic Congress had] joint congressional committees [that] scrutinized the Iran-contra affair." Reagan, of course, was president, and as will be noted in the next chapter, Congressman Dick Cheney (R-WO) believed Congress had no business conducting these oversight inquiries.

- "In the 1990s, [the Republican Congress had] authorizing committees and appropriations committees in both houses review military operations [of a Democratic president] in Kosovo." GOP oversight of Clinton's national security operations was ongoing and persistent, not to mention insistent in wanting to know everything he was doing and how he was doing it. [Because Clinton was playing by the rules, the Republicans only wasted his time, which is what they wanted to do.]

Congress's neglect of oversight during the first six years of the Bush presidency, ignoring everything from homeland security to the conduct of the Iraq war, from allegations of torture at Abu Ghraib to the illegal surveillance of domestic telephone calls by the National Security Agency (NSA), is more than just a failure to uphold the institutional standards of Congress; it borders on complicity. Mann and Ornstein, who have spent the past several decades working with Congress, found the lack of oversight by the Senate, which has a constitutional role in national security matters, most troubling. Oversight by the Senate is part of its nature, an "intense pride in the heritage and trappings of the body [which are] almost part of its institutional DNA." Mann and Ornstein found watching Senate Republicans "disregard that heritage and its honor over the past few years ... particularly jarring."

"No congressional function has atrophied under unified Republican control more than oversight of the executive," Representative Price concurred. "The list of legitimate oversight inquires foregone—many of them explicitly blocked after Democratic requests—[was] long and varied," he said, noting that when one looks at how Democrats like Senator William Fulbright (D-AR) used his Senate Foreign Relations

Committee and Representatives John Moss (D-CA) and John Dingell (D-MI) used the House Commerce Committee to take on Republican and Democratic administrations alike, the failures of the GOP Congress become glaring, showing "the extent to which partisan loyalty and deference to a Republican president have trumped any sense of institutional identity or constitutional responsibility since President Bush took office."[25]

"Historically and philosophically, liberals and conservatives have disagreed with each other, not only over the ends political systems should serve, but over the means chosen to serve those ends," Alan Wolfe observed, placing oversight in its broader context, along with the bellicosity of the Republicans. Wolfe noted,

> Whether through the ideas of James Madison, Immanuel Kant, or John Stuart Mill, liberals have viewed violent conflict as regrettable and the use of political institutions as the best way to contain it. Conservatives, from the days of Machiavelli to such twentieth-century figures as Germany's Carl Schmitt, have, by contrast, viewed politics as an extension of war, complete with no-holds-barred treatment of the enemy, iron-clad discipline in the ranks, cries of treason against those who do not support the effort with full-throated vigor, and total control over any spoils won. From a conservative point of view, separation of powers, [which are at the heart of congressional oversight] is divisive, tolerance a luxury, fairness another word for weakness, and cooperation unnecessary.[26]

When the Democrats took control of the Congress in January 2007, I expected to see much more aggressive oversight of the Bush/Cheney administration than has occurred. On the House side only Henry Waxman (D-CA), chairman of the Government Operations Committee, and John Conyers (D-MI), chairman of the House Judiciary Committee, have done serious digging. On the Senate side, Pat Leahy (D-VT), chairman of the Senate Judiciary Committee, has been active, investigating the politicization of the Justice Department. These men are all seasoned politicians, so they hit the ground running.

"Step Four: Spend, Spend, Spend"

Republicans, when out of power, like to boast of their prowess at budget cutting, deficit reduction, and fiscal conservatism. Yet when in power they have far outspent Democrats, whom they have long charged with fiscal irresponsibility. Most American know that when Bill Clinton left office the nation had a significant budget surplus ($236 billion), and polls report that they now recognize that the nation has a serious deficit ($300 billion). What did Congress do with the money? Taibbi asked that question, and answered, "In the age of Jack Abramoff, that is an ugly question to even contemplate. But let's take just one bill, the so-called energy bill, a big, hairy, favor-laden bitch of a law that started out as the wet dream of Dick Cheney's energy task force and spent four long years leaving grease-tracks on every set of palms in the Capitol before finally becoming law in 2005. Like a lot of laws in the Bush era, it was crafted with virtually no input from the Democrats, who were excluded from the conference process."

Pork-barrel spending, which sends federal dollars to local projects that ingratiate legislators with their constituents, has been a part of legislative processes since before the nation's founding. Legislative leaders of both parities use such appropriations to help their members get reelected, and within limits it is an acceptable method that benefits everyone. But used excessively and secretly, as has been the case under Republican control of Congress, it can lead to corruption. Pork is most commonly added to appropriation bills by "earmarks"—that is, by specifically designating how and where federal funds are to be spent. "Congress allocated a record $71.77 billion in 2006 to 15,832 special projects, more than double the $29.11 billion spent on 4,155 pork-barrel projects in 1994, when Democrats last controlled Congress, according to the nonpartisan Congressional Research Service,"[27] Matt

Taibbi discovered. He also found that by 2000 the GOP Congress had passed 6,073 earmarks, and by 2005 the number had risen to 15,877. As Taibbi observed, the Republicans got better at pork every year: "It's the one thing they're good at."

Mann and Ornstein also noted the "startling rise of earmarks," which they viewed as further evidence of the decline in the deliberative process under the GOP. Mann and Ornstein examined the particularly egregious abuses of such spending in the area of public works, citing data that showed an increase in pork spending directly traceable to the Republicans, to wit: "Over the past ten years, pork-barrel spending has increased exponentially, from 1,430 projects totaling $10 billion in 1995 to 10,656 projects totaling $22.9 billion, in 2004." As pragmatists and students of the legislative process, Mann and Ornstein share my view that "pork itself is not evil or even necessarily bad.... But you can reach a point where all the standards fall by the wayside and scarce funds are seriously misallocated—with important programs getting diminished funding so that picayune projects can prevail." They provided a striking example: "Over the past fifty years there have been 9,242 earmarks in highway bills. Of those, 8,504, or 92 percent, have been inserted in the three highway bills enacted since Republicans took the House ten years ago."[28] This is how you finance the building of a bridge to nowhere, as Senator Ted Stevens did, until he was forced to unfund the project.

David Price, who is on the House Appropriations Committee, was deeply troubled by not only the broken processes, but the policies being produced by them. He addressed the distorted spending of Republicans on the floor, where he gave his Bible-thumping conservative colleagues a reminder:

> Mr. Speaker, colleagues will remember the biblical story of the prophet Nathan coming to the mighty King David. Nathan told David a story about a rich man who had many sheep but who took the one little ewe lamb of a poor man to feed a visiting friend. David flew into a rage at the rich man and proclaimed that anyone who would do such a thing deserved to be put to death for abusing

his power and showing so little compassion. And Nathan said to David, "You are that man." This story should lead us to look into the mirror: Are we in danger of becoming "that man"? The Republican budget removes support for housing, education, Medicaid, community development, and small business lending. It raises taxes on the poor. And it does all this so the Republicans can afford new tax cuts for the wealthiest among us. If there was ever a moral issue before this Congress, it is that one.

Then, addressing both Republicans and Democrats, he reminded them that "as Members of Congress, we have a responsibility to be good stewards of the resources of our government and not simply look to our immediate desires but also to the needs of our children and our children's children, including their need to be free of a crippling debt. Republicans claim to be the party of moral values, but their budget belies their claim."[29]

"Contemporary conservatism is first and foremost about shrinking the size and reach of the federal government," Alan Wolfe explained when discussing the fiscal philosophies of Democrats vis-à-vis Republicans. The conservative's mission, he made clear, is ideological. "It does not emerge out of an attempt to solve real-world problems, such as managing increasing deficits or finding revenue to pay for entitlements built into the structure of federal legislation. It stems, rather, from the libertarian conviction that the money government collects in order to carry out its business properly belongs to the people themselves. One thought, and one thought only, guided Bush and his Republican allies since they assumed power...: taxes must be cut, and the more they are cut—especially in ways benefiting the rich—the better." Wolfe said that conservatives regularly find themselves in a bind once in office because they are

under constant pressure from constituents to use government to improve their lives. This puts conservatives in the awkward position of managing government agencies whose missions—indeed,

whose very existence—they believe to be illegitimate. Contemporary conservatism is a walking contradiction. Unable to shrink government but unwilling to improve it, conservatives attempt to split
the difference, expanding government for political gain, but always
in ways that validate their disregard for the very thing they are expanding. The end result is not just bigger government, but more
incompetent government.[30]

Another result of the Republican approach has been good old-fashioned corruption.

"Step Five: Line Your Own Pockets"

The existence of long-rumored high-level bribery schemes became public in 2005 with the increasingly serious reports of the criminal swath
cut by Republican lobbyist Jack Abramoff, who arrived on the cover of
Time magazine in early 2006 as "The Man Who Bought Washington."
When Abramoff cut a deal with the government,[31] pled guilty, and
went to jail for five years and ten months, it sent a chill through Washington that is yet to thaw, and this ongoing investigation had forced the
retirement of a number of prominent Republicans, like Senator Conrad
Burns (R-MT), who lost his reelection bid because of his assistance to
Abramoff (although he has not yet been indicted), and Representative
Bob Ney (R-OH), who plead guilty and went to jail for thirty months.
Many lesser figures—including congressional staffers and people who
worked with or for Abramoff—have also been badly tarnished if not
jailed as a result of this association. The rumors still suggest that a few
major figures in Washington may still be in serious trouble.

The most stunning financial corruption case, however, was that of
California Republican congressman Randy "Duke" Cunningham, who
had been a highly decorated Navy pilot and later a "Top Gun" Navy
pilot instructor. Many who know Cunningham have told me that the
man was "truly money hungry but stupid," qualities that do not make

for a successful criminal. (Unfortunately, it is not an unusual situation among the new breed of conservative office seekers.) In 2004 congressional staffers voted Cunningham the "No Rocket Scientist" ranking in *Washingtonian* magazine.[32] Nonetheless, Cunningham's résumé looks impressive, including even an MBA, which he earned in night-school study at National University in San Diego. It seems that when Duke discovered he was not very good at business, however, he ran for Congress, where fellow Republicans in Washington loved him because of his distinguished service record. No doubt Cunningham loved Congress, too. While he was not good at business he was good at getting government defense contracts for his friends, constituents, and those who paid him handsomely for his assistance.

Few people in Washington could figure out how Duke Cunningham supported his notably lavish lifestyle until it became clear that he was on the take. He appears to be headed for the *Guinness Book of World Records* for the amount of bribes he accepted, which totaled $2.4 million (accounted for so far)—the largest known ever for a member of the U.S. Congress. Evidence of his crimes was so powerful and abundant that his lawyer reported that they had no defense, so he urged his client, then sixty-four years of age, to make a deal with the government, unless he wanted to die in prison. Duke agreed to assist the government in nailing defense contractors who were buying business in Washington, and he was sentenced to eight years in prison, where he now resides. For Taibbi, Duke Cunningham represented "Congress in the Bush years, in a nutshell—a guy who takes $2 million in bribes from a contractor, whooping it up in turtlenecks and pajama bottoms with young women on a contractor-provided yacht named after himself (the 'Duke-Stir'), and not only is he shocked when he's caught, he's too dumb to even understand that he's been guilty of anything."[33]

"Holding the reins of power is a heady experience," Mann and Ornstein confirmed. They, too, were troubled by the GOP's attitude as they came to believe "in the late 1990s and through the first Bush term" that "anything goes." Mann and Ornstein explained that the GOP's desire to hold power and advance their ideological vision required a formidable political machine, one greased by money, staffed by loyalists in lobbying shops, and unabashedly adept at smash-mouth politics. Highlights—or lowlights—included the unprecedented re-redistricting effort in Texas in 2002, which after strenuous efforts that shattered any remaining bipartisanship in the state resulted in an election triumph for the GOP and then subsequently to the indictment of Tom DeLay and two of his cronies. The anything-goes atmosphere also led to the rise and fall of Jack Abramoff, whose multiple scandals, most playing off his access to Tom DeLay and other influential Republicans in Congress, along with players in the White House, the Interior Department, and such outside groups as Americans for Tax Reform, threatened to mushroom into the biggest corruption scandal in Washington in 125 years.[34]

Both Eilperin and Price reached similar conclusions about the corruption infecting the Republicans, although Price is a bit blunter. Eilperin correctly anticipated its negative impact on the GOP's maintaining control of Congress,[35] while Price reported the situation as he found it, namely that the House Republicans had "flat-out rejected any semblance of real ethics reform to rein in the abuses of power in Congress. They refused to even consider dozens of proposals from both Democrats and Republicans that would have strengthened the provisions of the lobbying reform bill and stopped the abusive practices that [had] become all too common within the ruling party." He found the term "do-nothing Congress" had become "more appropriate by the day."[36]

Wolfe, too, expressed concern about a vital part of the corrupting machinery, the infamous Republican K Street Project, named after the street where many lobbyists have their offices, which "was designed not only to allow lobbyists to make contributions to legislators in return for laws that benefit themselves—this has always been part of the politics of democracy—but to transform lobbying, which has usually been understood as bipartisan in nature, into an arm of one political party;

in return for access to government, Republicans insisted that lobbying groups fire Democrats from their leadership positions and replace them with Republicans." Recognizing the damage that the Abramoff plea had done to the K Street Project, Wolfe observed that "although Democrats will surely insist that lobbyists stop hiring only members of the majority party, no one seriously expects that lobbying will return to its once bipartisan days." Wolfe's concerns, expressed in 2006, were well placed. Although the Republicans are keeping tight-lipped about it, I am told that the K Street crowd is doing everything possible to help get Republicans back in control of Congress. They dream of returning to those days when the GOP ran Congress, and GOP leaders like Tom DeLay boasted that he had lobbying firms writing the laws.

While Matt Taibbi's five steps could easily have been labeled "Five Easy Steps to Ruining Congress," the views of Mann, Ornstein, Eilperin, Price, and Wolfe suggest that there is a consensus of analysis on this subject. Mann, Ornstein, Eilperin, and Wolfe also offered explanations for why GOP leaders are unable to manage the Congress, and the party's utter disregard for the constitutional process when they find such compliance politically inconvenient. A glaring example of this was the ease with which they simply ignored the basic requirement of bicameralism, which is symptomatic of both their incompetence and a characteristic "in your face" dishonesty.

Republican Disregard for Constitutional Fundamentals

The requirement that both the House and Senate agree upon legislation before it is sent to the president—bicameralism—is a fundamental precept of the Constitution, part of the system of checks, balances, and separation of powers.* Another basic principle is that all federal

---

*Because the concept of separation of powers is so fundamental to our system of government, and it is mentioned throughout the following pages, I have provided

officials, from the president on down, take a solemn oath to "preserve, protect and defend the Constitution of the United States." In addition, the president further pledges to "faithfully execute the Office of President of the United States" and "take care that the Laws be faithfully executed." Members of the House and Senate likewise pledge to "well and faithfully discharge the duties of the[ir] office."* If these oaths have one underlying rationale, it is to guarantee the responsibility of officeholders to keep the government operating, a point President Lincoln made during his first inaugural address. In the context of the Confederate states leaving the Union, Lincoln broadly discussed his constitutional oath of office. He viewed the Union and its government as perpetual, and stated that the "Constitution and the laws" must continue "unbroken." In Lincoln's vision, it was the president's duty to keep the government operating: "The power confided to me will be used to hold, occupy, and possess the property and places belonging to the Government and to collect the duties and imposts.... The mails, unless repelled, will continue to be furnished in all parts of the Union. So far as possible the people everywhere shall have that sense of perfect security which is most favorable to calm thought and reflection." He closed this address by noting, "*You* have no oath registered in heaven to destroy the Government, while I shall have the most solemn one to 'preserve, protect, and defend it.'"

Is there any time when a president can halt the government in its

_____

additional background information about it. See Appendix A: Separation of Powers: An Essential Process Envisioned by the Framers.

*The presidential oath is set forth at Article II, sections 1 and 3: "I do solemnly swear (or affirm) that I will faithfully execute the Office of President of the United States, and will to the best of my Ability, preserve, protect and defend the Constitution of the United States." The congressional oath is generally required pursuant to Article VI, clause 3, and pursuant to the rules of the House and Senate: "I do solemnly swear (or affirm) that I will support and defend the Constitution of the United States against all enemies, foreign and domestic; that I will bear true faith and allegiance to the same; that I take this obligation freely, without any mental reservation or purpose of evasion; and that I will well and faithfully discharge the duties of the office on which I am about to enter."

authorized operations? Or that Congress can refuse to provide the funding necessary for those operations absent a state of emergency? Obviously, they cannot. Notwithstanding endless lip service about their fidelity to the Constitution, Republicans have shown that they cannot be bothered with constitutional basics like bicameralism, and they actually think it clever to blatantly ignore their oaths and effectively allow the government to be closed down because they refuse to engage in the necessary deliberative processes when they cannot have their own way.

Mann, Ornstein, Eilperin, Price, Wolfe, and Taibbi make the point that when Republicans run Congress they often simply change the rules of the game as they proceed, whether that involves cutting Democrats out of conference deliberations, holding open voting beyond the fifteen-minute rule to twist arms to get votes they need, or similar violations of what is called regular order. But their behavior is far worse than merely breaking the rules of the House (or Senate), for they also have no hesitation about cavalierly ignoring the Constitution. Although these often involve highly technical points, I have selected an example with more serious ramifications: a $2 billion mistake that the Republicans refused to fix. Given the way they ran the Congress, mistakes happened frequently, and when they were discovered, they usually were corrected. But not when it is politically inconvenient.

After months of haggling, the Senate passed the Deficit Reduction Act of 2005, a law that would purportedly reduce the deficit. (In fact, it has failed to do so.) The means the bill employed were grim: It placed much of the financial burden upon the elderly, the poor, and the young, hacking away at benefits previously available under Medicare, Medicaid, and student loan programs. To pass this measure in the Senate required Vice President Dick Cheney to fly back from the Middle East to cast a tie-breaking vote. The Scrooge-like Deficit Reduction Act did pass the Senate 51 to 50, ironically enough, just before Christmas 2005. In one provision of the bill, the Senate voted that oxygen equipment used in the home was to be paid for by Medicare for only up to thirty-six months. (Previously, the law had sensibly paid these expenses as long as needed by the patient.) The Senate placed an even tighter cap of thirteen months' payment for other durable equipment, like wheelchairs and hospital beds. When the bill was sent back to the House, a Senate clerk mistakenly put the thirty-six months, from the vote on the oxygen provision, where the thirteen-month cap for other equipment was intended—thus providing up to thirty-six months' coverage for all such equipment. It was a $2 billion error that benefited Medicare patients.

On February 1, 2006, the Deficit Reduction Act squeaked through the House after heavy lobbying by Republican leaders, by a vote of 216 to 214. When this measure was returned to the Senate, however, the Senate clerk simply changed back the provision that had been mistakenly sent to the House to reflect the Senate-passed version. (That is, the clerk restored the Senate's thirteen-month cap for the other durable equipment, notwithstanding the fact that the House had voted for the longer thirty-six-month cap.) Nonetheless, House speaker Dennis Hastert (R-IL) and president pro tempore of the Senate Ted Stevens (R-AK) certified the Senate measure and sent it to the White House, where the president quickly signed it.

When Democratic members of the House learned that Speaker Hastert had sent the president legislation that was substantially different from what the House had passed—different to the tune of $2 billion—they were understandably dismayed. They had already been effectively shut out of the process: The entire legislative package of cuts had been agreed upon behind closed doors without any Democrats present—standard procedure in the GOP-controlled Congress—and the actual vote in the House had been taken after midnight, another ploy frequently relied upon by the GOP leaders. But sending a bill to the president that had not actually been passed by the House only added injury to insult. Typically, when such mistakes occur, they are corrected with appropriate legislation, which is often done by unanimous consent of both the House and the Senate. This time, however, House Democrats refused to capitulate. They decided they would demand a record vote—the kind that, for good reason, frightened Republicans who had been beating up on the elderly, the poor, and the young in an election year—and they wanted the vote to be taken on the entire bill, not merely on corrective legislation, because they believed that Republicans might not have a majority again, given the harsh measures in the bill. Instead, Senate GOP leaders simply changed the House-passed bill to make it the same as the Senate's, and Speaker Hastert simply acceded on behalf of the House, removing the thirty-six months (and $2 billion) that had already been approved by the House.

Clearly, this action and the resulting "law" were unconstitutional. California Democratic congressman Henry Waxman solicited the views of a number of constitutional experts on the question. Columbia University School of Law professor Michael Dorf advised that "Article I, Section 7 of the Constitution specifies that a bill becomes a law when passed by both houses of Congress and signed by the President. [This Act] was not passed by the House of Representatives. Thus, it is not a law." University of North Carolina School of Law professor Michael Gerhardt similarly said, "This legislation in question does not satisfy the requirements of the Bicameral Clause of the Constitution." And American University law professor Jamin Raskin reported, "The Deficit Reduction Omnibus Reconciliation Act of 2005 may be something but it is not law within the meaning of the Constitution." George Washington University law professor Jonathan Turley noted, "Obviously, the Speaker cannot certify a different bill as the will of the House of Representatives. If he could do that, he could become a House unto himself." Georgetown University law professor David Vladeck observes that these actions violated "one of the most fundamental guarantees in the Constitution."[37] Remarkably, the White House had no comment—rather casual behavior for a president who demands "strict construction" interpretation of the Constitution. No congressional Republicans gave any indication of being offended by this activity, either.

The principle of bicameralism is as crucial as it is simple. During the debates of the Constitutional Convention, the need for a bicameral legislature was addressed by James Wilson, who later became a justice of the U.S. Supreme Court, where he became known for his scholarship. At the nation's founding, Wilson observed: "Despotism comes on mankind in different shapes.... If the Legislative authority be not restrained, there can be neither liberty nor stability; and it can only be restrained by dividing it within itself, into distinct and independent branches. In a single house there is no check, but the inadequate one, of the virtue & good sense of those who compose it."[38] As the *Washington Post* commented on the Deficit Reduction affair: "It's grade school stuff: To become law, a bill must pass both houses of Congress in identical form and be signed by the president or approved over his veto." But in this instance, the *Post* noted, "complying with the Constitution would be really, really inconvenient to President Bush and Republican congressional leaders," so they ignored the Constitution.[39]

At least one prominent Republican was troubled enough by this congressional action and decided to test its legality. Jim Zeigler, a Mobile, Alabama, attorney, filed a lawsuit seeking a declaratory judgment that the Deficit Reduction Act of 2005 violated the Constitution. Zeigler, who served as a Bush delegate to the Republican National Conventions in 2000 and 2004, sued Attorney General Alberto Gonzales and the Unites States attorney for the Southern District of Alabama, where he filed his lawsuit. In addition, the public interest group Public Citizen filed a lawsuit in Washington, D.C. Prevailing in court, however, is going to be very difficult. As I will explain in chapter 3, the federal courts, which are now under the control of the Republicans, have abdicated their responsibility as a check on the other branches unless a policy matter of particular interest to conservatives is concerned. Even if the case lands in the courtroom of a Democratic trial judge, he or she would likely be reversed by a conservative court of appeals.

Republicans have repeatedly and deliberately thrown monkey wrenches into the gears of government, well aware that they could bring the entire machinery to a halt. The news media has portrayed such behavior as budgetary brinksmanship, or fiscal chicken, or mano a mano contests between the branches to see who would blink first, but they do not in any case take it very seriously.* This mind-set started with Ronald Reagan, who uttered a now famous hyperbole in his first inaugural address, "Government is not the solution to our problem; government is the problem." By then his attitude toward government was already well known. For example, in 1976, after losing the presidential nomination to Gerald Ford, Reagan observed that "if government would someday quietly close the doors; if all the bureaucrats would tiptoe out of the marble halls; it would take the people of this country quite a while to miss them or even know they were gone." Once he became president, Reagan made good on his vision rhetoric and literally shut down the government—several times.

Columbia Law School professor Alfred Hill, in an informal opinion published long afterward, concluded that Gingrich & Company, when they similarly closed down the government, had also acted inappropriately. Professor Hill noted that "government shutdowns in the 1990s represented a tactic new to the American political experience and raised serious constitutional questions." During one shutdown, "The chief judge of the United States Court of Appeals for the 6th Circuit, speaking as chairman of the steering committee of the Judicial Conference [which oversees the administration of the federal courts], said that a 'breakdown of constitutional order' was threatened unless an appropriation for the judiciary was made by the first week in January." (As it happened, the shutdown ended that week.) Professor Hill cited a number of other examples of how the denial of funds results in the suspension of countless laws, like those involved in enforcing "environmental protection and pollution control, inspection of food and drugs, operation of the veterans hospitals, the role of the Securities and Exchange Commission in the prevention of securities fraud, and the collection of economic data by various government agencies"—to name a few.

---

*For additional background information about government shutdowns, see Appendix B: Republican Appropriations Process Abuses: Shutting Down the Government.

But he found that the "Constitution is equally implicated when only a single governmental program mandated by statute is suspended by unconstitutional means." Hill concluded that Gingrich and the GOP leaders' (and by implication Reagan's) actions in "1995 and 1996 appear to have been unprecedented." As members of Congress who have "sworn to support the Constitution" they "are obliged to respect its requirements"—which includes maintaining an ongoing government. Congress cannot "refuse to appropriate for any reason it pleases. Congress may never ignore the dictates of the Constitution."[40]

While shutting down the government for political purposes is about as deliberate a breakdown of government as is imaginable, most Americans paid little attention to the matter, if they were even aware of it, because they were not affected. To the best of my knowledge, no one was seriously harmed by these actions, although millions of people were greatly inconvenienced. Eighty-four percent of those polled by Pew thought the shutdown had not had any impact.[41] Similarly, I suspect, most people would care even less—unless personally affected—that the GOP's 109th Congress, ending in January 2007, could not even get itself sufficiently organized to pass the annual spending bill, resulting in the government's operating for the year on continuing resolutions. There is a clear pattern in the GOP's handling of the nation's finances—they are a disaster.

In 1974, in memory of Richard Nixon's refusal to spend appropriated funds and to impound the money against its wishes, Congress enacted the Congressional Budget and Impoundment Control Act, a law that has since been amended many times and that has done much more than merely to address the Nixon problem.[42] Pursuant to this law, and in response to the president's budget, Congress adopts its annual budget resolution, which covers the following fiscal year, as well as the four succeeding ones. This resolution, which by law is to be adopted by April 15, is distributed to the House and Senate committees with jurisdiction over spending, and sets the ceilings for how much can be appropriated. While it is not a law, it is enforced by parliamentary procedures in both the House and Senate.

Remarkably, the GOP Congresses have not only had great difficulty meeting the April 15 deadline, but for the fiscal years 1999, 2003, 2005, and 2007 it simply failed to produce any budget resolution at all.

Under the law, neither the House nor Senate can proceed to floor consideration of either revenue or spending measures for a fiscal year until the budget resolution for that year has been approved—although the House can act on regular appropriations after May 15. If no member of the House or Senate raises a point of order to enforce this rule, it can be (and often is) skirted. By tradition, appropriations bills begin in the House. However, when the House has gotten bogged down, the Senate has broken with this tradition to meet its own constitutional responsibility. To say that the congressional budgetary and appropriation processes are archaic, convoluted, and excessively complex—and I have not even discussed hearings, markups, and floor proceedings—is an understatement. These processes are an unmitigated mess, and conservatives have taken advantage of their weaknesses, engaging in conspicuously unconstitutional behavior by literally stopping government operations for want of appropriated funding.

The *Kiplinger Letter* foresaw the problems that would face the 109th Congress. In its April 21, 2006, prognostication it announced, "Budget squabbles will dog Congress all year." More to the point, this well-informed inside Washington tipster (with information that had to have come from the GOP leadership) reported that the "GOP-led House and Senate won't reach agreement on a budget for fiscal 2007. Leaders are caught between fiscal conservatives seeking to cut spending and GOP moderates teaming up with Democrats to hike it by several billion for education, science, labor, health, transportation, parks and more." Kiplinger correctly predicted that "Republicans will resort to short-term spending bills in the fall to avoid a government shutdown while regular spending bills are stalled. They'll delay tough budget calls until after the Nov. elections gambling that they'll still be in control of both chambers of Congress."[43] When the Republicans lost their gamble, however, and returned to Congress as lame ducks, they refused to process nine of the outstanding spending bills. The GOP left town, many forever, without enacting appropriations bills that represented

more than $400 billion in spending on almost every domestic pro-
gram. "They're going to leave a mess as they go out," Democratic
House speaker-to-be Nancy Pelosi told the *San Francisco Chronicle*.
"It's really sad. The Republicans never miss an opportunity to miss an
opportunity."[44] Such blatant behavior left even a few Republicans red-
faced. "I think it's shameful," Representative Jack Kingston (R-GA), a
twelve-year member of the House Appropriations Committee, told the
Chronicle. "We were fired, as Republicans, for cause and the cause was
we didn't perform."[45] Representative Jo Ann Emerson (R-MO), noted,
"There's so much to do and we're punting. It's irresponsible. There's no
excuse for it."[46] There was also plenty of finger-pointing. "The breakdown of regular order this cycle, indeed the failure to get our bills done,
should be fairly placed at the feet of the departing Senate majority leader
[Bill Frist]," claimed Representative Jerry Lewis (R-CA), the outgoing
House Appropriations Committee chairman.[47] The *Washington Post*
(January 2, 2007) editorially agreed: "They didn't quite trash the place
on their way out, but congressional Republicans—specifically, the Senate leadership under outgoing Majority Leader Bill Frist (R-Tenn.)—
engaged in the legislative equivalent of vandalism when it came to getting
spending bills passed: They didn't." The *Post* called it an "abdication of
responsibility."*

The nine spending bills the GOP abandoned were also loaded with
"thousands of controversial earmarks—special items that members in-

*Tip of the hat to Matt Taibbi, one of the few to report on what this really
meant: "Congressional laziness comes at a high price. By leaving so many appropriations bills unpassed by the beginning of the new fiscal year, Congress forces
big chunks of the government to rely on 'continuing resolutions' for their funding.
Why is this a problem? Because under congressional rules, CRs are funded at the
lowest of three levels: the level approved by the House, the level approved by the
Senate or the level approved from the previous year. Thanks to wide discrepancies
between House and Senate appropriations for social programming, CRs effectively
operate as a backdoor way to slash social programs. It's also a nice way for congressmen to get around having to pay for expensive-ass programs they voted for, like No
Child Left Behind and some of the other terminally underfunded boondoggles of
the Bush years."

serted into the pending spending bills at the last minute without going through the usual appropriations process," the *Chronicle* added. The
Democrats quickly announced that they would freeze the earmarks,* and
when they took control of the 110th Congress in January 2007, they made
good on their word. Among the many rules changes they implemented
was to require that both the House and Senate demonstrate transparency
and accountability with earmarks. "Under the new rules, lawmakers must
submit a written outline of the project for which they are requesting an
earmark, listing its purposes and beneficiaries. They must also certify that
they have no financial stake in the project in statements posted on the
Internet within 48 hours after the earmark request is submitted. More
information must also be posted 48 hours before it comes to a vote," a
news report explained in summarizing the new procedures.[48]

By early February 2007, the Democratic House had cleaned up
much of the fiscal mess left behind by the GOP. As the *New York Times*
(February 3, 2007) described the effort, the "Democratic-led House
has made the most of a sorry budgetary business, stripping out billions
of dollars in earmarked pork from a spending measure urgently needed
to keep the government running this year.... This stopgap measure
roughly duplicates the spending levels of last year's budget, but has
enough room for important changes neglected by the last Congress."
The House had passed a "rare piece of legislative sausage devoid of expensive, toothsome pork."[49]

The perception that the GOP Congress was not working was undeni-
ably widespread. A leading Republican strategist and head of the Tarrance
Group polling organization, Ed Goeas, after studying voters' perceptions of Congress shortly before the 2006 midterm election, concluded,
"Washington is broken and needs to be fixed." Goeas discovered that

---

*In *Conservatives Without Conscience* (p. 130) I discussed earmarks, noting,
"Under GOP congressional leadership, 'earmarks' (meaning pork) spending has
soared. According to the *Wall Street Journal*, at the end of 2005 there were a stagger-
ing 13,998 earmarked expenses, costing $27.3 billion. When the Republicans took
control in 1995 there were only 1,439 earmarked items."

92 percent of American voters believed that all members of Congress put their partisan interests before those of the public.[50] The fact of the matter is 92 percent of Americans have it exactly correct.

Why *is* Congress broken? Mann, Ornstein, Eilperin, and Wolfe attribute the problem to polarization. Mann and Ornstein wrote that the rise of partisan polarization is distorting congressional processes and disrupting regular order. It was the Republican Party that had "manipulated the process to serve partisan interests far beyond what the Democrats did during their forty-year reign in the House."[51] They noted, "Bad process leads to bad policy—and often can lead to bad behavior, including ethical lapses.... The need for change, we believe, is compelling and urgent."[52] Juliet Eilperin included page after page of discussion of polarization's negative impact, for she holds it responsible for nearly every breakdown in her comments quoted earlier. She found that redistricting and the creation of safe House seats also contribute to the problem, and argued for reshaping the political map. One of her thoughts seems especially well taken: "Chipping away at the power of incumbency and of extreme partisans—by shifting the way districts are drawn—will not produce instant results. The parties have drifted apart, and their members are still nursing the wounds of a two-decade-long political battle. It will take years to rebuild relationships on Capitol Hill. But many representatives, particularly those focused on legislative substance, are seeking a rapprochement."[53]

Alan Wolfe observed that "conservative democracy has made its greatest inroads in the U.S. House of Representatives," and noted that research "has shown [that] the introduction of moral and cultural issues into the legislative process encourages members of the House to take extreme positions on which negotiation and compromise become difficult or impossible."[54]

Long before reading these analyses I had reached the conclusion that it was indeed political polarization that was literally destroying the House—an institution for which I have great affection, for I started my government career there working for the minority on the Judiciary committee. I have been watching Congress for four decades. I have close friends who are members of both the House and Senate; I have other friends who serve on the staffs of key committees in both bodies. As I have observed and they have acknowledged, Congress has become a very different place because of the hyperpartisanship of conservative Republicans, who have devoted the past two and half decades to dividing the country into polarized political camps. This has proven to be the only way they can win elections and, in turn, gain government power. Because of their fear that liberals and progressives might just get the country operating fairly and equitably, they have a deep and abiding interest in keeping that power firmly in their own hands.

Politics of Polarization: The GOP's Wedge-Driving Legacy

Today, political affiliation will determine for many what newspapers and magazines they read, what television programs they watch, which bloggers they link to, and what Web sites they prefer, for it is political persuasion that drives their judgment. Republicans discount information from what they perceive as liberal sources, and Democrats respond similarly to conservative sources. Each has its own reality, and seeks to distort what it perceives to be the reality of its opponents. While the nation has been headed in different directions for decades, it is in Congress that such polarization first became highly visible, emerging when the GOP took control in 1994 and growing steadily thereafter. When George W. Bush arrived in the White House it grew exponentially. "Before the Supreme Court decided the outcome of the presidential election of 2000," writes political reporter Thomas Edsall, "Matt Dowd, the former Democrat who had become George W. Bush's chief pollster, sent a memo to the architect of Bush's political career, Karl Rove, declaring, in effect, that the center of the electorate had collapsed." Edsall, who interviewed Dowd—apparently as he was beginning to become disenchanted with Bush & Company*—learned that Dowd's study was "based on a detailed historical examination of poll data from the previous five decades," and provided the information that enabled "Bush to abandon the themes that had guided him as Texas governor and as a candidate for president. Dowd's analysis destroyed the rationale for Bush to govern as 'a uniter, not a divider.' The memo freed Bush to discard centrist strategies and to promote instead polarizing policies designed explicitly to appeal to the conservative Republican core."[55] Based on Dowd's analysis, Rove and Bush went to work to divide the nation even more deeply. Starting in 2002 they helped elect more members of the hard right to Congress. Democratic speaker of the House Nancy Pelosi made it clear when the Democrats won control of the Congress in 2006 that she had no interest in polarized politics, and Democrats have sought to tone down both the divisiveness in Washington and the incivility that became the norm under the GOP.

The polarization that divides us today can be traced to a confluence of events that developed over the course of several decades. First came the collapse of the New Deal coalition that had given the Democratic Party a monopoly in the South. As Daryl Levinson and Richard Pildes explained, this artificial "monopoly was created and sustained by the elaborate system of electoral laws and representative institutions designed, at the end of Reconstruction, to drastically disenfranchise [blacks, who were] a substantial portion of the electorate (as much as one-half in some states), with the aim of eliminating partisan competition." Thus, "disenfranchisement artificially cemented one-party Democratic control. Only national intervention, in the form of the 1965 Voting Rights Act and the constitutional decisions of the Warren Court, began to dismantle this collusive regime."[56] Republicans eagerly exploited this situation, as when Richard Nixon adopted a Southern

---

*In a front-page *New York Times* story it was later reported that Dowd had lost faith in Bush, and was speaking out about his disillusionment. See Jim Rutenberg, "Ex-Aide Details a Loss of Faith in the President," *New York Times* (April 1, 2007) A-1.

strategy to win the heart of conservative Democrats and bring assorted racists, bigots, homophobes, and gun lovers (a group that often displayed the traits of authoritarianism) into the Republican Party.[57]

Republicans did not so much woo Southern conservatives as use hardball strategies to corral them, going directly after their hearts and minds with "wedge issues" to drive them into the GOP ranks. Political reporters started commenting upon this tactic in the mid-1980s. For example, *Washington Post* reporter David Broder, while following the campaign of Republican congressman Carroll Campbell for the governor's chair in South Carolina, reported that the congressman was asked how he, as a Republican, thought he could win the governorship of a state where Democrats had held the post for all but four years in the previous century. Broder said that Campbell's answer (which he characterized rather than quoted) "was to find an issue that would drive a wedge into what [Campbell] described as the 'unnatural' and 'unstable' Democratic coalition," which consisted of two bases: (1) blacks and (2) low-income, mainly rural, whites. Campbell was armed with several issues to achieve that goal, "including the purely symbolic question of flying the Confederate flag over the state capitol, which still bears the scars of Sherman's artillery."[58] Campbell eventually won the contest, and served as governor of South Carolina from 1987 to 1995.[59]

In fact, this rather crude political tactic was new only to the national media. In 1992, when former Nixon aide Patrick Buchanan was running against President George H. W. Bush for the GOP presidential nomination, the *Boston Globe* visited the National Archives to examine Buchanan's White House advice to Nixon, and they discovered that it was he who was the father of the wedge issue. The *Globe* summed up its findings: "As an ardent right-wing strategist for Nixon, Buchanan pioneered the political technique of using 'wedge' issues—for example, using race to divide Northern and Southern Democrats and to alienate blue-collar workers from liberal Democratic positions."[60] Later that year *New York Times* conservative columnist William Safire, a good friend of Buchanan's, tried rhetorically to clean up the public perception of this nasty activity:

As a phrase, "wedge issue" is related to the '80s' "hot-button issue," which was an updating of the '70s' "polarization." "Wedge issue" is a political attack locution, usually used by liberals and moderates, aimed at politicians on the right who bring up sensitive cultural and social subjects during political campaigns. The dividing wedge, however, need not be racial: Free trade is seen by the right as a wedge issue to use to divide workers and environmentalists on the left.

Safire, who turned the use of wedge issues upside down, was cutting his old friend Pat Buchanan a good deal of slack, not to mention his former boss Richard Nixon. Contrary to Safire's statement, conservatives call wedge issues just what they are—wedge issues. Safire provided a nice example of their use by quoting political strategist James Carville, who said during the 1992 Clinton campaign against Bush I, when Bush I found he had no agenda to run on, that his opponent's campaign had to "dust off the Republican manual, which is to go to 'wedge issues': 'We can't lead the country, so maybe we can divide it.' "[61] That, of course, is precisely what they did.

Using the same tactic Bush II picked up seats in Congress for the GOP in 2002, and got himself reelected in 2004 by working only his base and alienating everyone else.

Still, there is no consensus among scholars about precisely how deeply the nation might be divided. Some believe that the distinction drawn between the Republican "Red" and Democratic "Blue" America is all media hype to attract audiences, while others find the current political polarization serious enough to threaten our democracy. This is the type of situation that can drive concerned scholars into a state of symposia. For example, the Center for the Study of Democratic Politics at Princeton University's Woodrow Wilson School of Public and International Affairs gathered some three dozen academics, working journalists, and think-tank scholars with current and former members of Congress for a two-day conference entitled "The Polarization of American Politics: Myth or Reality?"[62]

Given the diversity of views of the attendees, it was surprising that it included not a single outright polarization denier, for like scientists who claim global warming is a hoax and historians who insist the Holocaust didn't happen, a few academics argue that polarization is a myth. When polarization first surfaced, many conservatives disputed its existence, but as it grew more conspicuous, not to mention endlessly reported by the news media, conservatives took the position that it is no worse today that it has ever been, and perhaps not even as bad. Other who did acknowledge it questioned its relevance.* The Princeton conference, despite its title, nevertheless took the existence of polarization as a given and proceeded to sort the facts from fiction by addressing pertinent questions like "has the American public become increasingly polarized and if so in what ways?" The answer was both yes and no. According to the data, so-called political elites (people associated with the news media, academics, campaign workers, and politicians) may well be polarized on a number of divisive social issues, but ordinary Americans are not.[63] There is only one issue that has truly polarized the general public: abortion. On many social issues (homosexuality and interracial marriages, for example) the country is becoming more liberal, notwithstanding the strong opposition of conservative activists. The differences between political activists, in contrast, have "grown sharper since the 1976 election." Today the data show that more people live in geographic areas where like-minded people live, and the map of the South that was once "blindingly" blue (as it was in 1976 when Jimmy Carter ran for president) has become "glaringly" red. Since 1990

---

*As political scientists Michael Robinson and Susan Ellis wrote in the neoconservative journal the *Weekly Standard,* "We suspect that if the Democrats were still the majority party and still controlled Congress and the presidency, the professoriate and the press would probably consider these changes to represent good, responsible government, not dreaded polarization." They added, "Polarization is mostly an urban legend, imagined by the chattering classes of the metropolitan centers of politics and media. Still, as in any legend, there is truth here. But it isn't new and it isn't news." Michael Robinson and Susan Ellis, "Purple America: The Country Is Really an Even Mix of Red and Blue," *Weekly Standard* (Aug. 16, 2004) at www.weeklystandard.com/Content/Protected/Articles/000/000/004/466umchs.asp?pg=1.

research has also established that there has been a "marked decline in people's willingness to hear something they don't want to hear." Thus, they do not have any interest in hearing opposing views.[64]

Commenting on the increased polarization of Congress, one panel presented information that attempted to demonstrate "there is nothing particularly remarkable about the current level of polarization in Congress"; rather, what contributes to the sense of polarization is the period of time being measured. The "25 years of Cold War consensus [on many issues by members of Congress] that followed World War II . . . is the real anomaly," one panel member claimed. As an example, it was argued that if one examines the post–Civil War period as a point of comparison, today's polarization would not appear terribly significant.[65] With all due respect, I must state that this is misleading information. While I have no idea of the political persuasion of the panel member who made this argument, and I have no reason to believe he was politically motivated, his contention is one that is often made by congressional conservatives. Changing the frame of reference for measuring polarization from the last sixty years to a much earlier date (if not the entire two hundred plus years that Congress has been sitting) and claiming that polarization today is close to the historical norm, is nonsense. The argument relies on a highly distorted measurement method, one that essentially compares the proverbial apples to oranges. To reach back to include, for example, the acrimony of the tumultuous days of the Federalist period (1795 to 1800) or the rancor of the post–Civil War Reconstruction era (1865 to 1877) creates a highly distorted context. Most congressional scholarship makes a distinction between "premodern" Congress and "modern" Congress; depending on the scholar, premodern Congress is typically considered to include those up to and as late as the 1880s, while the modern Congress is said to have emerged after this period. In premodern Congress there was a "high turnover of membership, many contested elections, short sessions [with] relatively light workloads, chaotic floor proceedings, high turnover of committee personnel [and] shifting criteria for assignment, numerous criteria for appointment of committee chairs, and underdeveloped political party structure." Modern Congress, in contrast, is characterized by "low turnover of membership, few contested elections, long sessions [with] heavy workloads, orderly floor proceedings, low turnover of committee personnel [and] stable criteria for assignment, seniority the dominant criterion for appointment of committee chairs, and well developed political party structures."[66] Measuring contemporary Congress against the premodern one clearly leads to a distorted comparison. Based on my reading of history, and on the standards of the modern Congress, at least until January 2007, when Democrats pledged to end the polarization, the GOP Congress from 1995 to 2007 was the most polarized in the last century.

The Princeton conference session that included former and present members of Congress agreed that the 109th Congress was "bitterly divided" with "incivility rampant." The congressional panelists regarded civility as "a by-product of stability," and since the Democrat and Republican are close to parity (creating a politically unstable situation) the tone is frequently rancorous. When a party has a comfortable majority "it can afford to make nice," but not when it has only narrow margins. It was also noted that when chairmanships were awarded by seniority, everyone knew where he or she stood, but with the Republican leadership now selecting chairs, the resulting internal politics "exacerbates polarization." Another reason for the divisiveness is the high number of House seats that are safe because of GOP redistricting. As one panelist pointed out, members coming to Washington from safe seats "are less trained to listen and accommodate."[67]

When Republicans unofficially discuss polarization they make it clear that they do not regard it as a significant problem. Given that it has become the natural state in which they thrive, that attitude is hardly surprising. Republican congressman Tom Cole of Oklahoma made precisely such comments at the Princeton conference. Cole has a master's degree from Yale and a doctorate from the University of Oklahoma in British history, and before going to Congress he was an academic. Today he is the fourth-ranking member of the House GOP leadership. Cole said, "I get more concerns about polarization from academics and media and sort of political elites than I do from the average person on the street. They're generally not too concerned about it.... I would agree very much with one of the speakers this morning [who] talked about the differences between disagreements that are [about] whether this person is right or wrong about an issue as opposed to good or bad. That does make it a lot nastier. But whether it actually changes the process ... is quite another matter."*

When Tom Cole dismisses polarization as an issue of little concern to the average voter, he is wrong. While the term "polarization" in the context of politics may not be familiar to the average citizen, its impact and consequences certainly are: political fighting and refusal to cooperate: These are the very facets of politics that are rejected by large numbers of Americans. In their study *Congress as Public Enemy: Public Attitudes Toward American Political Institutions,* John Hibbing and Elizabeth Theiss-Morse found, "People do not wish to see uncertainty, conflicting options, long debate, competing interests, confusion, bargaining, and compromised, imperfect solutions"—all the things that polarization produces. Rather they "want government to do its job quietly and efficiently, sans conflict and sans fuss."[68]

Even more questionable was Tom Cole's contention that polarization in Congress has not had a negative impact. Although he is a highly intelligent, and seasoned, member of Congress, he is also an aggressively partisan conservative Republican, and that conclusion is typical of GOP propaganda. But another panelist, former Oklahoma Republican congressman Mickey Edwards, who spent a decade lecturing at Harvard's Kennedy School of Government and now does so at Princeton, challenged Cole on this point, arguing that when party loyalty is so strong that it trumps institutional loyalty, it is detrimental to the system of separation of powers, and checks and balances. "I have a

*In the summary of the proceedings prepared by Merrell Noden, Tom Cole's extemporaneous statement was edited to read: "I hear more about polarization from academics and politicians than I ever do from the average person on the street. The general populace isn't too concerned about it, though they do like to win. That does make it a lot nastier, but whether it actually changes the process, I don't know." This appears to be a clarification, but I read no real differences in the statements.

strong sense that because of their [referring to congressional Republicans] connection to the [Bush/Cheney] White House instead of their own institutional prerogatives and constitutional requirements," Edwards said, "there has been a great deal of abdication of the separation of powers and responsibilities that has diminished Congress, and, in so doing, somewhat betrayed the American people, who count on the Congress to act as a check on the executive branch." The same point has been made by Daryl Levinson and Richard Pildes, namely, "Under unified governments, smaller partisan majorities [are] able to effect major policy change without the full range of checks and balances that are supposed to divide and diffuse power in the Madisonian system." They continued, "The cardinal virtue of the Madisonian separation of powers is supposed to be that, by raising the transaction costs of governance, it preserves liberty and prevents tyranny," citing from the dissent by Justice Louis Brandeis in *Myers v. United States* that "the doctrine of the separation of powers was adopted by the Convention of 1787, not to promote efficiency but to preclude the exercise of arbitrary power."* And, Levinson and Pildes noted, "there is reason to fear that unified governments will do too much too quickly, too extremely, and with too little deliberation or compromise."[69] As recent history also shows, civil liberties of all Americans have suffered when Republicans control Congress and a warrior president is hell-bent on engaging America in conflict.

Contemporary conservative Republicans on Capitol Hill have used their leverage as lawmakers as no party has ever done before to try to build a permanent Republican majority. Many Republicans have asserted privately—and a few even publicly—that they would have succeeded in this goal if they had not been so blatant and greedy. If anyone thinks that they will not continue trying to achieve it, he or she does not understand the nature of authoritarianism. Conservative GOP leaders are the Energizer bunnies of American politics: Not only do they keep on

*272 U.S. 52, 293 (1926).

keeping on, endlessly proselytizing; they dearly want to regain control, so they can continue. Many of these broken processes have already been repaired, or are being repaired, by the Democrats, now that they again have majorities in both chambers of Congress. The more basic question this material raises is, why would anyone want to return the current generation of Republican leaders to the House and Senate? They should not, for the GOP has earned its place on the sidelines until it demonstrates that it is able to govern, and not merely rule.

Unlike the other branches, Congress is under repair. The Democrats have returned to regular order, civility has been increasingly restored to the House, legislation and spending bills are moving, and Congress as a whole has taken an aggressive stance with oversight of the executive—much to the displeasure of the Bush administration, which has had none for six years. Republicans are deeply worried that the Democrats might succeed in returning the House to its deliberative nature, as they are actually working five-day weeks and operating the Congress as a constitutional co-equal, rather than as an extension of the presidency. Republicans are also concerned about the damage to their party, and the nation, because of the damage caused by their president and vice president.

*The executive power shall be vested in a President
of the United States of America.*

—Article II, Section 1, U.S. Constitution

CHAPTER TWO

Second Branch:
Broken and in Need of Repair

On January 20, 2009, a new president of the United States of America will be sworn in. Unfortunately, that high office has suffered serious damage at the hands of George W. Bush and Richard B. Cheney. Given the excessive secrecy that has characterized this administration from the outset, it has taken time to discern and understand their agenda.* But in forcing the presidency off its constitutional foundations, as they have done, makes it difficult to keep their intentions secret indefinitely. By now it has become impossible to find another presidency in American history that has done as much violence to the Constitution. Politically, they have gotten away with it; historically, that does not appear to be the case, as many historians believe Bush and Cheney have given Americans the worst presidency ever. For this reason it is certainly both justifiable and appropriate to ask if Bush and Cheney represent the worst example ever of the American presidency.

---

*I have written about the secrecy of the Bush administration at length in *Worse Than Watergate: The Secret Presidency of George W. Bush* (2004). So excessive has that secrecy been that it provides sufficient evidence that the executive branch is seriously out of order. This secrecy has largely been used to hide even more serious problems: the efforts of Bush and Cheney to redesign the American presidency to make it the dominant branch—by ignoring the Constitution.

However that question may ultimately be answered, the fact that that question is being seriously and widely raised about a sitting president is powerful evidence of how badly Republican rule has damaged the second branch. The failed Bush/Cheney presidency should serve as the capstone of contemporary Republican presidential rule, by which I mean it is difficult to believe that the situation can get any worse, for the presidency cannot withstand another president and vice president of this ilk. Bush and Cheney have taken this institution to a place the Founders of this nation, and the Framers of the Constitution, so clearly sought to avoid.

Bush/Cheney Presidency as the Worst Ever

Historians and other students of the presidency began submitting negative evaluations of Bush and Cheney well before the end of their first term, and these critical assessments have only increased since.[1] Contrary to the claims (or wishes) of ardent Bush/Cheney supporters, the harsh judgments of the Bush administration have come not only from the usual political suspects, but rather from across the entire political spectrum, and are the conclusions whenever an honest and objective appraisal is made.

We can begin with the Republican right. America's leading conservative, William F. Buckley, Jr., the father of the modern conservative movement, told *CBS Evening News* in the summer of 2006 that, given Bush's record, if he were a European prime minister "he would retire or resign."[2] Pat Buchanan's *American Conservative* magazine has spent more than six years decrying the Bush/Cheney presidency. The headlines of the stories that historians will one day examine to understand this presidency from the point of view of the Buchananites only hint at the antipathy many conservatives have for this presidency: "Counterfeit Conservative" (March 27, 2003); "The Cost of Empire: President Bush's War Policy Marks the Beginning of the End of America's Era of Global Dominance" (October 6, 2003); "Free-Speech Zone: The Administration Quarantines Dissent" (December 15, 2003); "American Richelieu: Dick Cheney, the Hand Behind the Throne" (February 2, 2004); "The Anti-Conservatives: Who Convinced the President That Our Democracy Depends on a Worldwide Crusade?" (February 28, 2006); "Thou Shalt Not Speak Ill of Bush: A Republican Loyalist Is Fired for Sticking to Principle" (March 13, 2006); and "Cheney of Command: Ask the Veep Which Laws Bind the White House" (March 27, 2006).[3] Retired Dartmouth English professor Jeffrey Hart, a lifelong conservative and a former senior editor of the *National Review,* has impeccable conservative credentials. "The common denominator of successful presidents, liberal or conservative, has been that they were realists," Hart wrote in an essay for the *American Conservative* magazine in August 2006. "Because Bush is an ideologue remote from fact, he has failed comprehensively and surely is the worst president in American history—indeed, in the damage he has caused to the nation, without rival in the race for the bottom. Because Bush is generally called a conservative, he will have poisoned the term for decades to come."[4]

The moderate-to-left presidential biographer and syndicated columnist Richard Reeves asked in one of his columns: "Is George Bush the Worst President Ever?" Reeves had spoken with three well-known American historians, all of whom told him that they did not wish to state their belief publicly that Bush represented the low point of the American presidency. Reeves, accordingly, reported on the findings of a poll of 415 historians conducted by the History News Network at George Mason University.* Those results, as early as 2004, were stunning: 338 (81 percent) responded that they believed Bush was failing as president, and only 77 (19 percent) believed that he was succeeding. Remarkably, fifty historians said they believed Bush to be the worst

*See Robert S. McElvaine, "Historians vs. George W. Bush," History News Network (May 17, 2004) at hnn.us/articles/5019.html. I spoke with the editor of HNN, Richard Shenkman, who told me the poll was anonymous, and there was no effort whatsoever to stack it against Bush; to the contrary, while not scientific, it may have been close to the norms for scientific polling, he said.

president ever—even worse than James Buchanan, who has almost universally held that distinction for the past half century.[5] Reeves offered a bill of
particulars provided by those who judged Bush worse than Buchanan:

- Bush has taken the country into an unwinnable war and alienated
  friend and foe alike in the process.
- Bush is bankrupting the country with a combination of aggressive
  military spending and reduced taxation of the rich.
- Bush has deliberately and dangerously attacked the separation of
  church and state.
- Bush has repeatedly "misled," to use a kind word, the American
  people on affairs domestic and foreign.
- Bush has proved to be incompetent in affairs domestic (New Or-
  leans) and foreign (Iraq and the battle against al-Qaeda).
- Bush has sacrificed American employment (including the toleration
  of pension and benefit elimination) to increased overall produc-
  tivity.
- Bush is ignorantly hostile to science and technological progress.
- Bush has tolerated or ignored one of the republic's oldest problems:
  corporate cheating in supplying the military in wartime.[6]

Reeves noted that some of the historians in the HNN poll also believe that President Bush has surrounded himself with an inept if not
dangerous group of advisers, with several placing Vice President Dick
Cheney at the top of that list.

As the end of the Bush presidency draws into sight, more and more
knowledgeable people are assessing his administration. While there are
too many reports to distill them all,[7] a few examples will reveal the pattern of the critiques.

Princeton historian and presidential scholar Sean Wilentz has
weighed in at some length to offer an appraisal of the Bush administration. In a piece in *Rolling Stone* he explained why Bush was likely to be
judged a "colossal historical disgrace," comparable with the occupants
of history's bottom rung of "calamitous" presidents: Herbert Hoover,

Andrew Johnson, and James Buchanan, all of whom, when faced with "enormous difficulties, ... divided the nation, governed erratically and left the nation worse off." Wilentz believes that

> [N]o previous president appears to have squandered the public's trust more than Bush has, [and] [n]o other president—Lincoln in the Civil War, FDR in World War II, John F. Kennedy at critical moments of the Cold War—faced with such a monumental set of military and political circumstances failed to embrace the opposing political party to help wage a truly national struggle. But Bush shut out and even demonized the Democrats.... [H]istory may ultimately hold Bush in the greatest contempt for expanding the powers of the presidency beyond the limits laid down by the U.S. Constitution.... The Bush administration—in seeking to restore what Cheney, a Nixon administration veteran, has called "the legitimate authority of the presidency"—threatens to overturn the Framers' healthy tension in favor of presidential absolutism. Armed with legal findings by his attorney general (and personal lawyer) Alberto Gonzales, the Bush White House has declared that the president's powers as commander in chief in wartime are limitless. No previous wartime president has come close to making so grandiose a claim.[8]

Political scientist Robert Watson cataloged the qualities of presidents who presidential scholars almost universally agree were great—Abraham Lincoln, Franklin Roosevelt, George Washington, and Theodore Roosevelt, with Harry Truman, Thomas Jefferson, and Andrew Jackson not far behind—for "clues as to how Bush measures up." Watson summarized the traits of these great presidents as follows:

- humanity, compassion, and respect for others
- a governing style that unifies, not divides
- rhetorical skills and the ability to communicate a clear, realistic vision

- willingness to listen to experts and the public
- ability to admit error, accept criticism, and be adaptable
- engaged and inquisitive, with a sense of perspective and history
- integrity, inspiring trust among the people
- moral courage in not shrinking from challenges

"Unfortunately," Watson concluded, "Bush's presidency has been the polar opposite of this list." Bush, he says, displays traits that are typical of our worst presidents. For example, "Bush has been tone deaf, disinterested in advice and evidence that contradicts his beliefs, intellectually disengaged from the crises that have enveloped his administration, and arrogant in exercising power." As Watson observed, "Unlike Lincoln (who appealed to 'our better angels' in times of crisis) and FDR (who affirmed that 'the only thing we have to fear is fear itself'), Bush opted for the low road, governing on fear and distraction. Far from uniting the nation and reaching out, he has sealed himself off from the public, press and critics and divided this nation more sharply than anytime since the Civil War. Indeed, the president has long passed the point of simply being untrustworthy; he has made a mockery of the office."[9]

"A question that seems to be on everybody's mind these days turns out to be: Is George Bush the worst President in American history?" Nicholas von Hoffman, who writes for *The Nation,* asked on Presidents Day (2007). While noting that there are no valid criteria to make such a judgment, von Hoffman nevertheless surveyed the list of all past presidents and decided that James Buchanan was the worst, because of the "long-lasting" impact of his "political poltroonery," which resulted in the Civil War. As for Bush II, he finds it too early to make such a determination. "One of the criteria for being worst is how much lasting damage the President did. Buchanan, for instance, did more than words can convey. With Bush II the reckoning is yet to be made," von Hoffman concluded. What will that reckoning involve? Von Hoffman offered a few telling suggestions: "We know he is responsible for the death of a lot of people who never hurt him or us. We wonder if he has so disturbed the entire Middle East quadrant of the globe that years and years may pass while the people there and the people here suffer for what he has done. Will we get habeas corpus back? Will the thumb screw become standard operating procedure, or will it be returned to the Middle Ages whence George Bush found it?"[10]

For so many students of the presidency to reach such negative conclusions even before Bush has left office is unprecedented. Nobody can know for certain where Bush and Cheney will stand in history; presidential ranking is best taken as an engaging and sometimes enlightening parlor game.[11] There is no agreed-upon criteria, and those who propose the rankings have varying levels of knowledge of the presidents.[12] Still, what is most revealing in these early evaluations of the Bush/Cheney administration is the criticism of its handling of, and attitude toward, national security, which has become its defining issue. I happen to agree with Sean Wilentz's concerns about the expansion of presidential powers. This, of course, is precisely what got Nixon in trouble, for he did not want a merely strong presidency, but rather a superior executive branch that could dominate its constitutional co-equals. The debate about the breadth of presidential powers is, of course, an old one, and has provoked commentary literally since the nation's founding.[13]

The question remains, however, what this administration has done to invite such hostile commentary. That question is not very difficult to answer for anyone who has followed it closely. George W. Bush entered the presidency with no national security credentials whatsoever; that lack of experience was not perceived as a relevant issue during the 2000 campaign, because the world was relatively peaceful and because his running mate, Dick Cheney, did have extensive national security experience. Given those realities, it has long been apparent that the man behind the curtain, the shrouded figure who has been pulling the levers and pushing the buttons that have taken this administration in so many wrong directions, was none other than Dick Cheney. His almost single-handed guidance of the American presidency seemed dazzling at first, as he quietly worked his will before many people began to realize what he was doing. Often his hand is visible; in other situations it is not terribly difficult to discern his involvement. To understand the Bush administration, and to understand the thinking of those who now dominate the Republican Party, it is essential to understand Cheney. He does not respect the government created by our Constitution, and he has been urging presidents to ignore it—as he does—for decades. It is not necessary to investigate Cheney's entire biography to recognize that this man of consummate bad judgment has done great damage to our government. Accordingly, I have selected only a few issues where Cheney has consistently insisted on acting outside the boundaries of the Constitution by relying on unconvincing—when not preposterous—arguments that sustain his extraconstitutional activities.

For purposes of clarification, let me note that I have absolutely no personal bias toward Cheney. To my knowledge I have never met the man, nor have I had any direct or indirect personal dealings with him, although he was at the Nixon White House at the same time I was there. Yet to make the point as strongly as possible, as someone who has studied the presidency for over forty years, I believe that Cheney has been an unmitigated disaster for the institution. Acquaintances of mine who do know him well do not understand what has happened to the man. Brent Scowcroft, who was Bush I's national security adviser and remains a close friend of the former president, said, "I consider Cheney a good friend—I've known him for thirty years. But Dick Cheney I don't know anymore."[14] Others, too, no longer understand him. "I would rather believe [Cheney's] sick rather than just mean and evil," Representative Charles Rangel (D-NY) said of his former House of Representatives colleague.[15] I do not believe Cheney is sick, although it is difficult not to agree with Mr. Rangel's view.[16] In *Conservatives Without Conscience,* I set forth my studied view of the vice president, which set forth his long history of very bad judgment, a conclusion that he constantly reinforces.[17] So in many ways his performance as vice president is not as surprising as is George W. Bush's reliance on him. It became clear early that Dick Cheney had his own plans for the Bush presidency.

Cheney's Vice Presidential Mission: Neo-Nixonian Government

Why did Dick Cheney leave millions of dollars in salary and options behind at Halliburton, as CEO and chairman of the board, to become Bush's vice presidential running mate? Vice President John Adams, the first man to hold the post, called it "the most insignificant office that ever the invention of man contrived or his imagination conceived." A century and a half later the thirty-second vice president, John Nance Garner, said that becoming FDR's vice president (after having served as speaker of the House) was "the worst damn fool mistake I ever made"— although he would serve two terms in a job he dismissed as not worth "a warm bucket of piss." His successor, Harry Truman, described the vice presidency as being "about as useful as a cow's fifth teat." Clearly, the scope of the vice presidency has changed, and rather recently, which was surely the reason that Dick Cheney wanted the job.[18]

The office of the vice president (OVP) entered the modern era with President Jimmy Carter and his vice president, Walter Mondale. The relative importance of the office to the presidency can be gauged by tracing the physical location of the vice president's office. Until 1961, when Lyndon Johnson took office as John Kennedy's vice president, the OVP resided on the Senate side of the Capitol building. But Kennedy and Johnson relocated it in the Executive Office Building, adjoining the White House. Then Mondale took the OVP into the West Wing and transformed the post from a globe-trotting ambassador at ceremonial functions to the position of top assistant to the president, a far more influential post than a cabinet secretary or chief of staff.[19] Cheney has built on the Mondale model but has taken it even further—so far, in fact, as to create questions about the legitimacy of the office as currently structured.

In February 1999, at a dinner in Austin with Texas governor George Bush, Cheney, who had been helping to tutor the would-be presidential candidate in foreign policy and national security matters for months in anticipation of his run for the GOP nomination, was asked by Bush to join him as his running mate. Cheney turned him down, but agreed to head a vice presidential search team. By July 3, 2000, Cheney had narrowed the list of potential choices, and went to visit Governor Bush at his Crawford, Texas, ranch to give him an update on the "scrubbing" process he had been putting potential candidates through. After lunch, as Cheney later told Larry King, Bush again urged him to consider being his running mate. This time Cheney did not refuse, but indicated that he would talk to his family and check with his doctors (he'd survived three heart attacks and quadruple bypass surgery).[20] The rest, as they say, is history.

We will never know what was said between Bush and Cheney before their agreement was reached, but it clearly involved an understanding regarding the role that Cheney would play. It is unimaginable that Cheney would have agreed to accept a merely ceremonial role serving much as Bush senior had for Ronald Reagan. Cheney had witnessed the vice presidency become a significant post under Mondale, and given his knowledge of the workings of the White House and Washington, Cheney knew what he could accomplish in the job. A vice president is, in effect, elected by one person—the presidential candidate (or president, when filling a vacancy in the office under the Twenty-fifth Amendment). Presidents are not elected because of their vice presidential running mates. A vice president is accountable to no one, because he cannot be fired, even by a president. (Of course, a president can request that a vice president resign, but if he does not wish to do so, he can only be removed by impeachment.) Above all, Mondale's vice presidency showed that through loyalty to the president, and with proper staffing, a vice president with knowledge and skill in the ways of Washington could operate behind the scenes and have a tremendous impact on an administration, particularly in areas where a president is not knowledgeable. Cheney had to be painfully aware that Bush, if elected, would need a lot of assistance in national security matters, in dealing with Congress, and in negotiating his way through the various bureaucracies of Washington. The odds were good that Bush would win the presidency: He had all the money necessary to overcome all

the other GOP competitors; and he did understand presidential campaigns (having worked in all his father's races), assembling a first-rate
campaign team under Karl Rove, who had developed a solid strategy to
win. So Cheney decided to return to politics, where he could take care
of a lot of unfinished business.

Bush came to the Oval Office with little idea about how to govern.
He was process ignorant, and had neither the disposition nor inclination to wade into the minutiae of either policy or process. Cheney, on
the other hand, had some three decades of experience with both: He
was a true policy wonk, with strong convictions about how government should work, and as a former White House chief of staff and
secretary of defense, he understood the inside game of capital politics.
(Even while out of government, Cheney had remained involved with
Washington, residing at the American Enterprise Institute and then
running Halliburton, which derived significant earnings from work for
American and foreign governments.) During his long years associated
with government, Cheney had accumulated a good deal of baggage,
which he hauled back to the White House and unpacked issue by issue
as vice president. Volumes will be written one day about Vice President
Cheney. (The record, however, will never be complete, because he will
almost certainly destroy as much of the hard evidence as possible before
leaving, in utter defiance of the 1978 Presidential Records Act, which
requires all such records be maintained, but which Cheney regards as
unconstitutional.) For my purposes—to explore Cheney's central role
in pulling the American presidency off its constitutional foundations—
it is only necessary to examine his beliefs about presidential powers with
respect to national security, along with his deep aversion to the checks
and balances that are a vital part of the Constitution's separation of
powers. In fact, Cheney's viewpoint is representative of the thinking of
many conservatives, both in and out of government, people now filling
the ranks from which officials of future Republican administrations will
be drawn.

Although Cheney's first job on Capitol Hill was working for

Wisconsin Republican congressman William Steiger in 1968, he has
consistently shown antipathy toward Congress, in matters large and
small. Thus, in his official biography he prefers to state that his career
in public service began in 1969 "when he joined the Nixon Administration, serving in a number of positions at the Cost of Living Council, at
the Office of Economic Opportunity, and within the White House."
After Gerald Ford became president following Nixon's resignation,
Cheney became Donald Rumsfeld's deputy White House chief of staff,
and then (again according to Cheney's official biography), when Rumsfeld became Ford's secretary of defense, "in November 1975, [Cheney]
was named Assistant to the President and White House Chief of Staff,
a position he held throughout the remainder of the Ford Administration."[21] During his tenure at the Ford White House he observed the
workings of the presidency up close, and it was that experience that
appears to have traumatized his relationships with, and understanding of, Congress, for it was during those years that Congress began its
historic readjustment of constitutional powers, reigning in what Arthur
Schlesinger appropriately and enduringly labeled "the imperial presidency," by which he meant not a strong presidency but a superior and
dominating one, more akin to a modern monarchy.[22]

Most Americans found Nixon's imperial presidency—with its excessive secrecy, its abuses of power, its corruption of governmental
processes, and its effort to place the president and his men above and
beyond the law—deeply troubling. They were reassured when a long-
slumbering Congress awoke to renew the constitutional checks and
balances envisioned by the Framers, and brought the second branch
back within the bounds of the Constitution and laws of the land. But
not Dick Cheney. "Watergate, Cheney has long maintained, was not a
criminal conspiracy but the result of a power struggle between the legislative and executive branches," Joan Didion explained in her profile of
the vice president.[23] That era remains important to Cheney for all the
wrong reasons.

"Watergate—a lot of the things around Watergate and Vietnam,
both, in the seventies, served to erode the authority, I think, the president

needs to be effective," Vice President Cheney remarked during a flight to the Middle East in December 2005. It was late afternoon, and Air Force Two was headed toward Oman, when Cheney did something he seldom does—talk with the pool reporters. He was asked, based on his long experience at the top of government, for his "view of presidential powers, and the degree to which [he] felt over the last four years that [he] and [his] office need[ed] to play a role in reasserting those powers both vis-à-vis Congress, and in terms of expanding presidential powers to take account of the world that we live in now." The question struck a responsive chord, for Cheney answered it at great length, the essence of which follows.

"Yes, I do have the view that over the years there had been an erosion of presidential power and authority, that it's reflected in a number of developments," Cheney began, and named several of them. "The War Powers Act, which many people believe is unconstitutional. It's never really been tested. We sort of have an understanding when we commit force that the U.S., the government, the executive branch will notify the Congress, but making it clear we're not doing [as prescribed by that law, rather in] a different form [than] the War Powers Act." Then Cheney added, "I am one of those who believe that [law] was an infringement upon the authority of the President." He next mentioned (but either he or the transcript was garbled) "the Congressional Budget and Impoundment Control Act of 1974, which passed during the Ford administration that limited the President's authority to impound funds." Cheney vaguely alluded to "a series of things, Watergate—a lot of the things around Watergate and Vietnam, both, in the seventies served to erode the authority."

As the monologue continued he explained that he thought presidents needed all the authority they could get, and cited a source that contained his thinking about the powers of the president vis-à-vis the Congress. "If you want reference to an obscure text, go look at the minority views that were filed with the Iran-Contra* Committee,

*The so-called Iran-Contra affair, also referred to in chapter 1, arose in 1986 when two scandals conflated into one during the Reagan presidency. Contrary to

the Iran-Contra Report, in about 1987. Nobody has ever read them, but we—part of the argument in Iran Contra was whether or not the President had the authority to do what was done in the Reagan years. And those of us in the minority wrote minority views, but they were actually authored by a guy working for me, for my staff, that I think are very good in laying out a robust view of the President's prerogatives with respect to the conduct of especially foreign policy and national security matters. It will give you a much broader perspective." Anticipating that someone might actually take him at his word and have a look at those views, which take a savage view of Congress, not to mention the Constitution, Cheney added a bit of rhetorical cover, noting that he had served in the Congress for ten years. "I've got enormous regard for the [Congress],... but I do believe that, especially in the day and age we live in, the nature of the threats we face—it was true during the Cold War, as well as I think what is true now—the President of the United States needs to have his constitutional powers unimpaired, if you will, in terms of the conduct of national security policy. That's my personal view."[24]

Several people close to the vice president further explained his thinking on this subject to Jane Mayer of *The New Yorker* in 2006, when she was writing a profile of Cheney's longtime associate David Addington, who had become the vice president's chief of staff when I. Lewis "Scooter" Libby was indicted for perjury and obstruction of justice. In her piece Mayer quotes Michael J. Malbin, a political scientist who worked for Cheney when Cheney was the ranking Republican member of the joint House and Senate investigation of Iran-Contra, as

---

President Reagan's publicly stated policy, members of his administration helped arrange the sales of arms to Iran, an enemy of the United States, with the proceeds of the sales being used to fund the Nicaraguan Contra forces, contrary to a law passed by Congress and signed by President Reagan. Members of the Reagan administration openly lied to Congress about these activities, and when they were discovered, countless documents were destroyed, making it difficult for Congress, and later an independent counsel prosecutor, to reconstruct precisely what had happened.

well as when Cheney became secretary of defense. (Malbin's relationship with Cheney continued, indirectly, with his appointment from 1990 to 1994 to the National Humanities Council, a group of twenty-six citizens appointed to the post by the Bush I White House to advise the chair of the National Endowment for the Humanities, who at the time was Cheney's wife, Lynne.) It was Malbin who was the author of the "obscure text" to which Cheney referred.[25] As he told Mayer, "On a range of executive-power issues, Cheney thought that Presidents from Nixon onward yielded too quickly." California Democratic congresswoman Jane Harman, who at the time was the ranking Democrat on the House Intelligence Committee, told Jane Mayer that she had spent considerable time working with Cheney in recent years, and she thought Cheney and Addington were still fighting Watergate. "They're focused on restoring the Nixon Presidency," Harman told Mayer. "They've persuaded themselves that, following Nixon, things went all wrong."[26] In short, Cheney wants to resurrect Nixonian government, particularly in matters of national security.

Malbin's "obscure text," as Cheney explained, had been released in 1987 by the Republican members of the House and Senate joint committees as the minority report section of the "Report of the Congressional Committees Investigating the Iran-Contra Affair with Supplemental, Minority, and Additional Views."[27] Although the document reveals Cheney's long-held Nixonian mind-set, it shows his thinking is not as carefully considered or as well reasoned as that of Nixon, who had a solid analytical legal mind and usually recognized nonsense when he saw it. Cheney has no legal training and, it appears, limited analytical skills, for he cannot distinguish shoddy scholarship from the real thing, as evident from his pride in the Iran-Contra committee minority report, which is replete with errors.

Although Cheney told reporters that the 1987 minority report went unread, he and his cohorts at the time had actually leaked it before the majority made their report public, thus ensuring that it would draw early and widespread attention. In an editorial, the *New York Times* characterized the minority report for what it was—an effort by Republicans to trivialize the Iran-Contra scandal: "Eight Republican members of the Iran-contra committees say of President Reagan's role in the affair that he made 'mistakes in judgment, and nothing more.' They appear, in a minority report, to be more vexed at their committee colleagues for reaching harsher conclusions than at Mr. Reagan, Lieutenant Colonel North and others for bringing the nation low." The *Times* added, "The Iran-contra affair raised fundamental questions of law and policy. The Republicans who signed the minority report do a disservice to their party and country by dismissing it as simply an issue of perspective and a matter of judgment. Their report is surely a matter of judgment: poor and partisan."[28] Not only did the minority report twist history, and was replete with factual and other errors, but it sought to establish extreme standards for presidential powers vis-à-vis Congress. Since as vice president Cheney has sought to implement these standards, it is worth examining a few high points of the document more closely.

Foreshadowing the lack of institutional responsibility that became the norm during the period of Republican control of Congress (1995–2007), Wyoming representative Dick Cheney and his Republican colleagues on the Iran-Contra joint committee scolded Congress itself for passing laws that restricted President Reagan's covert activities in Nicaragua, and then investigating the Reagan administration when it violated those laws, even though Reagan had signed the legislation.[29] The minority report is, in fact, primarily a testament to the views of Cheney (and conservative Republicans) that the president of the United States must be the preeminent if not the sole authority in the conduct of the nation's foreign policy (and national security), and that the Congress—other than writing checks to finance the president's policies—has no real role whatsoever. (Conservatives become deeply conflicted, however, when the president is a Democrat, so rather than attack the institution, which they want to keep strong, they attack the occupant of the office.) Adopting this position is tantamount to ignoring the text of the Constitution, which vests a preponderance of foreign policy powers with Congress—a position that is quite clear.* (Because the Iran-Contra committee minority report has had both historical and contemporary significance—since it represents current GOP thinking—and it is illustrative of the Republican effort to diminish if not undermine congressional involvement in national security, it is long past due that scholars deconstructed this document and exposed its distorted scholarship.[30])

As political scientist and congressional powers expert Louis Fisher testified before the Senate Judiciary Committee: "The breadth of congressional power [in national security] is evident simply by looking at

*For example, Article I vests Congress with specific but broad powers relating to foreign affairs and national security, such as the power to lay and collect taxes, duties, imposts, and excises; to pay debts and provide for the common defense; to regulate commerce with foreign nations; to establish a uniform rule of naturalization; to define and punish piracies and felonies committed on the high seas, and offenses against the law of nations; to declare war, grant letters of marque and reprisal, and make rules concerning captures on land and water; to raise and support armies, but no appropriation of money to that use shall be for a longer term than two years; to provide and maintain a navy; to make rules for the government and regulation of the land and naval forces; to provide for calling forth the militia to execute the laws of the union, suppress insurrections and repel invasions; to provide for organizing, arming, and disciplining the militia, and for governing such part of them as may be employed in the service of the United States, reserving to the states respectively, the appointment of the officers, and the authority of training the militia according to the discipline prescribed by Congress; and to make all laws which shall be necessary and proper for carrying into execution the foregoing powers, and all other powers vested by this Constitution in the government of the United States, or in any department or officer thereof.

By comparison, Article II narrowly designated the president to be the commander in chief of the Army and Navy of the United States, and of the militia of the several states, when called into the actual service of the United States; he shall have power, by and with the advice and consent of the Senate, to make treaties, provided two thirds of the senators present concur; and he shall nominate, and by and with the advice and consent of the Senate, shall appoint ambassadors, and he shall receive ambassadors; and he shall take care that the laws be faithfully executed.

the text of the Constitution and comparing Article I to Article II.... The powers expressly stated give Congress the predominant role in matters of war. However, this purely textual reading misses what the American Framers did, why they did it, and how they broke with the reigning British models of executive power. Their study of history led them to place in Congress the sole power to take the country from a state of peace to a state of war. They left with the President, in his capacity as Commander in Chief, certain defensive powers to 'repel sudden attacks.' "[31]

Because Cheney has always been a backroom operator, it is not always easy to determine precisely what he was doing at any point during his career. But another conspicuous statement of his continued dissatisfaction with congressional exercise of its constitutional and institutional role vis-à-vis the president's regarding foreign policy surfaced when he published an essay shortly before President George H. W. Bush appointed him to serve as secretary of defense in 1989. This piece, written for the American Enterprise Institute (apparently drafted by Michael Malbin but released under Cheney's name) was entitled "Congressional Overreaching in Foreign Policy," and again criticized what its author viewed as congressional incompetence in handling foreign policy. "Broadly speaking," he wrote, "the Congress was intended to be a collective, deliberative body. When working at its best, it would slow down decisions, improve their substantive content, subject them to compromise, and help build a consensus behind general rules before they were to be applied to the citizenry. The presidency, in contrast, was designed as a one-person office to ensure that it would be ready for action." Cheney continued, "At its best Congress is a deliberative body whose internal checks and balances favor delay as a method of stimulating compromise. At its worst it is a collection of 535 individuals, separately elected politicians, each of whom seeks to claim credit and avoid blame. Whichever of these faces Congress may put on at any given moment, the legislative branch is ill equipped to handle many of the foreign policy tasks it has been taking upon itself lately."[32]

The essay reaches the conclusion that an elected temporary monarch would be more efficient and effective than a cumbersome tripartite government with conflicting and overlapping powers, not to mention 535 weak-willed elected representatives of the people. Cheney seems to be oblivious to the fact that the type of government he advocates is not, in fact, the government our Constitution provides. (There is a remedy, however, if he genuinely believes another system to be better: Amend the Constitution.) His argument also assumes that a more agile, energetic, and fast-acting chief executive is the better system, but history does not support that contention. Presidential leadership has consistently shown itself less wise and less prudent than the slower but more deliberative nature of the system we have. It was Congress that forced presidents out of no-win wars like Vietnam. The reason the nation's Founders empowered Congress was because they wisely realized that a president—like heads of governments throughout history—was prone to fighting wars for his own glory, without seeming able to easily bring those wars to an end.

When Saddam Hussein's Iraqi troops invaded Kuwait in 1990, Dick Cheney was the secretary of defense. "Cheney, who during Iran-Contra had already argued that an American president has sweeping authority over foreign policy, tried to persuade [George H. W.] Bush he could go to war without congressional approval and that the administration might lose [a request for approval] on Capitol Hill," reports James Mann, senior writer-in-residence at the Center for Strategic and International Studies.[33] Although Bush Senior was not as taken with Cheney's advice as his son would be,[34] Cheney's Pentagon moved into full war mode, regardless of what the president or Congress might do, and Cheney himself was busy secretly end-running the Pentagon military leadership with his own concocted high-risk plans of battle, which he tried but failed to sell at the White House.[35] As troops were being assembled and deployed toward the battle zone, the president weighed going to war without congressional authority—should Congress refuse him. Speaker of the House Thomas Foley advised the president of concern in the House, and handed him a document signed by eighty-one Democratic members who "insisted that war, if ultimately necessary, could be waged only with congressional authorization."[36] On November 8, 1990, two days after the midterm election, in which Republicans lost nine House seats and one Senate seat, Bush announced that he was deploying a force of another 200,000, which placed a total of 450,000 American troops in various forward staging areas to deal with Saddam's capture of Kuwait. Failure to even informally advise congressional leaders of this additional buildup—an obvious effort to keep the war out of the midterm election—angered many in Congress.

By December 1990, when Secretary of Defense Cheney testified before the Senate, he was questioned on whether Bush I was going to seek authorization for war, and play by the rules set forth in the Constitution or not. Senator Edward Kennedy (D-MA) asked Cheney outright, "Now, barring an act of provocation, do you agree that the president must obtain the approval of Congress in advance before the United States attacks Iraq?" a question he might well have phrased as: Do you believe the president is obligated to follow the Constitution? Cheney, true to his belief that Congress can be read out of the warmaking clauses of the Constitution, responded that he did "not believe the president requires any additional authorization from the Congress before committing U.S. forces to achieve our objectives in the Gulf." The reason, he said, was that "there have been some two hundred times, more than two hundred times, in our history, when presidents have committed U.S. forces, and on only five of those occasions was there a prior declaration of war. And so I am not one who would argue ... that the president's hands are tied, or that he is unable, given his constitutional responsibilities as commander in chief, to carry out his responsibilities."[37] Cheney had announced to Congress, in essence, that he did not need their authority to go to war. Not long after this testimony, Senator Kennedy observed, "We've not seen such arrogance in a president since Watergate."[38] Two decades later, Senator Kennedy could draw the same conclusion, because Cheney and other Republicans would make the same basic arguments—except they have pushed them even further—following the September 11, 2001, terrorist attacks.

Ultimately, Bush Senior rejected Cheney's position. By then congressional leaders had repeatedly warned him that he could not "order combat without congressional authorization."[39] Fifty-three members of Congress filed a lawsuit against Bush to require him to seek congressional approval for going to war against Iraq.[40] Before the lawsuit advanced very far, Bush did ask Congress for a resolution authorizing the use of force to deal with Saddam's invasion of Kuwait, but the request did not expressly acknowledge that he needed congressional approval—although it implicitly recognized that fact.[41] "After three days of solemn, often eloquent debate, Congress ... voted to give President Bush the authority to go to war against Iraq," the *New York Times* reported on January 13, 1991. The Senate approved the use of military force 52 to 47; the House approved the resolution 250 to 193.[42] It was the first time since the Gulf of Tonkin resolution authorizing the use of force in Vietnam that Congress had approved offensive military action. The House of Representatives also sent President Bush, and all future presidents and secretaries of defense, a special message: By a vote of 302 to 131 it passed a resolution asserting that Congress had exclusive constitutional authority to declare war.* The breakdown of the vote is telling: 260 Democrats and 41 Republicans along with one independent voted to support the wording and clear intention of Article I of the Constitution; 126 Republicans and 5 Democrats, all hard-right conservatives, (including Tom DeLay of Texas and two would-be presidents of the United States: Newt Gingrich of Georgia and Duncan Hunter of California)[43] voted against the resolution.[44]

Cheney's explanations of why a president does not need congressional approval are based on bogus legal and historical arguments that have been made before, but no one has pushed them longer or harder than he has, from the Iran-Contra minority report to his days as secretary of defense and for eight years as vice president. Although the argument is

---

*The specific language of H. Res 32 was: "The Congress finds that the Constitution of the United States vests all power to declare war in the Congress of the United States. Any offensive action taken against Iraq must be explicitly approved by the Congress of the United States before such action may be initiated."

pure sophistry, it has been repeated by conservative Republicans so often during the past four decades that it has become conservative canon.[45] Today, Cheney's claims of inherent presidential powers are being used to justify not only unauthorized wars, but also torture, warrantless surveillance on Americans, the authority to designate anyone the president chooses as an enemy combatant, and countless other extreme measures, not to mention asserting that such matters are also outside the jurisdiction of the federal courts (a policy the Supreme Court did ultimately limit). Given the ominous implications of these claims, and where they might take the country, I have addressed them directly in Appendix C by examining them in their most recent iteration by University of California at Berkeley School of Law professor John Yoo, the former Justice Department official who provided the dubious legal opinions underlying many of the Bush/Cheney presidency's extraordinary war measures.*

Cheney's Legacy: Beyond the Imperial Presidency

Dick Cheney's infatuation with Nixonian government has involved activities far more insidious than merely promoting unsound, inaccurate, and specious constitutional war powers arguments. He has also reinvigorated the efforts of conservative Republicans that began in the Reagan years to ignore, nullify, or simply violate the efforts by post-Watergate Congresses to check and balance the executive branch, and then to expand presidential powers far beyond those of even the imperial presidency.

To understand fully where Cheney seeks to take the presidency (acting with Bush's blessings, although he has no apparent interest in the details of what Cheney is doing and why) requires a bit of context.

---

*See Appendix C: Bush and Cheney's Radical Lawyer: The Remarkable Source for Unconstitutional War Powers.

Cheney has made it very clear that his efforts are reactions to what occurred during Watergate and afterward. There is no question that Nixon's presidency, if not Nixon himself, was a provocation to Congress, as only a constitutional co-equal could legitimately take action in response. This did not surprise Nixon, who understood exactly what he was doing when he pushed presidential powers beyond prior limits. In his memoir he acknowledged that he "had thrown down a gauntlet to Congress, the bureaucracy, the media, and the Washington establishment and challenged them to engage in epic battle."[46] Well before Nixon resigned he was losing that battle, and in the aftermath of Watergate, a justifiably annoyed Congress, which was feeling the pressure of an increasingly outraged American public, passed law after law to force the American presidency back onto its constitutional foundations.

Andrew Rudalevige, a Harvard-educated political scientist who teaches at Dickinson College, has studied the impact of Watergate on the presidency vis-à-vis the Congress. Rudalevige, who is too young to have firsthand memories of Watergate, and who appears to be a scholar without a partisan agenda, reported his findings in *The New Imperial Presidency: Renewing Presidential Power after Watergate* (Ann Arbor: University of Michigan Press, 2005). His analysis of the post-Watergate events is virtually identical to my own, but with several exceptions, which I will note. I was most interested in the condition in which Professor Rudalevige found the American presidency at the time Bush and Cheney arrived in Washington, because I believe that an honest evaluation would show that, notwithstanding Cheney's claims to the contrary, the presidency was anything but a weakened institution.

Rudalevige picks up the story at the beginning of Nixon's second term and follows the presidency through Reagan, Bush I, and Clinton, and into the first term of Bush II. "Throughout the 1970s [Congress] erected a latticework of statutes ... to strengthen the legislative hand in interbranch relations. From war powers to public records to executive ethics, from intelligence oversight to [prohibiting] impoundment [by presidents of appropriated funds], this wide-ranging array of new laws reshaped executive-legislative relationships in the substantive areas where congressional prerogative had been slighted," Rudalevige reported, observing that these post-Watergate efforts by Congress "were very much intended to shape politics, and policy, by laying out the formal and informal mechanisms [read: the processes] through which the players in the great game of governance were supposed to interact and come to decisions." Not surprisingly, Professor Rudalevige noted, Congress demanded a larger role for itself, as it "reclaimed control" over the nation's finances, in its constitutional role "in authorizing and overseeing America's military deployments and covert adventures," and in keeping "a close eye on executive corruption." Rudalevige quoted a leading study on the ebb and flow of congressional power, James L. Sundquist's *The Decline and Resurgence of Congress* (1981), which states that from Nixon's high point following his 1972 reelection, which was Congress's low point, there resulted "a collective resolve—a firmness and unity of purpose extraordinarily difficult to attain in a body as diffuse as the Congress—to restore the balance between the executive and legislative branches." Rudalevige found that Congress's efforts to regain its constitutional balance with the presidency focused on checking excesses in government secrecy, by reining in presidential war powers and intelligence gathering, particularly those covert operations undertaken in the name of national security that threatened the civil liberties of Americans. In addition, Congress modernized its budgetary processes rather than defaulting to the president's budgetary decisions, and it created an independent counsel law that made it possible for it to institute investigations and prosecute high-level executive branch misconduct.*

---

*Any list of enactments during this period would include the following: the Federal Advisory Committee Act; Freedom of Information Act Amendments of 1974; Congressional Budget Reform and Impoundment Control Act of 1974; Government in the Sunshine Act of 1976; Presidential Records Act of 1978; and Inspector General Act of 1978. Relating to national security: the Case-Zablocki Act of 1972; War Powers Resolution of 1973; National Emergencies Act of 1974; Hughes-Ryan Amendment in 1974; Jackson-Vanik Amendment in 1974; Clark Amendment in 1976; International Emergency Economic Powers Act of 1977; Foreign Intelligence

As these various laws were adopted, Rudalevige said, journalists began keeping score in the contests of "the President versus Congress." By 1976 "journalists thought Congress was ahead."[47] By 1980, it appeared to me that the legislative and executive branches were operating at an appropriate constitutional equilibrium, but Rudalevige reported that conservatives believed that Congress had overextended, resulting in their rallying around Ronald Reagan's arrival in the White House in 1981 as an opportunity to review presidential power.[48]

Rudalevige regarded "Ronald Reagan's aggressive use of executive tools" as marking the beginning of the White House efforts to roll back the post-Watergate reforms. "Reagan's White House counselor and attorney general Edwin Meese recalled in his memoirs that one 'major threat to constitutional government' faced by the Reagan administration 'was the legislative opportunism that arose out of the Watergate controversies during the early 1970s. Congress had used this episode to expand its power in various ways vis-à-vis the executive branch.' Reagan intended to turn this around," Rudalevige wrote, and explained, "By [Reagan's] second term, many academic observers believed he had succeeded."[49] I do not disagree with Rudalevige's point, but it does need clarification: In the post-Watergate years Congress sought to deconstruct the imperial presidency by returning a constitutional balance to government, where the branches were once again constitutional co-equals. Presidential government is precisely what the nation's Founders sought to avoid by creating the legislative branch, with House elections to be held every two years to keep it close to the people.

Rudalevige portrayed George H. W. Bush as less aggressive than Reagan, but still a president who lost little ground to Congress. In one area—the ability to operate the presidency in greater secrecy than Congress thought proper—Bush I was more successful than Reagan. Because of the Iran-Contra scandal and Reagan's need to appear to not be

Surveillance Act of 1978; Ethics in Government Act of 1978; General Accounting Office Amendments of 1980; and Intelligence Oversight Act of 1980.

involved in a cover-up, Reagan had turned over nearly everything Congress requested, including his personal diary. Rudalevige found Bush I savvier about the ways of Washington than Reagan, having served as a former member of Congress, head of the Republican National Committee (during Watergate, no less), and director of the CIA. Bush I managed to avoid capitulating to Congress not by invoking executive privilege (which had earned a bad name because of Nixon's misuse of it), but rather by calling his refusals to produce information everything *but* executive privilege: "deliberative process privilege," "attorney work product," "internal departmental deliberations," "secret opinions policy"—and other such invented terms. It was a creative tactic, and it worked.[50] (Bush II has successfully used the same ploys, at least during the first six years of his presidency.)

Rudalevige's analysis of President Bill Clinton's relationship with Congress is accurate, but as I see it, incomplete. He acknowledged that Clinton was under constant investigation by independent counsel Ken Starr (and earlier, special counsel Robert Fiske), who probed "Whitewater" (the money-losing investment Bill and Hillary Clinton made in an Arkansas land deal), "Fostergate" (even questioning if Bill or Hillary Clinton had murdered Deputy White House Counsel Vince Foster, rather than his committing suicide), "Travelgate" (examining the propriety of the Clinton White House's firing employees in the White House travel office), "Filegate" (determining how the Clinton White House obtained FBI files on prominent Republicans), and, of course, "Monicagate" (ascertaining whether President Clinton had committed perjury in a civil deposition regarding his affair with White House intern Monica Lewinsky). Starr, who was more partisan than any prosecutor should ever be, particularly one empowered to investigate the highest office in the land, used his grand jury subpoena like a club to beat not only the Clintons but the presidency as an institution by going to court to strip White House lawyers of the attorney-client privilege that had been enjoyed since the nation's founding. The Clintons, of course, were cleared of all criminal wrongdoing except in the president's civil deposition, which would become the basis for the first-ever vote to impeach an elected president, by the Republican-controlled House. Clinton was found not guilty by the Senate.

What Rudalevige has *not* noted is that from 1995 until even after Bill Clinton had departed from the presidency in 2001, the Republican-controlled Congress—particularly the House of Representatives—investigated every issue that Ken Starr was investigating, as well as many more. Republicans in Congress blatantly abused their congressional oversight of the executive branch, using it like a weapon, constantly calling witnesses and demanding documents. Anyone who does not believe that such continuous investigative activity—from a prosecutor with endless resources to dozens of congressional committees—does not hamper a president's ability to govern does not understand how the governing process truly works. It is remarkable that, under the circumstances, Clinton accomplished as much as he did, and although what was done to him was unseemly, unfair, and uncalled for, the GOP never paid politically for the shame it brought on Congress.*

When Starr finished his investigations the independent counsel law was dead, because it contained a sunset provision, and no Congress, regardless of who is in control, is interested in renewing it after seeing what Starr did with it. In truth, the Bush/Cheney presidency has benefited from Republican abuses of both the independent counsel law and Congress's impeachment powers during the Clinton years. With no independent counsel, they have escaped a number of criminal investigations and prosecutions. The creation of a special counsel by the attorney general to investigate the leak of the identity of CIA covert operative Valerie Plame Wilson was something of a fluke, and Special Counsel Patrick Fitzgerald (the U.S. attorney from Chicago)

---

*Republican leaders are well aware that such abuses of Congress's investigative powers have no lasting impact on the party. Nonetheless, GOP leaders assigned these endless investigations to committee chairmen from safe Republican congressional districts, like Dan Burton of Indiana, then chairman of the Government Operations Committee. Although abusive oversight does not appear to cause problems for the party, a member from a marginal district could lose his or her seat by attacking a president.

was remarkably restrained in his investigation. The target of his inquiry should have been Dick Cheney, but he settled for Cheney's chief of staff, Lewis I. "Scooter" Libby, after he lied to the grand jury. Libby was indicted and convicted of perjury, falling on his sword for his friend, mentor, and boss Dick Cheney. Bush II, meanwhile, has escaped an impeachment investigation only because Democratic House speaker Nancy Pelosi has indicated that she would not subject him to what GOP speaker Gingrich subjected Clinton to, when, in fact, crimes and impeachable conduct far more serious than lying about illicit sexual activity in a trumped-up, politically motivated, civil lawsuit against the president have been blatantly undertaken by the Bush administration (for example, lying to Congress about the reasons for going to war in Iraq, employing torture contrary to federal criminal statutes and treaties, openly conducting electronic surveillance of Americans without warrants—to mention only a few).[51]

In tracking the presidency from Nixon to Bush I, Rudalevige reached solid conclusions about its post-Watergate nature; he also assessed the status of the institution that Bush and Cheney found when they arrived at the White House in January 2001. It is nothing like the presidency that Dick Cheney claims he and Bush inherited; it was neither lacking in powers or authority, nor had it been weakened by Congress. It was not a presidency that could honestly be described as Ed Meese had when Reagan arrived in Washington. On the contrary, over the years following Nixon's departure his Republican successors had managed to return the institution to its pre-Watergate imperial stature, and in fact it has become far stronger than Nixon ever envisioned. Rudalevige and others have suggested how this happened, and the short explanation attributes it to a remarkable lack of political gumption on the part of congressional Democrats. By the time Bush and Cheney came to power the presidency had been thoroughly reinvigorated:

- It had a wide array of unilateral administrative tools, from executive orders to regulatory review, at its disposal.
- It had extensively exercised executive privilege, if not always by

name, to withhold information from the public, Congress, and (less successfully) the courts.

- It had expanded its law enforcement authority to overcome many of the post-Vietnam limits on surveillance of suspicious groups and activities.
- It had never been formally limited by the War Powers Resolution and resisted most effective oversight over intelligence activities.
- It had been granted, if temporarily, unprecedented line-item veto authority over spending, and Congress had proven unable or unwilling to abide by the deadlines and discipline of the Congressional Budget Act.
- The Independent Counsel Act had expired, leaving no independent mechanism for investigating criminal behavior within the executive branch (and executive office).[52]

Dick Cheney's contention that the institution of the presidency was something less than it had been before Vietnam and Watergate is more than an exaggeration; it is simply untrue, an unsupportable claim. Cheney has made many absurd claims (Osama and Saddam were allies; Saddam was getting uranium from Niger; Saddam had weapons of mass destruction; Democrats are all cowards; the vice president's not an "entity" within the executive branch, etc., etc.), but he has harped on the weakness of the presidency since the day he arrived back in Washington for a reason. He is not trying to restore the imperial presidency; he knows that is no longer necessary, having been accomplished by Reagan and Bush I. (In fact, the conservative Cato Institute declared that even Clinton operated an imperial presidency.)* Cheney has convinced

*The Cato Institute report stated: "As William Jefferson Clinton came to power in January 1993, there was some reason to hope that the imperial presidency would be scaled back. Clinton, after all, was the first post–Cold War president and a member of a political party that had in the wake of the Vietnam War striven to restrain presidential aggrandizement in foreign policy. Such hopes proved illusory." See Gene Healy, "Arrogance of Power Reborn: The Imperial Presidency and Foreign Policy in the Clinton Years," Cato Institute (Dec. 13, 2000) at www.cato.org/pub_display.php?pub_id=1248. Note: Both the title and the lead sentence of the executive

Bush that his legacy should be to take the presidency to an even more powerful and awesome level. Conservative commentator and columnist George Will saw that agenda coming before Bush even formally announced his intentions to run for the presidency. Recall that it was Dick Cheney who became one of the first tutors to Governor George Bush in 1999, when he began his bid for the White House. On a visit to Bush in Texas that year to talk with the team he had assembled to work on his presidential campaign, Will noticed what the governor and his staff were reading and how they were thinking. "They are recasting conservatism by expunging the traditional conservative ambivalence about presidential power," Will reported at the time. "Hence the presence on the cluttered desk of chief speechwriter Mike Gerson of Terry Eastland's book, *Energy in the Executive: The Case for the Strong Presidency.* Eastland's title comes from Alexander Hamilton's Federalist Paper No. 70: 'Energy in the executive is a leading character in the definition of good government.'" Will explained the philosophy that would turn out later to be Bush's guiding principle: "Eastland's thesis is that 'the strong presidency is necessary to effect ends sought by most conservatives.'"[53] Strikingly, Will concluded his report with a savvy prediction: "A second Bush presidency would be more muscular than the first in exercising executive power." Will, clearly, anticipated this direction long before 9/11, which shows what terrific cover the issue of terrorism has provided for Bush and Cheney. Will's reading of the Bush team's goals provides strong evidence that, even in a hypothetical world in which 9/11 did not occur, we still would have witnessed a concerted grab for executive power by Bush and Cheney.

Terry Eastland's call for conservatives to embrace a strong presidency, and George Will's perception of its significance, reveal a milestone in conservative thinking. Will said that, as the Republicans took note of the emboldened post-Watergate Congress, "congressional supremacy [became] the conservative aspiration." Conservatives suspected that

summary, as well as the report itself, are based on the assumption that Clinton inherited an imperial presidency. Cato faults him for not paring it back.

if "Congress really [could] be a co-equal branch, [then] controlling it might even be preferable to holding the presidency, which is the engine of energetic government." Here Will makes a very important point. "Energetic government" is emblematic of liberal and progressive administrations, not conservative ones. The conservative canon that emerged during the post–World War II period, developed by conservative thinkers like James Burnham, whom George Will has always held in high esteem, opposed strong presidents, particularly those who overpowered Congress. Why, then, the turnabout? As Will explained, "Those ideas died during such Republican debacles as the 1995 government shutdown and the rout of Republicans during budget negotiations with Clinton. These [experiences] gave Republicans their own monomania: they must win the White House, and do so with an executive unapologetic about wielding power."

Works like Terry Eastland's book, and the unabashed insistence of movement conservatives (principally the authoritarian conservatives like the religious right, social conservatives, and the neoconservatives) on increased presidential power, do not fit very comfortably with the traditional conservative values like those of George Will. He hastened to remind his readers, "Conservatives are viscerally suspicious of power made potent by being concentrated in one person, and are wary of the plebiscitary idea of democracy inherent in the idea of a 'presidential nation.'" Eastland's book aimed to overcome such conservative concerns by providing an intellectual and constitutional foundation for all conservatives to embrace a strong presidency. It is, however, a very weak base, deeply flawed as history and constitutional law, and closer to cheerleading for presidential hubris, excessive secrecy, and monarchical-like authority than a solid justification for a strong presidency. Not surprisingly, it was reviewed almost exclusively by conservative publications like the *Wall Street Journal,* the *Washington Times,* and the *National Review.* One line in the *Wall Street Journal*'s review, which is taken from Eastland's book, is particularly worth noting: "At the end of Ronald Reagan's presidency his approval rating was the highest of any president since World War II. 'Like dying rich,' said columnist Charles Krauthammer, 'this is a great moral failure.' "[54] Conservative advocates of a strong president as envisioned by Eastland no doubt believe that a president who has performed truly well during his term of office will be thoroughly despised by the American public but admired by the Charles Krauthammer types. Apparently, this is the model that Bush and Cheney have chosen to follow.

Cornell Law School professor Cynthia Farina called this vision of greatly enhanced presidential leadership the "new presidentialism,"[55] but in fact it is most commonly known by the rather mundane and unthreatening label of "the unitary executive" or "unitary executive theory." (There is, additionally, one rather ominous version of this term as well: the "unitary rational actor.") Most Americans who have heard the expression "unitary executive" did so during the confirmation hearings of Judge Samuel Alito to become an associate justice on the Supreme Court, when with varying degrees of explanation, it was reported in the mainstream media.

When it was first conceived, the unitary executive theory was rather innocuous. But its aims were broadened quickly, and have been steadily distorted and corrupted. Simply stated, the unitary executive means that the president controls the entire executive branch, including all of the independent regulatory agencies created by Congress. In national security matters, it designates the president as the "sole organ," and as commander in chief he alone can decide when to go to war or when to make peace. In its most extreme form unitary executive theory can mean that neither Congress nor the federal courts can tell the president what to do or how to do it, particularly regarding national security matters. It establishes a unilateral presidency that overpowers the other branches, nullifies the separation of powers, thus eliminating checks and balances. It is presidential autocracy, and a totally logical consequence of authoritarian conservatism. Conservatives carried it from the Reagan presidency to the Bush I presidency, and most recently into Bush II's administration, expanding its reach and impact along the way. In its earlier phases, when it was limited to regulatory agencies, it did not go unnoticed by Bill Clinton; when he found it sitting on the shelf at the Justice Department, he could not resist employing it. But he did so much to the chagrin of conservative Republicans. Clinton realized that a theory that had been designed to enable the president to *reduce* federal regulations in health, safety, and environmental matters (the goal of Reagan and Bush I, and later Bush II) could also be employed to *increase* regulation, which Clinton did regarding the environment, health, and safety.

Today, it is very alive, and a very viable theory underlying the American presidency, for Bush and Cheney have pushed it further than their predecessors. While countless Justice Department memoranda and legal opinions developed during the Reagan administration gave birth to this legal bastard, and conservative lawyers have continued to feed it to give it added strength.

Former Clinton White House counsel Beth Nolan clarified its meaning for the Senate Judiciary Committee during the Alito hearings, for it was new to most members of Congress. Nolan testified that this simple term had complex and potentially powerful implications:

> "Unitary executive" is a small phrase with almost limitless import: At the very least, it embodies the concept of presidential control over all executive functions, including those that have traditionally been exercised by "independent" agencies and other actors not subject to the president's direct control. Under this meaning, Congress may not, by statute, insulate the Federal Reserve or the Federal Election Commission, to pick two examples, from presidential control. The phrase is also used to embrace expansive interpretations of the president's substantive powers, and strong limits on the legislative and judicial branches. This is the apparent meaning of the phrase in many of this administration's [referring to Bush II's] signing statements.*

Nolan noted that Judge Alito had embraced the concept of the unitary executive in a speech to the Federalist Society in November 2000.

---

*Signing statements are addressed shortly in this chapter.

(Alito was working in the Office of Legal Counsel [OLC] at the Reagan Department of Justice at the time this theory was first concocted.)[56] Nolan was struck by the theory's "broad reading" of executive power but "narrow view of Congressional power." She offered an example:

[W]hen the Reagan Administration undertook the covert arms-for-hostages operation that eventually grew into the Iran-Contra scandal, it triggered the requirement of the National Security Act that the Administration provide Congress "timely notification" of the covert operation. To determine the boundaries of this requirement, OLC read the phrase "timely notification" against the background of its view of the President's constitutional authority. OLC expressed the President's authority in sweeping terms: "The President's authority to act in the field of international relations is plenary, exclusive, and subject to no legal limitations save those derived from the applicable provisions of the Constitution itself." The same opinion offered as limited a view of Congressional power,... opining that "the Constitution gave to Congress only those powers in the area of foreign affairs that directly involve the exercise of legal authority over American citizens." In a footnote appended to this statement, OLC made clear that by "American citizens" it meant "the private citizenry" and not the President or other executive officials. If such claims are taken seriously, then the President is largely impervious to statutory law in the areas of foreign affairs, national security, and war, and Congress is effectively powerless to act as a constraint against presidential aggrandizement in these areas.[57]

Judge Alito could not have been surprised when his position on unitary executive theory became a critical issue in his confirmation, and many people believe it was one of the key reasons Bush selected him. Yet Alito's answers to all questions relating to this radical theory were, as one journalist wrote, "either confused or less than candid." For example, Alito was asked about a very recent dissenting opinion of Justice Clarence Thomas in *Hamdi v. Rumsfeld* (2004), claiming that the Founders intended that the president have primary responsibility and the power necessary to protect the national security and conduct the nation's foreign relations. Thomas's dissent was a pure expression of unitary executive theory, written in unitarian-executive-speak:

> The Founders intended that the President have primary responsibility—along with the necessary power—to protect the national security and to conduct the Nation's foreign relations. They did so principally because the structural advantages of a *unitary Executive* are essential in these domains. "Energy in the executive is a leading character in the definition of good government. It is essential to the protection of the community against foreign attacks." The Federalist No. 70 (A. Hamilton). The principle "ingredien[t]" for "energy in the executive" is "unity." This is because "decision, activity, secrecy, and dispatch will generally characterize the proceedings of one man, in a much more eminent degree, than the proceedings of any greater number." [Emphasis added.]

When asked about Thomas's opinion, Alito's memory failed him—as it did every time this subject arose; Alito did not recall Thomas's even using the term "unitary executive." With Alito's confirmation to the Supreme Court there now are three justices who subscribe to this radical theory of expanded presidential powers: Antonin Scalia, Clarence Thomas, Samuel Alito; it is widely believed that Chief Justice John Roberts does as well.

We have never had a strong, modern conservative presidency with a solidly conservative Supreme Court to cheer the institution along to greater strengths. Understandably, members of the Senate Judiciary Committee wanted to explore Alito's opinions on this improvised legal-historical-constitutional theory, but they learned little of his thinking. They, however, let the future justice know their thinking. Then chairman of the Senate Judiciary Committee, Arlen Specter (R-PA), told Alito of his concerns:

In speeches to the Federalist Society, you identified yourself as a strong proponent of the so-called unitary executive theory. That's a marginal theory at best, and yet it's one that you've said you believe. This is not an abstract debate. The Bush administration has repeatedly cited this theory to justify its most controversial policies in the war on terrorism. Under this theory, the Bush administration has claimed the right to seize American citizens in the United States and imprison them indefinitely without a charge. They've claimed this right to engage in torture even though American law makes torture a crime. Less than two weeks ago, the White House claimed the right to set aside the McCain torture amendment that passed the Senate 90-9.

"What was the rationale?" Specter asked rhetorically, and then answered the question himself, since Alito had nothing to say. "The unitary executive theory."

Senator Edward Kennedy (D-MA), also a member of the Judiciary Committee, held a press conference at the Center for American Progress where he likewise expressed his apprehension about Judge Alito's advocacy of "the gospel of the unitary executive." Because Alito refused to discuss the subject, Senator Kennedy had turned to the work of law professor Steven Calabresi, one of the originators of the theory and a cofounder of the Federalist Society. Kennedy said Professor Calabresi openly "acknowledged that, if the concept is implemented, it would produce a radical change in how the government operates." Drawing from a 1992 *Harvard Law Review* article by Calabresi, Kennedy warned, "The practical consequence of this theory is dramatic: It renders unconstitutional independent agencies and counsels to the extent that they exercise discretionary executive power." He continued,

Independent agencies such as the Federal Election Commission, created to see that our voting laws are properly enforced and interpreted, would be subject to the president's control. The same is true of the Securities and Exchange Commission, which is charged with preventing corporate abuses such as we recently saw in the case of

Enron, with tragic consequences for American workers. It would compromise the historic independence of the Federal Reserve Board, giving the president unprecedented and dangerous power to manipulate the economy. It would compromise the mission of every agency created to protect hardworking Americans from the exploitation of those who care only about profits, not the health and welfare and the very safety of their employees. Nor is the impact of this bizarre theory limited to the independence of administrative agencies. It has a major effect on other assertions of presidential power as well. Discussing President Bush's aggressive claims for unprecedented executive power in the field of national security, even Professor Calabresi stated recently that without accepting such a theory, "there would be no way that President Bush's anti-terrorism policies could be constitutionally justified."[58]

Among the witnesses the Senate Judiciary Committee called to get a better understanding of the concept of the unitary executive was Harvard Law School professor and Constitution expert Laurence Tribe. Senator Kennedy asked how the unitary executive theory concept "would change the relationship between the executive and Congress." Professor Tribe responded: "Well, it would make it much harder for Congress to say [to a president] 'You cannot interfere with the SEC in the following way. You can't override the directives of the Fed[eral Reserve Board].' Even the independence of the Federal Reserve Board, which could be distinguished on grounds that historically, monetary control was outside the executive power [fall within this theory].... In theory, it could take over the conduct of all of the [federal regulatory] agencies because there are only three branches of government and [they would claim the Federal Reserve Board] belongs in the executive." Professor Tribe added, "Now let me, if I might, just say why this distinction between scope, the reach of his authority, and control is not a coherent one. Yes, it is true that the unitary executive theory would not suddenly add to the executive branch a distinct lump of lawmaking powers; for example, the power that Truman exercised [during the Korean war, when he sought to seize the nation's steel mills, which were about to be shut down by a strike]. The president couldn't suddenly, under the unitary executive theory, gain the power of eminent domain. But the president does have the power to disregard acts of Congress that would impinge on his carrying out of an executive function."

A number of law professors have prominently assisted with burnishing the theory of the unitary executive, among the most active of whom are Professors Steven Calabresi (Northwestern), Anthony Colangelo (Columbia), and brothers Christopher (Vanderbilt/University of Pennsylvania) and John Yoo (Berkeley). Loyola Law School professors Karl Manheim and Allan Ides, however, have no interest in aiding and abetting this troubling theory, and have written a not excessively technical but thorough summary analysis of it, which is available online.[59] Professors Manheim and Ides note the efforts by Calabresi, Colangelo, and the Yoos to "doctrinally ground [the unitary executive] in the text of the Constitution," and then to claim that it "reflects the original understanding of constitutional structure, which, in their estimation, envisioned strict lines of separation between legislative, executive and judicial functions."[60] To promote the theory of the unitary executive, the leading proponents have flooded the market with their claims, placing lengthy articles wherever they found status-enhancing and willing publishers: *Harvard Law Review* (1992), *Yale Law Review* (1994), *Arkansas Law Review* (1995), *Case Western Reserve Law Review* (1997), *Michigan Law Review* (2001), *Vanderbilt Law Review* (2002), and *Iowa Law Review* (2005). But this outpouring of legal "scholarship" strongly suggests that there is more than meets the eye going on. Louis Fisher, when examining the dubious work of John Yoo relating to war powers, explained how easy it is for a well-credentialed law professor to bootstrap his point of view by placing it in a prestigious law journal. Fisher's observation about John Yoo is applicable to all such efforts by conservative legal scholars to bootstrap the unitary executive (Fisher's citations omitted):

Law reviews are student-run publications. Thousands of manuscripts are submitted to the articles editors but they are not peer-reviewed by scholars and experts. Instead, the articles editors look through submitted articles and choose what to print. How do they react to a manuscript that is destined to run 139 pages, fastened down with 625 footnotes, and one that offers a legal theory not seen elsewhere? They are very likely to publish it, regardless of its merits or how tenable the argument. Articles editors, talented and bright as they are, cannot provide a professional, expert read of a manuscript. They are no more learned in British history and the war power than a student at a medical school. In fact, students at a medical school do not pretend to have the competence to select and publish articles for a professional journal. Nor do students at any other graduate school. By allowing the publication of articles that have not been scrutinized and evaluated by specialists, the law review provides "a uniquely fertile breeding ground for the development of defective constitutional analysis." Editorial policy is often driven by a desire to publish articles "for their distinctiveness rather than their scholarly soundness." During the Reagan administration, a number of conservatives promoted the idea of an "inherent item veto," which would allow the President to exercise an item veto without the need for statutory authority or a constitutional amendment. This power, supposedly in existence ever since 1789, was not noticed until conservatives began advocating the idea in the 1980s. Almost all of the groundswell came from articles published in law reviews. The substantive arguments for the inherent item veto were so empty that the OLC, which generally defends executive power, issued a lengthy analysis in 1988 that found the concept wholly lacking in merit. On the hunt for originality, articles editors are eager to publish a manuscript that is likely to stimulate discussion, be cited by other law reviews, and perhaps be mentioned in decisions issued by federal or state courts. It is not at all unusual for a law review article, harebrained though it may be, to prompt dozens of counter-replies that go on for years until it is finally recognized by an exhausted readership that the ground is hopelessly arid. How this outpouring of articles contributes to scholarship, understanding, and progress is never explained.[61]

Bootstrapping legal arguments into controlling law has become a common practice by conservative constitutional legal scholars. Professor Herman Schwartz explains in *Right Wing Justice: The Conservative Campaign to Take Over the Courts* (2004) how conservatives have changed the law by writing law journal articles, then taking their invented ideas to court, where conservative judges have embraced them. When this happens at the level of the Supreme Court, of course, it becomes the law of the land. More specifically, Schwartz explained how conservative legal scholars created the modern "state's rights Constitutional theory," which has been used by conservatives "to undermine the constitutional basis for many social and environmental programs" by claiming that they are in the domain of the states, not the federal government. Schwartz argued that this body of law is "a judge-made product, crafted by five conservative justices on the Supreme Court, conservative lawyers, and others, most of whom are prominent and active members of the Heritage Foundation and the Federalist Society."[62] (These, of course, are the same organizations that are promoting the unitary executive theory as well.)

Alarmingly, Bush and Cheney operate as if the unitary executive was the established constitutional standard for the presidency. They have made this point time and again by asserting so in signing statements.* In

---

*In following the constitutional requirement of signing legislation into law, presidents since the early days of our nation (starting with James Monroe) have issued public pronouncements about such new laws. These are called "signing statements." They are different from veto statements, when a president rejects a bill and sends it back to Congress. Traditionally, these statements, when a president has approved a bill, have had no legal significance whatsoever but are merely presidential comments about the law. From time to time presidents have expressed displeasure with one or more provisions of a law, and have explained in signing statements why they have signed the bill into law rather than veto it. Bush has set a new record in the number of provisions he has objected to in bills he did not veto. Instead Bush has suggested he would not enforce a provision if he believed it in conflict with his presidential powers, including the unitary executive. This, obviously, is another effort to expand presidential powers through extra-constitutional tactics.

the spring of 2006 they finally attracted the attention of the mainstream news media when Charlie Savage, the Washington correspondent for the *Boston Globe,* wrote that "President Bush has quietly claimed the authority to disobey more than 750 laws enacted since he took office, asserting that he has the power to set aside any statute passed by Congress when it conflicts with his interpretation of the Constitution."[63] The concern is not that Bush has issued signing statements—they are, in fact, common with modern presidents—but rather the exceedingly high number of them. There are two metrics for counting signing statements: the number of bills the president signs and issues a statement with, or the number of provisions within a bill that the president addresses in a signing statement. Under either method of measurement Bush II has issued more statements than all presidents combined since the nation's founding. The following is an example of a typical Bush signing statement, issued on January 26, 2006, when the president signed into law H.R. 1815, the National Defense Authorization Act for Fiscal Year 2006. The act authorized funding for the defense of the United States and its interests abroad, for military construction, and for national security–related energy programs:

> The executive branch shall implement these provisions in a manner consistent with *the President's constitutional authority to supervise the unitary executive branch* and to recommend for the consideration of the Congress such measures as the President judges necessary and expedient. Also, the executive branch shall construe section 1206(d) of the Act, which purports to regulate formulation by executive branch officials of proposed programs for the President to direct, in a manner consistent with the President's constitutional authority *to supervise the unitary executive branch* and to require the opinions of heads of executive departments. In addition, the executive branch shall construe section 1513(d) of the Act, which purports to make consultation with specified Members of Congress a precondition to the execution of the law, as calling for but not mandating such

consultation, as is consistent with the Constitution's provisions concerning the separate powers of the Congress to legislate and the President to execute the laws.* [Emphasis added.]

According to attorney Joyce Green (see footnote), who has monitored Bush's signing statements on an ongoing basis, "Most media and web sources have failed to update their numbers since the early-2006 *Boston Globe* article, and few distinguish between the signing statement documents and the number of laws challenged. Therefore, reports of 750 signing statements are very common. At this point, it is more accurate to say that 147 signing statements challenge over 1,140 provisions in about 150 federal bills."** These are truly astounding numbers, and using the provisions rather than bills metric for his predecessors, we discover that Reagan issued 71 during his two terms; Bush I issued 232 in his one term; and Clinton issued 105 in his two terms.[64]

This, again, is Dick Cheney's invisible hand at work, and it is another effort overseen by David Addington. "David Addington was a key advocate of the ... more than 750 other signing statements the administration has issued since taking office," according to *U.S. News & World Report*.[65] At about the same time Charlie Savage reported: "Cheney's legal adviser and chief of staff, David Addington, is the Bush administration's leading architect of the 'signing statements' the president has appended to more than 750 laws. The statements assert the president's right to ignore the laws because they conflict with his interpretation of the Constitution."[66] But as Joyce Green discovered, the process actually starts in the Department of Justice and the Office of

*All signing statements—and comprehensive material relating to Bush's uses and abuses of these statements—can be found on a Web site operated by Oklahoma City attorney Joyce A. Green, described by the American Bar Association as "a concerned and public spirited lawyer" to whom they refer anyone interested in this subject. See www.coherentbabble.com/signingstatements/about.htm. Be sure to read her Frequently Asked Questions for an overview to her material, which covers virtually all the relevant literature, much of it available online.

**Ibid.

Management and Budget.[67] In fact, as a practical matter, it would not be possible for Addington to pour through thousands upon thousands of pages of legislation, not to mention check the underlying laws that are often being amended, and do any other work. Clearly Cheney and Addington have given the DOJ and OMB criteria for what they find unacceptable, because the signing statements are highly repetitious. Professor Philip Cooper, who specializes in public administration, reported that Bush "asserted constitutional objections to over 500 [provisions in bills he signed] during his first term: 82 of these related to his theory of the 'unitary executive,' 77 to the President's exclusive power over foreign affairs, 48 to his power to withhold information required by Congress to protect national security, [and] 37 to his Commander in Chief powers."[68]

It is not the use of signing statements that is a problem, for they have no legal consequence. During the Reagan years, Attorney General Edwin Meese arranged to have signing statements published by the West Publishing company in their compilations of legislation, but a president's statements are extraneous to the law. Reagan's Justice Department wanted them to be considered part of legislative history, but that has not really occurred. A few of Reagan's signing statements have been cited in Supreme Court rulings relating to presidential powers, namely *Bowsher v. Synar* (478 U.S. 717, 719 n.1[1986]), involving the limits of deficit spending, and *INS v. Chadha* (462 U.S. 919 [1983]), where the Court struck down the legislative veto. But it is rare that any court takes into account presidential signing statements. Likewise, it is not that Bush has issued statements asserting that he will not comply with a given provision in the law, for other presidents have taken that stance.

For example, it has long been the position of the Department of Justice that "the President may declare in a signing statement that a provision of the bill before him is flatly unconstitutional, and that he will refuse to enforce it." President Clinton's assistant attorney general for the Office of Legal Counsel, Walter Dellinger (later solicitor general), informed the Clinton White House that "in each of the last three Administrations [Carter, Reagan, and Bush I], the Department of Justice has advised the President that the Constitution provides him with the authority to decline to enforce a clearly unconstitutional law."[69]

Because of the media reaction to the revelation of the extent of Bush's signing statements the American Bar Association appointed a task force on presidential signing statements and the separation of powers doctrine to examine constitutional and legal issues raised by the practice. The bipartisan panel issued a report that went out of its way not to indict the Bush presidency or to pass judgment on what it had been doing. The study involved no independent investigation but rather based its findings on the best expert information available.[70] The task force recommended that Congress enact legislation that would provide a vehicle to test future presidents who used signing statements, again going out of its way to avoid citing Bush II—who in fact is the source of the problem. Their core recommendation was not widely embraced by constitutional and presidential scholars, for the ABA report was premised on there being something inherently wrong with signing statements, which is not the case: It is Bush's abuse of them that is extraordinary.[71]

No one outside the White House knows whether or not Bush is in fact not complying with particular provisions or merely saying he will not comply. If, in fact, Bush has refused to enforce the "1,140 provisions in about 150 federal bills" he should be impeached immediately—notwithstanding Speaker Pelosi's lack of interest—because it would be an extraordinary breach of his oath. Given Bush's characteristically truculent attitude, it is difficult to believe he is issuing these signing statements as a symbolic gesture. By refusing to employ his veto power yet telling Congress he will not enforce laws, he is gaming the system in a fashion never contemplated by the Framers of the Constitution. His statements are an insult to the lawmaking process, for which he claims he does not have to follow the constitutional rules. At minimum they reflect a deplorable attitude for a president of the United States; at worst Bush is engaging in impeachable behavior, but has yet to be caught. It is difficult for me to believe that he has not refused to enforce one or more laws, if not many, and in so doing has failed to follow a careful course similar to that pursued by Bill Clinton when he refused to execute a law.*

In January 2007, the House Judiciary Committee began looking at Bush's uses and abuses of signing statements. The chairman of the House Judiciary Committee, John Conyers, Jr., of Michigan, said he was launching an investigation to determine whether the Bush administration had violated any of the laws it claimed a right to ignore in presidential signing statements.[72] More significant than the witnesses who testified from the American Bar Association about their report, and the witness for the Bush administration, who assured the committee nothing was amiss, is the fact, reported by Charlie Savage, that Conyers is building up the staff of his committee to conduct oversight, but as yet they have not found widespread failure to execute the laws by Bush. So what is going on? Harvard professor of constitutional law Larry Tribe nicely summed up Bush's excessive use of signing statements:

> What is new and distressing in the current situation isn't primarily the frequency with which President Bush, in the course of signing rather than vetoing congressional enactments, says something about his equivocal intentions, or even his defiant views, in connection with their future enforcement or non-enforcement. Rather, what is new and distressing is the bizarre, frighteningly self-serving, and constitutionally reckless character of those views—and the suspicion that this President either intends actually to act on them with some regularity, often in a manner that won't be publicly visible at the time, or intends them as declarations of hegemony and contempt for the coordinate branches—declarations that he hopes will gradually come to be accepted in the constitutional culture as descriptions of the legal and political landscape properly

---

*Clinton's actions, based on the advice of his attorney general, are set forth in note 69 of this chapter.

conceived and as precedents for later action either by his own or by future administrations.[73]

Bush's use of signing statements, many of which claim that the reason he will not follow the law is because they violate the concept of the unitary executive, appears an effort to add credibility to this radical doctrine. By acting like a unitary executive and talking like a unitary executive Bush may actually have convinced himself that he has created a unitary executive. As Joyce Green noticed, the Bush administration constantly refers to the unitary executive not only in signing statements, but mentions it "regularly in court briefs defending exercise of the claimed powers, oral arguments in courts, SAPs [statements of administration policy], Executive Orders, Presidential Proclamations, congressional documents, executive agency reports, remarks by administration officials (in many contexts), and other government materials that are not as easily accessible to the general public."[74]

Bush's use of signing statements and his claims of being a unitary executive, like Cheney's long history of believing Congress an institution inferior to the presidency, are baseless. Similarly, his belief that group think is good and dissent is bad, and that deliberation is too cumbersome, slow, and difficult is foolish, for it rejects studies over the past half century that prove him to be very wrong.[75] Yet Bush and Cheney's thinking, and their corresponding actions, accurately represent the mentality of current Republican rule. Republicans in the House and Senate are deferential to this unpopular president not because it helps them politically—the 2006 election showed that was not the case—but rather because they share his beliefs. If this seems contradictory—and it does—remember that today's authoritarian conservatism is filled with irrational contradictions. Bush and Cheney head the GOP in word and deeds. All Republicans are defenders of the strong presidency not because of the good that strong presidents can do, but because of the rewards its power can bring to all Republicans, including themselves. Given the self-serving mind-set of Republicans, it is not difficult to understand how and why they have given us the worst presidency in modern history, if not ever.

Just as Republicans failed on Capitol Hill, they have failed at the White House, because they do not believe in concepts like the separation of powers—except when they are out of control of one or more of the elective branches. Though I have heard many Republicans praise the separation of powers doctrine, decade after decade their actions reveal that when in power they do not live by their words. From the beginning of our nation's history—from its conception, no less—separation of powers has been the uniquely distinguishing feature of our democratic republic. Presidential war powers that need no congressional approval (and make the executive branch strong), a presidency that acts on radical legal advice and embraces a concocted theory of presidential powers far greater than Americans rejected first with King George and more recently with Richard Nixon's imperial presidency, are no small threat to our government and its underlying principles. But add to this Republican attitude about executive power the actions they have taken with that power during four decades when their presidents have worked relentlessly to make the federal judiciary just another means to implement conservative politics, and the hazards for our democracy escalate significantly. Today as never before, that is the reality. The third branch is heading toward a troubling tipping point, thanks to Republican rule, with the potential of legitimizing an overly empowered, excessively energetic executive branch, while trimming the powers of Congress. That may sound like an overstatement. Regrettably, it is not.

The judicial power of the United States, shall be vested in one supreme court, and in such inferior courts that Congress may from time to time ordain and establish.

—Article III, Section 1, U.S. Constitution

CHAPTER THREE

Third Branch:
Toward the Breaking Point

Because few Americans have direct dealings with the third branch of the federal government, they have little awareness of its impact. For most of us the federal judiciary is the invisible branch. Yet its operations and decisions greatly affect us all, as much and in many instances more so than those of the other branches of government. It is the higher courts in the judicial pecking order of this branch—the U.S. Circuit Courts of Appeal and U.S. Supreme Court—that most commonly have an impact on our lives. As the Alliance for Justice noted, "Federal judges have an indirect, though strong influence over the quality of our air and water, rule on whether a woman's right to choose can be restricted, decide issues of worker and consumer safety, and sentence those convicted of federal crimes. They make decisions that determine the types of schools our children attend and the level of education they will receive there, as well as how far the government can go in limiting our rights in order to protect us from future attacks by terrorists."[1]

Knowledgeable Republicans recognize that their recent presidents have set about making the federal judiciary a conservative stronghold, and that they have largely succeeded. It has never been clear to me why Democrats have only selectively resisted these efforts by Republican presidents, but I do know that if another Republican president should follow Bush II, and another generation of conservative jurists is appointed, the federal judiciary will become a bastion of radical con-servatism with no interest in restraining presidential powers and no in-terest in personal rights and liberties, but great interest in servicing the law to meet the needs of social, religious, and business conservatives. Federal courts can achieve for conservatives what Congress cannot, be-cause conservatives cannot elect sufficient numbers of their own to the legislature to get the supermajorities needed to enact radical laws. It is only necessary to look at the Republican drive to politicize the Supreme Court to see how effective it has been. They have pushed and pushed until the federal judiciary is now poised at a dangerous balance. If it does tip to the hard right, this is going to be a very different nation.

Before reviewing this concerted effort by the Republican executive branch to make the federal judiciary an extension of the presidency, allow me to clear up a misunderstanding some have about how judges operate. It is important to understand how judges make their decisions, because anyone who does not believe that when conservative zealots are selected to be judges and justices that it does not radicalize the system has little appreciation for human nature.

Reality of Judicial Decision Making

Let me be as candid as possible and state that, if you show me an ap-pellate judge who says he or she never lets his or her politics or personal beliefs influence their decision making, I will show you a judge who is either a liar or without sufficient intelligence to be on a higher bench. Of course, good judges do try to keep their objectivity, but it is naive to believe that this is completely possible on anything other than the most mundane, inconsequential, or routine judicial business, which, fortu-nately, constitutes much of the day-to-day work of judges. Good federal judges double-check themselves, and they can—at least in private—be brutally honest about the difficulty of divorcing their jurisprudence from their politics, for their politics and political philosophies are part of who they are, and no one arrives on the federal bench who has not engaged in political activity at some level. After all, all federal judges are political appointees. The mere fact that good judges try to rid their decision making of personal political beliefs influences their thinking. Who truly knows how our unconscious beliefs affect our decisions?

Thoughtless judges, of course, will insist that they always keep their personal beliefs separate from their professional responsibilities, for to do otherwise would be unprincipled. They consult the body of the law and apply it. But this, too, is myth, not reality. Seldom is there such a thing as definitive as *the law.* There are always conflicting cases, differing rules and approaches toward constitutional and statutory interpretation, ambiguities inherent in language itself, and countless other factors that can come to play in making a judgment. Judicial decision making is not a mechanical process, as some pretend it to be.

For nonlawyers (and even for a few lawyers) there are degrees of confusion about the actual work done by judges, which is understandable. Judges encourage mystery. No other government official wears a black robe, sits on an elevated bench, and presides over highly ritualized procedures in which, the higher the court is located in the legal pecking order, the more secretive their methods, and the longer and more obtuse their written decisions. DePaul University professor of constitutional law Jeffery Shaman explained:

> During the nineteenth century a shroud of myth and fiction descended over the legal process. Law came to be seen as a science that could be mechanically applied by judges. According to this view, law and the judicial functions were thought to be essentially nonideological. Law was thought to be neutral, objective, and devoid of values. Hence, it was for the legislative and executive branches of our government, but not the judiciary, to make value judgments or policy choices. Judicial decisions then did not require the exercise of will or discretion, and certainly had nothing to do with making value choices. Judges were expected to be unconcerned about policy, or detached from it; it simply was none of their business.[2]

To a considerable degree, these processes remain shrouded, notwith-standing efforts to reveal how they really operate. For example, as early as 1881 Oliver Wendell Holmes, Jr., revealed that "the life of the law has not been logic: it has been experience," and that experience in-volves "the prejudices which judges share with their fellow-men."[3] In 1908 Roscoe Pound tried to further enlighten those outside the legal fraternity by discrediting the nineteenth-century notion of mechanical jurisprudence. Still, as late as 1936, as Professor Shaman noted, Su-preme Court justice Owen Roberts was still writing as if the Dark Ages of jurisprudence prevailed, in his *U.S. v. Butler* ruling:

> It is sometimes said that the court assumes a power to overrule or control the action of the people's representatives. This is a miscon-ception. The Constitution is the supreme law of the land ordained and established by the people. All legislation must conform to the principles it lays down. When an act of Congress is appropriately challenged in the courts as not conforming to the constitutional mandate, the judicial branch of the government has only one duty; to lay the article of the Constitution which is invoked beside the statute which is challenged and to decide whether the latter squares with the former. All the court does, or can do, is to announce its considered judgment upon the question. The only power it has, if such it may be called, is the power of judgment.[4]

Obviously, if the process was as detached and straightforward as Justice Roberts claimed, a well-equiped laptop computer could handle much of the work of courts today. Obviously it is not, and has never been, so uncomplicated, which has caused constitutional scholars and judges to develop "abstract rules that give an appearance of objectivity and neutrality while masking the human value choices," Professor Sha-man reported. He noted that in the decades "since the original framing of the Constitution, the Supreme Court has created a body of doctrine as it goes about interpreting the document. Through the continual in-terpretation and reinterpretation of the text, the Supreme Court perpetually creates new meaning for the Constitution." The effect of this ongoing revision is that "we have an unwritten Constitution."[5] Let me state that principle even more directly: We have a Constitution that means what those who sit on the Supreme Court tell us it means. One constitutional practitioner sums up the reality of judicial decision making by quoting a highly respected former Chief Justice, Charles Evans Hughes, who said that "90% percent of judicial decisions are based on bias, prejudices and personal and political motivations, and the other 10% is based on the law."[6] This fact makes the appointment of judges especially important to presidents, for their rulings are binding on all governments—federal, state, and local.

A leading mantra of contemporary conservatism is opposition to judges "who legislate from the bench" or who are "judicial activists." Conservatives demand judges who will apply the law as found in the Constitution or statutes enacted by Congress. Republicans seem utterly oblivious to the fact that it is conservative judges who have become the activists. The evidence for this contention is conclusive and indisputable for anyone making an honest assessment with any knowledge of the Supreme Court.* Terms like "judicial activism" or "strict construction," which was an earlier conservative rallying cry, have all become largely meaningless. Cass Sunstein, a law professor and creative researcher at the University of Chicago Law School, has focused on defining more precise terms to broadly describe the different approaches taken by appellate judges—against whom the charge of legislating from the bench or judicial activism is typically made.

Extrapolating, paraphrasing, and quoting Sunstein from his book

---

*See, for example, Thomas M. Keck, *The Most Activist Supreme Court in History: The Road to Modern Judicial Conservatism* (Chicago: University of Chicago Press, 2004). Professor Keck wrote that "when conservatives came to power in the federal judiciary after 1968, they were faced with a difficult choice: they could abandon liberal activism in favor of judicial restraint, or they could use their newfound control of the courts to help dismantle the edifice of modern liberalism" (p. 109). As Keck shows in overwhelming detail, they chose the latter—judicial activism—by any way that term can be defined.

Radicals in Robes: Why Extreme Right-Wing Courts Are Wrong for America (2005), I have summarized four positions or philosophies that he found current among federal judges, which he then used as categories into which judicial thinking can be placed. Notwithstanding the fact that there are always exceptions, his labels are quite comprehensive. I will summarize them all, but the two that are most relevant to this discussion are "minimalism" and "fundamentalism."

- *Perfectionism.* The perfectionist follows the text of the Constitution but is willing to interpret that text in a way that reflects his own beliefs about freedom of speech, equal protection under the law, the power of the president, and other fundamental questions. Former chief justice Earl Warren, who presided over a Court that banned racial segregation; required the voting rule of one person, one vote; prohibited compulsory school prayer; and provided broad protection for dissent is an example of a perfectionist who believed in rights that, as he read the Constitution, included them. This is a position favored by many liberals; conservatives condemn it as judicial activism. Today there are no true perfectionists on the Supreme Court, with the possible exception of Justice John Paul Stevens, who may be a closet perfectionist.
- *Majoritarianism.* This approach is embraced by some judicial conservatives, who say that judges must defer to the democratic process to resolve issues facing society. Accordingly, they want to reduce the role of the Supreme Court to allow the will of the majority of Americans to work its way through elected representatives. If a majority of voters want affirmative action, and to allow same-sex sodomy, it is not for the courts to rule otherwise. Justice Oliver Wendell Holmes was a majoritarian. Recently, this approach has found "significant support among lawyers and law professors, [but] it is hard to find a consistent majoritarian on today's Supreme Court."
- *Minimalism.* "Minimalists are skeptical about general theories of interpretation; they want to proceed one step at a time." They are restrained about getting involved. While "they insist that the Con-

stitution is not frozen in the past," they do not want the Supreme Court creating so-called new rights that lack solid "foundation in traditions and practices." They can be "either conservative or liberal." Justice Felix Frankfurter (from the left) and Justice Sandra Day O'Connor (from the right) were minimalists.

- *Fundamentalism.* "Fundamentalists believe that the Constitution must be interpreted according to the 'original understanding.'" They take the Constitution as meaning today what it meant at the time it was ratified in 1789. If the Constitution did not originally prohibit the federal government from discriminating based on race, prohibit Congress from banning child labor, or provide broad protection for political dissent, then there is no authority for such actions today.[7] (Justice Antonin Scalia is an archetypical fundamentalist.)

Today, perfectionism is rarely to be found in the federal system, and majoritarianism is also in a distinct minority; the contemporary debate primarily involves the minimalists versus the fundamentalists. Sunstein favors minimalism, but, as the title *Radicals in Robes* suggests, he is deeply concerned about the growing reliance on fundamentalism within the federal courts. "It is in constitutional law that fundamentalism can be shown to be destructive and pernicious," he wrote. "Fundamentalism would make Americans much less free than they now are." Sunstein acknowledged that he did not find it "at all pleasant to challenge, as wrong, dangerous, radical, and occasionally hypocritical, the many people of honor and good faith who have come to embrace fundamentalism."[8] But we should not lose sight of the fact that most of these people are authoritarian conservatives, and as such, are not likely to take offense at such criticism.

The prevalence of fundamentalism within the current federal judicial system can be traced to President Nixon's politicization of the federal judiciary, a process his GOP successors have only accelerated. As Sunstein noted, since Reagan arrived in the Oval Office, followed by Bush I and II, there has been "a disciplined, carefully orchestrated, and quite self-conscious effort by high-level Republican officials in the

White House and the Senate ... [to] radically transform the federal judiciary." Few people who are not Supreme Court watchers appreciate what Republican presidents have done to the highest court, not to mention the lower courts, of the land, and how they have done it.

Nixon's Politicalization of Supreme Court Appointments

All presidents have nominated Supreme Court justices and other federal judges who, to varying extents, have shared their political or judicial philosophy. But before Nixon's 1968 presidential campaign no presidential candidate had made the judicial philosophy of a potential candidate for the Supreme Court a major issue in his platform.[9] By doing so Nixon made judicial selection an important part of presidential politics, and for the past four decades, Republican presidents, assisted by conservative GOP senators, have pursued a concerted and sustained effort to seat "strict constructionist," "law and order," "conservative," and "nonactivist" justices on the Supreme Court.* Nixon's own strict constructionist selections were what court watchers would now call "conservative minimalists," although his last appointment was a fundamentalist.

*Notably, moderate Republican president Gerald Ford and moderate Democratic president Bill Clinton did not follow this pattern. During Ford's brief presidency he appointed a single justice, Jimmy Carter had no Supreme Court appointments, and Clinton filled only two vacancies. Neither Ford nor Clinton, however, sought to influence the Court philosophically, nor did they make judicial selection a major campaign issue. Supreme Court scholars acknowledge that both Ford and Clinton primarily looked for good judges and sought to avoid confirmation fights, not wishing to spend their political capital.[10] For fuller analysis of the Ford and Clinton appointments, see note 10. Both men's nominees were noncontroversial, all judicial minimalists who were easily confirmed: Ford's John Paul Stevens was received a Senate vote of 98 to 0, Clinton's Ruth Bader Ginsburg was approved by a vote of 96 to 3 (with three ultraconservatives opposing her), and Clinton's Stephen Breyer was passed by 87 to 9 (drawing a only bit more GOP opposition).

Nixon selected four members of the Supreme Court: a chief justice (Warren Burger) and three associate justices (Harry Blackman, Lewis Powell, and William Rehnquist), but began playing hardball politics with the Court even before he was elected president. In June 1968, acting eight months before the end of Lyndon Johnson's term as president, Chief Justice Earl Warren announced he was stepping down, giving LBJ ample time to fill the vacancy. Nixon understood that the politically savvy Warren was attempting to preempt him, as by then he appeared to be the likely winner of the election. Nixon accordingly sent word to the Republicans in the Democratic-controlled Senate to urge them to block Johnson's naming of a new chief justice. Johnson nominated his earlier appointee (and crony), associate justice Abe Fortas, to be the chief justice, and another Texas crony, Judge Homer Thornberry, to take the Fortas seat. During Fortas's confirmation hearing, Republicans, joined by conservative Southern Democrats, challenged Fortas over his rulings relating to obscenity, but this failed to knock him out of play, and the Senate Judiciary Committee sent his nomination to the full Senate. As the nomination was headed for a vote, the Senate Republicans got a tip that Fortas had been paid an amount equal to a third of his Supreme Court salary to teach a seminar at American University, an honorarium that had been raised by one of his former law partners. This negative information, and the Southern Democrats' opposition to Fortas's civil rights rulings, provided the pretext for the Republicans in launching the first Senate filibuster against a Supreme Court nominee. LBJ's White House could not muster the supermajority votes (then sixty-seven) to end the filibuster, so Fortas requested his name be withdrawn.

Chief Justice Earl Warren then agreed to remain until the end of the Supreme Court's next term (June 1969), which meant that Nixon, as the new president, would have the selection of the chief justice. Nixon felt obligated to offer the job to two prominent Republicans, but both former Eisenhower attorney general Herbert Brownell and former GOP presidential candidate and Wall Street lawyer Thomas Dewey turned it down. Nixon then nominated a chief justice from central casting, War-

ren Burger, a judge on the U.S. Court of Appeals for the District of
Columbia with flowing white hair. Burger, a conservative minimalist,
was easily confirmed.

With Burger safely installed, the president and his attorney general,
John Mitchell, went to work to open another vacancy on the Court by
forcing Fortas off. Their tactic involved an ugly bluff that Nixon's Justice Department was going to open a grand jury investigation on Fortas's dealings—while on the Supreme Court—with a financier who was
already under investigation by the Justice Department, with Mitchell
hinting he would soon be calling Fortas's wife (an attorney and partner
at Fortas's former law firm), as well as other former law partners, before
a grand jury. The threat worked. Rather than put his wife and partners through this ordeal, Fortas, who knew precisely what Nixon and
Mitchell wanted, resigned from the Court, leaving Nixon his second
vacancy.

During the 1968 campaign Nixon had used his so-called Southern
strategy, which included pledging to appoint a strict constructionist to
the Supreme Court.[11] To fill the empty Fortas seat Nixon went to the
South and nominated an experienced, moderately conservative judge
from the U.S. Court of Appeals for the Fourth Circuit, Clement Haynsworth, who enjoyed a reputation as a good intellect and able jurist. By
this time, however, Democrats in the Senate were determined to get
back at Nixon for what had been done to Fortas (in fact, several members of the Senate even told Judge Haynsworth that they were going to
vote against him because of Nixon's treatment of Fortas, so he should
not take it personally), and Haynsworth was rejected by the Senate,
55 to 44.

Many Supreme Court historians believe that Nixon then intentionally made the disastrous selection of G. Harrold Carswell, a newly appointed Georgia federal appellate judge, out of anger and to strike back
at the Senate, but that was not the case. Carswell had been recommended
by Assistant Attorney General William Rehnquist, who had been assist-
ing Mitchell in identifying potential nominees. All that Nixon knew
about Carswell was that Mitchell had recommended him, and that FBI

director J. Edgar Hoover had personally cleared him. Within days of his nomination, however, reports started to surface in the press that Carswell was a bigot who was frequently abusive toward African Americans in his courtroom, and that he loved to tell foul, racist jokes. (Not until years later was it discovered that J. Edgar Hoover—who always became directly involved with Supreme Court nominees—had called one of his trusted special agents in charge in the South to get background information on Carswell. Hoover was told Carswell was good for the FBI, which was all he needed, but in fact, no background investigation was ever conducted on the judge.) Nebraska Republican senator Roman Hruska, who was managing Carswell's confirmation effort, said all that needed to be said when he stepped out of the Senate chamber during the debate on Carswell to speak with the press on the matter. In his deep, rumbling voice Hruska protested into the microphones, "Even if he is mediocre, there are a lot of mediocre judges and people and lawyers. They are entitled to a little representation, aren't they, and a little chance?" Carswell was rejected by the Senate vote of 51 to 45.

To Nixon these rejections only made for good politics. He went on television and assured the people of the South that he was doing everything in his power to get them appropriate representation on the Supreme Court, but the Senate would not approve a Southern judge. Chief Justice Burger, who had an open channel to the president through Attorney General John Mitchell, suggested appointing his friend from Minnesota (Burger's home), the federal circuit court judge Harry A. Blackmun, a conservative minimalist. Nixon met with Blackmun, liked him, and sent his nomination to the Senate, where he was quickly confirmed.

In 1971 Nixon had two more appointments. He selected Lewis Powell, a Virginia lawyer and former president of the American Bar Association, and a minimalist; he was easily confirmed. Nixon's last appointment, his assistant attorney general in charge of the Office of Legal Counsel, William Rehnquist, did not have as easy a time of it, but was eventually approved. Rehnquist was the first fundamentalist to be seated on the modern Supreme Court, and he would set a pattern for other fundamentalists who found it necessary to make their way through the confirmation process by deception. (I'll return to the subject of Rehnquist when I discuss Reagan's appointing him to be chief justice, for the central issue of his second confirmation hearing would be whether he had been truthful with the Senate during the first proceeding.)

Nixon's judicial legacy, aside from placing Rehnquist on the Court, was his influence on the process by politicizing presidential decisions in judicial appointments. Blocking Lyndon Johnson from selecting a new chief justice, and then scheming to force a sitting justice off the Court, were ruthless power plays. Once Nixon had torn up the judicial pea patch, so to speak, much to the delight of conservatives, his Republican successors realized that this field was too politically fertile to abandon, and no president has ever plowed this ground more effectively than Ronald Reagan. More accurately, Reagan further politicized the third branch by seeking to place solid conservatives throughout the federal judiciary, in courts high and low, in an effort to tilt the entire federal judiciary to the hard right.[12]

Reagan's Hard Right Push While Perfecting Nixon's Politicized Process

Like Nixon, candidate Ronald Reagan used his potential selections to the Supreme Court as part of his campaign against incumbent president Jimmy Carter. "Reagan's [1980] campaign had gone 'flat,' as [a longtime Reagan political adviser] Stu Spencer put it in mid-October," Reagan biographer Lou Cannon reported. "On October 14, for the only time in the campaign, pollster Richard Wirthlin's trackings showed Carter marginally ahead. So Reagan's campaign strategists rummaged about for a new issue and came up with the idea of putting a woman on the Supreme Court. At a news conference in Los Angeles on that day, Reagan promised he would name a woman to 'one of the first Supreme Court vacancies in my administration.' "[13] And like Nixon, Reagan would honor that campaign promise. In February 1981, only weeks after Reagan had entered office, Associate Justice Potter Stewart sent word that he would step down at the end of the term (in June). When Attorney General William French Smith submitted a list of candidates that included both men and women, Reagan made clear his intent to keep to his pledge.[14] Smith decided to start the process with Arizona Court of Appeals judge Sandra Day O'Connor, so he dispatched a young assistant in his office, Kenneth Starr, along with the assistant attorney general in charge of the Office of Legal Policy (the office responsible for judicial selections), Jonathan C. Rose, to interview her in Phoenix, as well as others who knew her. Starr and Rose were favorably impressed, and two days later Judge O'Connor flew to Washington for secret meetings with Attorney General Smith, presidential counselor Ed Meese, White House chief of staff James Baker, and communications adviser Michael Deaver. O'Connor quickly earned the support of them all, and then of her classmate at Stanford Law School, Associate Justice William Rehnquist, and of Senator Barry Goldwater, her senator and friend. Lou Cannon reported that when Reagan met with O'Connor he was "charmed" by her and thought she was the right choice to be the first woman on the Supreme Court. Six days after their meeting the president sent her nomination to the Senate.[15]

Movement conservatives from the religious right, however, did not believe that O'Connor was sufficiently conservative, so they organized a number of protests against her. Reverend Jerry Falwell of the Moral Majority announced that all "good Christians" should be concerned about O'Connor's nomination (which led Senator Barry Goldwater to respond, "Every good Christian ought to kick Falwell in the ass"*[16]). Women's groups and many prominent and highly respected liberals in the Senate, including Senator Edward Kennedy (D-MA) and Representative Morris Udall (D-AZ), were quick to make their support for O'Connor known. On September 15, 1981, the Senate Judiciary Com-

*Actually the senator suggested that good Christians should kick Falwell in the "nuts" but the media changed the anatomical reference. (Based on personal conversations with Senator Goldwater.)

mittee approved her nomination unanimously, in a 17 to 0 vote. Six days later the Senate confirmed her by a vote of 99 to 0. Justice Sandra Day O'Connor was a conservative minimalist, and Professor Sunstein considered her the epitome of this school of thinking and "the Court's leading minimalist."

Appointing the First Fundamentalists: Rehnquist and Scalia

Terry Eastland's *Energy in the Executive: The Case for the Strong Presidency* asserted that one of the indicia of a strong president is his ability to select judges with the proper "judicial philosophy." Eastland is blunt in his explanation of why this is critical for a president: He can then "influence the direction of the courts through his appointments" because the "judiciary has become more significant in *our* politics." (Emphasis added.) In other words, the choice has nothing to do with running government well but instead suits the needs of conservative politics. Eastland goes so far as to claim that presidents have a constitutional mandate to politicize the federal judiciary, as if these appointments were merely lesser officers of the presidency, available to further his will both when in office and after he has departed. To subtly augment his point, Eastland repeatedly quotes James Madison (without identifying the source) as referring to federal judges as "shoots off the executive stock."[17] While Eastland recognized that once his choices are appointed a president loses control, he assured that "if a president carefully selects his nominees with judicial philosophy in mind, he can reasonably expect to see that philosophy applied in the way cases and controversies are decided. He can expect a jurisprudential legacy."[18]

Eastland, who himself served in the Justice Department at the time of Scalia's selection, said, "There is probably no better example of how a president should work in an institutional sense in choosing a nominee than the Reagan administration process that resulted in the Scalia selection in 1986."[19] He broadly described that process—again, not one of finding the best justice, but rather of finding one who will implement the president's political philosophy from the bench:

> The administrative effort that led to the Scalia selection began in 1985, long before anyone knew a vacancy might occur, when Attorney General Edwin Meese III asked Assistant Attorney General William Bradford Reynolds to advise him just in case. Reynolds assembled a team of Justice Department officials who examined about twenty prospects, most of them sitting federal judges, many appointed by Reagan. The group reviewed everything known about the candidates. And it focused especially on judicial philosophy. Each candidate's published writings, including judicial opinions, and speeches were collected and placed in notebooks, and then read and assessed by three-person units assigned by Reynolds.... As the final leg of the process, Reynolds convened sessions during which the group debated the relative merits of the candidates. The Reynolds team concluded by giving equal priority to two individuals: Bork and Scalia. Neither was ranked over the other; *both were regarded as the best available, most well-qualified exponents of Reagan's judicial philosophy.* Moreover, both men were seen as giants in the law, men who could someday rank among the few greats who have served on the Court. When Burger indicated his intention to resign, Reynolds was able to advise Meese without delay, recommending that the President pick Bork or Scalia as part of a two-step approach in which [Associate Justice] Rehnquist would be named to take Burger's place, with Scalia or Bork simultaneously named to replace him. Agreeing, Meese forwarded the advice to Reagan, who ultimately made the only remaining decision when, after interviewing both candidates, he chose Scalia.[20] [Emphasis added.]

Even though Democrats controlled the Senate, Scalia—the most conservative jurist ever to sit on the contemporary Supreme Court—went through his confirmation proceedings without a problem, because he had three factors in his favor: He had very strong credentials, he was the first Italian American to be selected for the High Court, and his confirmation followed that of Rehnquist. No one doubted Scalia's brilliance.[21] No member of the Senate with a significant Italian American constituency (and that means much of the Senate) could politically risk challenging this son of Italy.[22] But most important, Rehnquist, who had gone through the process first, had already drawn all the fire, which spared Scalia, for few truly understood the radical nature of his conservatism. After a perfunctory hearing the Judiciary Committee approved Scalia's nomination by a unanimous vote: 18 to 0, and the full Senate went on to approve him 98 to 0.[23]

William Rehnquist's two confirmations established a pattern that other judicial fundamentalists have gone on to follow when nominated for a seat on the Supreme Court, in which they seek to hide the depth of their conservatism. (A few commentators believe that Sandra Day O'Connor kept her moderation hidden so that Reagan would appoint her: "O'Connor, when asked by Ken Starr, then an assistant [to the] attorney general, who vetted her, whether she had supported a 1970 bill to decriminalize abortion in Arizona, told him she could not remember. Starr did not check it out—she had voted for the bill and Reagan, misled, vouched for her anti-*Roe* [*v. Wade*] credentials."[24]) Rehnquist tried to go the "I don't remember" route, and when that did not work, he literally concocted answers no one believed. His conspicuously false testimony did not offend his conservative Republicans supporters, however, so he was made chief justice. It has remained a disquieting fact that Rehnquist perjured himself to become chief justice, not once but several times.*

Rehnquist's problems began during his first confirmation in November 1971, when press reports raised additional charges—similar but more serious than those that had surfaced during these first confirma-

---

*I have written about this at length in *The Rehnquist Choice: The Untold Story of the Nixon Appointment That Redefined the Supreme Court* (New York: Free Press, 2001), 270–84.

tion hearings—that Rehnquist had challenged and harassed black and Hispanic voters as an attorney in Phoenix during the 1962, 1964, and 1968 elections. Although conservative Southern Democrats (who were still prevalent in the Senate at that time) and Republicans had nominal control of the Senate Judiciary Committee, Democrats controlled the Senate, and they refused to vote to approve his nomination until he responded to these new charges. Rehnquist was forced to submit a sworn affidavit denying the accusations, which had been brought by six people who attested that, as a poll watcher, he had challenged them improperly as voters. Rehnquist, in his affidavit and an accompanying letter to Committee Chairman James Eastland, flatly denied the charges, which effectively ended the matter. Questions of his challenging voters improperly echoed through the Senate floor debate in 1971, but they did not threaten his confirmation.

Fifteen years later, however, when Reagan nominated him to be chief justice, these questions returned with a vengeance and became focal points of his second confirmation proceeding. No longer was the issue merely Rehnquist's behavior at the polls, but his testimony to the Senate in 1971. The evidence is compelling that Rehnquist was not truthful with the Senate in either 1971 or in 1986. His flat denial that he had ever challenged any voter—even for legitimate reasons—was foolish. I don't believe Rehnquist personally "harassed" black and Hispanic voters; that was not his style or nature. But I have no doubt that he challenged black and Hispanic voters at a time when it was perfectly legal in Arizona to do so. After reading and rereading his testimony, it appears to me that what he was really saying to the Senate was that he was not quite sure himself of his behavior, but he could not bring himself to tell the truth. Thus, his 1971 blanket denial forced him to remain consistent to that account in 1986, and since his blanket denial was a lie, he had to continue lying. His false statement to Congress in 1971 was a crime, but the statute of limitations had passed. His false statement to Congress in 1986, however, was pure perjury.

There were other matters he clearly lied about as well: in particular, his work for Associate Justice Robert Jackson as a law clerk. During his confirmation hearing a 1952 memo he had written leaked, in which he had urged that Jackson not vote for the historic civil rights decision *Brown v. Board of Education,* which would overturn *Plessy v. Ferguson's* "separate but equal" schools. Rather than admit that that had been his position at the time (and that he had since seen the error of his thinking), Rehnquist took the position that his memo actually represented Jackson's position. It was an absurd contention, and a defamation of the dead justice for whom he had worked.

A number of scholars who have sifted through the relevant documents—Rehnquist's testimony and the papers of Justice Jackson—have confirmed that this was another Rehnquist falsehood. For example, in 1988 Professor Bernard Schwartz, who specializes in the Court's history, was given access to Justice Jackson's draft concurring opinion in the *Brown* case, which had not previously been available. The draft reveals that Jackson was convinced school segregation was unconstitutional and wrong, prompting Professor Schwartz to write: "It is hard to believe that the man who wrote the sentences holding segregation invalid in his draft held the view only a few months earlier attributed to him by Chief Justice Rehnquist—'that *Plessy v. Ferguson* was right and should be re-affirmed.' So inconsistent, indeed, is this view with the Jackson draft that one may ask . . . what might have happened had Jackson's unequivocal draft statements on the invalidity of segregation been available when the Senate voted on the Rehnquist nomination . . . ?" In 1996 Professor Laura Ray examined the relationship between Justice Jackson and Rehnquist. When she turned to the 1952 memo she found there was "room for considerable skepticism concerning Rehnquist's claim that the memo reflected Jackson's views." After parsing the evidence, including the writings of scholars who had preceded her, she concluded: "On balance, then, it is hard not to agree, . . . that Rehnquist was expressing his own views in the *Brown* memo. With [the top] seat on the Supreme Court almost in his grasp, Rehnquist may well have retreated from an uncomfortable position taken almost twenty years earlier in the only way that seemed open to him. That such a step might unfairly tarnish the reputation of Justice Jackson years after his death does not seem to have been a concern."*[25]

It was very difficult for the next authoritarian conservative nominated to the Supreme Court to dissemble. Judge Robert Bork's radical positions were well-known even before Reagan placed him on the Circuit Court of Appeals for the District of Columbia. When Associate Justice Louis Powell resigned in the summer of 1987, Reagan and his aides hoped Bork's nomination might revive his faltering presidency, which was sinking under the Iran-Contra scandal and the criminal investigation of his attorney general, Ed Meese.[26] Bork, whom Reagan's own staff had described as a "right-wing zealot," was chosen to please the right-wing base, although he was publicly packaged as a moderate conservative, because Reagan needed all the support he could get. Selling Bork as a moderate was like selling tobacco as beneficial to health— a disingenuous if not insincere claim. Bork, of course, went down in eternal flames, but the failed Bork confirmation story has never really ended. Conservatives have sought to avenge his rejection, an ongoing effort that has helped fuel the drive of authoritarian conservatives to take control of the federal judiciary.

Slouching Toward Extremism with Robert Bork

Judge Robert Bork's defeat made him both a martyr and a verb.** Countless books and articles have been written about the Bork confirmation

---

*Having been personally involved as White House counsel in promoting Rehnquist for the seat on the Supreme Court, and based on my many conversations with him over the years, I thought I knew him. I did not. To set the record straight, which I did in 2001 with *The Rehnquist Choice,* I included these charges and asked my editor to send a copy of the book to the chief justice, which he did. I also publicly invited any and all of Rehnquist's law clerks to refute them. Neither he, nor anyone else, has done so, for they cannot. The sixteenth chief justice of the United States lied to win his confirmation.

**According to *Safire's New Political Dictionary* the word "bork" means to

proceedings, mostly by conservatives who still have difficulty grasping that many conservative senators voted against him because he was so far over the top; not surprisingly, they provide less-than-accurate accounts of what actually transpired. Conservatives who share Bork's views do not want to see themselves as extremists, so they need a good tribal myth to explain his rejection. Terry Eastland, director of public affairs at the Justice Department at the time, has contributed generously to this conservative mythology. He claimed that "corrupted liberalism" defeated Bork, along with ruthless left-wing interest groups and a lack of conservative support.[27] (A review of the mainstream news coverage reveals that the claim that Bork had little outside conservative support is inaccurate.[28]) "This corrupted liberalism was present in the vicious attack against Robert Bork that distorted his substantive record," Eastland wrote, as if the Senate and cognoscenti were not well aware of that record. More specifically, Eastland, Judge Bork himself, and other conservatives have never forgiven Senator Edward Kennedy for his description of "Robert Bork's America," which he publicly proclaimed within hours of the nomination's announcement:

> [In Judge Bork's America] women would be forced into back alley abortions, blacks would sit at segregated lunch counters, rogue

---

"attack viciously a candidate or appointee, especially by misrepresentation in the media." Safire states:

> The verb first appeared in print in 1988, enclosed in quotation marks, as in the *Chicago Tribune* of November 20, 1988: "Honest disagreement is one thing: 'borking' is something else." In February 1989, Republican Senator M. Wallop of Wyoming commented on "CBS This Morning": "I feel strongly that he [Senator John Tower] is being borked.... The charges that have been leveled at him have all proved groundless, baseless." On the same program on July 9, 1990, it was reported that "an opponent of Judge Clarence Thomas said yesterday, 'We're going to bork him.'" The verb is also proving useful to right-wingers seeking to retaliate for Judge Bork's defeat. A recent *New Republic* essay by Ruth Shalit discusses Democratic nominees to the Supreme Court and is headlined "Borking Back," with the subhead "The right gets even."

police could break down citizens' doors in midnight raids, school-children could not be taught about evolution, writers and artists could be censored at the whim of government, and the doors of the federal courts would be shut on the fingers of millions of citizens for whom the judiciary is the—and is often the only—protector of the individual rights that are the heart of our democracy.... No justice would be better than this injustice.

Eastland claimed that Kennedy's "speech inspired Washington-based liberal groups to unite in opposition." Surely Senator Kennedy would take that as a compliment, although it, too, was not true: There was an instant response and public reaction when Bork's nomination was announced. By any standards of conservative oratory, Eastland's complaint against Kennedy is a reach: "Kennedy's rhetoric violated the norms for deliberative democracy; it was a popular speech of the most demagogic kind."[29]

Eastland added a further twist to the myth of Bork's defeat by attributing it partly to Reagan. If Reagan had been minding the store, there would have been no Iran-Contra scandal. If Reagan had appointed Bork instead of Scalia, Rehnquist would have drawn the fire for Bork. If Reagan had personally entered the battle, he could have won the seat for Bork. "Reagan should have used rhetoric to counter Kennedy; his speech should and need not have been demagogic, however. Reagan could have attacked Kennedy's speech precisely as demagoguery, arguing that such language, in addition to being untruthful and unfair, should have no place in the advise-and-consent process." Thus, he complained, when Reagan finally give a speech on Bork's behalf, it was too late; it took place after the hearings, and only CNN carried it.[30] All these facts are correct, but Eastland's spin on them is fantasy. The truth of the matter is that Kennedy's hyperbole was based in fact, and since Reagan was engaging in presidential politics with the High Court, Kennedy's reaction was not inappropriate, nor even close to out-of-bounds (which it would have been had the charges had no factual basis whatsoever) in this high-stakes contest. As for Reagan's doing more to help, Eastland overlooks the fact that Reagan's credibility had by then been compromised because of Iran-Contra, which left him with no political capital to offer Bork.

Eastland and the other Bork mythologists have also tended to simply ignore the events that preceded Bork's nomination. "The turning point in Bork's confirmation came not in 1987 when he was nominated, but in 1986 when partisan control of the Senate switched from the Republicans to the Democrats," political scientists Jeffrey Segal and Harold Spaeth have explained. Reagan campaigned actively to retain Republican control of the Senate during the 1986 midterm contests, making Supreme Court appointments a campaign issue as he traveled throughout the South, where he frequently attacked Senator Kennedy.[31] His stump speech for North Carolina senator Jim Broyhill was typical.

Since I've begun appointing federal judges to be approved by people like Jim Broyhill in the Republican Senate, the federal judiciary has become tougher, much tougher, on criminals. Criminals are going to jail more often and receiving longer sentences. Over and over, the Democratic leadership has tried in the Senate to torpedo our choices for judges. And that's where Jim Broyhill can make all the difference. Without him and the Republican majority in the Senate, we'll find liberals like Joe Biden and a certain fellow from Massachusetts deciding who our judges are. And I'll bet you'll agree: I'd rather have a Judiciary Committee headed by Strom Thurmond than one run by Joe Biden or Ted Kennedy.[32]

Senator James T. Broyhill lost in North Carolina, and Democrats regained control of the Senate by a 55 to 45 majority, winning Republican seats in Alabama, Florida, Georgia, and North Carolina. More important for understanding the Bork nomination, it was *how* Democrats won that had a bearing on Bork's loss. A *New York Times* report—with the headline "Blacks Cast Pivotal Ballots in Four Key Senate Races, Data Show"—foretold Bork's fate. "Democrats owe their new majority in the Senate, at least in part, to the black vote. The black vote was crucial in four of the eight states the Democrats took from Republicans to regain control of the Senate, . . . according to political analysts and reviews of the polls of voters."[33] Southern Democrats owed their Senate seats to black voters, and as surely Reagan and his aides knew when nominating Bork, those same black voters would be deeply opposed to Judge Bork, for his positions on civil rights were an anathema to all who cared about equality in America. Constitutional law professor Herman Schwartz has summarized Bork's stance on this subject:

> Bork condemned the Fourteenth Amendment's Equal Protection Clause decisions outlawing the poll tax (to him it was just "a very small tax"), the decisions establishing the one-person, one-vote principle, abolishing school segregation in the District of Columbia, barring courts from enforcing racially restrictive housing covenants, preventing a state from sterilizing certain criminals or interfering with the right to travel, and prohibiting discrimination against out-of-wedlock children. . . . Bork's hostility to governmental action on behalf of minorities did not stop with his critique of court action. In 1963 he criticized a section of the proposed Civil Rights Act of 1964 that required white businesses to serve blacks as resting on a principle of "unsurpassed ugliness."[34]

Even before they nominated Bork the Reagan White House understood they were in for a fight, and on the day of the announcement (July 1, 1987) a "senior White House official acknowledged the potential of a difficult Congressional battle and said Mr. Reagan was aware of it in making the choice," the *New York Times* reported. The story also stated that "the President would try to insure Judge Bork's confirmation by waging an active campaign."[35] By this time, Howard Baker had left the Senate to become Reagan's White House chief of staff.* No one in

---

Washington Post reporter Peter Baker (unrelated to Howard Baker) later wrote that "Democratic leaders agreed to forgo impeachment proceedings against Ronald

Washington was better at counting votes in the Senate than the former majority/minority leader of the Senate. On July 2, 1987, "officials close to" Baker told the *New York Times* that Baker "had some doubts about nominating" Bork, but he had not objected to the president's decision. "Baker had doubts whether ... [Judge Bork] could be confirmed, and that even if Judge Bork eventually won, a prolonged and bitter battle could expend too much of the president's political capital and energy.... Baker believed that Mr. Bork's chances of being confirmed would turn on how effectively he testifies," the *Times* reported.[36] Contrary to the account of Eastland and others, President Reagan realized that Bork might not make it, but not unlike Nixon sending Haynsworth and Carswell to the Senate to please the conservative base, he went ahead with his choice.

Conservatives also claim that Judge Bork never had a chance at the hearings, with Eastland going so far as to claim that "the Senate Judiciary Committee positioned the table at which Bork sat in such a way as to create for him the least favorable television shots."[37] But Robert Bork on his best day was never going to look like Gregory Peck, who came out of retirement to be filmed on the steps of the Supreme Court warning Americans what Judge Bork might do to their privacy, their civil rights, and their free speech. Peck was a difficult act to follow, but it was not the position of his chair in the hearing room that made Bork look bad, but rather his arrogance, his hubris, and his occasional cold-bloodedness, not to mention his equivocations and occasional "confirmation conversions," where he did what nobody else could do: He made himself a terrible witness who did not appear to be truthful. Those confirmation conversions surprised even his supporters. Although he had once claimed that the First Amendment protected only "political

Reagan for the Iran-Contra affair once former senator Howard H. Baker Jr. took over as White House chief of staff, pledging to put things back on track." Peter Baker, *The Breach: Inside the Impeachment and Trial of William Jefferson Clinton* (New York: Scribner, 2000), 19.

speech," during the hearings he said that news, opinion, literature, and other forms of speech were also covered; likewise, he abandoned his claim that the equal protection clause of the Fourteenth Amendment did not apply to women. Bork's hearings, one of the great public discussions of the Constitution, provided a valuable education for many who watched them. His radical conservatism, however, failed to gather public support.* Bork was not defeated in a cliff-hanging vote on the floor of the Senate; the tally was not even close. He was denied a seat on the High Court by a decisive vote of 58 to 42, with many conservative Southern Democrats voting against him.[38]

Bork's judicial philosophy was rejected by the Senate on October 23, 1987, but the impact of his nomination on the federal judiciary continues. His confirmation has become the norm against which all later confirmations of conservatives have been calculated by the White House, particularly those of Clarence Thomas, John Roberts, and Samuel Alito. Many legal scholars note the ongoing influence of Bork's judicial philosophy on fundamentalist judges and justices. Should the fundamentalists obtain a majority on the Supreme Court—and that is the direction Republican presidents are taking the nation—"Robert Bork's America" may become a reality.

In Judge Bork's place, Reagan nominated another hard-right conservative (and judicial fundamentalist), Judge Douglas Howard Ginsburg, whom the president had earlier placed on the D.C. Circuit, but Ginsburg withdrew when it was revealed that he had a serious conflict-of-interest problem that he had ignored when working at the Department of Justice, and that he had smoked dope as both a student and professor

---

*The *New York Times*/CBS poll told the story. Before his hearing "12 percent said they had an unfavorable opinion of Judge Bork, 11 percent had a favorable opinion and 77 percent were undecided or had no opinion." After he testified "26 percent said they had an unfavorable opinion of Judge Bork; 16 percent a favorable opinion and 57 percent were undecided or had no opinion." Philip Shenon, "Poll Finds Public Opposition to Bork Is Growing," *New York Times* (Sept. 24, 1987), A-20.

at Harvard Law School. This last disclosure, when combined with the fact that his wife was a doctor who had performed abortions, made him less than acceptable to the religious right. Reagan next nominated a federal judge from the Ninth Circuit, Anthony M. Kennedy, a moderate conservative (a conservative minimalist) who was easily confirmed. Justice Kennedy, along with Reagan's first selection, Justice Sandra Day O'Connor, would become the swing votes on the Court—and their refusal to vote in lockstep with Rehnquist and Scalia annoyed Reagan's conservative supporters endlessly.

Bush I and II: Continuing Reagan's Push to the Right

Like Reagan, neither George H.W. Bush nor George W. Bush is an attorney, which meant that their involvement in selecting justices would be political, not intellectual. Both men relied on their White House counsels and attorneys general, along with other aides, to suggest appointments. Both focused on lower federal courts as well as the Supreme Court, but Bush II far exceeded his father is tilting the federal judiciary to the hard right.[39] Bush I would make two Supreme Court appointments: David Souter and Clarence Thomas. Bush II *should* have only two High Court appointments: John Roberts and Samuel Alito, as I will explain.

President George H. W. Bush

Most Republicans and conservatives believe President George H.W. Bush's selection of former New Hampshire Supreme Court justice David Souter was the worst mistake of his presidency. How, they asked, could Bush have picked Souter from a list that included "Fifth Circuit Court of Appeals judge Edith Jones of Houston, Solicitor General Kenneth Starr, and D.C. federal appeals judges Lawrence Silberman and Clarence Thomas"[40]—all dyed-in-the-wool conservatives? It was not difficult.

Bush believed everyone on his list of leading contenders was a solid conservative, based on recommendations from his attorney general, Richard Thornburgh, and White House counsel, C. Boyden Gray. According to Thornburgh, he and Gray favored Souter while White House chief of staff John Sununu (the former governor of New Hampshire, who had placed Souter on the New Hampshire Supreme Court in 1983), along with Vice President Dan Quayle, preferred Judge Edith Jones.[41] (It is surprising that the ultraconservative Federalist Society, which schools future conservative lawyers and incubates conservative judges, did not take away C. Boyden Gray's membership over his recommendation of Souter. But this may explain how the Federalist Society came to have a large role in selecting judges for both Bush I and II.)

President Bush first met with Judge Edith Jones, whom he thought was terrific. Then he received a visit from David Souter, and knew he had found his candidate. Republican senator Warren Rudman, who had hired Souter to be one of his deputies when he was attorney general of New Hampshire, had to convince Souter to travel to Washington to meet with Bush, and put him on a plane to fly there (giving Souter, who discovered he only had three dollars in his wallet, one hundred dollars to cover his expenses). Rudman later recounted: "David and the president hit it off extremely well. They came from similar backgrounds: Yankee, white Anglo-Saxon Protestant families that believed in the old values of hard work, integrity, and public service. The president was impressed by David's intelligence, modesty, and duty."[42] Before going into the Oval Office meeting, Souter had called a friend in New Hampshire and asked him to tell his mother where he was and that he would be home soon, for he did not believe he was seriously in the running. When he came out of the Oval Office, he was accompanied by the president, who was taking him to the press room to announce his selection for the Court.

Souter was dubbed the "stealth nomination," because notwithstanding all his years of public service in New Hampshire, this Rhodes Scholar and Harvard undergraduate and law school graduate had written no law journal articles, and his opinions as a New Hampshire Supreme Court justice were so routine as to be nonrevelatory about his philosophy. The Bush White House assured the conservative base that the selection was a "home run." The confirmation proceeding was uneventful; Bork's shadow still lay over the confirmation process, and David Souter was about as dissimilar from Bork as possible. As Henry Abraham described it, "Unlike the colorful, outspoken, contentious Bork, Souter's personality exuded diffidence, quiescence, and low key.... Soft-spoken, even-tempered, he remained polite, almost courtly, throughout five days of marathon testimony." The Senate Judiciary Committee recommended him by a vote of 13 to 1, and the Senate confirmed him by a vote of 90 to 9.[43]

Conservatives were not sure what to think, given the scant record, and because during Souter's first few years on the Court he voted with Scalia and wrote few opinions. But by the time Bush I had been defeated for reelection, many felt he had given them the worst justice ever, for Souter soon joined with Sandra Day O'Connor and Anthony Kennedy to form a moderate core that foiled conservatives consistently. But before he was voted out of office Bush did have a chance to redeem himself with the GOP base, and he did so with a vengeance. When Justice Thurgood Marshall, the first African American to sit on the High Court, announced his retirement in July 1991, Bush's aides knew exactly whom he should nominate: Clarence Thomas, whom he had placed on the D.C. Circuit a little over a year earlier. C. Boyden Gray and Bush's judicial "Rasputin," Lee Liberman—who had been a cofounder of the Federalist Society when she was at the University of Chicago Law School—believed that with Thomas they had a "black Bork."[44]

Thomas was young (in his early forties) and highly conservative, and he would be the second African American on the Supreme Court. Bush called him "the most qualified man in the country" for Justice Marshall's seat; the American Bar Association did not agree. Since the late 1940s the ABA has issued ratings of nominees for the federal bench to help the Senate and the public by offering an unbiased examination of a nominee's "integrity, professional competence and judicial temperament." The ABA interviews school officials where the nominee received his or her education and others in the legal community familiar with the nominee, from professional peers to judges, the results of which are kept confidential, except for their conclusion. They have three rankings: well-qualified, qualified, and not qualified. The fifteen-member panel vote on Thomas resulted in twelve saying he was "qualified" and two saying "not qualified," with one member not voting. "Of the last nine Justices confirmed going back to 1969, there were no votes of unqualified. The records are unclear as to whether there were any votes of unqualified against some earlier Justices," the *New York Times* noted.[45] For the president to send a nominee to the Supreme Court with anything less than a uniformly well-qualified rating is irresponsible, but such decisions have become part of the politicization of the judiciary.

While conservatives were thrilled with the choice of Thomas, civil rights, women's, and environmental groups were terrified, and for good reason. Thomas, a product of affirmative action, was opposed to it. He had no interest in civil rights but rather believed in a "color-blind" Constitution, notwithstanding the fact that our Constitution is anything but. If Bush had made a mistake with his conservative base with Souter, he had gone to the other extreme with Thomas. The White House strategy was crude but effective: They would use Thomas's color as a wedge with the civil rights community, because he would pick up some blacks' support notwithstanding his dismal record in protecting their civil rights. This would enable Bush to put a hard-right conservative on the Supreme Court that might not otherwise ever be approved by the Senate.

Thomas's public statements about women's rights provoked Eleanor Cutri Smeal, the president of the Fund for the Feminist Majority, to testify before the Senate Judiciary Committee that "over the past decade, Judge Thomas repeatedly expressed his views in numerous law review articles, speeches, and essays in newspapers," which she had reviewed. "There is nothing in his record, performance, or writings—not a shred of evidence—that indicates any willingness to protect civil liberties or civil rights for women," she told the committee. "Quite the contrary, his record is chilling."⁴⁶ Environmentalists were concerned because of his rulings as a judge on the D.C. Circuit Court of Appeals, where he consistently took the position of conservative jurists—or a fundamentalist view—that denied plaintiffs the right to contest the failure of federal regulatory bodies to enforce environmental laws or simply ruled against them when they did get into federal court.⁴⁷

Thomas's confirmation hearings took place in two rounds, with the second one unplanned. Well coached by the Bush White House, the Justice Department, and his mentor, Senator John Danforth (R-MO), for whom he had worked when Danforth was attorney general of Missouri, and later as a legislative aide in the Senate, Thomas did as he had been told, saying as little as possible, being as polite and deferential as possible, and working to get the process over as quickly as possible by giving short and bland answers. Still, he was not a good witness. For one thing, he was conspicuously untruthful. Most memorable during the first round—because it was so unbelievable—was his claim to Senator Patrick Leahy (D-VT) that he had no position on *Roe v. Wade,* the Supreme Court's 1973 decision legalizing abortion, and that he had never discussed the case with anyone.⁴⁸ Even Thomas's sympathetic biographer, conservative writer and attorney Andrew Peyton Thomas (no relation to Clarence Thomas), failed to vouch for Thomas's response about *Roe* to Senator Leahy, as he tried to show it was not perjurious.⁴⁹ But his biographer agreed that Thomas crossed the line when he told Leahy that notwithstanding his citing *Roe* in his writings, he "did not and do[es] not have a position on the outcome," and conceded that "these representations about *Roe* proved a laughingstock." So unbelievable was Thomas's position on *Roe* that even his foremost supporter was ready to abandon him. Paul Weyrich, a key figure and strategist for social and religious conservatives who was running a war room to counter any negative statements about Thomas as the proceeding unfolded, disputed his testimony about *Roe* based on his own dealings with Thomas. "Weyrich remembered that Thomas had expressed an opinion on ... abortion in prior meetings with him. He found Thomas's lack of candor 'disingenuous' and 'nauseating.' ... Weyrich seriously considered withdrawing his support of Thomas."[50] (Soon enough Clarence Thomas would put the lie to his own testimony with his action as a justice.[51]) Even in this first round of his confirmation hearings it was clear that Thomas was going the route that Rehnquist had traveled: Say whatever was necessary to win confirmation, regardless of the conspicuousness of the lie. Regrettably, it would get even worse.

When the first round of hearings ended, the Senate Judiciary Committee believed they had finished their task, but by now the Anita Hill time bomb was ticking. The committee split with a 7 to 7 vote, which meant it would issue no recommendation to the full Senate. "Not [his] conservative ideology, nor the interest group opposition, nor the questions of qualifications were enough to bring Thomas down," observed one team of political scientists when the head count as of October 4, 1991, just four days before the scheduled Senate vote, showed "only about forty senators opposed the nominee."[52] In fact, the Senate Judiciary Committee had been sitting for weeks on Anita Hill's explosive charges of sexual harassment by Thomas when she had worked as a staff attorney for him, when he was an assistant secretary at the Department of Education, and then when he was chairman of the Equal Employment Opportunities Commission. Committee investigators had been examining the charges, but Hill—a professor of law at the University of Oklahoma—was reluctant to come forward. A friend from her days in Washington had recalled she had been told by Hill about Thomas's behavior years earlier, and with Hill's consent, she had informed the Senate Judiciary Committee. But not until late in the proceedings were members of the staff able to convince Hill to lodge a formal charge with the committee, so it could be fully investigated. When she did, the FBI commenced an investigation, and on October 6, as the nomination was headed for a vote in the full Senate, Nina Totenberg of National Public Radio and Timothy Phelps of *Newsday*, the Long Island daily, reported that they had learned of Anita Hill's charges. The time bomb had exploded.

The situation became ugly quickly. Anita Hill testified before the committee, with great specificity, about how Thomas had pursued her to date him, talked about the size of a porn star's breasts, told her about his sexual prowess and the size of his penis, discussed his favorite pornographic movies (which featured *Long Dong Silver*), and asked her "Who put this pubic hair on my Coke?" It was the most explosive hearing ever on Capitol Hill (at least until the Monica Lewinsky scandal about consensual sex, which was far more graphic and colorful, or off-color, depending on one's point of view). At around 9:00 P.M. on Friday, October 11, 1991, following Ms. Hill's devastating testimony, Clarence Thomas returned to the hearing room to respond to her charges. He was outraged and famously attacked the committee:

> I would like to start by saying unequivocally, uncategorically, that I deny each and every single allegation against me today that suggested in any way that I had conversations of a sexual nature or about pornographic material with Anita Hill, that I ever attempted to date her, that I ever had any personal sexual interest in her, or that I in any way ever harassed her. A second, and I think more important point, I think that this today is a travesty. I think that it is disgusting. I think that this hearing should never occur in America. This is a case in which this sleaze, this dirt, was searched for by staffers of members of this committee, was then leaked to the media, and this committee and this body validated it and displayed it at prime time over our entire nation. How would any member on this committee, any person in this room, or any person in this country, would like sleaze said about him or her in this fashion? Or this dirt dredged up and this gossip and these lies displayed in this manner? How would any person like it? The Supreme Court is not worth it. No job is worth it. I'm not here for that. I'm here for my name, my family, my life, and my integrity. I think something is dreadfully wrong with this country when any person, any person in this free country would be subjected to this. This is not a closed room. There was an FBI investigation. This is not an opportunity to talk about difficult matters privately or in a closed environment. This is a circus. It's a national disgrace.

He leaned back in his chair, and then he remembered there was one other point he had wanted to make, for he had carefully planned his outrage, including playing the race card:[53]

> And from my standpoint as a black American, as far as I'm concerned, it is a high-tech lynching for uppity blacks who in any way deign to think for themselves, to do for themselves, to have different ideas, and it is a message that unless you kowtow to an old order, this is what will happen to you. You will be lynched, destroyed, caricatured by a committee of the U.S. Senate rather than hung from a tree.[54]

Charge and denial; he said; she said. Who was telling the truth? Since that hearing people have chosen sides largely based on their political beliefs, but by doing so they are not paying sufficient attention to the situation and the evidence. Ms. Hill had absolutely no motive to lie, and Clarence Thomas had a seat on the Supreme Court at stake. The evidence that has emerged since the hearing overwhelmingly supports Anita Hill, while there is not a scintilla of evidence to support Clarence Thomas. To the contrary, it indicates that he also lied in denying Hill's charges.

David Brock, the former journalistic hatchet man for conservative causes, later revealed in his mea culpa *Blinded by the Right: The Conscience of an Ex-Conservative* (2002) what was happening within the Thomas supporters' camp. He explained that they had decided, with no support for the theory, that Hill's testimony was a trick of liberals who sought to deny a conservative his seat on the Supreme Court. Accordingly, following Hill's testimony, the White House went to work with lawyers from the Federalist Society, combing for anything and everything to discredit her. As Brock reported, "The Federalist team had worked through the night to attack and discredit specific aspects of Hill's testimony. One of the most striking anecdotes that Hill had related was a story in which Thomas had turned to her in his office and said, 'Who put this pubic hair on my Coke?' *The Exorcist* contained a scene involving pubic hair and a glass of gin, and sure enough, Senator [Orrin] Hatch [(R-UT), an active member of the Federalist Society], held up a copy of the book ... and accused Hill of lifting that detail in her testimony from the novel." Brock related that the Federalist lawyers also found an obscure 1988 sexual harassment case where the complaining witness had mentioned the porn character "Long Dong Silver," just at Ms. Hill had in her testimony, so Orrin Hatch accused Hill and her "slick lawyers" of inventing these charges by culling bits and pieces from such public material. Senator Arlen Specter (R-PA), a former prosecutor, took Hill through round after round of brutal cross-examination, seeking to make her out a liar, and at one point he accused her of perjury. Specter submitted to the committee a pseudo-psychological analysis of Ms. Hill, claiming that she had imagined all these activities. Senator Alan Simpson (R-WY) suggested he had received damaging and derogatory material about Ms. Hill, raising questions about her sexual proclivities and smearing her as best he could. It was brutal but effective.

The entire episode played out quickly. On October 6, Totenberg and Phelps reported Hill's charge. Hill and Thomas testified on Friday, October 11, and Saturday October 12. Four strong and unchallenged witnesses corroborated Hill on Sunday morning, October 13, and witnesses for Thomas appeared that afternoon, offering platitudes about what a fine fellow he was. The Senate voted on October 15. The projected vote count was close, but the White House believed they would prevail because public opinion was with them. "A majority of the American people, both men and women, believed Thomas's denials of Hill's charges, [and the polls further showed] that African-Americans overwhelmingly rallied behind Thomas after the charges were leveled, and that a majority of the public supported his confirmation. Thomas's support in the polls was cited by those favoring his confirmation as evidence of his veracity and fitness for the Supreme Court." (Almost a year would pass before it was shown that these "fast reaction" polls were dead wrong, and strikingly off the mark.)[55]

Inexplicably, the chairman of the Judiciary Committee, Senator Joe

Biden (D-DE), and the other Democrats on the committee made no effort to protect Anita Hill as the Republicans savaged her. Not only did they not protect her, but they elected not to release information that corroborated her testimony. The committee had learned that Clarence Thomas was indeed a regular customer at a pornographic film rental store, but apparently, they judged it more prejudicial than probative. Anita Hill had also provided the names of persons who had come forward to remind her that back in 1981 and 1982, when Thomas's actions occurred, that she had told them of his behavior. The committee allowed only a few of these witnesses to testify. They also chose not to make part of the record the fact that Anita Hill had taken a lie detector exam from one of the best polygraph experts in Washington, and passed it effortlessly.[56] Anyone who doubts that Anita Hill was telling the truth, or still suspects that her charges were fabricated by left-wing opponents of Clarence Thomas, must read the compelling investigative report done by Jane Mayer and Jill Abramson in *Strange Justice: The Selling of Clarence Thomas* (1994). After two years of meticulous research they provide clear and convincing information that supports the truth of her claims, as well as evidence that Anita Hill was not the only woman Thomas had harassed sexually.

Clarence Thomas was confirmed by the lowest margin of votes for any nominee to the Supreme Court: 52 to 48. He has not distinguished himself as a justice other than to reinforce the worst fears of his opponents that he would vote as a rock-solid conservative, further augmenting a fundamentalist bloc on the Court.

President George W. Bush

On July 1, 2005, Associate Justice Sandra Day O'Connor announced her retirement after a quarter century on the Court, and a little over two weeks later, on July 19, 2005, Bush nominated D.C. Circuit Court of Appeals judge John Roberts to replace her. As the Senate was preparing to hold confirmation hearings on Judge Roberts, however, Chief Justice William Rehnquist (for whom Roberts had once clerked) died.

Within forty-eight hours Bush withdrew Roberts's nomination as a replacement for O'Connor and resubmitted it for consideration as chief justice. Bush requested that the Senate process the Roberts nomination on an expedited basis, so he could preside as chief justice at the opening of the fall term, on October 3. The Senate, under the control of the Republicans at the time, complied, armed with a convincing rationale for hurrying the nomination through the process (even though, in fact, the Supreme Court can operate without a chief, and has on many occasions). This rush to confirm meant Judge Roberts was not examined quite as closely as might have occurred under normal circumstances. Judge John Roberts, whom Bush had placed on the D.C. Circuit Court of Appeals, had left a relatively thin public record of his views and philosophy. Although he had worked at the Reagan Justice Department (and in the White House counsel's office, as well), and he had argued a significant number of cases before the Supreme Court for both the government and while in private practice, the positions an attorney takes on behalf of a client before the Court may or may not reflect his or her personal views. Former Supreme Court law clerk and fellow FindLaw columnist Edward Lazarus offered his take after the nomination was announced: "Roberts's writings as a young Turk in the Reagan Justice Department suggest that, at least at one time, he was a hard-edged 'movement' conservative. But unlike with Bork, Roberts's rough edges seem to have been smoothed away: He now projects the image of a modest and thoughtful legal craftsman who, despite strong conservative convictions, is the kind of collegial and open-minded conservative with whom liberals can have a meaningful dialogue."[57]

This was the widely held view, even though neither Republicans nor Democrats were very sure where Roberts stood on many issues. It was clear, in any case, that he was every bit as conservative as the man whose seat he was hoping to assume, William Rehnquist. Roberts was also telegenic, articulate, personable, and impeccably prepared at his confirmation hearing: He provided what sounded like valid answers to the questions but effectively volunteered little about his beliefs that was not already known. As a sophisticated Supreme Court practitioner, he knew how to walk around or jump over the potential land mines during a confirmation, and on September 22, the Senate Judiciary Committee sent the Roberts nomination to the full Senate by a vote of 13 to 5, with Democratic senators Ted Kennedy, Richard Durbin, Charles Schumer, Joe Biden, and Dianne Feinstein opposing the nomination. On September 29, 2005, Roberts was confirmed by the full Senate with a vote of 78 to 22.[58] (The 44 Democrats in the Senate at the time were split, with 22 voting for confirmation and 22 against, with many both publicly and privately complaining that they did not know much about the nature of Roberts's conservatism.) Because Roberts was not changing the balance of the Court, there was no talk from the Democrats about mounting a filibuster.

Justice O'Connor's seat still needed to be filled, however, so on October 3, 2005, President Bush nominated his White House counsel, and longtime friend and personal attorney, Harriet Miers for the position. By October 27, however, Miers asked the president to withdraw her acceptance of the nomination after encountering widespread opposition from conservatives. The attacks were vicious, as movement conservatives did not believe she was sufficiently hard core in her beliefs. Four days later, on October 31, Bush nominated Judge Samuel Alito, whom his father had placed on the Third Circuit Court of Appeals in 1990.

Judge Alito's confirmation hearing took place January 13–19, 2006. Like John Roberts, Alito was given a highly qualified rating by the American Bar Association.[59] Also, like Roberts, Alito was a good witness, although a less-charismatic presence than the new chief justice. His testimony only served to confirm that the entire process has become little more than a great charade. Members of the Senate Judiciary Committee understand that nominees will not testify as to how they might actually decide a specific case, for to do so would be to prejudge the case without hearing the specific evidence or arguments. It would show a lack of "judicial impartiality," as if the nominee was in fact truly impartial on all the issues, particularly the hot-button issues that interest the committee. Nominees will, however, discuss their judicial philosophy. So rather than a committee member's asking if the nominee would overturn *Roe v. Wade,* he will ask if the nominee believes in precedent and *stare decisis* (to adhere to decided cases), or the right of privacy, or some other principle that they are obviously going to agree with, the game being how close the questioner can move the nominee to saying, Yes, I will/will not overturn this or that ruling. Members of the committee know very well that Bush would not send anyone to the High Court unless his aides believed the nominee would please the ultraconservative base of the GOP, particularly after the Miers fiasco.

It is generally acknowledged that the confirmation process no longer works, and Bush and his nominees took full advantage of its weaknesses. "The confirmation process broke down ... because the Bush [II] Administration learned the wrong lesson from the failed Bork nomination. It decided it could still nominate extremists, as long as their views were not well known. The previous Bush [I] administration tried a similar approach with Clarence Thomas' nomination, but the current White House turned the effort to hide nominees' views into an art form," Senator Edward Kennedy stated.*[60] Kennedy has served on

*I was invited by the Senate Judiciary Committee to testify at the hearings on both Roberts and Alito, but other standing commitments made it impossible. I did, however, agree to submit my statement for the record for John Roberts's hearing to be chief justice, which I had planned to attend until the committee had a scheduling change. I informed the committee that I was not testifying for or against the nominee; rather, my interest was in drawing the attention of the committee to process—in the instance of Judge Roberts and the refusal of the Bush administration to release his documents from his time serving in the Reagan Justice Department (although they did release many of his documents as a young lawyer in the office of the White House counsel). I suggested that the committee examine judicial nominees regarding the process by which they had been vetted, which is ignored by the committee, but I assured them it had not been ignored by the White House. See "Testimony of John W. Dean Before the Senate Judiciary Committee Hearings on the Nomination of Judge John Roberts to Be Chief Justice of the United States," *Confirmation Hearings on the Nomination of John G. Roberts, Jr., to Be Chief Justice of the United States*, Hearings Before the Committee on the Judiciary, 109th Congress, First Session (Sept. 12–15, 2005), 814.

the Senate Judiciary Committee for forty-three years and participated in the confirmation of every justice now on the Court (plus several who are no longer there), a wealth of experience that gives him a sense of how well the process is working. He finds it wanting, and as his Exhibit A is the manner in which Roberts and Alito were able to mislead the Senate.* Kennedy said:

> Senate Democrats pressed the two nominees on their views on critical issues, including executive power, civil rights, and the environment. In many of these areas, the nominees had a written record that suggested that they were right-wing partisans with strong views. But ... when the Democrats asked the tough questions, both nominees refused to answer, except by distancing themselves from their earlier writings and insisting they would seek to be as neutral as a baseball umpire. Unfortunately, those bland reassurances proved to be enough for a majority of the Senate. Now that they are sitting Justices, Roberts and Alito are justifying every concern we expressed when they were nominated. The men who promised to be neutral umpires look more and more like loyal members of the President's team.[61]

Comparing Roberts's and Alito's testimonies before the committee with their decisions after arriving on the Court, Senator Kennedy found

---

*No one disputes that injecting presidential politics into the Senate confirmation process of federal judges and justices has destroyed it. Political grandstanding for and against nominees, the presence of television, nominees coached to say nothing and senators coached to say too much, and public interest groups running grassroots campaigns for and against a nominee to influence votes of senators have turned the proceedings into a political circus, because GOP presidents keep pushing the envelope. Much of what has gone wrong can be traced back to Nixon's 1968 campaign, when he first raised the stakes and urged Senate Republicans and Southern Democrats to block the elevation of Justice Fortas to be chief justice. The confirmation process has been going downhill ever since, and Republican presidents, who couldn't care less what they are doing to the Senate, have clearly been winning the game.

striking differences. He stops just short of accusing them of lying, but he has no doubt that the Senate was misled.[62]

The question remains: Exactly *how* conservative are Roberts and Alito? Are they judicial fundamentalists or conservative minimalists? It is important to know how close the Supreme Court is to becoming controlled by a solid fundamentalist bloc because—as I will explain—it is difficult to believe Americans want that to happen. Clearly both Justices Antonin Scalia and Clarence Thomas are fundamentalists. Chief Justice Rehnquist was a fundamentalist, so the question is whether there are now three or four fundamentalists on the Supreme Court. This question is also worth considering given the age and health of Justices John Paul Stevens and Ruth Bader Ginsburg, neither of whom are fundamentalist nor likely to vote with the fundamentalist bloc. Many recent High Court watchers worried when a conservative majority arrived on the Court, but that was unnecessary hand-wringing; there has been a conservative majority on the Supreme Court for over a decade. What is at issue now is whether it will take one or two more appointments to create a fundamentalist Supreme Court.

Cass Sunstein appears confident that Chief Justice John Roberts is a conservative minimalist. Writing in the *Los Angeles Times,* in a May 2006 op-ed titled "The Minimalist," Sunstein described how judicial minimalism results in narrow rulings that deal with nothing more than the issues before the Court, and based on what he has observed of the new chief justice, he feels John Roberts is not only following that path, but sending signals about what he is doing. Sunstein reported that at a commencement address at Georgetown University Law Center, Roberts "offered an original, substantive and unambiguous defense of narrow, minimalist rulings." As Sunstein explained,

> Roberts made several approving references to Justice Felix Frankfurter, one of American history's great minimalist judges who consistently called for narrow rulings, especially on the issues that divide the nation most sharply. Writing more than 50 years ago, Frankfurter said that the court has an obligation "to avoid putting

fetters upon the future by needless pronouncements today." It was advice Frankfurter followed himself. In his opinion voting to strike down President Truman's 1952 seizure of the nation's steel mills, Frankfurter refused to say much about presidential power in general. He emphasized that "rigorous adherence to the narrow scope of the judicial function" is especially important when national security is at risk, notwithstanding the national "eagerness to settle— preferably forever—a specific problem on the basis of the broadest possible constitutional pronouncement." Roberts referred, with unmistakable enthusiasm, to Frankfurter's suggestion that courts should focus on the concrete issue and "not embarrass the future too much."[63]

Professor Sunstein's name also came up throughout Samuel Alito's hearings, because he had undertaken a study of Judge Alito's fifteen years on the Third Circuit bench, reviewing all 240 of his opinions, which included 41 dissents. Based on this study, which Sunstein discussed with *Newsweek* before the hearing, he was not certain if Alito was a fundamentalist, although he did not believe him to be a minimalist. While he did not think that Alito is another Scalia, he did consider him to be "a very conservative judge.... He's had more than three dozen dissenting opinions and the overwhelming majority of them are more conservative than the [Third Circuit] court itself.... This is particularly noteworthy because the court he is on is already very conservative."[64] In an online interview on *Washingtonpost.com*, when asked if he thought Judge Alito was a minimalist conservative, Sunstein answered: "I'm not sure whether Alito is a minimalist. He doesn't speak of the 'original understanding' in his lower court opinions, but from what I've seen, he's more predictable than minimalists tend to be. On the other hand, he doesn't favor ambitious, broad rulings."[65] Clearly, Professor Sunstein was conflicted before Alito was confirmed, so I contacted him to get an update. My question: "Before Alito's confirmation you publicly (*Newsweek, Washingtonpost.com*) were not certain whether Judge Alito was a conservative minimalist or a fundamentalist. He did not seem to fit into either category. Have you reached any judgment on Justice Alito? And do you still feel Chief Justice Roberts is a conservative minimalist?" His response: "Roberts is a minimalist in the sense that he doesn't like broad, ambitious rulings. But minimalists are by nature unpredictable. Not having a framework, they surprise people. Roberts has issued, at last count, zero surprises. Thus far, his voting record looks much more ideological than I expected. He's not a fundamentalist à la Scalia, because he lacks a broad theory. Maybe it's best to say he's a methodological minimalist with highly predictable and, in that sense, highly ideological voting patterns, at least thus far. I tend to think Alito falls in the same category. Still very early, but that's how it appears to look, yes?"[66]

I certainly hope Professor Sunstein is correct, but as he says, it is too early to tell for certain. It does seem clear, however, that unlike Scalia and Thomas, neither Roberts nor Alito is a pure fundamentalist from the outset of his Supreme Court career. Others I have spoken with, though, view these two new appointees a bit differently, including two friends who are seasoned and sophisticated Supreme Court watchers. The first, the author of several well-known books about the Supreme Court, said, "I have no hope for Alito. I have read enough of his career to realize he is always looking for a leader. He thinks that is Scalia— whither Nino goeth, he will goeth. Roberts is, I think, another matter. He is obviously very smart. I think Rehnquist is his model, and he will stay just clear enough from Scalia et al. to be evaluated independently. He is a minimalist—when that is useful to gain his ideological goal. Just like Rehnquist. But he knows how to use activist means to achieve those goals. Just like Rehnquist."

My other professional Court analyst, a former Supreme Court law clerk, now an appellate advocate who teaches about the Court, offered a more pessimistic reading:

Which leaves our friends Roberts and Alito: I am quite torn about them. There is a strong argument that both of these guys are "closet fundamentalists" who use the rhetoric of conservative minimalism.

Both men came of age in a highly ideologically charged Reagan Justice Department, and my gut tells me that both of them are closer to Scalia and Thomas than we may think. In their heart of hearts, I fear that they are fundamentalist true believers who have behaved as moderates in order to move up the ladder. Now that they have life tenure, they could just as easily move right than to the center. I also think that there's a chance, based on early voting and performance at oral arguments, that Alito may turn out to be somewhat more moderate than Roberts, and that it is John Roberts who is truly the biggest wolf in sheep's clothing. Thus, I would argue that it could be as [many] as four fundamentalists—two openly so [Scalia and Thomas and] two [Roberts and Alito] almost always reaching the same results but dressing their decisions up in the language of conservative minimalism.

Needless to say, only time will reveal if George W. Bush has placed two judicial fundamentalists who are also authoritarian conservatives on the Supreme Court. What is clear, however, is that there is a powerful conservative core in the current Supreme Court, which has moved it much further to the right than it had been during the previous four decades. My own read of the situation is that Roberts and Alito are likely to vote so consistently with Scalia and Thomas that it is tantamount to having a four-member fundamentalist bloc, if, in fact, one does not already truly exist.

Equally clear is that if Bush II has another Supreme Court appointment by reason of an unexpected vacancy before the end of his term in January 2009, Senate Democrats must flatly tell the president that they will not fill the vacancy until after the November 2008 election, and give the appointment to the next president.[67] Republicans have consistently made Supreme Court appointments part and parcel of presidential elections and presidential politics. With the 2008 campaign in full swing, this issue is too important to be made by a deeply unpopular lame-duck president who for years has carried very low approval ratings. It should be for the voters to decide in 2008 whether they want

Republicans to tip the Court to fundamentalism, or Democrats to bring it back into balance. They should understand the consequences that another Republican president will bring, for there is no way a Republican can get elected without that unwritten pledge to continue doing what his predecessors have done, and add more fundamentalists to the Supreme Court. Because authoritarian conservatism is no longer in ascendancy but remains in control of the Republican Party, its adherents' last and best hope to survive and rebuild is the Supreme Court. If they control the Court they know they can slowly but steadily impose their will on America and, they believe, resume their plans to create a permanent authoritarian conservative majority. The conservative bloc of the Court is both the residue of their past success and their hope for the future.

American Law Radicalized by a Fundamentalist Supreme Court

Cass Sunstein is not alone in expressing concern about the direction of the Supreme Court as it has become more and more radical.* New York City attorney Martin Garbus has provided a chilling picture of where he believes the current conservative justices will take the law:

> Imagine the effect on our lives if workplace standards for health and safety were severely cut back; if abortions were banned, no exceptions; if minimum-hour and wage laws were so reduced as to be meaningless; if child labor laws were abolished or weakened; if there were no gun control at all. Imagine what our world would look like if the law abolished equal rights, by use and misuse of

*The principal critiques of the federal judiciary I have consulted include Herman Schwartz's *Right Wing Justice: The Conservative Campaign to Take Over the Courts* (2004) and the writings of Martin Garbus, who blogs at HuffingtonPost .com and is the author of *Courting Disaster: The Supreme Court and the Unmaking of American Law* (2002) and *The Next 25 Years: The New Supreme Court and What It Means for Americans* (2007).

dubious terminology like *color-blind* and *reverse discrimination;* if the state took money from public schools and gave it to parochial schools; if regulatory agencies like the Food and Drug Administration, the Securities and Exchange Commission, the Federal Trade Commission, or the Environmental Protection Agency were so gutted or handcuffed as to be completely ineffectual; if Congress' ability to pass needed social legislation ended. All this and more are the declared goals of the Radical Right who now dominate the Republican Party on matters related to the judiciary. The judicial revolution that began under Richard Nixon, which accelerated during Reagan's second term and peaked in the past five years, has become a runaway train.[68]

What will happen if or when the fundamentalists obtain a solid majority of the High Court? The changes will be dramatic, but not immediate; the process does not work that way. Rather, they will revise the law incrementally. Some changes, like those relating to the other branches of government, will occur sooner than others, such as those relating to rights and liberties. If Supreme Court justices proceed too quickly, it could outrage the public—even though much of that public has slept through everything the Supreme Court has done since its inception, although *Dred Scott v. Sandford* and *Bush v. Gore* did attract some attention (the first gave us the Civil War and the second, George W. Bush, Dick Cheney, and the Iraq War). Justices have only the powers of reason to enforce their decision, and should the public, and in turn the Congress and the president, reject their ruling(s), they have a serious problem. Judicial fundamentalists are more likely to effect changes in the law by selecting and resolving particular cases and controversies and working slowly and steadily to implement their radical transformation of existing jurisprudence, making it all seem very logical, reasonable, and consistent. Fundamentalists will not need to start with a blank slate, since the conservative bloc of the Court has been building a foundation for judicial fundamentalism for many years.

Here, then, is a look at what law might become under judicial fundamentalism. While it is obviously hypothetical, it is grounded in reasonable projections of the fundamentalists' positions. This analysis is far from complete but sufficient to provide a sense of how fundamentalists view constitutional law. I offer it as a warning, and sincerely hope that I am wrong, or that the fundamentalists never have the opportunity to prove that I am correct.

Unilateral and Unitary Presidentialism

Fundamentalists take the view that the president's unilateral powers in national security are almost unlimited. As Sunstein explained, "National Security Fundamentalists understand the Constitution to say that when national security is threatened, the President must be permitted to do whatever needs to be done to protect the country. If he cannot provide that protection, who will?"[69] (This is precisely the position that the Bush administration has taken under the legal advice of John Yoo.) Fundamentalists embrace the unitary executive theory and see few needs for restrictions on presidential powers in the modern era. The only relevant check on the presidency is the quadrennial election. Thus, if a president abolishes independent regulatory agencies (like the Securities and Exchange Commission, the Consumer Product Safety Commission, or the Federal Communications Commission), voters can wait four years to remove him from office if they do not approve of his actions.

Elimination of Campaign Finance Restrictions

Judicial fundamentalists do not believe campaign finance reform is consistent with the First Amendment. How can we claim to have free speech if the government is regulating how much a person can contribute to support a particular candidate or idea? (Of course, the other side of that coin is, how can speech be considered "free" if only wealthy people have access to it?) Fundamentalists will tolerate fewer restrictions on campaign contributions and reject attempts at election law reform.

Restricting Congressional Powers

The Supreme Court's efforts to cut back the powers of Congress began under Chief Justice William Rehnquist, when Clarence Thomas brought another fundamentalist vote to the panel. One scholar notes that in "its view toward federal legislation power ... the later Rehnquist Court has been the least deferential of any in the history of the U.S. Supreme Court [toward Congress], striking down thirty provisions of federal law from 1995 to 2001."[70] Efforts by Congress in such areas as regulating health and safety standards or protecting the environment will face growing difficulty under a fundamentalist Supreme Court.

Business Will Have a Friendly Court

Fundamentalists, as one commentator stated it, "see the overriding principle of the law as the maximization of wealth, not social justice, as they aggressively champion corporate interests."[71] Fundamentalists, for example, want to protect "commercial speech"—in other words, advertising which, of course, is vital to countless businesses but which has never been covered under the First Amendment. Traditionally, the First Amendment has been viewed as relevant to political speech, in which public questions, including criticism of government and its officials, are discussed and debated; selling sodas, cigarettes, or cars has not been envisioned as needing the same degree of protection. Sunstein reported that Justice Clarence Thomas has said that "he would rule that the First Amendment protects commercial advertising to the same degree that it protects political speech."[72] This would make it unconstitutional to restrict ads on television for tobacco and liquor, or any other demonstrably harmful product. False and misleading advertising would be for the marketplace to sort out, not government bureaucrats. The FCC could no longer fine a broadcast by shock-jock Howard Stern on commercial radio. Sunstein observes that "fundamentalists are transforming the First Amendment into a species of laissez-faire economics."[73]

Direct Impact of Judicial Fundamentalism on Individuals

For the past five decades, it has traditionally been the role of the federal judiciary to help the less fortunate and those whom fortune has short-changed, a role that began to change as Republican presidents added conservatives to the Court. Fundamentalists will make the federal judiciary a benefactor for the rich and fortunate, while its decisions will provide little support for those who most need it. Below I have listed alphabetically key areas of law that a controlling bloc of fundamentalists will address:

- *Abortion.* The 1973 *Roe v. Wade* ruling that legalized abortion will either be overturned or so limited as to be meaningless. Both Chief Justice Roberts and Justice Alito said during their confirmations that they believed precedent is important, so it is most likely the Court will gut this ruling slowly, so that it will not be a meaningful precedent. Rather than overturn *Roe* they will dilute it. This change, of course, will most affect the reproductive freedoms of lower-income women.

- *Affirmative Action.* Myriad affirmative action programs provide opportunities for racial minorities in areas of education, business, government, the military—to name only a few. Such programs seek to provide advantage to Americans who were long subjected to the disadvantages of blatant discrimination. In the 1960s and 1970s "affirmative action" programs were enacted by Congress and adopted by institutions to give such people a chance to catch up with those who did not suffer such economic and political handicaps. Fundamentalists dislike these laws and programs, for they claim that the Constitution should be color-blind and that any attempt to address an imbalance is "reverse discrimination." Fundamentalism seeks to abolish such programs, and when they have a majority these programs will go from endangered species to extinction.

- *Bill of Rights.* The Bill of Rights—the first ten amendments to the Constitution—originally applied only to the federal government, not to state governments. When the Fourteenth Amendment was adopted in 1868 as a means to limit Southern state governments from threatening the rights and liberties of former slaves, many proponents of the amendment intended that its language protecting "privileges and immunities" include the rights covered by the Bill of Rights. In 1873, however, the Supreme Court, in a 5 to 4 decision, so narrowly construed the privileges and immunities clause of the amendment (in *The Slaughterhouse Cases*) as to blunt this broader reading.[74] However, by 1897 the Supreme Court began applying the Bill of Rights to the states through the due process clause of the Fourteenth Amendment, which is known as the "incorporation doctrine." During the 1940s, 1950s, and 1960s the Supreme Court slowly but steadily incorporated item after item in the Bill of Rights—such as freedom of religion, freedom of speech, freedom of the press, and the procedural safeguards of the Fourth, Fifth, and Sixth amendments to criminal defendants. Fundamentalists reject this doctrine, and as Martin Garbus explained, "Thomas, Scalia, Roberts, and Alito are dead set against the application of many of the Bill of Rights amendments against the states. So, for the first time, there are four solid votes to overturn more than sixty years of settled law."[75] Needless to say, this will have very dramatic consequences, enabling, for example, states to have official religions, and it would allow them to censor speech through measures like closing down news outlets. (China will have no powers greater than those of the states without a Bill of Rights.)

- *Civil Rights.* Civil rights are not favored by judicial fundamentalists—not because they are racists or misogynist, but rather because it seems that they do not approve of the way the federal government has addressed problems confronting African Americans and women. For example, although extensive congressional hearings found that threats against women had an impact on interstate commerce, the fundamentalists thought otherwise. They said such violence did not substantially affect interstate commerce and struck down provisions of the Violence Against Women Act that enabled women to file lawsuits for sex-related violence in federal courts against their attackers, relying on both the Commerce Clause and the Fourteenth Amendment. Fundamentalists do not believe that the equal protection language of the Fourteenth Amendment even applies to women, so the government can discriminate against women as it sees fit. Under the fundamentalist view there are no constitutional restrictions on either federal or state governments regarding discrimination based on race or sex.[76]

- *Cruel and Unusual Punishment.* Fundamentalists fully embrace the death penalty. They do not believe it is cruel and unusual to put juvenile offenders to death, nor the mentally incompetent. Because they reject the doctrine of incorporation, they do not believe that the Eighth Amendment's ban on cruel and unusual punishment applies to the states, so the states can do as they wish. As for the negative view the rest of the international community has regarding America's use of capital punishment, Justice Scalia recently explained how fundamentalists think: "There exists in some parts of the world sanctimonious criticism of America's death penalty, as somehow unworthy of a civilized society. (I say sanctimonious, because most of the countries to which these finger-waggers belong had the death penalty themselves until recently—and indeed, many of them would still have it if the democratic will prevailed.)"[77] Given that rationale, it is equally unlikely that fundamentalists would have any problem with "aggressive interrogation techniques" (known to the rest of the world as torture) against suspected terrorists.

- *Environmental Protection.* Fundamentalists believe that there is no constitutional foundation for a federal Environmental Protection Agency. They have instead protected a number of businesses from environmental regulation by accepting the argument that such regulation is the same as taking property under the principles of the Fifth Amendment (which covers cases like condemnation), in which case the government should compensate the property owner. They have also found a very easy way to deal with nongovernmental environmental groups that file federal lawsuits to enforce the law—they simply throw them out of court.

- *Free Speech.* Under judicial fundamentalism the "Constitution would provide far less protection than it does now to free speech," Sunstein says. "There is a plausible [fundamentalist] argument that on the original understanding, the federal government could punish speech that it deemed dangerous or unacceptable, so long as it did not ban such speech in advance." Sunstein doubts the fundamentalists would go that far, but they might not prohibit the government from regulating "libelous speech, blasphemous speech, and commercial advertising."[78]

- *Gay Rights.* When a minimalist majority of the Supreme Court overturned sodomy laws, the fundamentalists fumed. Justice Scalia's dissent in *Lawrence v. Texas* provides a précis of their thinking:

> Today's opinion is the product of a Court, which is the product of a law-profession culture, that has largely signed on to the so-called homosexual agenda, by which I mean the agenda promoted by some homosexual activists directed at eliminating the moral opprobrium that has traditionally attached to homosexual conduct.... It is clear from this that the Court has taken sides in the culture war, departing from its role of assuring, as neutral observer, that the democratic rules of engagement are observed. Many Americans do not want persons who openly engage in homosexual conduct as partners in their business, as scoutmasters for their children, as teachers in their children's schools, or as boarders in their home. They view this as protecting themselves and their families from a lifestyle that they believe to be immoral and destructive.[79]

- *Guns.* The Second Amendment reads: "A well-regulated Militia, being necessary to the security of a free states, the right of the people to keep and bear Arms, shall not be infringed." The Supreme Court has not ruled on the Second Amendment since 1939 in *U.S.*

v. Miller, which was a less-than-clear holding on the right to bear arms. Conservatives and gun aficionados, however, are working at getting a case before the High Court as soon as possible, now that they have a conservative majority. Fundamentalists believe that the Second Amendment makes most laws that attempt to control guns unconstitutional. Suffice it to say that with a fundamentalist-dominated Supreme Court, the National Rifle Association could close down its operation, for it will have lost its raision d'être.

- *Habeas Corpus.* Conservatives on the Supreme Court have already vastly restricted their jurisdiction over habeas corpus petitions. Justice Clarence Thomas, whose view is representative of fundamentalist thinking, argued that existing federal habeas corpus statutes, which have been used by state prisoners to obtain a federal court review of their convictions, should not be permitted because such "review 'disturbs the State's significant interest in repose for concluding litigation … and intrudes on state sovereignty to a degree matched by few exercises of federal judicial authority.' "[80] Fundamentalists do not much care what state governments do—except when it affects the conservative agenda.

- *Religion.* Given the fact that fundamentalists do not believe that the First Amendment applies to the states by reason of incorporation through the Fourteenth Amendment, the wall of separation between church and state will crumble quickly. In addition, fundamentalists do not accept the separation arguments even where the First Amendment does apply, for the Constitution states nothing about "separation," only that the national government not "establish" a national religion. Under judicial fundamentalism it would not be unconstitutional for a state to embrace a particular religion and tax citizens to support that religion. In short, school prayers will return, public buildings will be adorned with postings of the Ten Commandments, and public events will begin and end with a prayer. Grants of federal funds to religious organizations will become the norm, and prohibitions that might result in the loss of charitable tax status for politically active churches will be abolished. The dreams of the religious right will come true.

- *Sex.* The Supreme Court under the fundamentalists will define obscenity by what offends them, not according to some vague community standard. They will encourage the closing of sex parlors and strip joints; magazines like *Playboy, Penthouse,* and *Hustler* may not survive; and sexual censorship of the public airways will increase. Judicial fundamentalists want to reverse the permissiveness that they believe their predecessors have tolerated. Justice Scalia, in his dissent in *Lawrence v. Kansas,* rejected the majority opinion's claim of "*an emerging awareness* that liberty gives substantial protection to adult persons in deciding how to conduct their private lives *in matters pertaining to sex.*" (Emphasis in original.) Scalia said, "Apart from the fact that such an 'emerging awareness' does not establish a 'fundamental right,' the statement is factually false." Fundamentalists, like Scalia, take solace in the fact that "States continue to prosecute all sorts of crimes by adults, [even] sodomy laws, too, have been enforced 'in the past half century,' in which there have been 134 reported cases involving prosecutions for consensual, adult, homosexual sodomy." Under a fundamentalist Supreme Court there will be substantially more prosecutions and convictions for sex-related offenses, even among consenting adults.

- *Standing to Sue.* "Standing" means that a person bringing the lawsuit has a sufficient personal stake in the matter being adjudicated. "In essence the question of standing is whether the litigant is entitled to have the court decide the merits of the dispute or of particular issues," the Supreme Court has said.[81] There is a complex body of jurisprudence that has developed around this concept, but for purposes of this analysis the relevant point is that fundamentalists have constantly refined such procedural matters to make it increasingly difficult for plaintiffs to use the federal courts to redress their grievances. Fundamentalists use standing to keep the federal courts out of areas they do not believe should be litigated. For example, members of Congress who have sued the president in an attempt to compel him to execute the laws or honor treaties are regularly tossed out of federal court for lack of standing.

Fundamentalists will make it virtually impossible—it is already close to being so—for a public litigant to sue a regulatory agency whose decision they disagree with and have an interest in. They will narrow even further the ability of the public to use the Freedom of Information Act to obtain information that is often essential to filing a lawsuit relating to policy actions or decisions by the executive branch. The standing jurisprudence of the fundamentalists will also render decision makers in the executive branch effectively immune for even their most egregious decisions. Conservatives and fundamentalists would like to put the federal courts out of business, with one exception: They will go out of their way to protect property interests, particularly those of large corporations. Disturbing as it is, standing is only one of many such procedural blocks fundamentalists have developed to limit the responsibilities of the federal judiciary.

- *Voting.* Until 1962 the Supreme Court refused to enter this "political thicket," taking the position that it was a question to be resolved by the political branches of government. But that year, in *Baker v. Carr,* they decided by a 6 to 2 vote to consider the constitutionality of gerrymandered districts, and in a series of cases that followed, created the standard of "one person, one vote."[82] Judge Bork, a fundamentalist, has called the one-person, one-vote doctrine a "fiasco," and complains that it "does not result in equality of representation" and "in no way reduces gerrymandering, which means some persons' votes are deliberately submerged and made ineffective."[83] In case after case that has come before the Supreme Court, fundamentalists have made it clear that they are not interested in finding a solution to this problem. They are not, in general, keen on voting laws. Justice Thomas has consistently ruled to cut back the reach of the Voting Rights Act. He is highly critical of efforts by federal courts to eliminate discrimination against African American voters, calling it "political apartheid" and asserting that other justices are acting on "the implicit assumption that members of racial and ethnic groups must all think alike on important matters of public policy and must have their own 'minority preferred' representatives holding seats in elected bodies if they are to be considered represented at all."[84]

The Constitution simply did not anticipate the ability of a political party's ideology to trump and effectively eliminate the separation of powers. The system was not designed to accommodate the concerted efforts of these Republican presidents to tilt the federal judiciary by appointing uniformly thinking conservative judges and justices to the bench, but that is what has occurred. Over the past four decades Nixon, Reagan, Bush I, and Bush II have restructured the federal judiciary, not merely with those who now sit on the federal benches, but with the legacy of those who held their seats before them issuing decisions that provide a conservative base for a fundamentalist federal judiciary.

Conservative Republicans embrace all of these radical changes in American law, and believe that a solid fundamentalist majority throughout the federal judiciary is exactly what the country needs. But such a federal judiciary will never reflect the will of the majority of Americans, and as such will be judicially out of touch with reality. Too often it is forgotten that the Supreme Court, like every other institution of government, must not be at odds with the people for whom they work—namely, the citizens of our country. But that is where the GOP insists on taking the federal judiciary. Professor Sunstein noted that fundamentalists and ultraconservative Republicans have become virtually indistinguishable, for "fundamentalists read the Constitution not to fit the original understanding [the doctrine that they claim to embrace] but the views of the extreme wing of the Republican Party." And they are "now mounting an assault on the very idea of judicial independence—and are seeking to produce a federal judiciary that operates as an arm of the political branches."[85] If there is still any question that the Supreme Court and lower federal courts are controlled by conservative Republicans, we need only consult the chart below, which shows the current balance of sitting judges listed by the president appointing them:

	ALL JUDICIAL POSTS	APPOINTED BY DEMOCRATIC PRESIDENTS	APPOINTED BY REPUBLICAN PRESIDENTS
Vacant	55 (6.3%)		
Bush II			269 (30.5%)
Clinton		335 (38%)	
Bush I			104 (11.8%)
Reagan			90 (10.1%)
Carter		21 (2.4%)	
Ford			3 (0.3%)
Nixon			4 (0.5%)
Johnson		1 (0.1%)	
Total (all courts)	881 (100%)	356 (40.5%)	471 (53.3%)

Chart based on data (as of June 2007) from the Alliance for Justice (see www.afj.org/judicial/judicial_selection_resources/selection_database/byCourtAndAppPres.asp)

Republicans are not satisfied with a *conservative* federal judiciary; they want a fundamentalist one, and they are frighteningly close to achieving that goal. The question raised in this chapter, as in the earlier chapters, is what should or should not be done, what will and will not work, and does anyone really care that Republicans are insisting on operating each of the three branches outside the precepts of the Constitution?

Democracy is like sex—it works best when you participate.

—Anonymous (sign in store on East Nineteenth Street, Manhattan)

CHAPTER FOUR

Repairing Government:
Restoring the Proper Processes

In the preceding chapters I have examined key processes related to the proper operations of the legislative, executive, and judicial branches to make the point that under Republican control none of these branches has operated as envisioned. Congress under Republican rule has proven to be incapable of deliberation, timely annual appropriations, and necessary oversight of a Republican president, all fundamental constitutional responsibilities of the legislative branch. Modern Republican presidents, in turn, believe that they must dominate the entire federal establishment, and in so doing override the fundamental safeguard of our system's checks and balances. Corrupting the independence and impartiality of the federal judiciary has been a priority of Republican presidents, who have devoted four decades to selecting primarily judges and justices with a radical conservative political philosophy. As a result these Republican-appointed jurists, who now constitute the prevailing majority, are no more objective and open-minded on countless issues that regularly come before the federal courts than the Republican National Committee.

Republicans have simply dismantled or ignored countless well-established processes found in the rules, customs, norms, traditions, laws, and constitutional mandates of the federal system. Refusing to govern by traditional standards, they create their own self-serving schemes that often *they* do not even attempt to justify, while at other times they rely on legal opinions that should result in disbarment of the attorneys who issue them. Ironically, conservatives were once sticklers who insisted that everyone play by the established rules; now they invent their own to fit their needs as required. Thus, we find Republicans demanding that lobbyists contribute to the party in substantial amounts before they are entitled to talk with GOP congressional leaders—an extortion operation worthy of the Mafia. We have an unaccountable Republican vice president secretly running the government because the president is not interested. We had the five conservative Republican justices who claimed allegiance to states' rights—two of whom hoped to retire with conservative replacements (Rehnquist and O'Connor)—inventing a new one-time-only process (which, as they explained in their ruling, should be ignored by other courts) that enabled them to intervene to resolve the Florida vote count in *Bush v. Gore* and short-circuit both state *and* federal procedures—just the way banana republics resolve their elections. One thing that conservatism does not wish to conserve are processes that block their efforts to gain power.

Proper process can be viewed as operating government the way it was designed to function to serve all Americans, and not merely one political party. If a process is not working, it can be changed by amending the rules, creating new laws, or even amending the Constitution. But there is another, more encompassing and equally appropriate way to view proper process, based on an even more fundamental set of standards for government operations.

Few Americans, I am sure, are aware of the institutional processes that I have addressed broadly in the earlier chapters of this book as a survey of the havoc Republicans have inflicted on the federal system. We do not, however, need to understand these institutional operations to recognize proper process. Polling data shows that Americans who are not privy to the workings of Washington can certainly recognize when matters are amiss. The Pew Research Center reported in late March 2007 that Democrats are believed to be better at managing the federal government than Republicans, with 47 percent of respondents reaching this conclusion. When the issue was management skills, the Democratic Party emerged with "a 16-point advantage over the GOP in this area." In addition, "by a margin of 43% to 25% more Americans say the Democratic Party, rather than the Republican Party, governs in a more honest and ethical way."[1] These are process evaluations. Pew pollsters do not ask respondents why they think Democrats can manage the federal government better or more honestly, but the responses appear to be associated with the broader public reaction to Republican rule and growing unhappiness with it. In another March 2007 survey Pew found a strikingly "dramatic shift in party identification that has occurred during the past five years.... In 2002, the country was equally divided along partisan lines: 43% identified with the Republican Party or leaned to the GOP, while an identical proportion said they were Democrats. Today, half of the public (50%) either identifies as a Democrat or say they lean toward the Democratic Party, compared with 35% who align with the GOP."[2] Thus, these polling responses also indirectly indicate that Republican malfeasance and poor management have not escaped the public's attention.

Americans are actually aware of many process matters, like Bush's increasing troop levels in Iraq (88 percent aware), that the Democrats control of the House of Representatives (76 percent aware), and that the United States has a trade deficit (68 percent aware).[3] Other polls measure public attitudes toward the Congress, the president, and the Supreme Court, and these job assessments certainly involve public perception of the processes associated with these institutions. For example, the ABC News/*Washington Post* poll charting the job performance of Congress (from March 1997 to November 2006) shows that the average annual approval is 46 percent and the disapproval is 49 percent—measuring predominately the years the GOP controlled Congress.[4] Presidential job ratings for George W. Bush range in the *Newsweek* polls from his post-9/11 high of 88 percent approval to his still downward-trending low of 28 percent as of May 2007.[5] The U.S. Supreme Court is consistently ranked the most favorably of all the three branches and varies little from poll to poll and year to year, with an average approval rating between

55 to 60 percent.[6] It has been argued that the reason different branches have different approval/disapproval ratings is because of the visibility of their respective processes.[7] Congress, which has the most open processes of the three branches, consistently has the lowest approval rankings. The Supreme Court, where process is almost invisible, has the highest rankings. As George W. Bush's processes—his refusal to play by the rules—have become more apparent along with the highly negative impact of his presidency on the United States, his approval ratings have gone lower and lower.

Think how differently the Bush presidency might be viewed if, in taking the nation to war in Iraq, he had respected the proper processes. "War is not a military activity conducted by soldiers, but rather a social activity that involves entire nations," noted Lieutenant Colonel Paul Yingling, a professional solider trained in political science. Drawing on world history, he explained that all wars require sacrifices that come from the people of a nation, who "supply the blood and treasure required to prosecute the war." The great military theorist Carl von Clausewitz insisted that leaders must have popular support to go to war, and that the "greatest error the statesman can make is to commit his nation to a great conflict without mobilizing popular passions to a level commensurate with the stakes of the conflict."[8] Sending the nation to war in Iraq on false pretenses and then declaring the mission accomplished when it clearly was not were colossal blunders by Bush—the very antithesis of what history teaches and Clausewitz counsels. Bush has entangled the nation in a no-win war that he now perpetuates so it can be lost by Democrats in one of two ways: The Democratic Congress finds the spine and sufficient Republicans to override a veto, forcing him to end the war—which Republican hawks will call surrender—or the war will be ended in the next Democratic president's term. Either way Bush and the Republicans will claim the war was lost because of Democrats. This, clearly, will be duplicity parading as hypocrisy, but by now we are familiar with such norms of Republican politics, and they are remarkably effective.

The social sciences in general, and political science in particular, have paid pitifully little attention to the workings of process. The dearth of process study is surprising, given its importance to our political system. Take any significant policy issue—the war in Iraq, the Israeli-Palestinian conflict, terrorism, health care, immigration, food contamination, budget deficits, and fixing social security, to randomly name only a few of an eternal list. Endless studies and reports are generated on these problems, which seldom provide answers rather than the point of view of those issuing the documents. If these policy issues were easy, they would have long since been solved. In fact, they are all difficult to understand fully; circumstances surrounding them are changing constantly, and it is never easy to determine with any certainty the best answer for the nation. Process can be complex, as well, but it is seldom as complex as policy, and unlike policy, process is not as susceptible to change. The scholarly study and media attention that have been devoted to process have provided great insights into the working of our system, including the fact that Americans do not need to understand the mechanics of a "motion to recommit" to recognize that congressional processes are proper, or that they need to understand unitary executive theory to perceive that a president is engaged in a power grab, or that they need to be familiar with the jurisprudence of federal court jurisdiction to grasp when the federal judiciary is taking better care of big business than average citizens.

Public Perceptions of Process

There are, of course, many people like myself who believe that what is happening in this country cannot be truly comprehended without examining political processes. I find that point of view particularly true of those who have had the opportunity to either work inside the system or report and write about it—former and current government officials, journalists who cover Washington, historians who write about Washington, academics and scholars who study government and politics. They, and I, have become convinced that a proper process—using that phrase in a dual sense as the discussion that follows will explain—produces good policy. And, in turn, compromised processes will lead to bad policy. If candidates for federal offices spent more time developing and refining their thoughts about employing proper processes, we would all be better off, for it would improve policy.

To learn how process is viewed generally, I have relied on the groundbreaking work of John Hibbing and Elizabeth Theiss-Morse, which I discussed briefly in the introduction, for it provides a useful map. Their research has gone largely unnoticed, notwithstanding the fact that it upsets much conventional wisdom. In discussing their findings (off-the-record) with their professional peers, I discovered that those familiar with it find that it has been undertaken with the rigor required of any scientific inquiry; I also found that their peers were surprised that their studies have not drawn more attention, given their significance. When examining their findings I realized that my own view of process—with reference to whether those running the legislative, executive, and judicial branches were operating pursuant to the established and normal standards—is too narrow, if not unnecessarily technical, as well.

Hibbing and Theiss-Morse explain how we all tend to view process. Because politics is often complex, we employ mental techniques that help us make sense of it all. We simplify the political world by relying on our fixed notions (biases); on earlier conclusions we have made about people, professions, groups, and organizations (stereotypes); or on ideas we have accumulated based on our experiences (frameworks). We use this accumulated knowledge as preexisting mental reference points to assist in understanding political events and activities. In short, we take what we think we do know and use it as a peg on which to hang what we do not know, for this enables us to reach conclusions with which we are comfortable without expending a lot of mental exertion. These existing attitudes or beliefs also provide places to mentally catalog new information easily.

It seems we make such judgments fairly automatically. In my own case, for example, before I began reading about the Republican presidential contenders in early 2007, I had already sorted them in my mind as to which, if any, were authoritarian conservatives. Clearly, I have a negative bias toward authoritarian conservatives, because everything I know about them is troublesome, if not dangerous, for our democracy. Thus, as the prospective candidates surfaced in 2006 and early 2007, I categorized them as high, medium, or low authoritarians.* In initially assessing these candidates, however, I found myself using my knowledge of process. Having strong (and experience- and study-based) opinions about what it takes to be an effective president, I cannot but react to the recent trend of electing national leaders whose principal political credential has been to serve as a governor: Consider Georgia governor Jimmy Carter, California governor Ronald Reagan, Arkansas governor Bill Clinton, and Texas governor George W. Bush. Each of these men required well over a year if not more to figure out how processes operate in Washington, and some never did. All these former governors had to rely heavily on their vice presidents, or their staffs, or both, who had Washington-based experience, until they learned their way. Voters often believe that by selecting a Washington outsider they can change the way business is done in Washington, but it seldom works that way. So, with my process framework, I find myself hoping that, regardless of which party prevails in November 2008, Americans will elect a president who knows the ways of Washington, because he or she will be better able to get down to the business of governing faster—for a four-year term is surprisingly short.

Another example, paraphrased and modified from Hibbing and Theiss-Morse: A presidential candidate gives a speech on health care reform to a business group that opposes such reform. A member of the audience may connect with, understand, or interpret that speech

---

*My highs: former speaker Newt Gingrich (whom I discussed in *Conservatives Without Conscience*) and former New York City mayor Rudy Giuliani. Mediums: Representative Duncan Hunter; former Massachusetts governor Mitt Romney; former Arkansas governor Mike Huckabee; Kansas senator Sam Brownback; and Arizona senator John McCain. Lows: Senator Chuck Hagel; former senator Fred Thompson; and former Virginia governor Jim Gilmore.

through a number of existing mind-sets. The information could be viewed in terms of the issue or policy involved (health care reform); the person delivering the speech (the candidate); the method of delivery (no notes, no podium, and a lone microphone, speaking confidently and passionately); the political affiliation of the speaker (Democrat); the reason for the speech (he or she is running for president—does he or she look like a president?), or the particular audience involved (business people).[9]

Because we all rely on our existing belief systems to reach conclusions about politics and government operations, we are in some sense preprogrammed, but we also have a dominant disposition toward political matters, an inclination, a predilection, or what Hibbing and Theiss-Morse describe as one of four possible "political propensities." We look initially, if not primarily, at (1) the person; (2) political party affiliation; (3) policy involved; or (4) the process. As a process person I would interpret the hypothetical event in the previous paragraphs as follows: The candidate has guts, and is not hiding behind a podium. The candidate knows what he or she is talking about because it is an extemporaneous speech. Because I have only newspaper knowledge of health care reform, I am impressed by the candidate's seeming expertise and passion for the position.

The way a candidate handles himself or herself when campaigning is very much a part of process. The Bush White House raised to new heights the use of mediagenic settings to make a weak and inarticulate speaker look strong.

Although psychology, sociology, and other social sciences have explored our cognitive approaches to political questions they, too, have all overlooked process. Hibbing and Theiss-Morse filled this gap, and in so doing found that 14 percent of their respondents view the world of politics through "process."[10] If this number is extrapolated to all Americans, it represents roughly 20 million people who have a process propensity. With the possible exception of policy, process far exceeds other attitudes and beliefs in interpreting politics.[11] Process-propensity individuals stand out in several ways. They are "more highly educated than average, and have high levels of efficacy, interest, and involvement in politics"—meaning they are knowledgeable, get involved in politics, are good at it, and find it personally rewarding. They are "engaged in the political system, both psychologically and behaviorally." For these reasons, they are "citizens who are in a good position to make a difference." It was further discovered that people with a process propensity constituted the largest percentage of their respondents broadly described as political "experts." Political expertise was determined by a quick test used to rank the political sophistication of interviewees. Although expert-level responses would not earn anyone a Ph.D. in political science, the questions did elicit knowledge of current political affairs and process: the ability to identify key foreign leaders, key members of a president's cabinet, and the general fiscal condition of the U.S. government.[12]

Does this mean that to understand process a person must be well acquainted with and involved in public affairs? Absolutely not. To the contrary, people can be "notoriously uninformed about political institutions and processes" and have no "direct experience with decision-making procedures," yet understand processes.[13] They do not have to be familiar with parliamentary procedure to understand congressional processes; they need know nothing about the operations of the National Security Council or the Office of Management and Budget to understand the presidency; and no citizen is required to be conversant with the rules of evidence to sit on a jury or understand what happens in a court room.

"People think about process in relatively simple terms," Hibbing and Theiss-Morse discovered.[14] They concluded that in political situations "process concerns come down to only one thing and that is whether or not people believe decision makers are acting in their own self-interest." Accordingly, there is no need to take into account "decision makers being thorough, collecting all the relevant data, considering all possible alternatives, and listening closely to the people."[15]

It is not necessary to consider what constitutes regular order in the House or abuse of the filibuster in the Senate or the influence of presidential signing statements or which judges speak to the Federalist Society and why. It all comes down to one reality—and this is a key to their findings: If people feel an official is taking care of himself or herself or some special interest rather than the larger public, it is that behavior which becomes the focus of voters' attention, if not anger.[16] Thus, in the end, proper process for all Americans comes down to "perceptions of the motives of the decision makers, nothing more, nothing less."[17] This means that a given decision must have not only have been made fairly, but it must be perceived as a fair treatment of the matter as well.[18] "Far from requiring citizens to be students of the internal operations of political institutions, judgments influenced by process can be made by anyone who has an opinion of whether politicians are self-serving or not." Hibbing and Theiss-Morse offer a method to verify their conclusion: "We would encourage those who claim the common people are not knowledgeable enough to make process determinations to go to any bar in the country and ask the patrons whether they think politicians are out to benefit themselves or not," they wrote, only partially tongue in cheek. "If the patrons say they do not know or have not thought about this aspect of process, this would be strong evidence that we are incorrect—but we are not worried."[19]

To summarize, there are two ways to determine if government officials are engaging in proper process. The first way is to acquaint oneself with the established processes and procedures of the institutions of the national government. In chapters 1 through 3, I have attempted to show that Republicans are not inclined to follow the well-established and fundamental processes when they control the elective branches of government. The second way to view the propriety of process is to examine whether the process in question is neutral, fair, and unbiased in both fact and appearance, and whether the politician or official using the process is doing so to serve the public rather than his or her self-interest, or on behalf of special interests. Not surprisingly, in applying either test, the process is working only when it does serve the public interest.

Regrettably, there are many people who have no interest whatsoever in politics and government. Americans are notoriously uninvolved in their democracy. To understand the role of process in our system it is also instructive to examine those who have dropped out of the system and actually seek to avoid such process. Ignorant and apathetic voters, and dropouts, probably frown at the sign in the shop on East Nineteenth Street in Manhattan that says: "Democracy is like sex—it works best when you participate."[20] A charming thought, if a questionable simile. (If democracy were, in fact, like sex, it would be impossible to prevent people from participating.) If I ever come across this shop, I plan to offer them an additional sign that sums up the GOP attitude about process: "If democracy were like sex—Republicans would make it illegal, except for themselves."

Ignorant and Apathetic American Voters Are Content—and Irresponsible

Voter ignorance or apathy in the United States has long been a dreadfully serious and well-known problem. Students of voter behavior issue periodic reports with shocking if unremarkable findings that lead one to wonder how people manage to remain so uninformed. Over the years—actually, over the decades—the figures have not changed significantly, so the data from 2004 are as good as any and probably not far from what they have been since these embarrassing records were first kept in the 1930s. The most recent study from the Pew Research Center, for example, is titled "Public Knowledge of Current Affairs Little Changed by News and Information Revolutions—What Americans Know: 1989–2007." This was not a study of voters per se, but rather of all Americans. Pew developed a set of twenty-three core questions that it asked 1,502 subjects to answer. Only eight answered all the questions

correctly. (I confess to missing one; my news-junkie wife got them all.)
At the other end of the scale, five people could not answer any correctly. If Americans were graded as students (90 percent and above, A;
80 percent, B; 70 percent, C; 60 percent, D; and below 60 percent, F),
Pew reports that "fully half would have failed, while only about one in
six would have earned an A or B."* Registered voters do not do much
better than Americans as a whole.

So just how ignorant are American voters? The answer, of course,
is *really* ignorant. The Cato Institute conducted a study just before the
2004 presidential election. In its results Cato reported, "Particularly
significant is the fact that, on many issues, the majority is not only ignorant of the truth but they are actively misinformed. For example ...
58 percent believes that the administration's [false claim that there was]
a link between Saddam Hussein and 9/11, and 57 percent believes that
increases in domestic spending have *not* contributed significantly to the
current budget deficit." Ignorance runs wide and deep. "Most of the
time, only bare majorities know which party has control of the Senate,
some 70 percent cannot name either of their state's senators, and the
vast majority cannot name *any* congressional candidate in their district
at the height of a campaign." Cato observes that "voters are ignorant
not just about specific policy issues but also about the basic structure
of government and how it operates." This study concluded the situation is not likely to get much better. "A relatively stable level of extreme
ignorance has persisted even in the face of massive increases in educational attainment and an unprecedented expansion in quantity and
the quality of information available to the general public at little cost."
The Cato report grimly concluded that any and all "efforts to increase
the stock of knowledge possessed by voters are unlikely to be no more
than modestly effective."[21] In the end, the institute found that about a
third of all voters are hopelessly ignorant.[22] (This figure clearly does not
include those who are not even interested in voting.)

*This April 2007 report with the twenty-three-question quiz can be found at
people-press.org/reports/display.php3?ReportID=5319.

How many Americans do vote? The answer is surprisingly few. Among the 172 nations of the world for which records are maintained, the 2004 nationwide voter turnout of 48.3 percent of the eligible voters in the Kerry versus Bush presidential race ranks the United States 139 among the world's democracies, slightly ahead of Botswana (46.5 percent) and Zambia (40.5 percent). Most developed democracies have far greater turnout, like Germany (80.6 percent), Sweden (83.6 percent), France (84 percent), and Italy (92.5 percent).[23] In the United States about 50 to 60 million eligible voters do not bother the register, and 70 to 90 million who could vote fail to do so.[24]

Notwithstanding decades of scholarly study, no one knows precisely why American voters are so apathetic.[25] In the context of process, John Hibbing and Elizabeth Theiss-Morse offered one of the better explanations: "Participation in politics is low because [many] people do not like politics even in the best of circumstances." Why don't they like politics? Mincing no words, Hibbing and Theiss-Morse explained: "People love contests, people love athletic competition, people love television shows pitting one side against the other, people crave picking a side and being a part of a group with a shared concern. Why, then, since politics is laced with conflict, sides, shared concerns, and groups, do people despise politics? *Because they believe politicians are playing them for suckers.*"[26] (Emphasis added.) This is the gut reaction that many people have, and as a result they prefer to simply opt out of government and politics altogether. Then there are those who are conflict averse, or who believe political debate is so contrived that they find it tiresome, or who simply find the business of government irrelevant to their own lives. Accordingly, they want invisible government and politics—or stealth democracy, as Hibbing and Theiss-Morse describe it.[27]

It is very difficult to determine how many people would actually prefer invisible government and politics, because such a measurement would be difficult to take. Hibbing and Theiss-Morse were only able to measure it indirectly, through responses to their survey questions that suggested that respondents had a favorable attitude toward government operations.[28] Given the fact he has been working with this data and thinking about the implications of their findings for over a decade, I contacted John Hibbing to see if he could suggest an estimate of the percentage of Americans who do favor such invisible government. He replied:

> At the risk of sounding like an academic, it is a bit tricky to offer a precise figure on the percent of people who prefer relatively un-seen governmental processes. The reality is probably a spectrum of sorts, making it difficult to know where to draw a clear line between those who prefer visible government and those who want somebody else to take care of things without any muss or commotion. Even over time, preferences toward the tangible presence of government changes. As the Iraq War becomes more salient and more disliked, people become less likely to want government to be invisible. If you have to attach numbers, *I would say at least a third are stealth democrats at heart* but that is more impressionistic than based on a particular survey item or items.[29] [Emphasis added.]

After years of my own reading about voter ignorance and apathy, along with countless suggestions for addressing it, I have come to the conclusion that there are no known fixes. I have decided, therefore, that it is not worth worrying about, because when politics or govern-ment does directly affect the lives of Americans, they can and do get interested very quickly. People who are ignorant or apathetic have, in all but the rarest of situations, made a rational choice. I have spoken with many of them and found them remarkably content with their position. Of course, they are shirking their responsibility of citizenship, but there is no law that demands that everyone must be a responsible citizen. Ironically, ignorance and apathy do not necessarily go hand in hand with a lack of awareness of the processes of politics and government, as polls I have cited indicate. To some degree, I believe that almost every-one is interested in process as Hibbing and Theiss-Morse describe it, by which I mean that no one wants to be taken advantage of, screwed, or shortchanged by the system, or have his tax dollars wasted by Washington—not even those who would prefer an invisible democracy.

Restoring Proper Processes

Breakdowns in the three branches of the federal government do not call for new government reforms. The breakdowns I have described did not develop because any of the three branches has fundamentally flawed processes. Rather, as I have made clear, they occurred because contemporary Republican leaders simply do not govern or rule by long-standing and well-understood procedures. The solution to the problem is surprisingly simple: Run the government as it is supposed to be run. If Republicans are not willing to do that—and I believe they are not philosophically capable of it—they should not be trusted to control America. Given the droves of people who have left the GOP in the past six years—many of whom, I believe, are disgusted with the behavior of elected Republicans—this is not as difficult as it might seem. One of the best ways to keep Republicans out of power is to encourage their cheerleaders—pundits like Rush Limbaugh, Sean Hannity, and Ann Coulter—to continue serving as spokespeople and catalysts for authoritarian conservatism. Few want to go where they would take this country, as Republican losses in the 2006 election were solid signs that Americans are not interested in GOP authoritarianism. It was a hopeful indication that the electorate is weary of the vituperation and polarization, and seeks instead to return to the quiet center where this country has always operated at its best.

Since Democrats took charge of Congress in January 2007, they have returned the legislative branch to traditional standards and procedures, and back toward the center. Proper process has resulted in the entire atmosphere on Capitol Hill changing for the better. One senior Republican staffer said he managed to survive and become a minority staffer only because, unlike the Republicans, who cut the minority staffs to almost nothing when they were in control, the Democrats have not retaliated with a similar ploy. This longtime Republican staffperson, who has worked on Capitol Hill since 1995, told me it was as if someone had finally opened the windows to let fresh air into the Capitol building. Civility is returning as well. Republicans who feared Democratic reprisals were surprised when Democratic leaders refused to play payback politics. While incivility had never been as rampant in the Senate, nor had the processes become as distorted there, Democratic speaker Nancy Pelosi's efforts have helped restore the deliberative processes of both chambers. She set the tone not only with her words that "cooperation, consensus, and compromise" would be the Democrats' approach in returning to "regular order," but by her deeds as well. As an act of goodwill toward the minority, she provided former speaker Dennis Hastert with "prized real estate on the first floor of the Capitol that boasts a reception area, a private kitchen and a spacious personal office with a commanding view of the National Mall."[30] (It is not easy to imagine Newt Gingrich or Dennis Hastert doing the same for a former Democratic speaker.) Democrats have also increased the diversity within the staff of both the House and Senate by hiring more African Americans, Asians, and Hispanics.[31] Democratic leaders made significant changes in the rules that focused on three areas the GOP had allowed to collapse: ethics, civility, and fiscal responsibility.

To end the Republicans' infamous and corrupt K Street Project, Democrats amended the House code of official conduct to prohibit "Members from threatening official retaliation against private firms that hire employees who do not share the Member's partisan political affiliation." To bring into focus the fuzzy rules that facilitated lobbyist Jack Abramoff's wining, dining, and arranging tickets to sporting events and foreign golfing vacations, the Democrats banned lobbyist gifts exceeding one hundred dollars in any calendar year, including the value of tickets to sporting events. In addition, tight restrictions, prohibitions, and disclosure requirements were added for members and staff regarding lobbyists paying for travel. Travel on corporate jets was banned. Finally, the Ethics Committee was instructed to provide annual training for all members and their key staff, plus all new employees, within sixty days of starting to work at the House.[32]

To further civility in the House, Democrats adopted new rules that prohibit "the Speaker from holding votes open for longer than the scheduled time for the sole purpose of changing the outcome of the vote"— ending the outrageous gamesmanship that became a regular occurrence under Republican leaders, and which created ill will throughout the House. (GOP leaders had regularly refused to close votes within the normal fifteen-minute time period as they busied themselves twisting arms to get GOP members to change their votes.) In addition, Democrats have ended the GOP practice of shutting the opposition party out of conference committee meetings (where differences between House- and Senate-passed legislation are resolved, but where Republicans had made it a practice to produce legislation that had not been voted on or even seen by any Democrat). The new rule further prohibits "the consideration of a conference report that has been altered after the time it was signed by the conferees" (another remarkable practice Republicans had perfected under their control.)[33] Because revenue and appropriations laws begin in the House, Democrats have amended the rules to prohibit legislation that would increase the nation's budget deficit, placing the government back on a sound fiscal practice known as "pay-as-you-go." In addition, Democrats have changed the rules regarding earmarks by ending the GOP practice of trading them for votes, and by requiring members to disclose their requests and certify that neither they nor their spouses have any financial interest in them.

Professional Congress watchers have been monitoring both the House and Senate under Democratic control, and have agreed that "Congress is certainly working harder," for Speaker Pelosi and Senate majority leader Harry Reid (D-NV) have made five-day workweeks the norm in their respective chambers. Thomas Mann, and research assistant Molly Reynolds, looked at the results for the first three months of the GOP-controlled 109th Congress and the Democratic-controlled 110th and found a substantial increase in activity across the board under the Democrats. For example, the House was in session only 27 days (164 legislative hours) during the first three months of 109th, but in the 110th it has been in session 49 days (407 legislative hours). The Senate was in session for 35 days (244 legislative hours) during the 109th, while it has been in session 51 days (388 legislative hours) during the first three months of the 110th. Mann and Reynolds reported a corresponding increase in committees marking up legislation, roll call votes, and related legislative activity.[34] Honoring their 2006 campaign pledge, House Democrats enacted a number of important substantive laws well within their first one hundred legislative hours back in control: legislative implementation of the 9/11 Commission's recommendations and a minimum wage increase, and legislation to promote stem cell research, to permit negotiation for lower prescription drug prices under Medicare, to cut interest rates for college student loans, and to cut subsidies for big oil companies. (Senate Republicans, meanwhile, vowed to subvert as much as they can of the House's work by threatening to filibuster.) Most important, Congress has resumed its vital role—considered by many to be more important than writing laws—of executive branch oversight. After six years of facing negligible opposition from Congress, the Bush administration has found itself in trouble. If Republicans had engaged in even minimal oversight, scandals like the firing of U.S. attorneys for political reasons would never have occurred, or revealed that the man Bush had named his second attorney general, Alberto Gonzales, was less than competent—a fact even Republicans agree on.[35] Lack of GOP oversight has, ironically, hurt the Republican Party most, for Democrats will find no shortage of misfeasance, nonfeasance, and malfeasance before Bush and Cheney depart at noon on January 20, 2009.

Cheney's mission to strengthen the presidency, particularly in foreign affairs, by rewriting the Constitution and ignoring the law has only confirmed that unchecked presidential power is dangerous. Cheney has privately told many people that if Richard Nixon had fought a better fight, he would have survived. That was not remotely possible, but it is indicative of Cheney's judgment and his attitudes toward the presidency. It also explains the obstinacy of Bush, and their unshakeable conviction in their failed policies. As we saw earlier, conservative thinkers believe any leader who is popular when he ends his term has not been a strong leader. For example, they applaud Great Britain's prime minister Margaret Thatcher, who left office when her approval ratings were at the historic low of 29 percent.[36] The warped thinking that equates strength with unpopularity is pure authoritarianism, and the type of Machiavellian thinking more suited to an autocracy than a popular democracy. With their record low approval rating, both Bush and Cheney will undoubtedly be celebrated by conservatives as notable successes.

Similarly, the fact that Bush and Cheney operate outside the parameters of the Constitution and the rule of law also accords with the latest conservative canon. Harvard professor of government Harvey C. Mansfield, an instructor of choice for conservative students, approvingly referred to John Yoo in an essay for the *Wall Street Journal* defending presidential powers that exceed the rule of law. Remarkably, Mansfield argued that, in a contest between a strong executive who believes he needs to take action and the constraints of law, the Constitution inherently empowers the president to do whatever he deems is necessary. Mansfield, like Yoo, simply overlooks a century of serious scholarship to claim that the Framers of the Constitution embraced political theorist John Locke's conflicted view of executive power, adding the extraordinary claim that the Framers adopted Locke's view of the all-powerful executive as part of the Constitution. Mansfield wrote:

> Locke was a careful writer, so careful that he did not care if he appeared to be a confused writer. In his "Second Treatise of Government" he announces the supremacy of the legislature.... But as the argument proceeds, Locke gradually "fortifies" (to use James Madison's term) the executive [including] the prerogative, defined as "the power of doing public good without a rule." Without a rule! Even more: "sometimes too against the direct letter of the law." This is the very opposite of law and the rule of law—and "prerogative" was the slogan of the king's party in the same war. Thus Locke combined the extraconstitutional with the constitutional in

a contradiction; besides saying that the legislature is "the supreme power" of the commonwealth, he speaks of "the supreme executive power." ... The American Constitution adopted this fine idea and improved it. The American Founders helped to settle Locke's deliberate confusion of supremacy by writing it into a document and ratifying it by the people rather than merely scattering it in the treatise of a philosopher.[37]

With all due respect, this is flummery mixed with twaddle and trumpery.* Mansfield's reading of constitutional history is at odds with most every constitutional scholar who has examined this question. He is at odds with two centuries of constitutional interpretation by the Supreme Court. "The record is overwhelmingly clear that the Framers consciously and deliberately broke with the British model of John Locke," countered Louis Fisher of the Library of Congress.[38] In the first sixteen pages of his book *Presidential War Power* (2004), Fisher effectively does away with the notion that the Framers wrote Locke into the president's executive powers. I have never tallied the number of scholars who agree with this reading of history, but from what I have examined only conservative scholars—like John Yoo—seem to be able to channel the Founders to know what they were really thinking but never managed to record for history. "The Framers did not incorporate John Locke's notion of the royal prerogative to act in time of emergency or crisis into the Constitution.... Rather, if the president ... believed he needed to react to an emergency situation, he had to act unconstitutionally and seek ratification or indemnification from Congress or accept punishment for his action," explained University of Pittsburgh School of Law professor Jules Lobel.[39]

Our tripartite government has been operating for over two centu-

---

*It is tempting to fully deconstruct Mansfield's assertions, but since I have done so with John Yoo in Appendix C, I have resisted. Suffice it to say that conservative scholarship has sunk to desperate lows.

ries. There is very little in the Constitution that describes how any of
the divisions were to operate, particularly the judiciary. For example,
the Constitution did not expressly provide for the Supreme Court and
lower federal courts to have judicial review of legislative or executive
actions, a power that effectively makes the third branch a constitutional
co-equal. It was Chief Justice John Marshall who laid the groundwork
for judicial review, drawing on the structure of the Constitution itself,
along with the practices of colonial and early state courts. Even today,
some of the finest legal minds would reduce the power of the federal
courts by eliminating judicial review. Still others claim that what federal
courts must do is restore "the lost constitution" or the "constitution in
exile"—namely, the way the document was read before courts incor-
rectly (in their view) interpreted it after the 1930s.

Clearly, two hundred–plus years of analyzing the document has
resulted in little consensus, although there have been long-standing
norms and agreed-upon procedures about how the government was
to function. Nowhere in all the scholarship that our Constitution and
courts have provoked, however, can I find anyone who claims or believes that there should be uniformity in constitutional thinking, and
that a legitimate way to achieve it is for presidents to appoint as many
like-thinking judges and justices as possible until the entire federal judiciary is composed of philosophical clones.

Today, the GOP demand for ideological purity for federal judges
weakens the third branch as a constitutional co-equal, and weakens its
institutional judgment. Empirical data establishes that diversity and dissent create sounder judgment in any organization, particularly courts.[40]
Nothing should be more troubling to Americans who vote in the next
several presidential elections than the looming prospect of a sold bloc
of judicial fundamentalists controlling the federal judiciary. Obviously,
there is only one way to prevent this: It is to not vote for another GOP
president until the federal judiciary is back in balance. This book is
being written in mid-2007, and the Republican candidates—both
those officially declared and unofficially testing the waters—are already

parroting the familiar mantra that, if they are elected president, they will select judges and justices "who don't legislate from the bench." This, of course, is nonsense. With the exception of Representative Ron Paul—a libertarian who is never going to be president—every single Republican candidate can be counted on by the conservative base to continue doing exactly what Nixon, Reagan, Bush I, and Bush II have done, and that is to place as many judicial fundamentalists on the federal bench as they can push through the Senate.

Although Congress is on the mend under the Democrats, it has a good way to go to repair the damage done at the hands of the GOP. Anyone concerned about its well-functioning future, however, should not forget that Democrats did not win control; rather, Republicans lost it. Republicans are making a major effort to regain a majority of the House in the 2008 elections, and to stanch their potential losses in the Senate. Conservative antigovernment philosophy works best when conservatives are in the minority, for they then have no responsibility to accomplish anything. In that position they are very good at obstructionism and using their minority status to make the Democrats look bad. This, in fact, is how they won control of Congress in 1994. Although they claimed, of course, that it was their Contract with America that earned them the House, that argument has proven it is to be pure myth; as Media Matters recently pointed out by collecting the devastating data from poll after poll taken in 1994, only 30 percent of Americans were even aware of this Contract, a number that was hardly sufficient to gain a majority in the House.[41] No, Republicans achieved that victory by doing their best over the course of a number of years to destroy the place and then put the blame for it on the Democrats. Because that tactic worked so successfully, they are again reverting to this mode of behavior. This is exactly the kind of abuse of process that Americans understand, so Democrats running for Congress who fail to bring it to the attention of voters are not only missing an opportunity but are allowing Republicans to engage in conduct that should never be considered acceptable.

In almost four decades of involvement in national politics, much of them as a card-carrying Republican, I was never concerned that the GOP posed a threat to the well-being of our nation. Indeed, the idea would never have occurred to me, for in my experience the system took care of excesses, as it certainly did in the case of the president for whom I worked. But in recent years the system has changed, and is no longer self-correcting. Most of that change has come from Republicans, and much of it based on their remarkable confrontational attitude, an attitude that has clearly worked for them. For example, I cannot imagine any Democratic president keeping cabinet officers as Bush has done with his secretary of defense, Donald Rumsfeld, and attorney general, Alberto Gonzales, men whom both Democrats and Republicans judged to be incompetent. Evidence that the system has changed is also apparent when a president can deliberately and openly violate the law—as, for example, simply brushing aside serious statutory prohibition against torture and electronic surveillance—without any serious consequences. Similarly, but on a lesser scale, Alberto Gonzales faced no consequences when he politicized the Department of Justice as never before, allowing his aides to violate the prohibitions regarding hiring career civil servants based on their party affiliation, and then gave false public statements and testimony about the matter. When the Senate sought to pass a resolution expressing "no confidence" in the attorney general, the Republicans blocked it with a filibuster. The fact that Bush's Justice Department has become yet another political instrument should give Americans pause. This body was created by Congress to represent the interests of the people of the United States, not the Republican Party, but since the system no longer takes account when officials act outside the law (not to mention the Constitution), Republicans do so and get away with it.

In the past the White House (whether occupied by Republicans or Democrats) placed tight restrictions on who could contact the Department of Justice regarding pending business. It was typically limited to only the president, the vice president, the White House chief of staff, and White House counsel, who were authorized to speak with the attorney general, the deputy attorney general, or the top assistant and associate attorneys general. However, in the Bush White House no less than a startling 471 White House aides are authorized to speak with thirty senior Justice Department officials.[42] It is not an exaggeration to say that the Bush administration has made the Justice Department a political extension of the White House in the area of law enforcement, which is unprecedented and seriously dilutes the credibility of the government when it goes to court. It will take years to depoliticize the Justice Department, and countless nonpolitical career attorneys—including some of the most experienced and able men and women to ever serve in the department—have left because of the way Bush's people have run it. Ironically, when Republicans find Democratic officials with even a toe across the line, they raise unmitigated hell for that official. But when a Republican official crosses the line, Republicans close ranks around the miscreant, as they have done with the former chief of staff to the vice president, I. Lewis "Scooter" Libby.

Libby, a sophisticated Washington attorney, leaked Valerie Plame Wilson's covert CIA identity. Libby had leaked her name as part of the effort to discredit Valerie Wilson's husband, former ambassador Joe Wilson, who had traveled to Niger to determine for the CIA if Saddam Hussien had purchased uranium—a claim that would be made by the Bush White House. When Ambassador Wilson wrote a *New York Times* op-ed putting the lie to that claim, Scooter Libby led the attack against him, notwithstanding the fact that Wilson was telling the truth. One of his tactics was to claim that Wilson's wife, a covert CIA operative, had sent him on a boondoggle. Libby, as Cheney's national security adviser, was quite familiar with the potentially dire consequences of leaking the identity of a covert agent. When special counsel Patrick Fitzgerald (the U.S. Attorney in Chicago) was appointed to investigate, Libby lied to the FBI and then to the grand jury about how he had learned of Valerie Wilson's CIA connection, claiming a newsman had told him, when, in fact, he had been told by the vice president. Although Special Counsel Fitzgerald found no criminal statute had been violated in leaking Valerie Wilson's name, he indicted and convicted Scooter Libby for false statements, perjury, and obstruction of justice. Even before federal judge Reggie Walton (a Bush appointee) sentenced Libby to thirty months in prison and a $250,000 fine, Republicans were demanding that Bush pardon him or commute his sentence.

Republicans have offered an array of explanations and justifications for Libby's amnesty, but when one cuts through the smoke, what they are really arguing is that one of their own should not be punished for criminal behavior. It is an absurd position. Conservatives once claimed they stood for law and order, and that no person was above the law, but their words belie their true beliefs as expressed in their actions. Frankly, I hoped that Bush would let Libby off, as it would have served as a particularly egregious and conspicuous example of the Republican double standard—the authoritarian's "do as I say, not as I do" mentality. Voters understand hypocrisy, and another solid abuse of process (and power) could only help the Democrats get back into the White House.

Having watched the GOP's evolution as it embraced the radicalism of authoritarian conservatism, slowly ceding control to its most strident faction, the authoritarian conservatives, I can no longer recognize the party. These new conservative leaders have not only sought to turn back the clock, but to return to a time before the Enlightenment when there were no clocks. As former vice president Al Gore nicely stated it, Republicans have undertaken an "assault on reason." Indeed, they have rejected their own reasoned philosophy by ignoring conservatism's teachings—based on well-documented history—about the dangers of concentrations of power. They have done so by focusing on the presidency as the institution in which they wish to concentrate the enormous powers of the federal government. Nixon led the way, and Reagan, Bush I, and Bush II learned from his mistakes. Nixon scowled as he scolded and secretly investigated his opponents in the name of national security; his GOP successors have smiled and reassured Americans they are operating to protect them as they have proceeded to convert the American presidency into an elective monarchy, with its own high council, which was once known as the federal judiciary.

Fortunately, the power of the authoritarian conservatism that has so dominated the Bush/Cheney presidency is waning, although it is not likely there will ever be less than about one in four Americans who will follow such authoritarian leadership without question.[43] For authoritarian conservatism to win another presidential contest, its candidate would have to attract independent voters in addition to their hardcore base. But polling of independents reveals that they have largely become disgusted with the Republicans, and lean heavily toward the Democrats. In surveying *all* of the Republican contenders for the GOP nomination, I have found that, to the man, they all are far more authoritarian than even the most authoritarian of the Democrats. This raises the almost certain likelihood that, regardless of how great a distance any of these GOP candidates might attempt to place between himself and the Bush/Cheney presidency during a general election campaign, in fact, if elected he is going to continue in the vein that has already caused this nation so much trouble. (There is no doubt that the GOP will select an authoritarian standard-bearer, because these are the people who are most active in the primaries and the most devoted workers in the general election. It is almost impossible for a low authoritarian to win the Republican nomination, as the party is now structured.)

As I was writing this closing section, an old friend from the Nixon White House called. Now retired, he is a lifelong Republican who told me that he voted for Bush and Cheney twice, because he knows them both personally. He asked how my new book was coming, and when I told him the title, he remarked, "*I'll* say the government's broken." After we discussed it, he asked how I planned to end the book, since the election was still a good distance away. I told him I was contemplating ending midsentence and immediately fading to black—the way HBO did in the final episode of *The Sopranos*—but that I would settle for a nice quote from him, on the record. He explained that he constantly has to bite his tongue, and the reason he does not speak out more is because one of his sons is in an important (nonpolitical) government post, and we both know that Republicans will seek revenge wherever they can find it. How about an off-the-record comment? I asked. That he agreed to.

"Just tell your readers that you have a source who knows a lot about the Republican Party from long experience, that he knows all the key movers and shakers, and he has a bit of advice: People should not vote for *any* Republican, because they're dangerous, dishonest, and self-serving. While I once believed that Governor George Wallace had it right, that there was not a dime's worth of difference in the parties, that is no longer true. I have come to realize the Democrats really do care about people who most need help from government; Republicans care most about those who will only get richer because of government help. The government is truly broken, particularly in dealing with national security, and another four years, and heaven forbid not eight years, under the Republicans, and our grandchildren will have to build a new government, because the one we have will be unrecognizable and unworkable."

Those comments summed up our current situation—and our possible future—as eloquently as anything I could have wished.

ACKNOWLEDGMENTS

Living in an information age makes it increasingly difficult to know when information is reliable, given its quantity so greatly exceeds its quality. Finding and reporting dependable information (and pointing out the fallibility of bad information) strikes me as one of the principle responsibilities of a nonfiction author who writes about public affairs. Accordingly, I have turned to sources whose work I have been reading for many years because of the trustworthiness of their information: scholars like Henry Abraham, Bruce Ackerman, Martin Garbus, Thomas E. Mann, Norman J. Ornstein, Sean Wilentz, and Alan Wolfe. More than merely acknowledging these people, I wish to encourage others to find their work. So, too, with the writings of Louis Fisher, Cass Sunstein, John R. Hibbing, and Elizabeth Theiss-Morse, all of whom I owe special thanks for their assistance, which I have cited in the narrative.

Historian Stanley Kutler was most helpful in looking at the politicalization of the federal judiciary, as was Charles Curtis, an attorney from Madison, Wisconsin, whom Stanley introduced me to when I was visiting the only city in America where I found Al Franken's former radio show advertised on the sides of the buses. In addition, I found several books that are cited in this work at a used bookstore in Madison, as well as at the University of Wisconsin's bookstore. Stanley and Chuck Curtis are joined by a few "off-the-record" folks who provided advice about my material on the Supreme Court, and because of their relationship to the Court, they prefer to remain in the background. Bob Altmeyer continued my tutorial on authoritarianism. Maureen, my wife, plowed through the final version of this book to make certain I had not written something "too textbookish." She, along with my most able and much appreciated literary agent, Lydia Wills, provided a solid sounding board.

Viking has done a remarkable job in moving this project along quickly. They, too, deserve acknowledgment for their indispensable contribution: Sharon Gonzalez is the production editor; Rachel Burd is the copy editor; Jacqueline Gallai is the production manager; Francesca Belanger did the interior design; Maggie Payette did the cover; Ben Petrone and Kate Lloyd will be doing publicity, as they did for my last book; Nancy Sheppard is the marketing director; and Laura Tisdel is the assistant to my editor, to whom I will turn next. But first, I must note that this entire team is headed by Viking's president, Clare Ferraro, who has created not only a successful publishing house but the most author-friendly publisher I have encountered, and I have had the pleasure of doing my seventh and now eighth books with her.

Rick Kot—whom his assistant Laura describes as my "dashing editor," for indeed he is, but more important he is a real editor—gets inside a manuscript to understand it and make sure the best book possible comes out. Ronald Reagan used to tell the joke about the man who gave his son—who was an eternal optimist—a pile of horse manure, only to watch the kid dive into the mess, declaring, "I know there is a pony in there somewhere." Whether it is optimism or professionalism, Rick plows through my manuscripts seeming to know there is a book in there somewhere. For that I am grateful, because his keen eye and fine touch sure helps.

Appendices

APPENDIX A

Separation of Powers:
An Essential Process Envisioned by the Framers

When the fifty-five delegates from the thirteen independent states, which were loosely joined in a collective working relationship under the deeply flawed Articles of Confederation, met in Philadelphia during the summer of 1787, they were introduced to the relatively untested concept of government. It was explained to them by the young and articulate governor of Virginia, Edmund Rudolph, who presented the plan that had been prepared by his fellow Virginian, James Madison. That plan envisioned three separate branches of the government—legislative, executive, and judicial—with each empowered to check and balance the other. Madison believed, based on his study of governments old and new, that there were three basic forms a government might take: monarchy (the one), oligarchy (an elite few), and democracy (the many). But because each form had serious drawbacks, Madison sought to take the best of each to create a "republic"—a form that had been adopted in varying degrees by many of the American colonies. Republics, of course, had been around since the days of the Greeks and Romans; the term "republic" is a Latin word meaning "public thing," a form of government in which sovereignty resides with the people, who elect agents to represent them in the political decision-making process.[1] Madison's plan for a republic combined elements of each type of government, a mixing of forms, with an executive who incorporated the strength of monarchy without the evils of a king, and a Senate that embodied the wisdom of an oligarchy but balanced the self-interest of such elites with a House composed of representatives who spoke for the people of the nation.[2] Madison and his compatriots were mistrustful of a pure democracy, for none had worked well in the past, plus the country was too large and diverse to directly involve its population. Later, Madison nicely explained the differences in Federalist No. 14: "In a democracy, the people meet and exercise the government in person; in a republic they assemble and administer it by their representatives and agents. A democracy consequently will be confined to a small spot. A republic may be extended over a large region."[3]

Under this Virginia Plan, as Madison's proposal became known, the concept of a separation of powers with checks and balances was widely embraced, but the plan's call for a popularly elected lower house of the legislature to select the members of the upper house troubled delegates from smaller states, who feared that the larger states might dominate the new national government to their disadvantage. Small-state delegates preferred the plan offered by William Paterson of New Jersey, which called for a unicameral (one-chamber) legislature, in which each state would have a vote—not unlike the Congress of the Articles of Confederation. Under Paterson's New Jersey Plan the state governments, not the people, would elect members of the new congress. The New Jersey Plan was, in fact, only a slight modification of the government under the Articles of Confederation, while the Virginia Plan was a dramatic departure, an entirely new form of national government. Under both plans, as initially introduced, the legislature would select the chief executive (as the British Parliament selects the prime minister of Great Britain).

After much debate the delegates reached a number of compromises. They rejected another unicameral legislature like the Continental Congress; rather, the new Congress would be bicameral: a House of Representatives elected by the people of each state for terms of two years, based on population, from districts within each state; and a Senate in which each state would be represented by two members, who would be elected by the state legislatures for terms of six years. Most of the delegates approved of Madison's concept of the separation of powers, with each branch of the government checking and balancing its co-equal branches. They also considered the bicameral system as providing a further check and balance within the system, since both chambers had to agree to identical language before legislation could be presented to the president for approval (or, if the president disapproved, both chambers had to override the president's approval by a two-thirds majority) to become law. The new federal government took its sovereignty (and power) directly from the people, rather from each of the states, as with the Articles of Confederation.

This legislative branch was the centerpiece of the new government, and the powers to be delegated by the people to Congress were set forth in the Constitution in considerable detail. In light of concern that the legislative branch might have too much influence over the executive branch if Congress selected the president, the parliamentary concept was abandoned, and in its place the Framers created the electoral college, where electors from each state—in the same proportion as their representation in Congress—would assemble every four years to select the president. Other than providing details of how the president would be elected, however, few specifics were set forth regarding the executive branch other than defining the president's appointment and treaty powers, and designating the president as commander in chief to assure civilian control over whatever military Congress created. Even less was specified regarding the judicial branch; instead, Congress was charged with creating the judicial branch, as it was the executive departments and agencies. "So anxious were [the Framers] to affirm legislative supremacy in the new government that they failed to flesh out the executive and judicial departments," explained historian Robert Remini, "thereby assuring that the legislature would retain control of the structure and authority of both those branches."[4]

Creation of our government did not begin with the Constitutional Convention and end with the ratification of nine of the thirteen states, however. "When precisely did 'the Founding' end?" Yale political scientist and historian Bruce Ackerman has asked. In his revelatory work *The Failure of the Founding Fathers: Jefferson, Marshall, and the Rise of Presidential Democracy* (2005), he argued persuasively that the founding period commenced with the Philadelphia Convention of 1787 but did not conclude until after election of Thomas Jefferson as president in 1800. "Everybody recognizes that the proposal and ratification of the Bill of Rights were essential parts of the original deal—and so the common understanding of 'the Founding' proceeds into the 1790s. At that point things become a little hazy, but one final event stands out: *Marbury v. Madison* [the 1803 ruling by Chief Justice John Marshall's Supreme Court that they had the power to review the constitutionality of laws enacted by Congress and signed by the president] is presented as the triumphant conclusion of the story."[5]

It is not necessary to resolve the debate of when the founding actually ended to appreciate that the actions of the early Congress and presidencies constituted part of the founding, setting the course for the nation and establishing the government itself. During the North Carolina ratification debates, James Iredell, who would be appointed by Washington to the first Supreme Court, declared, "The first session of Congress will probably be the most important of any for many years." Indeed, it has been described by some as a second constitutional convention. "As the first session unfolded," historian Forrest McDonald wrote, "the doings in the Congress amounted to a second constitutional convention, for they organically defined, shaped, and gave life to a government that the Constitution only authorized."[6] Historian Samuel Eliot Morison aptly described the situation: "The Federal Constitution was so flexible and open to such varied interpretation that the solution of those difficulties it had been created to overcome depended more upon precedents created, traditions begun, and policy followed during the ensuing years than upon the actual words of the document." Or, as he more bluntly stated, "This new government had to create its own machinery."[7]

One concept runs from the opening days of the Constitutional Convention through the founding Congress and early presidencies right down to this day: the essential nature of Madison's checks and balances to the integrity of American government. No more interesting and provocative analysis of this fundamental precept of the American system of government exists than one written by Professors Levinson and Pildes for the June 2006 *Harvard Law Journal,* which actually examined how the separation of powers works *in fact,* rather than in theory. Professors Levinson and Pildes argue that the Madisonian vision of separation of powers, with its related checks and balances, has, in fact, been trumped by political parties. "The success of American democracy overwhelmed the Madisonian conception of separation of powers almost from the outset, preempting the political dynamics that were supposed to provide each branch with a 'will of its own' that would propel departmental 'ambition ... to counteract ambition.'"[8] This in turn, they argue, made the underlying theory of the separation of powers largely "anachronistic." When they looked at government they found that when different political parties control the different branches—creating a divided government—then the parties working through those branches operate as Madison had hoped, but Levinson and Pildes argued that it is not on behalf of protecting the institutional powers that the checking and balancing occurs, but rather it is the influence of party politics operating through that divided branch:

> Contrary to the foundational assumption of constitutional law and theory since Madison, *the United States has not one system of separation of powers but (at least) two.* When government is divided, party lines track branch lines, and we should expect to see party competition channeled through the branches. The resulting interbranch political competition will look, for better or worse, something like the Madisonian dynamic of rivalrous branches. On the other hand, when government is unified and the engine of party competition is removed from the internal structure of government, we should expect interbranch competition to dissipate. Intraparty cooperation (as a strategy of interparty competition) smoothes over branch boundaries and suppresses the central dynamic assumed in the Madisonian model. The functional differences between these two

systems of separation of powers—[all] party separated and party unseparated.[9] [Emphasis added.]

This is a powerful analysis, and well taken. Thus, notwithstanding the fact that political parties undertake much of the system of checks and balances envisioned by Madison, they are not the only checks.[10] As I scan history, however, I tend to believe that Levinson and Pildes have it half right. For modern presidents and Congress, Democrats under a unified government (thus, with Democrats controlling both Congress and the White House), Congress has been remarkably institution minded, and the separation of powers has remained viable. On the other hand, conservative Republicans—as I have demonstrated throughout this book—easily place party loyalty before the responsibilities of the government institution in which they serve.

For a few examples it is only necessary to examine Senator Harry Truman's (D-MO) relentless investigations of Franklin Roosevelt's administration (before Truman became vice president), or Senator William Fulbright's (D-AK) investigations of both the Kennedy and Johnson presidencies. On the House side, the list would include countless institution-minded members, who sought no higher office but held the president of their party responsible through aggressive oversight, like Wilbur Mills (D-AK), when chairman of the Ways and Means Committee, or Adam Clayton Powell (D-NY), when chairman of the Education and Labor Committee, or John Dingell (D-MI), Jack Brooks (D-TX), and Emanuel Celler (D-NY), who as committee chairs gave Democratic presidents fits. The most recent unified government under Democratic control, the Clinton administration and the 103rd Congress, showed that congressional Democrats simply do not automatically capitulate to presidents of their party, even as parties have become more cohesive. On the other hand, Levinson and Pildes have it exactly right for the modern Republican Party.

Today Democrats control the House under a highly institution-minded speaker, Nancy Pelosi, and those who chair the key committees of the House: Charles Rangel (D-NY) of the Ways and Means

Committee, Henry Waxman (D-CA) of the Government Reform Committee, John Conyers (D-MI) of the Committee on the Judiciary, Tom Lantos (D-CA) of the International Relations Committee, Barney Frank (D-MA) of the Financial Services Committee, and, of course, John Dingell (D-MI) of the Energy and Commerce Committee. While these individuals are all good Democrats, they are also congressional institutionalists, unlike many of the GOP party hacks they have replaced. Similarly, in the Senate under Democratic control, is there any greater protector of that institution than Robert Byrd of West Virginia, now in his ninth (six-year) term, and chair of the Appropriations Committee? Senator Byrd guards the prerogatives of the Senate regardless of the party in power at the White House. Others who have made their careers in the Senate, and who will not let their party affiliation trump their institutional duties, include Senator Carl Levin of Michigan (in his fifth term), chair of the Armed Forces Committee; Senator Edward Kennedy of Massachusetts (in his eighth term), chair of the Health, Education, Labor, and Pensions Committee; Senator Patrick Leahy of Vermont (in his seventh term), chair of the Senate Judiciary Committee; and Senator Daniel Inouye of Hawaii (in his eighth term), chair of the Commerce, Science, and Transportation Committee. Again, while this is only a sample, all these senators are loyal Democrats, but their belief in the Senate's institutional role and the separation of powers has been established as a fact, decade after decade.

There are few concepts in our Constitution more basic—or important—than its separation of powers. Nowhere in that founding document are these words actually used; rather, they are inherent in the structure, as was first explained to Americans in *The Federalist Papers*. Since adoption, these constitutional divisions of power have successfully protected our democracy from tyranny for over two hundred years, yet there are growing numbers of conservatives who are critical of the concept because it slows down the ability of any branch from operating with the greatest efficiency. They forget that the Framers designed a system that was not supposed to be efficient, but rather one that checks the power of its co-equals. No student of government would deny that dictatorships are more efficient, but not very good at protecting the liberty and freedom of citizens. Conservative Republicans love to talk about the checks and balances inherent in the separation of powers; they simply are not very good at employing them, for they have allowed their constant reach for power to dictate conduct, whether in or out of power. Republican failures in the legislative, executive, and judicial branches are directly related to refusal to honor this fundamental precept. It appears that the anti-authoritarian nature of the separation of powers is simply incompatible with contemporary conservative Republicanism.

APPENDIX B

Republican Appropriations Process Abuses:
Shutting Down the Government

Not everyone is familiar with the appropriations process, which is the way many government officials would like to keep it. No processes are more essential and important to Washington insiders, as money is literally the lifeblood of the government, as it is of any organization. Republicans have engaged in striking misuses of these processes. It is difficult to think of a clearer example of broken government than one that is intentionally closed down as a political ruse, which is what the Republican leaders—both presidents and congressional leaders—have repeatedly done. Accordingly, I have divided this appendix into two sections: first, a very brief and quite broad primer on the essentials of the appropriation process; and then a description of the Republicans' gambit.

The Appropriations Process in a Nutshell

Since the First Congress in 1789, an initial order of business has been to raise revenue, pay debts, and appropriate funds for the operation of a government seeking to "establish Justice, insure domestic Tranquility, provide for the common defense, promote the general Welfare, and secure the Blessing of Liberty to ourselves and our Posterity." Congress was given the exclusive power of the purse, and it has no responsibility higher, nor more demanding, than managing the nation's finances and fiscal well-being. Only Congress can tax, and only Congress can authorize and appropriate spending from the U.S. Treasury. Specifically, the Constitution provides that Congress is to "make all Laws which shall be necessary and proper" to implement their responsibilities.* In addition, the Constitution states: "No Money shall be drawn from the Treasury, but in Consequences of Appropriations made by Law."** James Madison wrote in Federalist No. 58: "This power over the purse may, in fact, be regarded as the most complete and effectual weapon with which any constitution can arm the immediate representatives of the people, for obtaining a redress of every grievance, and for carrying into effect every just and salutary measure."

Congress controls spending for all branches of government, a responsibility it once took very seriously. While I have long been impressed that Democratic leaders have always placed those who are among their best and brightest members on finance-related committees in both the House and Senate, when the Republicans gained control of Congress, they promoted less than top talent for seats on the Budget and Appropriations committees, basing their choices more on loyalty to the leadership and ability to raise money from lobbyists for GOP campaign coffers than for background and skills that might benefit these committees. (The disgraced Duke Cunningham, whom the GOP leaders seated on the Appropriations Committee, is not untypical of the type of talent they relied upon.) To appreciate the seriousness of the GOP's behavior, a few key concepts need to be grasped, starting with "authorization legislation," "appropriations measures," and "budgets:"[1]

*Article I, Section 8.

** Article I, Section 9. In further implementation of this provision, Congress enacted the Antideficiency Act—31 U.S.C. 1341(a)(1)(A)—in 1870, during the Grant administration, that prohibits the executive branch from spending more money than the appropriated amount, and can only spend appropriated funds for the purpose designated by the Congress.

Authorizing Legislation. One of Congress's duties is to create departments (e.g., Homeland Security, most recently), agencies (e.g., the Federal Communications Commission or the Securities and Exchange Commission), and programs (e.g., Social Security, Medicare, and the Small Business Improvement Act). Before these departments, agencies, and programs are entitled to funding by an appropriation, the authorizing committees (which are distinct from the appropriating committees) must recommend, and Congress must approve, authorizing legislation by stating the amount that should be appropriated for each fiscal year. Obtaining money from the Treasury is a two-step process (actually four steps, since the same process must be repeated in both the House and Senate). Sometimes authorizing committees set the amount for several fiscal years; at other times they require the department, agency, or program head to return to Congress to seek reauthorization annually. Requiring regular reauthorization gives Congress the ability to determine how well or poorly a department, agency, or program is operating. Authorizing legislation is like any other law, and it must be enacted by both the House and Senate, and approved by the president, or his veto must be overridden by a vote of two thirds of both the House and Senate. Without an authorization there can be no appropriation.

Appropriations Measures. As noted, the Constitution states that money can only be spent from the Treasury when appropriated. By long tradition and law, most appropriations are enacted on an annual basis. The federal government's fiscal year for accounting purposes begins on October 1 and ends on September 30 of the following calendar year. (Fiscal years are identified by the calendar year in which it ends, so FY 2008 began on October 1, 2007.) Because presidential terms begin on January 20, a new president always inherits his predecessor's budget.

Both the House and Senate have created subcommittees of their Appropriations committees to handle *regular appropriations* bills (as well as *supplemental appropriations* bills, which provide for additional funding during a fiscal year), and when these bills are enacted into law, the funded department, agency, or program can incur obligations and make payments out of the Treasury. An appropriation is not a cash payment, but rather a grant of authority to write checks that the Treasury will pay. When Congress fails to complete the appropriations process by October 1 (i.e., the beginning of the new fiscal year), to keep government operations going, typically temporary funding is provided. Because it is always enacted as a joint resolution of the House and Senate—and also must be signed by the president to become effective—this stopgap funding is known as a *continuing resolution,* or CR.

CRs are the normal device utilized to keep the government operating when a fiscal year ends while work on spending legislation it still ongoing. These often hurt the government, however, for they keep funding at the level of the prior fiscal year, and fund programs at their lowest level, not to mention the fact that they ignore new programs and continue to fund ones that should be cut off. They are also dangerous when used excessively (as has become the norm): "A long-term continuing resolution that funds government operations at [previous-year] levels would have disastrous impacts on the war on terror, homeland security, and other important government responsibilities," the chairman of House Appropriations Committee warned in 2003. "It also would be fiscally irresponsible," said Representative Bill Young (R-FL). Repeated use of continuing resolution is an "indication of the complete failure of the legislative process," added Representative Charles Stenholm (D-TX). "It's a failure. You can't sugarcoat it."[2] Yet this occurred predictably, year after year, when the GOP controlled Congress.

Federal Budgets. When Warren Harding became president in 1921, he created a Bureau of the Budget to centralize the funding of departments and agencies of the executive branch, rather than the existing system, in which each department and agency head negotiated for funds with Congress.[3] President Nixon modernized the Bureau of the Budget, giving it increased management and fiscal supervision of the executive branch, renaming it the Office of Management and Budget (OMB). Presidents initiate the appropriation process by sending their

annual budget to Congress on or before the first Monday in February.*
The president's budget, which is prepared by the OMB, sets forth the
president's request for funding for the departments, agencies, and programs, and contains the spending limits for the executive branch. After
a president submits his budget to Capitol Hill, all of the departments,
agencies, and programs he has included provide detailed justifications
for their financial needs to the House and Senate appropriations committees that have jurisdiction over them.

These are but the basic steps of a highly convoluted process, and
both House and Senate have adopted special rules regarding debating
and amending this legislation, as well as procedures for resolving differences between them. This information will help provide a context for
the Republican—and I can find no examples of these activities undertaken by the Democrats—tactic of literally stopping government for
lack of funding. Although it has been a few years since the GOP has
played this game, it has never repudiated it.

Republican Government Shutdown Ploys

The government of the United States can never sleep, never take
a holiday, nor close down its operations. The Constitution, and the
government it created, is constantly in operation, with its employees
and officials always on call, if not on actual duty. The Framers created
machinery that was designed to run until modified by constitutional
amendment or superceded by a revolution by the American people,
deciding that they wanted a different government. Congress has passed
laws for these essential and critical operations to assure that they always
have the resources needed to fulfill their responsibilities. The fact that
not every government operation is essential does not mean, however,
that it is unimportant.

Starting with President Ronald Reagan, Republicans have thought

*31 U.S.C. 1105(a). In transition years, adjustments are made for new
administrations.

it clever to block the appropriation processes, a game that the public has largely ignored, even though it has literally cost taxpayers billions. The initial Reagan government shutdown occurred in November 1981, when the president exercised his first veto, rejecting a federal spending bill. Democrats believed that the bill they had passed was agreeable to the White House; the president, however, who was all grins and delighted with himself, called his cabinet into an "emergency" session, where he announced, "There's no cash to meet the payroll"; accordingly, they were instructed to send home all "nonessential" employees. Speaker of the House Tip O'Neill (D-MA), who liked Reagan, also understood that the president did not know what he was doing. Reagan knew "less about the budget than any other president in my lifetime. He can't even carry on a conversation about the budget," O'Neill confided.[4] Clearly, the shutdown was an idea cooked up by the president's staff, who convinced him that it was a way to force the Democratic Congress to toe the line on spending. The next day Congress passed a continuing resolution to keep the government funded, and Reagan backed down.

While many government operations do not require annual appropriations, "about 40% of total federal spending" is subject to the annual appropriation process.[5] Mail, border operations, tax collection, prison guards, the military, air traffic controllers, social security checks, and other such vital functions are not affected by such a shutdown, but all nonessential services are closed. When the president refuses to sign a continuing resolution, knowing it will result in countless laws not being executed, he is blatantly violating his oath of office and the duty imposed on him by the Constitution. This first Reagan shutdown (in 1981) cost somewhere between $65 million and $80 million, depending on whose estimate is relied upon.[6] In 1984 he tried the tactic again, this time hoping to force the House of Representatives to provide funding for the Nicaraguan Contras. It did not work, but it set the tone for the lawlessness that would follow in the Reagan White House, ultimately leading to the Iran-Contra scandal.[7] Iran-Contra independent counsel Lawrence Walsh later explained:

President Reagan was determined that the Contras should be supported to prevent the spread of communism in Central America. His political advisers, however, persuaded him to refrain from raising this generally unpopular issue in the 1984 presidential election. Accordingly, Reagan signed the appropriation acts containing the Boland Amendments [which cut off funding], but he had no intention of abiding by the restrictions.[8]

The third Reagan shutdown occurred in October 1986, when he did not like the spending bill Congress had assembled. After four brief continuing resolutions, he decided to close the government and headed off to Reykjavik, Iceland, to meet with Soviet leader Mikhail Gorbachev, leaving almost half the government and most of Washington in chaos. Outside of Washington the situation merited barely a mention, other than a passing referral in lead stories about Reagan in Reykjavik.[9] Ironically, though by this time Reagan's aides had convinced Congress to assist the Contras, just two weeks after this shutdown, on November 3, 1986, *Al-Shiraa,* a Lebanese weekly, reported that the United States had been secretly selling arms to Iran, and within a few weeks it would become public that the proceeds of those purportedly prohibited arms sales had been "diverted" to the Contras in Nicaragua, contrary to the Boland Amendment. The Iran-Contra scandal had arrived.

President George H. W. Bush closed down the government in 1990, after "six stop-and-go months of negotiations between the White House and Congress" to agree upon a a bipartisan deficit reduction package."[10] It was a delicate deal, however, because conservatives are opposed to all tax increases, and this package contained "such politically painful measures as tax increases on beer, wine, liquor, cigarettes and gasoline, and spending cuts in numerous popular programs."[11] As the spending bill headed for final action, a test vote was taken, and it was clear the deal had fallen apart; as conservatives broke rank on the tax increases, Democrats did the same over the cuts in popular programs. Bush Senior, who had personally lobbied for the package, was furious—he could not blame the Democrats because GOP minority leader Newt Gingrich

grich (R-GA) had helped kill the package—and Bush had even enlisted lobbying efforts from former presidents Ford and Reagan: "President Bush, still smarting over the crushing defeat of the bipartisan deficit-reduction package, began shutting down all but essential government operations early today after refusing to sign a short-term spending measure approved by Congress to keep the government running for a week," the *Washington Post* (October 6, 1990) reported. Senate majority leader George Mitchell (D-ME) cautioned that closing was "unnecessary and extremely unwise," for it would "not advance the president's position during the negotiating process."[12] Capitol Hill, for its part, was equally annoyed with the president's action, so within a few days it passed another continuing resolution that was veto-proof (the Senate approved it by unanimous consent, and the House by a vote of 362 to 3). With the outline of a revised agreement in place, Bush had no choice but to agree.[13] (This episode led Newt Gingrich to conclude that he had learned a useful new trick: Because no president dared to keep the government closed more than a few days, if Congress could take the heat of public disapproval, they could force a president's hand.) In the end, after months of protracted negotiations, Bush would be forced to break his now notorious 1988 campaign pledge: "Read my lips. No new taxes." His government shutdown, in the end, backfired, and his flip-flop on taxes would be a contributing factor in his defeat in 1992.

When Republicans took control of the House of Representatives in January 1995, a key part of the leadership's strategy was to radically change the operations of vital committees like Appropriations and Budget. Needless to say, Speaker Gingrich understood these were the most powerful committees on Capitol Hill, so he tossed aside the traditional seniority system to select chairmen who were loyal soldiers (and good fund-raisers). Bipartisanship was of no interest to Republicans, and they forced their own members to toe the party's line in both floor and committee votes.* (Breaking with longtime norms of the House

---

*The partisanship of the Appropriations Committee during the GOP-control years could be seen in the partisan votes (where a majority of each party votes in op-

even further, GOP majority leader Dick Armey advised those running the authorization committee to start writing laws by adding them to appropriations legislation, which cannot be amended on the floor. But he also told them that unless the authorizing legislation was approved by the GOP leadership, it would be subject to a point of order, which could kill it.)[14]

By October 1995, the GOP leaders, working with their chairs of the Budget and Appropriations committees, were ready for their coup de grace: forcing President Clinton to accept their "massive, far-reaching bill intended to balance the budget over seven years, cut taxes for American families and dramatically change the face of the federal government."[15] It was the centerpiece of the GOP's Contract with America. The GOP package eliminated three cabinet departments (Education, Commerce, and Energy), along with every federal program that conservatives disliked that they believed they could chuck without getting tarred and feathered back home, and cut spending for such sacred programs as Medicare. Although House Republicans had a sufficient majority to pass their budget, they did not have enough votes to override the president's inevitable veto. But Gingrich believed he had a tool as powerful as a president's veto: the extraconstitutional power to shut down the government by refusing to pass a budget, and literally putting the government out of business until Clinton yielded to the GOP's wishes.

Journalists David Maraniss and Michael Weisskopf, in their book *Tell Newt to Shut Up!* (the title taken from a message to the speaker Gingrich from rank-and-file Republicans), vividly described the standoff: "For months Washington had been obsessed with the notion of a train wreck coming down the line: Gingrich and his budget-cutting revolu-

---

position to the other). For example, between the 96th and 102nd Congresses, 55.2 percent of the votes in the House Appropriations Committee were partisan, but by the 104th (after the GOP took control), 77.8 percent of the votes were partisan (and it only became more so). See John H. Aldrich and David W. Rodhe, "The Republican Revolution and the House of Appropriations Committee," *Journal of Politics* (Feb. 2000), 17, Table 2.

tionaries steaming in from one direction, Clinton and his veto rolling in from the other. Perhaps the fact that it was so visible for so long made few people believe that it would actually happen in the end. Certainly one side would stop, or both would move off to a track of compromise. But the train wreck did happen. Many times, in fact. A series of train wrecks began that day in mid-November and continued into the first two weeks of 1996."[16] Maraniss and Weisskopf note that there "was debris everywhere" and many casualties, with "Gingrich perhaps the most seriously wounded." In dealing with Clinton, Newt was playing out of his league. "Gingrich's self-confidence was eroded when he finally tried to negotiate a budget deal himself, a task at which he proved inept, his trips to the White House ending in confusion and dismay as time after time he was seduced by Clinton and the atmosphere in the Oval Office."[17] Clinton later recounted his side of the story:

Not surprisingly, the Republicans tried to blame me for the shutdown. I was afraid they'd get away with it, given their success at blaming me for the partisan divide in the '94 election. Then I got a break when, at a breakfast with reporters, ... Gingrich implied that he had made the CR even harsher because I'd snubbed him during the flight back from [former Israeli prime minister Yitzhak] Rabin's funeral by not talking to him about the budget and asking him to leave the plane by the back ramp instead of the front one with me. Gingrich said, "It's petty but I think it's human, nobody has talked to you and they ask you to get off the plane by the back ramp.... You just wonder where is their sense of manners?" Perhaps I should have discussed the budget on the way home, but I couldn't bring myself to think about anything but the purpose of the sad trip and the future of the peace process. I did visit with the Speaker and the Congressional delegation, as a photograph of Newt, Bob Dole, and me talking on the plane showed. As for getting off the back of the plane, my staff thought they were being courteous, because that was the exit closest to the cars that were picking up Gingrich and the others. And it was four-thirty in the morning; there were no cameras around. The White House released the photo of our conversation, and the press lampooned Gingrich's complaints.[18]

Gingrich closed down the government for a total of twenty-seven days, which cost it about $1.4 billion in lost revenue and increased expenses.[19] Although the public was little affected—other than by the closure of operations like national parks, social security offices, and veterans' affairs offices—about 40 percent of the nation followed the story and judged it important.[20] Correctly, the public blamed Gingrich and the GOP Congress, not Clinton, for the situation.[21]

Why are shutdowns important? Because government should not be a game of Blindman's Bluff. Indeed, all federal officials are oathbound not to do what Republicans have repeatedly done when cutting off funding for government operations.

APPENDIX C

Bush and Cheney's Radical Lawyer:
The Remarkable Source for Unconstitutional War Powers

This appendix has two purposes. First, it is an extended footnote that explains why it is necessary to view the legal arguments of conservative attorneys such as John C. Yoo, who provided key legal opinions upon which the Bush administration has relied in its war on terror, with great skepticism at minimum, and more safely with total disregard. And second, it is an examination of a few of the key arguments that conservatives rely on in claiming remarkable authority for Republican presidents (such as finding "inherent powers" in the Constitution; reading the commander in chief clause as bestowing other powers; and claiming that because past presidents have gone to war without congressional authority, all presidents can do likewise) and of how attorneys like Yoo have distorted constitutional interpretation to an extent that borders on fraud.

Since the September 11, 2001, terror attack, Bush and Cheney have insisted on operating outside of the well-established parameters of the Constitution, all in the name of fighting their alleged "war" against al-Qaeda and other international terrorist groups. They have claimed extraordinary presidential powers, largely by relying on so-called inherited constitutional powers of the presidency, and justify their actions based on both public and private (they call it classified) legal advice that assures them they are indeed fighting a war, which, in turn, has created an emergency situation authorizing their use of heretofore illegal tactics to defend the nation's security. Were the stakes not so high, such hubris would be almost comedic; under the circumstances it is frightening and inexcusable.

The legal Svengali behind much of the astonishing Constitutional analysis that has supported the radical program of Bush and Cheney is the young, ultraconservative lawyer John Choon Yoo, who has been mentored by the most extreme of Washington's conservatives. Yoo clerked for Judge Laurence H. Silberman of the U.S. Court of Appeals of the D.C. circuit, and then for Justice Clarence Thomas of the U.S. Supreme Court; he then served as general counsel of the U.S. Senate Judiciary Committee from 1995 to 1996, when Orrin Hatch chaired the committee. It was while he was on a leave of absence from the University of California at Berkeley School of Law, serving as a deputy assistant attorney general in the Department of Justice's Office of Legal Counsel, that the attacks of September 11, 2001, occurred. This was John Yoo's moment, for he had studied the laws relating to war, and as he (and other conservatives) saw it, 9/11 placed the United States in a state of perpetual war.

In his position at OLC Yoo would become the leading legal adviser to the Bush White House. It appears that President Bush launched his war against terrorism based on a legal opinion issued over Yoo's signature on September 25, 2001.[1] Yoo is probably best known, however, as the author of the so-called torture memos, which legitimized the Bush administration to employ hard-line (and unlawful) interrogation tactics against suspected terrorists—tactics that most of the world considers torture but that Yoo, and those he has advised, describe as "aggressive interrogation techniques."

Although John Yoo is only one of a covey of influential young conservative attorneys, his theories have been so integral to the actions of the Bush/Cheney presidency that he calls for particular attention. Because much of Yoo's work for the government remains classified, he cannot discuss some of it openly; still, he has addressed the thinking behind his work in his books *War by Other Means: An Insider's Account of the War on Terror* (New York: Atlantic Monthly Press, 2006) and *The Powers of War and Peace: The Constitution and Foreign Affairs after 9/11* (Chicago: University of Chicago Press, 2005).

Yoo's War by Any Means

As a result of 9/11, we are fighting something akin to World War III, according to Professor Yoo, who believes that the United States is engaged in a full-scale, all-out, no-hold-barred conflict with terrorists— a fact he asserts at the outset of *War by Other Means*. In that work he immediately takes to task those who do not share his assessment, for he claims that "critics of the Bush administration's terrorism policies believe that terrorism is a *crime*. They say that terrorism, even attacks as destructive as those on 9/11, by definition *cannot justify war*, because we are not fighting other nations." (Emphasis added.)

In making this point, however, Yoo demonstrates at the very outset of his work a striking lack of intellectual honesty. Earlier I had read highly critical reports, written by legal scholars who had examined his legal opinions authorizing the use of torture, that all but accused him of fraud. Thus, when I noticed misleading information at the very opening of *War by Other Means* I decided to pause to take a closer look. (Others have questioned his scholarship in this book, as well;[2] for example, in a review of *War by Other Means* Georgetown law professor David Luban reported that "Yoo argues forcefully and intelligently, but not always honestly. Half-truths, straw men, double standards, selective quotations, significant omissions, and caricatures of his opponents' positions—all are characteristic of *War by Others Means*."[3]) Given the important role he has played in the Bush administration, the question must be asked: How does one know when Yoo is being honest or when he is distorting the truth? The only answer is to check because he cannot be trusted.

To make his point about Bush critics viewing terrorism as criminal activity rather than as war, for example, Yoo cited the opinions of several high-profile scholars (including some who have been critical of his own work). When he discussed these critics, however, he gave a false impression by suggesting that they all "say that terrorism, even attacks as destructive as those on 9/11, by definition cannot justify war." In one passage, Yoo stated:

> Former Clinton Justice Department official and Harvard law professor Philip Heymann states that "war has always required a conflict between nation states."[4] Former senator and presidential candidate Gary Hart and historian Joyce Appleby put the view nicely: "The 'war on terror' is more a metaphor than a fact. Terrorism is a method, not an ideology; terrorists are criminals, not warriors."[5] Yale professor Bruce Ackerman begins a recent book by declaring: " 'War on terror' is, on its face, a preposterous expression," and devotes his first chapter to arguing that "this is not a war."[6] [Citations found in original, with different numbers.]

In this quotation, however, Yoo failed to mention or even suggest that Bruce Ackerman's following chapter argued that terrorism "is not a crime." Likewise, Yoo does not explain the true positions of Gary Hart or Phillip Heymann. (I am passing over historian Joyce Appleby, because I could find no indication that she has addressed how the war on terror should best be conducted beyond her op-ed with former senator Hart.) To move from Yoo's characterization of the views of these people to their true opinions reveals the extent of his distortions.

Bruce Ackerman actually wrote that "the criminal law is fundamentally inadequate as a complete response to our present predicament"— making the very point that Yoo did. More important, Yoo never addressed precisely why Ackerman rejected the "war on terror" label. Ackerman's reasoning is quite compelling: He demonstrated how labeling terrorism as a war confuses the public in a manner that makes it too easy for a president to engage in additional wars. In the Ackerman book Yoo quotes from, *Before the Next Attack: Preserving Civil Liberties in an*

Age of Terrorism (2006), Ackerman explained the negative implications and destructive impact of "war talk" like that employed consistently by people like John Yoo.* "The war against Afghanistan is distinct from the one against Iraq," Ackerman explained. "But once the public is convinced that a large 'war on terrorism' is going on, these old-fashioned wars can be repackaged as mere battles—as in President Bush's famous description of Iraq as 'the central front' in the war on terror.... Once the president convinces the public that an invasion of a 'rogue state' is merely a 'battle' in the 'war on terrorism,' he is well on the way to winning his battle against Congress over final decision-making authority."

In addition, his concern about this undoing of the checks and balances of our constitutional system, which leads to "presidential uni-lateralism" in war making, historian Ackerman made clear that not all wars are the same. For lawyers, he said, "war is war, that is that: it is easy for lawyers to extend precedents upholding presidential power in big wars to cases involving minor skirmishes." But precedents from the Civil War, where the existence of the nation was at stake and Lincoln jailed "American citizens on his own say-so" while suspending "their constitutional right to ask the courts for a writ of habeas corpus demanding their freedom," or World War II, when "Roosevelt invoked extraordinary powers as commander in chief to order 120,000 Japanese—mostly citizens—into internment camps" are "irrelevant" to the war on terror, Ackerman argued. "Terrorism is a very serious problem," he acknowl-

---

*In fact, Ackerman asked us to "consider this particularly chilling statement from Professor John Yoo...: 'The world after September 11, 2001,... is very different.... It is no longer clear that the United States must seek to reduce the amount of warfare, and it certainly is no longer clear that the constitutional system ought to be fixed so as to make it more difficult to use force. It is no longer clear that the default state for American national security is peace.'" Ackerman added, "And it will never be clear, until the public and the legal community repudiate the mindless war-talk which swirls around us." Bruce Ackerman, *Before the Next Attack: Preserving Civil Liberties in an Age of Terrorism* (New Haven, Conn.: Yale University Press, 2006), 17.

edged, "but it doesn't remotely suggest a return to the darkest times of the Civil War or World War II." Under no circumstances, even a worst-case scenario, can any terrorist group pose comparable problems to the United States, Ackerman pointed out.[7]

Professor Yoo also misrepresented the position of former senator Gary Hart, who served as the cochairman (with former senator Warren Rudman) on the United States Commission on National Security in the 21st Century, which issued a detailed report on September 15, 1999, with the following lead conclusion: "America will become increasingly vulnerable to hostile attack on our homeland, and our military superiority will not entirely protect us." The Hart-Rudman commission, which was clearly far ahead of Bush and Cheney in understanding the national security problems facing the nation, further concluded that "terrorists ... will acquire weapons of mass destruction and mass disruption, and some will use them. Americans will likely die on American soil, possibly in large numbers."[8] To deal with these problems, Senator Hart's commission recommended that "U.S. military, law enforcement, intelligence, economic, financial, and diplomatic means must be effectively integrated for this purpose."[9]

Finally, Yoo's reference to Harvard law professor Philip Heymann's statement that "war has always required a conflict between nation states" correctly quoted Heymann, but by including him under the banner of supporting a "law enforcement" approach to dealing with terrorism completely misrepresented Heymann's position. In his book *Terrorism, Freedom, and Security: Winning Without War* (2003), Heymann did not dismiss war against terrorists but rather examined the term "war," which has been used "metaphorically to indicate any massive commitment of attention, energy, and resources to a dangerous problem," like the wars against "poverty, crime, and drugs," as well as to refer to real wars involving the military, which have "always been temporary states—not states of prolonged, even indefinite, duration." Contrary to the impression Yoo gave his own reader, Heymann did not reject the notion of fighting terrorists through wars; to the contrary, Heymann wrote, "Although these traditional characteristics of the term 'war' do not fit comfortably with its use to describe the aftermath of the attacks of September 11, that does not preclude stretching the concept if that has desirable consequences." While he explained how the term can be stretched, he believes that doing so is "dangerous in the longer run."

Viewing the fight against terrorists in terms of war hurts rather than helps win that fight, Heymann asserted, because not all terrorist groups are the same. If a tactic in the fight against terrorists is labeled war, "we are less likely to develop different remedies for different dangers," Heymann noted, and concluded:

> Finally, a definition of the situation we face as "war" strongly suggests that our primary reliance will continue to be on military force.... If use of the military was in fact the most promising avenue to deal with the variety of forms of terrorism that threaten us, there would be nothing affirmatively misleading (although nothing very helpful) about describing the situation we face as "war." The danger is that, for several reasons, the use of the term "war" points us in the wrong direction. The very term suggests a primacy for military force; that's what war has always been about. The military is the group to whom we have generally turned in situations of grave danger from hostile forces. In that sense, we may be captives of the dictum that "to a man with a hammer, everything looks like a nail." Finally, the military, recognizing the vulnerabilities of its traditional strategies for fighting wars to what it calls "asymmetrical threats," has vested its pride in efforts to meet such low-level threats. But a little thought reveals sharp limits on the usefulness of military force against terrorists sheltered by a sympatric population or even against a state harboring terrorists.

Contrary to Yoo's statements, Heymann did not reject war in favor of law enforcement, but instead made a strong case for why the military alone simply will not be able to prevent terrorism, which is also going to require "ordinary policing" both in the United States and abroad— work for which our armed forces are not trained, nor truly suitable.[10]

(Phillip Heymann's position is, in fact, strikingly similar to that in the *9/11 Commission Report,* included in the section: "More Than a War on Terrorism."*[11]

John Yoo needs a state of war, or a state of perpetual emergency, to help bolster his remarkable claims for presidential powers. In times of war and emergency, Americans have given their leaders added authority, often without questions. Thus, Yoo claimed, "If an emergency because of terrorist attack allows the government to exercise the same powers as in wartime, then labeling the post–9/11 world an emergency rather than a war is of no real difference."[12] In fact, we are not in a state of war or ongoing emergency, both of which might justify the use of extraordinary powers to protect the nation. No sane person doubts that terrorists can (and no doubt will) do terrible things to us, and it is even possible that they may detonate an atomic bomb in New York City, Chicago, or Los Angeles. Still, even the worst-case scenario does not begin to compare to the devastation that a nuclear power like the Soviet Union could have brought upon the United States during the cold war. In short, we have faced far greater threats than terrorism and dealt with them diplomatically and intelligently. Indeed, the entire cold war represents the triumph of diplomacy, starting with the doctrine of containing communism following World War II through the economic collapse of the Soviet Union four decades later. Rather than going to war when the Soviets placed missiles in Cuba, President Kennedy ignored the table-pounding generals chomping for battle and relied on a nonconfrontational naval quarantine of Cuba and heavy back-channel diplomacy. Bush Senior knew better than to invade Bagh-

---

*To bolster his case for war and against law enforcement in fighting terrorists, Professor Yoo made references without citation or attribution: "Bipartisan studies of the failing that led up to 9/11 refer to the inadequacy of the criminal justice approach to deal effectively with an ideologically motivated military organization like al Qaeda" (*War by Other Means,* 3). This appears to be a reference to the 9/11 Commission, yet the 9/11 Commission clearly embraced law enforcement as a principal means of fighting terrorists. See *9/11 Commission Report,* chapter 12: What to Do? A Global Strategy, and chapter 13: How to Do It? A Different Way of Organizing the Government.

dad after repelling Saddam Hussein from Kuwait; unfortunately his son did not. Fortunately, a few have attempted to place terrorism in its proper perspective, although when one thoughtful scholar did just that, he was ignored. In *Overblown: How Politicians and the Terrorism Industry Inflate National Security Threats, and Why We Believe Them* (New York: Free Press, 2006), Ohio State University political science professor John Mueller not only placed contemporary terrorism in perspective, but showed how we have consistently tended to misread our perils, and refuse to learn from our history.*

John Yoo is representative of a current school of radical Republican legal scholars seeking to enhance the powers of the presidency by stretching the Constitution beyond its limits. Under the Yoo view of the Constitution, a president can unilaterally, without the approval of Congress and beyond the jurisdiction of the federal courts: make war; violate treaties; imprison anyone the president designates an "enemy combatant" for as long as he wishes without charges or access to counsel; use torture when interrogating any terror suspect or anyone the president says is a terror suspect; kidnap such suspects and transport them to friendly foreign countries that employ torture (called "extraordinary rendition"); create military tribunals to determine punishment (even death) of captured combatants with no true procedural safeguards; and engage in warrantless wiretapping and electronic surveillance irrespective of the prohibitions of the Foreign Intelligence Surveillance Act. In addition, should any innocent person be seriously injured by such conduct and seek remedy, he can be blocked from litigating such a claim by the president's invocation of a "state secrets" privilege that prohibits even federal courts from dealing with the matter.

Lawyers like Yoo and his former colleagues at the Department of Justice have based their arguments on a number of claims, most prominently: the president has inherent powers under the Constitution;

---

*He has posted several papers on his Web site that outline his thinking. See John Muller; papers on the Web, at psweb.sbs.ohio-state.edu/faculty/jmueller/links.htm.

that as commander in chief he is authorized to undertake such actions; and, in some instances, the claim is based on the precedent of a predecessor's action. Allow me to explain briefly why most of these arguments are what has been defined and described by Princeton philosopher Harry G. Frankfurt so memorably as "bullshit."*

The Claim of Inherent Constitutional Powers

So stunning are the Bush administration's claims to inherent presidential powers under the Constitution that they prompted Louis Fisher, a political scientist and constitutional scholar who has spent his career working as a nonpartisan professional at the Library of Congress (and earlier served several decades at the Congressional Reference Service), to assemble a group of highly credentialed experts—of all political persuasions—to examine them. The forum for this undertaking was a special issue of the *Presidential Studies Quarterly*, a blind, peer-reviewed journal of the nonpartisan Center for the Study of the Presidency.[13]

Fisher observed in the special issue of *PSQ* that "at no time in America's history have inherent powers been claimed with as much frequency and breadth as the presidency of George W. Bush."[14] Bush and Cheney have effectively changed the very nature of our nation's government "from one of limited powers to boundless and ill-defined authority. . . . Across a broad front, the presidency of George W. Bush claims inher-

---

*See Harry G. Frankfurt, *On Bullshit* (Princeton, N.J.: Princeton University Press, 2005), 22:

> The notion of carefully wrought bullshit involves . . . a certain inner strain. Thoughtful attention to detail requires discipline and objectivity. It entails accepting standards and limitations that forbid the indulgence of impulse or whim. It is this selflessness that, in connection with bullshit, strikes us as inapposite. But in fact it is not out of the question at all. The realms of advertising and public relations, and nowadays the closely related realm of politics, are replete with instances of bullshit so unmitigated that they can serve among the most indisputable and classic paradigms of the concept.

ent powers to create military commissions and determine their rules and procedures; designate U.S. citizens as 'enemy combatants' and hold them indefinitely without being charged, given counsel, or ever tried; engage in 'extraordinary rendition' to take a suspect from the United States to another country for interrogation and possible torture; and authorize the National Security Agency to listen to phone conversations between the United States and a foreign country involving suspected terrorists."[15]

What constitutes inherent powers? Turning to the leading legal reference, *Black's Law Dictionary*, Fisher reported that the current, eighth edition (2004) defines inherent power as "a power that necessarily derives from an office, position, or status." Although John Yoo may have found such powers in the Constitution, Fisher, who has been studying the document a good deal longer, cannot: "The assertion of inherent power in the president threatens the doctrine of separated powers and the system of checks and balances. Sovereignty moves from the constitutional principles of self-government, popular control, and republican government to the White House."[16]

Former Reagan Justice Department senior official and Harvard lawyer Bruce Fein examined Bush's claim of "inherent constitutional power to target American citizens on American soil for warrantless electronic surveillance" and found it to be "nonsense on stilts." Fein observed that "in the midst of the Korean War, President Harry Truman seized private steel mills to avert a threatened strike that could have upset the supply of steel used in weapons manufacture. The Supreme Court rebuked the president's claim of inherent constitutional power as commander in chief to justify a seizure that Congress had declined to authorize."[17]

Georgia State University College of Law professor and former attorney with the Justice Department's Office of Legal Counsel Neil Kinkopf asserted that "it is fairly clear that the president does not have inherent power."* He observed that "the Constitution was adver-

---

*In addition to disposing of the matter of inherent powers, Professor Kinkopf upped the ante by recasting the question "to ask whether the president holds power

tised—by Publius [James Madison, writing in *The Federalist Papers*] at least—in a way that rejects inherent presidential power." He further wrote that "Chief Justice John Marshall early on established structural analysis as a crucial method for interpreting the Constitution. In a host of cases considering contentious issues of first impression, John Marshall turned to the nature and character of the Constitution as a guide to the meaning of its provisions. For Marshall, the fact of the Constitution's writtenness was key to resolving these questions. In *Marbury v. Madison,* for example, he emphasized that the Constitution establishes the federal government as a government of limited and enumerated powers," and rejected inherent powers. Professor Kinkopf said that the closest the Supreme Court has come to recognizing inherent powers was in the dicta (the opinions of judges that are unrelated to the actual resolution of a case and go beyond the matters at issue, therefore not considered as precedents) of Justice Sutherland in the ruling in *United States v. Curtiss-Wright Export Corp.,* where he wrote that the "Union existed before the Constitution ... [resulting in] the investment of the federal government with powers of external sovereignty [that] did not depend on the affirmative grants of the Constitution." But, Kinkopf noted, "the Supreme Court has never adopted the *Curtiss-Wright* dicta. In fact, the Supreme Court resoundingly rejected the existence of inherent powers."[18] Kinkopf quoted Justice Jackson's opinion in the leading presidential power holding, where he noted the request

> that we declare the existence of inherent powers *ex necessitate* [of necessity] to meet an emergency asks us to do what many think would be wise, although it is something the forefathers omitted. They knew what emergencies were, knew the pressures they engender for authoritative action, knew, too, how they afford a ready

---

that is broadly or commonly beyond the authority of Congress to limit"—as Yoo and others have argued. He then disposed of the notion that there is any such presidential power.

pretext for usurpation. We may also suspect that they suspected that emergency powers would tend to kindle emergencies. Aside from suspension of the privilege of the writ of habeas corpus in time of rebellion or invasion, when the public safety may require it, they made no express provision for exercise of extraordinary authority because of a crisis. I do not think we rightfully may so amend their work, and, if we could, I am not convinced it would be wise to do so.[19]

University of Pittsburgh School of Law professor Jules Lobel, in the special issue of *PSQ*, analyzed the nation's founding and concluded, "The framers of the Constitution clearly rejected any claim that the president had inherent powers over the initiation and prosecution of wars." He added,

The Framers did not incorporate John Locke's notion of the royal prerogative to act in time of emergency or crisis into the Constitution. The early leaders of the Republic accepted Locke's thesis that, at times, the executive had the prerogative to take emergency action "without the prescription of the law and sometimes even against it. An emergency permitted the disregard of even the 'direct letter of the law'" [Locke citation omitted]. But for the founders of the American Republic, this prerogative power was not part of the constitutional authority provided to the president. Rather, if the president or any other military official believed he needed to react to an emergency situation, he had to act unconstitutionally and eventually seek ratification or indemnification from Congress or accept punishment for his actions.[20]

The Bush administration tacitly acknowledged this fact—not to mention its own criminal misconduct—when it quietly added a provision to the Military Commission Act of 2006 (MCA) that rewrote the War Crimes Act retroactively to November 26, 1997, making those offenses that were considered war crimes before the MCA was adopted no longer punishable under American law.[21] If it truly believed it had the inherent powers that John Yoo and others claim, it would not have worried about its criminal liability.

Barnard College and Columbia University political scientist Richard M. Pious titled his essay for the special *PSQ* issue "Inherent War and Executive Powers and Prerogative Polices," and noted, "Scholarship about claims of inherent executive, war, and diplomatic powers [citations omitted] makes it clear that presidents do not possess a monopoly of prerogative power in war and foreign affairs, and in fact they cannot even claim all 'executive' powers, as the Constitution has always had, in the words of delegates at the ratifying conventions, 'blended' executive powers shared by president and Senate."[22] Professor Pious, who discussed scholarly analysis versus what the executive and judicial branches are actually doing from the viewpoint of a political scientist, offered the most chilling analysis of any of the *PSQ* essays. He pointed out that

> presidential practice, congressional legislation, and judicial case law have all moved us far toward a "unitary executive" that possesses, if not a monopoly of prerogative in theory, the actual control of war-making and foreign affairs in fact. If, as [Edward S.] Corwin says, the Constitution provides "an invitation to struggle" for control over the conduct of foreign affairs, there is a question political scientists must answer: why have presidents since Nixon almost always won in courts and usually gained support in Congress, irrespective of the weight of constitutional scholarship that undermines their more extravagant claims of prerogative?

The short answer is that presidents simply plow ahead; courts do not wish to get involved; and the Congress is either unaware or, of late, misled. Pious cited, for an example, the provision of incorrect information to Congress as a means for a president to obtain an authorization. "This was the tactic used by President George W. Bush when he exaggerated the weapons of mass destruction threat from Iraq and the links of the

Baathist regime to al Qaeda prior to the Iraq War of 2003."[23] Professor Pious summed up the situation from a real-world point of view: "There is no question that the weight of scholarship favors doctrines that limit executive power and provide for both interbranch policy codetermination and checks and balances. The scholars have won the battle of constitutional analysis, but they have lost the war over executive powers." The result:

> The exercise of inherent executive power usually is not checked by Congress or courts, but at best under some circumstances is constrained by the party system and public opinion when issues of legitimacy are trumped by doubts about authority (in the sense that there are questions about the viability of policy). In such a case either the president changes course because of his own political calculations, or else a successor in the White House makes the changes. Where the weight of constitutional scholarship and the mechanisms of institutional checks and balances have failed, public opinion and the sentiments of the electorate—the "auxiliary precautions"—sometimes succeed.[24]

The *PSQ* editors nicely summarized the analysis offered by Stanford University political scientist and Pulitzer Prize–winning historian Jack N. Rakove, who writes frequently about the origins of the Constitution:*

*Professor Rakove, along with seven other historians, filed an *amicius curiae* (friend of the court) brief with the U.S. Supreme Court in the case of *Hamdan v. Rumsfeld*, addressing a central issue of the case of whether "the inherent powers of the President" authorized the creation of a military tribunal to try Hamdan. Directly addressing the claims of John Yoo and other legal scholars, the brief explained that "the adopters of our Constitution rejected a monarchical conception of executive prerogative, and instead maintained and extended the legislative supervision and control of executive power that were the profound legacy of Anglo-American constitutional history since the early seventeenth century" (2006 U.S. S.Ct. Briefs LEXIS 19). The Supreme Court did not decide this issue, but the brief makes a powerful case that there are no such inherent powers.

Claims for the inherent authority of the executive over issues of national security imply that the adopters of the Constitution relied on prior British definitions equating executive power and royal prerogative. These claims cannot survive the scrutiny of key sources, including ... the Federal Convention's debates over the presidency, and the famous 1793 exchange between Hamilton and Madison over the nature and sources of presidential power. When Hamilton relied on the Vesting Clause [of Article II of the Constitution] to stake his claim, he was engaging in interpretive *innovatio,* not providing a historically faithful account of how the presidency had been contrived.[25]

As Rakove characterized the debate between Madison and Hamilton, while Hamilton was embracing newfound presidential powers for President Washington, "on the merits of the underlying claims about the nature and extent of the constitutional authority, it was Madison who was far more faithful to the original meaning, intention, and understanding of the Constitution, and Hamilton who was engaged in a brazen act of interpretive *innovatio* [a Latin term that means 'to be known.']." As Rakove later stated, Hamilton, when "playing fast and loose with the facts," was the "keenest original student of executive power."[26]

Finally, the *PSQ* special issue turned to Abraham D. Sofaer, a former law professor at Columbia University (1969–1979), a former federal district court judge (1979–1985), a former legal adviser to the U.S. Department of State (1985–1990), and currently with Stanford University's Hoover Institution. Judge Sofaer liked the questions posed by the panel, but chose instead to focus on the workings of the "mixed" government the Framers had designed. In so doing, he noted, "Claims that the Framers intended to create a 'unitary' executive underlie the recent wave of assertions that the president has all the inherent and exclusive powers he and his lawyers consider necessary to win the War on Terror. These claims have often been baseless."

■   ■   ■

Cleary there is a wide scholarly consensus that there are no inherent powers in the presidency. Congress has adopted emergency statutes that cover many situations, but if the president encounters a terror situation in which the law fails to give him the tools he needs to deal with an emergency, he should do as President Jefferson did first, and President Lincoln did later—deal with the situation, then go to Congress and explain why it was necessary to act beyond the law and Constitution, and seek ratification after the fact.

The Commander in Chief Clause Does Not Empower Presidents

Reliance on the commander in chief clause is one of many fallacious arguments that are made for presidential war powers. John Yoo finds powers in this clause that would make the president the equivalent of the once-powerful British monarchy, an argument that he supports with a phantasmagorical reanalysis of the history that influenced the Framers of the Constitution—history that all other scholars over the past two hundred some odd years have apparently gotten wrong. One of his stunning conclusions is that, rather than rejecting the model of the British monarchy that the nation had fought a revolution to escape (and which they had said rather unflattering things about in the Declaration of Independence, particularly its war powers), King George III was actually the model the Framers emulated in writing the Constitution. And the Constitution they created (again, contrary to two centuries-plus understanding,) placed the president, in times of war, just like a monarch—beyond the powers of Congress and the federal courts. While the topic is only addressed in passing in Yoo's book, in his memoranda that have surfaced he basically subscribed to the position adopted by William Rehnquist when he was an assistant attorney general advising Nixon: namely, that the commander in chief clause was an independent grant of authority to the president. (No one is ever going to accuse the late chief justice Rehnquist of being a very good historian, however.) In short, for years—thanks to Rehnquist—the Department of Justice has found more in this clause than the Founders had in mind.

The Constitution states: "The President shall be the Commander-in-Chief of the Army and Navy of the United States, and of the Militia of the several states, when called into actual service of the United States." What does it mean to be commander in chief? That this term was so well understood at the time the Constitution was written appears to explain why there was no debate whatsoever on this clause at the Constitutional Convention of 1787. Alexander Hamilton explained the authority of the commander in chief in Federalist No. 69: "It would amount to nothing more than the supreme command and direction of the military and naval forces, as first General and Admiral," and unlike British kings, the president as first general did not have authority for "the *declaring* of war and to the *raising* and *regulating* of fleets and armies—all which, by the Constitution under consideration, would appertain to the Legislature." (Emphasis in original.) Similar explanations were provided at the ratification conventions, such as that given by Richard Spaight, who had represented North Carolina at the Constitutional Convention in Philadelphia. When concern was expressed that Congress did not have control of "the direction of the motions of the army," Spaight acknowledged that the president commanded the army and navy, but added, "Congress, who had the power of raising armies, could certainly prevent any abuse of that authority in the President, [for] they alone had the means of supporting armies, and that the President was impeachable if he in any manner abused his trust."[27] James Iredell, who later served on the Supreme Court, also explained to the North Carolina ratifying convention that the

> King of Great Britain is not only the commander-in-chief of the land and naval forces, but has power in time of war, to raise fleets and armies. He also has the power to declare war. The president has not the power of declaring war by his own authority, nor that of raising fleets and armies. The powers are vested in other hands.

The power of declaring war is expressly given to Congress, that is, to the two branches of the legislature.... They have also expressly delegated to them the powers of raising and supporting armies, and of providing and maintaining a navy.[28]

In short, the text of the Constitution is too precise, the history of the Framers' decision making too clear, and the ratification process too well recorded to come to any other rational understanding than that the war powers reside with Congress and the commander in chief clause did not empower presidents to make war. This fact, however, has not prevented arguments to the contrary, and given the circumstances in which some of them were presented, they are compelling.

Abraham Lincoln, for example, devised the argument that he could launch a war to preserve the nation by wedding the commander in chief clause to the clause requiring the president "to take care that the laws be faithfully executed." Esteemed constitutional scholar Edward S. Corwin explained, "From these two clauses thus united Lincoln proceeded to derive what he termed the 'war power,' to justify a series of extraordinary measures," such as raising an army and navy; paying out millions in unappropriated funds from the Treasury; prohibiting use of the post office for "treasonable correspondence"; imposing new passport regulations of all traveling to or from foreign countries; blockading Southern ports; suspending the writ of habeas corpus; and ordering the arrest and military detention of persons believed to be engaging in, or even contemplating, "treasonable practices."[29] He also based the Emancipation Proclamation on his powers as commander in chief, claiming freeing slaves was a matter of "military necessity."[30] The result was, "For a brief time, America had a "constitutional dictator."[31] But Lincoln's situation was unique: He was faced with a true and sustained emergency; he had a rebellion to quell. Both Congress and the Supreme Court recognized this fact, and ratified his actions. The Supreme Court, however, only ratified Lincoln's defensive actions. Thus, in upholding the president's naval blockage of rebellious states, the Court explained that the president was "bound to resist by force," for Lincoln had not "initiated the war"; rather, he found it necessary to address the "challenge without waiting for … Congress" to act.[32] Although Lincoln brought the commander in chief clause into play, absent an emergency it had little impact. Any intellectually honest scholar or lawyer who has studied the history of the Constitution and the rulings of the Supreme Court will concede that the commander in chief clause was designed by the Framers to grant presidents very limited powers.

Predecessors' Precedents

The claim of precedence established by prior presidents is the single most difficult point to counter, and for that reason it is the one that presidents—and their secretaries of defense—rely on most often. The contention is very simple: Other presidents have done it, so why shouldn't I do it as well? While these claims are specifically employed with regard to war powers, their implications are even broader. I became familiar with this thinking as Nixon's White House counsel. My predecessor in that position, John Ehrlichman, and I had a number of conversations about Nixon's war powers. In those days the White House counsel was only involved tangentially in such issues, because the National Security Council relied on its own legal apparatus, including direct pipelines to the Departments of Justice, State, and Defense. On one occasion, Ehrlichman told me that Nixon had a list of some 160 incidents during which presidents had used force without congressional consent, dating back the to the administration of President Washington. But "the Boss," as Ehrlichman called the president out of earshot, felt that "Harry Truman had no congressional authorization, and went to war in Korea, relying on his powers as commander in chief. Lyndon Johnson was escalating in Vietnam way beyond anything Congress authorized, based on his powers as commander in chief." With Ehrlichman I typically enjoyed being mildly adversarial, but I was nonetheless surprised at his reaction when I said that yes, both Truman and Johnson were operating outside the Constitution. He thought about my remark for a silent few seconds, and our conversation ended with one of his memorable comments: "Well, my boy, two wrongs don't make a right. But in law and politics, they are very solid precedents."* Years later I was amazed to find Ehrlichman's cynical aphorism repeated by conservative writer Victor Lasky in his Nixon apologia *It Didn't Start with Watergate.* Early in his book Lasky observed, "Two wrongs don't make a right; but in law and politics, two wrongs can make a respectable precedent."[33]

Unfortunately, Ehrlichman and Lasky, and others who would adopt this cynical mentality, appear to have a good point. For example, in law, there is a doctrine know as *stare decisis* (a Latin phrase meaning to abide by or adhere to decided cases), which is designed to give stability to the law by allowing it to evolve in a measured manner. The doctrine, however, can also serve to keep intact badly decided prior cases, and make them controlling rules.[34] To claim that acts of prior presidents create a political *stare decisis,* as Lasky in effect did to justify Nixon's abuses of power and bad behavior, is ludicrous. Lasky merely wanted to make Nixon look good by dredging up the dark side of other presidencies to look for similar behavior: Franklin Roosevelt (anti-Semitic slurs, civil liberties violations, misuses of the FBI, court packing, undeclared war making, and unauthorized wiretapping), Harry Truman (anti-Semitic slurs and wiretapping), John Kennedy (assassination of foreign leaders, a bungled Bay of Pigs invasion, misuses of the Internal Revenue Service, links to the Mafia, ruthless campaign tactics, wiretapping, and womanizing), and Lyndon Johnson (ties to convicted Senate aide Bobby Baker, campaign finance violations, misuses of the CIA, misuses of the FBI, cover-up of the Jenkins affair [a senior White House aide was arrested for homosexual activity], surveillance of Martin Luther King, Jr., ruthless campaigning, wiretapping, and womanizing).[35] Lasky's defense failed,

---

*Those not of the Watergate generation will not likely recall Ehrlichman's remarks, which became part of the vernacular at the time. When he ordered me to handle L. Patrick Gray, whom Nixon had nominated to be director of the FBI but whose nomination was doomed, Ehrlichman said to "leave him twisting in the wind." Watergate, of course, gave us "stonewalling." And for the true buff there was Ehrlichman's "modified-limited-hangout" to describe what Nixon might say about it all.

however. When one looks closely at his examples—and it is necessary to look beyond his book—what emerges is that these unseemly matters in other presidencies certainly occurred, but they were the exception to the rule; in the Nixon White House they were the rule—standard operating procedure, which is very different. Still, it cannot be denied that Ehrlichman—far more cleverly than Lasky—had a point that two or more political wrongs for a matter like presidential powers will stand, unless checked by Congress or the federal courts.

Louis Fisher, who analyzes these matters largely from a congressional point of view, has examined and reexamined the various lists of precedents for presidents to go to war without congressional authority, and has found only three clearly unconstitutional wars (and he certainly does not accept the claim that two constitutional wrongs make a fair precedent). Take, for purposes of discussion two key presidents who provide an interesting contrast. Lincoln exercised extraconstitutional powers during the Civil War but asked Congress to ratify his actions, which it did, after the fact. Fisher noted: "[Lincoln appreciated] that the superior lawmaking authority was Congress, not the president," and that "Lincoln never claimed authority to act outside the Constitution." He added: "Lincoln and his advisors never argued that he could take unilateral military action against other nations without prior approval by Congress.... Lincoln acted defensively, not offensively." In short, there was nothing unconstitutional about the way Lincoln handled the crisis of the Civil War.

On the other hand, Fisher believes that President Harry Truman is responsible for establishing the precedent that has been abused by his successors, when in 1950 he sent troops to Korea without the approval of Congress. Fisher stated that Truman was the first president in a century and a half to go to war in violation of the Constitution, as well as in violation of legislation (and a personal commitment to Congress) requiring that the president first obtain the consent of Congress before committing American troops to a United Nations peacekeeping effort. Although Truman conferred with Congress and kept them aware of his activities after the North Koreans (then a puppet of Moscow) launched a surprise attack on South Korea, he nonetheless entered a major war without congressional authorization. Although Truman had a compliant Congress* and considered seeking a resolution from it approving his actions, Senate Democratic majority leader Scott W. Lucas of Illinois counseled him against doing so. Truman told a meeting of Senate leaders that "it was necessary to be very careful that he would not appear to be trying to get around Congress and use extra-Constitutional powers."[36]

Fisher, like many scholars, does not believe that congressional acquiescence justifies an unconstitutional war. In short, before sending troops to Korea Truman should have obtained formal congressional authorization. Yet when examining what actually happened, I find that the precedent that Truman set was actually rather limited. Congressional leaders, and the Congress itself, informally approved his actions, and advised him not to seek a formal resolution. Fisher argued that this advice from his party's leaders did not preclude his obtaining formal congressional approval.[37] Nonetheless, it appears that those who rely on the Truman precedent are grossly abusing it when they flatly claim, as Yoo did in his September 25, 2001, opinion supporting President Bush's desire to go to war against terrorists anywhere and without the approval of Congress, as follows: "Perhaps the most significant deployment without specific statutory authorization took place at the time of the Korean War, when President Truman, without prior authorization from Congress, deployed United States troops in a war that

*The *New York Times* (June 28, 1950) headlined the congressional reaction "Legislators Hail Action by Truman: Almost Unanimous Approval Is Voiced in Congress by Both Sides—House Cheers." Only two members of Congress openly objected to Truman's action: Far-left American Labor Party representative Vito Marcantonio of New York City decried Truman in the House, according to the *New York Times,* and conservative Ohio Republican senator Robert Taft attacked Truman in the Senate. The *New York Times* that day also reported Taft charging that Truman had "usurped the powers of Congress" with the headline: "Taft Says Truman Bypasses Congress: But He Supports President's Decision on Korea—Calls on [Secretary of State Dean] Acheson to Resign" (June 29, 1950).

lasted for over three years and caused over 142,000 American casualties."[38] This statement would be correct only if it read with "the informal consent of Congress."

Defensive Powers of the President

Writing in the *Indiana Law Journal* (Fall 2005), Louis Fisher noted that "one area of the war power that the Framers assigned to the President, to be taken on his initiative, was of a defensive nature": the authority to repel sudden attacks against the United States. Although it was not expressly set forth in the Constitution, Fisher explained the source of this power, which I have both paraphrased and quoted: This presidential power emerges from the Constitutional Convention of 1787, when the delegates made a change in an early draft of the proposed constitution that authorized Congress to "make" war. Charles Pinckney expressed concern that, by nature, a legislative body was "too slow" in an emergency situation to protect the country; in addition, Congress would only meet but once a year, and then only briefly. James Madison and Elbridge Gerry offered a motion to insert "declare" in place of the word "make," and, according to Madison's notes of the debate, leaving to the president "the power to repel sudden attacks." This motion was approved, and is from this brief and passing remark in the debate on the Madison-Gerry amendment that authority is claimed for the president to use force in a defensive manner.[39]

In the special issue of *PSQ,* Jack Rakove reviewed this debate, from August 17 and 23, 1787, which he noted has been "much scrutinized by scholars" and concluded that this change of Congress's power from "make" to "declare" resulted in "implicitly 'leaving to the Executive the power to repel sudden attacks.'"[40] When this issue arose during the Nixon administration *Time* magazine consulted with constitutional scholars, and the consensus in the early 1970s was that "according to James Madison, the President would ... have 'power to repel sudden attacks.' To many scholars the implication is clear. The President was to initiate emergency defensive operations; Congress was to remain responsible for all offensive ones."[41] This is the understanding of every constitutional scholar with whom I have spoken over the past three decades.

Notwithstanding the rather clear meaning of this debate, John Yoo again simply stood history on its head, and quite incredibly wrote in *The Powers of War and Peace* that "changing the phrase from 'make' to 'declare' reflected an intention to prohibit Congress from encroaching on the executive power to conduct war."[42] New York University School of Law professor Stephen Holmes, whose review of the book ("The Tortured Logic of John Yoo") criticized both its content and methodology, explained how Yoo rewrote history and summed up his deceptive techniques:

> To make his contrarian claim ring true, Yoo whites out contrary evidence and draws dubious conclusions on the basis of fragmentary and carefully selected facts. He disregards the main thrust of the historical record and misrepresents the parts he acknowledges. He ferrets out (and exaggerates the importance of) scattered shreds of evidence that, at first glance, seem to back up his predetermined narrative. This cherry-picking of the sources may explain why he fits so comfortably into an administration known for politicizing intelligence, smothering doubts, silencing critical voices and fixing the facts around the policy.... The footnotes and citations teem with ambiguity and complexity, while the summary statements snap dogmatic simplicities.... The nimbleness with which, on several occasions, he simply inverts the manifest significance of historical texts that contradict his preset beliefs can only be called athletic.

As for the much-scrutinized August 1787 debate, Holmes wrote:

> Yoo's fictionalizing of the founding period is best exemplified by his lengthy discussion of the August 17, 1787, debate at the Constitutional Convention in Philadelphia. The surviving notes of this debate are admittedly garbled, cryptic and open to interpretation. But two things come through with ringing clarity. First, the word "declare," as the Framers used it, had a loose and fluctuating

meaning. Second, most participants in the discussion agreed on the importance of limiting the President's war powers by granting important war powers to Congress. This consensus stemmed from a conviction that war is the nurse of executive aggrandizement and that the President, whose powers balloon unnaturally in wartime, has a dangerous incentive to contrive and publicize bogus pretexts for war.[43]

Nonetheless, it is in this manner that John Yoo continues to work diligently to bolster the powers of the presidency—Republican presidencies anyway.

NOTES

Preface

1 Noam Chomsky, *Hegemony or Survival: America's Quest for Global Dominance* (New York: Henry Holt and Company, 2003), 1–2.

Introduction: Process Matters

1 William Safire, *Safire's New Political Dictionary* (New York: Random House, 1993), 614–15.

2 Disdain, particularly by a number of high-profile political journalists, for process matters has been a growing trend. I first noticed it in early 1996, when Washington writer (a former speechwriter for President Jimmy Carter), journalist (now the national correspondent for the *Atlantic*), and editor *(Washington Monthly, Atlantic,* and *U.S. News & World Report)* James Fallows published his unsparing critique of political reporting in *Breaking the News: How the Media Undermine American Democracy.* Among Fallows's observations were the persistent tendency of reporters to ask presidential candidates not "what" questions, but "how" questions, which are process questions. Notwithstanding widespread election postmortems on campaign coverage, which Fallows points out resulted in journalists acknowledging "that they should try harder to ask questions their readers and viewers seemed to care about—that is, questions about the difference political choices would make in people's lives" as they headed into the 1996 presidential race, Fallows found nothing had changed. Rather, they were still asking "questions no one but their fellow political professionals care[d] about"—and typically doing so with "discourtesy and rancor." As Fallows put it, the top political reporters "ask questions no one but their fellow political professionals cares about." As it happens, Fallows's point of view is not supported by empirical data, as I will show.

3 David Corn, "The No-Nuke Deal," *The Nation* (online), "Capitol Games" (posted May 24, 2005) at http://www.thenation.com/blogs/capitalgames?pid=2747.

4 Fox News Transcript, Jim Angle, "Interview with Michael Barone," *Fox Special Report with Brit Hume* (April 22, 2005).

5 CNN Transcript, *Paula Zahn Now*, "Gore Endorses Dean; Interview with Senator John Kerry" (Dec. 9, 2003) at http://transcripts.cnn.com/TRANSCRIPTS/0312/09/pzn.00.html.

6 NBC News Transcript, *Meet the Press* (Jan. 18, 2004).

7 Joe Klein, *Politics Lost: How American Democracy Was Trivialized by People Who Think You're Stupid* (New York: Doubleday, 2006), 236.

8 Fox News Transcript, *Fox Special Report with Brit Hume* (Jan. 30, 2002).

9 Fox News Transcript, *Fox Special Report with Brit Hume* (March 18, 2002).

10 Fox News Transcript, *Fox Special Report with Brit Hume* (Dec. 16, 2004).

11 Fox News Transcript, *Fox Special Report with Brit Hume* (Jan. 9, 2004).

12 David S. Bernstein, "Can Mitt Win?" *The* (Boston) *Phoenix* (Nov. 21, 2006) at http://www.thephoenix.com/article_ektid27996.aspx.

13 Fox News Transcript, *The Beltway Boys* (March 23, 2002).

14 Pew Research Center for the People and the Press, "Candidate Qualities May Trump Issues in 2000" (Oct. 18, 1999) at http://people-press.org/reports/print.php3?PageID=264.

15 Pew's pollsters asked Americans what they hoped to learn about presidential candidates over the coming year (as the 2000 presidential race approached). There were two real bell-ringing responses: 82 percent said that learning about the candidates "reputation for honesty" was very important (with 13 percent saying it was somewhat important), and 71 percent said it was very important to learn "how well a candidate connects with average people" (with 23 percent saying this was somewhat important). These were the strongest responses to the three dozen questions on the poll. The only other information voters expressed serious interest in was "a candidates voting record or policy positions in public offices he or she previously held," which 58 percent thought was very important (and 33 percent somewhat important). However, over half of the respondents to the poll conceded that they had virtually ignored "news about candidates for the 2000 presidential election." (Respondents were read a list of stories and were

asked to tell the pollster if they happened to follow the news story very closely, fairly closely, not too closely, or not closely at all. News about presidential candidates had been followed by 17 percent very closely, 32 percent fairly closely, 28 percent not too closely, and 16 percent not closely at all. This poll question was asked on three occasions, and I have listed the highest response. To me, not too closely and not closely at all are virtually ignoring the reporting. See Question No. 3[b] at http://people-press.org/reports/print.php3?PageID=267.)

Based on Pew's data, The Project for Excellence in Journalism (PEJ) issued a report in February 2000 that drew policy versus process conclusions. PEJ speaks with authority to journalists and news editors. PEJ, which is nonpartisan, nonideological, and nonpolitical, was created in the early 1990s by journalists "alarmed about the core values in journalism," according to Hugo de Burgh, ed., *Making Journalists* (New York: Routledge, 2005), 215. PEJ undertakes empirical studies to evaluate the performance of the press. Initially, it was associated with the Columbia University Graduate School of Journalism, but has recently become a part of the Pew Research Center for the People and the Press. (PEJ has a terrific Web site at http://www.journalism.org.) PEJ did not like the early news coverage of the 2000 presidential race, which they said, "paints a picture not of a contest of ideas between men but of a massive chess game of calculation and calibration in which little seems spontaneous or genuine." (In fact, modern presidential elections are not contests of ideas; rather, given our antiquated electoral system, they can be accurately described as "massive chess games.")

In 2004, PEJ examined 817 stories from 13 publications, including a number of blogs, along with cable and network programs from October 1 to 14, 2004, tracking coverage starting with the eve of the first debate and the day following the last debate. Again, PEJ criticized the mainstream media for its fixation with "political internals," which was the focus of 55 percent of the major stories. (Project for Excellence in Journalism, "The Debate Effect: How the Press Covered the Pivotal Period—The Major Stories" [Oct. 27, 2004] at http://www.journalism.org/node/198.) As for the bloggers, they were no better. "Far from a new kind of citizen journalism, the most popular blogs took an inside baseball approach to assessing the debates (70 percent), echoing the mainstream media. In the contentious vice-presidential debate, not a single posting dealt with policy matters," the report noted. Averaging across all the blogs studied, PEJ found them focused on political internals/process or performance 50 percent of the time.

16 Jonathan S. Morris and Rosalee A. Clawson, "Media Coverage of Congress in the 1990s: Scandals, Personalities, and the Prevalence of Policy and Process," *Political Communications*, vol. 22 (2005), 297, 301, 306, 310.

17 Dorothy Samuels, "Psst. President Bush Is Hard at Work Expanding Government Secrecy," *New York Times* (Nov. 1, 2004), A-24.

18 John W. Dean, *Conservatives Without Conscience* (New York: Viking, 2006), 131.

19 Examples based on skimming the platforms from 1960 to 2004 show an endless range of process issues have been addressed. To identify the source of the platform plank, I have designated the party (D or R) and year the matter was made part of the platform. Almost no area of the operation of the federal government is excluded over the span of several decades, such as: improving the national security policy machinery (D '60); revising ethics laws (D '60); assuring independence of regulatory agencies (D '60); improving training for federal employees (R '60); appointing federal judges based on qualification rather than party affiliation (R '60); changing the Electoral College (R '60); amend rules of House to expedite moving legislation to the floor (D '60); change Rule 22 of the Senate to only require sixty votes to end filibuster, decentralize Defense Department weapons procurement (R '72); attack on wiretapping and electronic surveillance by the Nixon administration (D '72); reorganization of federal regulatory agencies (R '72); end congressional seniority system (D '72); end congressional secrecy (D '72); regulate lobbying (D '72); reduce the burden of federal paperwork (R '76); a "top-to-bottom" reorganization of the federal government (R '76); make the federal government more accountable to the people (D '76); overhaul the civil service laws (D '76); assure individual privacy (R '80); temporary moratorium on any new federal regulations (R '80); bring an end to big government (R '80); reorganize the executive branch (R '80); pursue policies to increase voter participation and turnout (R '80); give Americans honest, open, and representative government (D '84); end packing federal courts based on ideology (D '84); universal, same-day, and mail-in voter registration (D '88); end federal deficit spending and reduce the deficits (D '92); end the "pathological" control of the Congress by the Democrats, who have controlled the House for thirty-eight years (R '92); reform the congressional budget process (R '92); increase the privatization of federal functions, turning to private enterprise to undertake appropriate government tasks (R '92); make the Corporation for Public Broadcasting self-sufficient, and their programming more balanced (R '92); legal reform to end frivolous lawsuits (R '92); end big government, slash burdensome regulations, eliminate wasteful programs, and

return governing to the people (D '96); transform FEMA into a "swift and effective agent of relief" for emergency disasters (D '96); limit the influence of special interests and increase the influence of average Americans (D '96); impose term limits on House committee chairs (R '96); streamline government (R '96); appoint only conservative judges to the federal bench and remove the American Bar Association from passing judgment on nominees (R '96); reform the intelligence agencies (R '96); run a "Government that's always open" (D '00); end stripping federal courts of jurisdiction (D '00); campaign finance reform to create fairer and more open elections not tied to special interests (D '00); provide the president a line item veto of spending bills (R '00); and create a "sunset commission" to get rid of programs that are duplicative, wasteful or inefficient, outdated or irrelevant, or failed (R '04).

20 Marguerite Allen, "Schakowsky Sees Discord in the Democratic Process," Evanston Roundtable (Dec. 1, 2004) at http://www.house.gov/schakowsky/article_12_1_04_evanston_Roundtable.html.

21 See Transcript, Jeff Berkowitz, "Emanuel and DeLay: A Shared Philosophy?" Public Affairs, City of Chicago, Cable Channel 21 (Nov. 5, 2005) at http://jeffberkowitz.blogspot.com/.

22 See http://www.janschakowsky.org/SchaBLOGsky/tabid/36/ctl/ArticleView/mid/512/articleId/392/Thank-You.aspx.

23 CNN, "Poll: 3 Out of 4 Say U.S. Government 'Broken'," (Oct. 23, 2006) at http://www.cnn.com/POLITICS/blogs/politicalticker/2006/10/poll-3-out-of-4-say-us-government.html. Other polls corroborate the CNN poll, with the situation deteriorating as the election approached. For example, the Rasmussen Reports headlined their August 28, 2006, poll making the same point: "Voters Everywhere Agree Political System 'Badly Broken.'" Rasmussen reported: "A plurality of voters in each of 32 states agree that the political system in the U.S. is 'badly broken.' Percentages range for a high of 63% in Vermont to 47% in Nebraska."

24 With its repeat showings, the series ran for nine nights in October, and according to *The New Yorker*, the series significantly boosted CNN's ratings. Ken Auletta, "Mad As Hell," *The New Yorker* (Dec. 4, 2006), 66.

25 Even though CNN's "Broken Government" was critical of both left and right, Democrats and Republicans, the Republican/conservative bloggers took offense to the series even being shown, while Democratic/progressive bloggers encouraged others to watch the series. Obviously, the mere existence of a broken government reflected poorly on the Republicans who had been in control, so the reaction of Republican bloggers was understandable.

26 Transcript, Wolf Blitzer, *The Situation Room* (Oct. 26, 2006).

27 For a small sampling, see: John R. Hibbing and Elizabeth Theiss-Morse, "Process Preferences and American Politics: What the People Want Government to Be," *The American Political Science Review*, vol. 95 (March 2001), 145–53; John R. Hibbing and Elizabeth Theiss-Morse, "What Would Improve Americans' Attitudes Toward Their Government?" Paper presented at Conference on Trust in Government, Princeton University, Nov. 30–Dec. 1, 2001; Elizabeth Theiss-More, "The Perils of Voice and the Desire for Stealth Democracy," *Maine Policy Review* (Winter 2002), 80–89; and John R. Hibbing and James Smith, "Is It the Middle That Is Frustrated? Americans' Ideological Positions and Government Trust," *American Politics Research*, vol. 32 (Nov. 2004), 652–78.

28 John R. Hibbing and Elizabeth Theiss-Morse, *Congress as Public Enemy: Public Attitudes Toward American Political Institutions* (New York: Cambridge University Press, 1995), 143–44.

29 Ibid., xiii.

30 John R. Hibbing and Elizabeth Theiss-Morse, *Stealth Democracy: Americans' Beliefs About How Government Should Work* (New York: Cambridge University Press, 2002), 37.

31 Hibbing and Theiss-Morse, *Congress as Public Enemy*, 14.

32 Ibid., 145.

33 Ibid., 146–47.

34 Ibid., 130, Table 7.1.

35 Ronald Reagan, "Inaugural Address" (Jan. 20, 1981) at http://www.reaganfoundation.org/reagan/speeches/first.asp.

36 Michael K. Deaver, ed., *Why I Am a Reagan Conservative* (New York: Morrow, 2005), 7, 39, 41, 87, 107, 129, 131, 133.

37 Tom DeLay with Stephen Mansfield, *No Retreat, No Surrender: One American's Fight* (New York: Sentinel, 2007), 143–44.

38 Alan Wolfe, "Why Conservatives Can't Govern," *Washington Monthly* (July/Aug. 2006) at http://www.washingtonmonthly.com/features/2006/0607.wolfe.html.

Chapter One: First Branch: Broken but Under Repair

1 Mann and Ornstein's work was embraced by such members of the Washington establishment as former Republican Speaker of the House Newt Gingrich, who said that today "the legislative branch is too weak, too dysfunctional, and too out of touch with modern times to fulfill its constitutional du-

ties" but "Mann and Ornstein understand well the glaring gap between the framers' design and today's reality"; former Democratic Speaker of the House Thomas S. Foley observed that in "the opinion of many Americans, Republicans and Democrats alike, the [Congress] simply does not work" and Mann and Ornstein show "what has gone wrong and why"; and former Senate Majority Leader Tom Daschle said Mann and Ornstein's work confirmed "what many of us have long known." Gingrich, Foley, and Daschle's statements are found in blurbs on the book jacket. See Thomas E. Mann and Norman J. Ornstein, *The Broken Branch: How Congress Is Failing America and How to Get It Back On Track* (New York: Oxford University Press, 2006).

2 For example, the *Washington Post* (Aug. 13, 2006) prominently and favorably reviewed the book. Reviewer Robert G. Kaiser, as associate editor of the paper, said, "The authors are members of what, sadly, may be a disappearing breed in Washington: independent-minded, knowledgeable experts whose concern for process is stronger than their desires for particular outcomes. They are means guys in an age dominated by ends." The book was also featured and discussed in publications ranging from *USA Today* (Aug. 8, 2006) to *U.S. News & World Report* (Sept. 11, 2006) to the *New York Times* (Aug. 10, 2006)—to mention only a few.

3 Juliet Eilperin, *Fight Club Politics: How Partisanship Is Poisoning the House of Representatives* (Lanham, Md.: Rowman & Littlefield, 2006), 2.

4 Ibid., 3.

5 Ibid., 11.

6 David E. Price, "Reflections on [Woodrow Wilson's book] *Congressional Government* at 120 and Congress at 216," *PS, Political Science & Politics* (April 2006), 232.

7 Alan Wolfe, "Why Conservatives Can't Govern," *Washington Monthly* (July/Aug. 2006) at http://www.washingtonmonthly.com/features/2006/0607.wolfe.html.

8 Matt Taibbi, "The Worst Congress Ever: How Our National Legislature Has Become a Stable of Thieves and Perverts—in Five Easy Steps," *Rolling Stone* at http://www.rollingstone.com/politics/story/12055360/cover_story_time_to_go_inside_the_worst_congress_ever.

9 Mann and Ornstein, *The Broken Branch*, 98, 105–6.

10 Taibbi, "The Worst Congress Ever."

11 Eilperin, *Fight Club Politics*, 30–35.

12 Ibid.

13 Taibbi, "The Worst Congress Ever."

14 Eilperin, *Fight Club Politics*, 30–35.

15 Price, "Reflections on *Congressional Government*," 231–32.

16 Wolfe, "Why Conservatives Can't Govern."

17 Mann and Ornstein, *The Broken Branch*, 98, 105–6.

18 Chris Bowers, "House 2008: Republican Targets and Defenses," MyDD (March 29, 2007) at http://www.mydd.com/story/2007/3/29/124442/644.

19 See, for example, Chris Cillizza, "Getting to 60 in the Senate," The Fix at http://blog.washingtonpost.com/thefix/2007/04/60.html.

20 Taibbi, "The Worst Congress Ever."

21 Mann and Ornstein, *The Broken Branch*, 170.

22 Eilperin, *Fight Club Politics*, 51–53.

23 Price, "Reflections on *Congressional Government*," 232–33.

24 Taibbi, "The Worst Congress Ever."

25 Price, "Reflections on *Congressional Government*," 233–34.

26 Wolfe, "Why Conservatives Can't Govern."

27 William Roberts and Charles R. Babcock, "Congress Failure to Curb Projects a Win for Lobbyist," Bloomberg.com (Sept. 15, 2006) at http://www.bloomberg.co.uk/apps/news?pid=20601070&sid=ahjtP7v6G1y8&refer=politics.

28 Mann and Ornstein, *The Broken Branch*, 175–79.

29 David Price, "A Budget Is a Statement of Moral Priorities," U.S. House of Representatives (March 17, 2005) at http://price.house.gov/News/Docu mentSingle.aspx?DocumentID=23920.

30 Wolfe, "Why Conservatives Can't Govern."

31 Karen Tumulty, "The Man Who Bought Washington," *Time* (Jan. 16, 2006) at http://www.time.com/time/magazine/article/0,9171,1147134,00.html.

32 Anonymous, "Best & Worst," *The Washingtonian* (Sept. 2004).

33 Taibbi, "The Worst Congress Ever."

34 Mann and Ornstein, *The Broken Branch*, 214.

35 Eilperin, *Fight Club Politics*, 133–37.

36 Price, "Reflections on *Congressional Government*," 233.

37 See John W. Dean, "The Broken Branch: An Unusual Lawsuit Takes Congress to Task for Shoddy and Partisan Lawmaking, in Which a Bill Is Unconstitutionally Being Treated as Law," FindLaw (March 10, 2006) at http://writ.news.findlaw.com/dean/20060310.html. (This column was written shortly after I spotted the egregious behavior. Many others later commented unfavorably on this behavior, and Public Citizen filed its lawsuit.)

38 Ibid.

39 Editorial, "Not a Law: A Bill Passed by Only One House of Congress Just Doesn't Count," *Washington Post* (April 1, 2006), A-16.

40 Alfred Hill, "Opinion: The Shutdowns and the Constitution," *Political Science Quarterly* (Summer 2000), 273–82.

41 Pew asked (during the period Jan. 11–14, 1996): "Were you or a member of your family personally inconvenienced by the recent partial shutdown of the federal government or not? If YES (the question was asked): Was it a major inconvenience or a minor inconvenience? Responses: 7 percent Yes, major; 9 percent Yes, minor/not sure; and 84 percent No, hasn't had any impact. See http://people-press.org.

42 The original law was prompted by Nixon's refusal to spend money that Congress had appropriated; rather, he impounded it. Many presidents had done this, starting with Thomas Jefferson in 1803, when he decided not to spend $50,000 appropriated for gunboats to use on the Mississippi River. Nixon believed he had constitutional authority as the chief executive to not spend. Presidents Truman, Eisenhower, and Kennedy had impounded funds. Nonetheless, Nixon's positions—partly because he was constantly expanding his presidential powers—angered Congress. When impeachment proceedings began, the House Impeachment Inquiry explored whether this was another impeachable offense, but decided Nixon actually had a respectable argument that he had authority. Meanwhile, Congress had been at work for years to get themselves back into the budget process, which had grown to major proportions. OMB had hundreds of experts, and Congress had only a few, so they enacted the Budget and Impoundment Control Act, eliminating any argument that the president could not spend funds, but more importantly establishing both a process and nonpartisan professional staff to assist Congress.

43 "Budget Squabbles Will Dog Congress All Year," *The Kiplinger Letter* (April 21, 2006), 1.

44 Edward Epstein, "Congress Goes Home with Budget Work Unfinished; Lawmakers Fail to Approve 9 of 11 Appropriations Bills," *San Francisco Chronicle* (Dec. 8, 2006), A-12.

45 Epstein, "Congress Goes Home with Budget Work Unfinished," A-12.

46 Deirdre Shesgreen and Adam Sichko, "Here's the Important Work Congress Got Done This Fall: Not Much. How the 109th Congress Got Away with 2-Hour Workdays and Renaming Post Offices," *St. Louis Post-Dispatch* (Dec. 10, 2006), B-1.

47 Shailagh Murray and Jonathan Weisman, "Democrats Freeze Earmarks for Now," *Washington Post* (Dec. 16, 2006), A-3.

48 Lyle Harris, "Ethics Reform Revived; Congress Reins in Pork Projects, Political Waywardness; Heavy on Disclosure, New Rules Weaken Lobbyists' Hold," *Atlanta Journal-Constitution* (Jan. 27, 2007), 10-A.

49 Editorial, "A Rare Bill in Congress," *New York Times* (Feb. 3, 2007), A-26.

50 See "Restoring Order: Practical Solutions to Congressional Dysfunction," The Reform Institute (Oct. 2006) at http://www.reforminstitute.org/uploads/publications/RestoringOrderFinal.pdf.

51 Mann and Ornstein, *The Broken Branch*, 175.

52 Ibid., 13.

53 Eilperin, *Fight Club Politics*, 132.

54 Alan Wolfe, *Does American Democracy Still Work?* (New Haven, Conn.: Yale University Press, 2006), 175 (citing the work of Elizabeth Anne Oldmixon, *Uncompromising Position: God, Sex and the U.S. House of Representatives* [Washington, D.C.: Georgetown University Press, 2005]).

55 Thomas B. Edsall, *Building Red America: The New Conservative Coalition and the Drive for Permanent Power* (New York: Basic Books, 2006), 50.

56 Daryl J. Levinson and Richard H. Pildes, "Separation of Parties, Not Powers," *Harvard Law Review* (June 2006), 2334. (This article can be found online at http://www.harvardlawreview.org/issues/119/june06/levinson_pildes.shtml.)

57 It is my belief that the contemporary GOP was built by the ironic flight of Southern racist Democrats to the party of Abraham Lincoln, and this view is widely shared. For example, Cliff Schecter, a former Rockefeller Republican, writes in the *Fordham Urban Law Journal* his witnessing this movement of the GOP to the right. His analysis is widely shared by former Republicans who left the party as the hard right took charge. "Today, the Republican Party, founded on an antislavery platform 147 years ago, seems, at times, more at home with former segregationists than civil rights crusaders, more comfortable with Bob Jones University [that forbade interracial dating] than Brown vs. Board of Education." Schecter traces a direct line from President Harry Truman's desegregation of the armed forces to Senator Goldwater's 1964 presidential bid, where he won Alabama, Georgia, Mississippi, Louisiana, and South Carolina, to Richard Nixon's "Southern Strategy" (which courted Southern Democrats using coded racial references regarding busing and law and order) to the "Reagan Revolution" (which embraced Reagan Democrats from the South and Southern evangelicals) to the rise of Southern Republicans like Trent Lott (R-MI) in the

Senate and Newt Gingrich (R-GA) in the House. Cliff Schecter, "Extremely Motivated: The Republican Party's March to the Right," *Fordham Urban Law Journal*, vol. 29 (Apr. 2002), 1663.

58 David S. Broder, "The Democrats' Enduring Strength in the South," *Washington Post* (Oct. 19, 1986), H-7.

59 By 1990 political reporters were writing about wedge issues. For example, see David Sarasohn, "The Wedge: New U.S. Political Tool," *The Sunday Oregonian* (July 29, 1990), D-8.

60 Editorial, "Buchanan's Paper Trail," *Boston Globe* (Jan. 12, 1992), 68.

61 William Safire, "Wedges Are the Way the Poll Bounces," *Houston Chronicle* (Sept. 20, 1992), 6. (Safire's *New York Times* Syndicate column ran in newspapers throughout the nation.)

62 A report of this December 3, 2004, conference, and transcripts of the seven panels, representing a wide spectrum of political views and perspectives, including an overview summary of the principal views expressed at the proceedings, are available at http://www.princeton.edu/~csdp/events/polarization .htm. (Report and Transcripts.)

63 Merrell Noden, (Summary) "Princeton University Conference: The Polarization of American Politics: Myth or Reality?" at http://www.princeton .edu/~csdp/events/polarization.htm. (Paraphrased.)

64 Ibid.

65 See Panel II—Trends in Polarization at http://www.princeton.edu/ ~csdp/events/pdfs/Polarizationfinal.pdf.

66 Randall B. Ripley, *Congress: Process and Policy* (New York: W.W. Norton & Company, 1983), 52–53.

67 Report and Transcripts.

68 John R. Hibbing and Elizabeth Theiss-Morse, *Congress as Public Enemy: Public Attitudes Toward American Political Institutions* (New York: Cambridge University Press, 1995), 147.

69 Daryl J. Levinson and Richard H. Pildes, "Separation of Parties, Not Powers," *Harvard Law Review* (June 2006), 2338 and n. 116.

Chapter Two: Second Branch: Broken and in Need of Repair

1 I have focused on the assessments of presidential scholars. But the general public view of Bush's potential place in history also places him toward the bottom. For example, for President's Day the Gallup poll, for the past several years, has been providing the public's ranking of America's greatest presidents

(and comparing it with the academic view). For 2007, Gallup pulled out of the data the rankings of greatest modern-day presidents (meaning they served post-1930), which produced the following:

1. Ronald Reagan
2. John F. Kennedy
3. Bill Clinton
4. Franklin D. Roosevelt
5. Harry Truman
6. Jimmy Carter
7. Dwight Eisenhower
8. George W. Bush
9. Gerald Ford
10. George H. W. Bush (the elder)
11. Richard Nixon

Note: George W. Bush, like Jimmy Carter and Dwight Eisenhower, received votes in the 2 percent range; Gerald Ford and George H. W. Bush (the elder) received votes in the 1 percent range; and Richard Nixon received less than a half percent. On the broader question of who was regarded as the greatest president, not merely those post-1930, Gallup reported: (1) Abraham Lincoln, (2) Ronald Reagan, (3) John F. Kennedy, (4) Bill Clinton, and (5) Franklin D. Roosevelt. By way of comparison, Gallup noted the bipartisan poll of academics who study presidents conducted by the *Wall Street Journal* in 2005 had the following results: (1) George Washington, (2) Abraham Lincoln, and (3) Franklin D. Roosevelt.

2 Thalia Assuras, "Buckley: Bush Not a True Conservative," *CBS News* (July 22, 2006) at http://www.cbsnews.com/stories/2006/07/22/eveningnews/main1826838.shtml.

3 See *The American Conservative* at http://www.amconmag.com/2006/2006_03_27/index1.html.

4 Jeffery Hart, "What Is Left? What Is Right? Does It Matter?" *The American Conservative* (Aug. 28, 2006), 16.

5 Robert S. McElvaine, "Historians vs. George W. Bush," *History News Network* (May 17, 2004) at http://hnn.us/articles/5019.html.

6 Richard Reeves, "Is George Bush the Worst President Ever?" Universal Press Syndicate at http://www.uexpress.com/printable/print.html?uc_full_date=20051202&uc_comic=rr.

7 There is a near endless supply of examples indicating that Bush will not

be viewed kindly by history. His hope, of course, is that he will be viewed well. To support my point, here are a few further samples of current opinion:

- Harold Meyerson, "President of Fabricated Crises," *Washington Post* (Jan. 12, 2005), A-21. ("But when historians look back at the Bush presidency, they're more likely to note that what sets Bush apart is not the crises he managed but the crises he fabricated. The fabricated crisis is the hallmark of the Bush presidency.")
- Susan Page, "Conflict Will Define Bush's Role in History; Even Some of the President's Advisers Say His Legacy Will Be Dominated by the War," *USA Today* (March 14, 2006), 1-A. ("As surely as Franklin Roosevelt is remembered most for his leadership during World War II and Lyndon Johnson for Vietnam, presidential scholars and some of Bush's own advisers predict that history will judge Bush by his decision to order a pre-emptive attack on Iraq on March 19, 2003, and by the long-term consequences of America's first war of the 21st century.")
- Susan Taylor Martin, "A Place in History Can Be Foreign," *St. Petersburg Times* (Aug. 13, 2006), 1-P. ("Bush's legacy may be less lustrous than he had hoped.")
- Kate Zernike, "Bush's Legacy vs. the 2008 Election," *New York Times* (Jan. 14, 2007). ("Like any president, however, he is concerned with how history will judge him. Mr. Bush has frequently likened himself to Harry Truman, an unpopular president when he left office, but one applauded by history. 'To coin a phrase, he's no Harry Truman,' said Robert Dallek, a presidential historian. 'Truman is now seen as a near great president because he put in place the containment doctrine boosted by the Truman Doctrine and the Marshall Plan and NATO, which historians now see as having been at the center of American success in the cold war. If you ask yourself, what is Bush's legacy, what is there?' Mr. Dallek asked. 'What's his larger design to meet the dangers of Islamic terrorism?'")
- David Greenberg, "All Our Favorite Presidents Are Dead," *Los Angeles Times* (Jan. 14, 2007), M-1. ("For many months now, George W. Bush has been speaking about Harry Truman—another president, maligned in his own time, whom history has come to treat more charitably for sticking to his guns in the early years of a long, global conflict. And although this comparison strikes most historians of the Cold War as strained, it's perhaps conceivable that some day Bush's successful steps in the war on terrorism will come to be seen as justifying his wrongs. A more likely

outcome, though, is that he'll follow in the steps of Lyndon Johnson—who also failed to end a degenerating war despite mounting popular discontent. For all his achievements, LBJ has emerged as the only postwar president [besides Nixon] who has failed to benefit from the ratings bounce that death or retirement brings.")

- Peter Beinart, "Cut Your Losses, Save Your Legacy," *Time* (Feb. 12, 2007), 6. ("Bush says he doesn't think about his legacy, but more and more, it's what he seems to think about most. I wish he wouldn't. In theory, thinking about your legacy should be humbling. But in Bush's case, it's making him increasingly reckless. Bush knows that historians will see him through the prism of Iraq: if the war is a failure, so is he. So he's paying any price to win. Were he focused on the present, he might see that the war is already lost. Instead, he's gazing over the horizon, trying to dig himself out of his Iraq hole and making it ever deeper as a result. Bush seems to think that historians smile upon Presidents who never give up, even when the going gets tough. But that's not quite right. Take Bush's hero, Truman, who regularly ranks among the top 10 Presidents of all time. One of the things historians admire about him is his willingness to acknowledge when victory was beyond reach.")

8 Sean Wilentz, "The Worst President in History? One of America's Leading Historians Assesses George W. Bush," *Rolling Stone* at http://www.rolling stone.com/news/coverstory/worst_president_in_history/page/1.

9 Robert P. Watson, "Under the Cold Eye of History," *South Florida Sun-Sentinel* (May 24, 2006), republished by CommonDreams.org, News Center at http://www.commondreams.org/views06/0524-31.htm.

10 Nicholas Von Hoffman, "The Worst President Ever," *The Nation* (Feb. 26, 2007) at http://www.thenation.com/doc/20070226/howl.

11 John W. Dean, "Ranking Presidents—Utter Nonsense or Useful Analysis?" FindLaw (May 11, 2001) at http://writ.news.findlaw.com/dean/20010511.html.

12 It is telling, however, that the judgment of presidential scholars about which presidents are the greatest has remained constant and consistent for many decades—Washington, Lincoln, and FDR—but the other rankings are regularly shuffled and reshuffled, and there has been little consistency of judgment about who should rank at the bottom and why. Wikipedia, the online encyclopedia, maintains summary tables and collections of the better established polls of presidential rankings. See "Historical Ranking of United States Presidents,"

Wikipedia at http://en.wikipedia.org/wiki/Historical_rankings_of_United_States_Presidents.

13 Few details about the second branch were agreed upon at the Constitutional Convention of 1787. Terms like "executive powers" and "commander in chief" were not spelled out, based on the assumption by the Framers that they had designed a system where the branches would check and balance one another, or as Madison famously said, the ambition would counteract ambition—part of the "tension" to which Wilentz refers. Conflicting views of presidential powers surfaced during the first presidency, when George Washington exercised unilateral authority when issuing a neutrality proclamation in 1793 to avoid drawing the nation into the war between Britain and France, and prompting the famous public debate (under noms de plume) between Secretary of the Treasury Alexander Hamilton and Congressman James Madison. (The Pacificus [Hamilton]–Helvidius [Madison] Debate of 1793 occurred when President Washington proclaimed the United States neutral in the war then under way between Britain and France. Hamilton's aggressive and expansive defense of the presidency alarmed Secretary of State Thomas Jefferson, who enlisted Madison to respond.) As political scientist Professor Andrew Rudalevige describes it, "[r]educed to its essence, the dispute was—and is—relatively straightforward: is a president limited to the specific powers affirmatively listed in the Constitution or granted in statute, or can he take whatever actions he deems in the public interest so long as those actions are not actually prohibited by the Constitution?" (Andrew Rudalevige, "The Contemporary Presidency: The Decline and Resurgence and Decline (and Resurgence?) of Congress: Charting a New Imperial Presidency," *Presidential Studies Quarterly* [Sept. 2006], 506.) This debate has recurred throughout our history. Professor Rudalevige quotes the classic examples of the differences, what might be described as the progressive/liberal versus the conservative position: "Theodore Roosevelt's iteration of Hamilton's position put it clearly: 'My belief was that it was not only [the president's] right but his duty to do anything that the needs of the Nation required unless such action was forbidden by the Constitution or by the laws.' Roosevelt's handpicked successor, William Howard Taft, clarified the opposing view. 'The President can exercise no power which cannot be fairly and reasonably traced to some specific grant of power or justly implied within such express grant as proper and necessary to its exercise,' Taft wrote. 'There is no undefined residuum of power which he can exercise because it seems to him to be in the public interest.'" The arrival and domination of authoritarian conservatism within the Republican ranks has resulted in a reversal of positions. Former president and chief justice Howard

Taft (not to mention his son Senator Robert A. Taft) would ask Dick Cheney how he can call himself a conservative.

14 Jeffrey Goldberg, "Breaking Ranks: What Turned Brent Scowcroft Against the Bush Administration?" *The New Yorker* (Oct. 31, 2005) at http://www.newyorker.com/archive/2005/10/31/051031fa_fact2?printable=true.

15 Daniel Wagner, "A Healthy Debate for Cheney, Rangel," *Newsday* (Oct. 4, 2005), A-9.

16 In *Worse Than Watergate*, I wrote about the secrecy that has shrouded Cheney's health. One of the reasons I believed this information important is that there are medical reports of personality changes of persons who have had quadruple heart bypasses and multiple heart attacks, as has Cheney. I could not find sufficient evidence to reach any conclusions. Cheney biographers Lou Dubose and Jake Bernstein have raised the same problem in *Vice: Dick Cheney and the Hijacking of the American Presidency* (2006) when they observed, "The possibility that Cheney's health problems and the medications his doctors prescribed for them affect his mental state is real. Yet the vice president has never released his full medical records for public review. Nor will he give the media the precise list of medications he takes."

17 In *Conservatives Without Conscience* (pp. 159–60), I wrote:

An examination of Cheney's career reveals that it is marked by upward mobility and downward performance. For example, the best thing Cheney did for Halliburton as chairman and CEO was to step down and help them get no-bid contracts to rebuild Iraq and federal help with their asbestos claims liability; Cheney's attempt to run for president failed at the conception stage; he was undistinguished as Secretary of Defense, and many believe he was actually disappointed when the cold war ended on his watch, and not by his doing; his years in Congress have left a voting record that any fair-minded person would be ashamed of; and he was way over his head as Ford's chief of staff, which resulted in the remaining Nixon staff's appreciating how good Haldeman had been in the job; and, of course, he helped Ford lose his bid to become an elected president in the race against Jimmy Carter.

Bad judgment is Dick Cheney's trademark. It was not George Bush who came up with the idea of imposing blanket secrecy on the executive branch when he and Cheney took over. It was not George Bush who conceived of the horrible—and in some cases actually evil—policies that typify this authoritarian presidency, such as detaining "enemy combatants" with no due process and contrary to international law. It was not George Bush who had the idea of using torture during interrogations, and removing restraints on the National Security Agency from collecting intelligence on Americans. These were policies developed by Cheney and his staff, and sold to the president, and then imposed on many who subsequently objected to this authoritarian lawlessness. It was Cheney and his mentor, Secretary of Defense Donald Rumsfeld, who convinced Bush to go to war in Iraq, which is proving to be a protracted calamity. As Colin Powell's former top aide, Laurence Wilkinson, rather bluntly puts it: In 2002 Cheney must have believed that Iraq was a spawning ground for terrorists, "otherwise I have to declare him a moron, an idiot or a nefarious bastard." Colonel Wilkinson, it appears, has a rather solid take on the vice president's thinking, for there is no evidence that Cheney believed—or had any basis for such a belief—that Iraq was a spawning ground for terrorism—before we made it into one.

18 The office of the vice president (OVP) received very little consideration at the Constitutional Convention of 1787, and it was not addressed until the end of the proceedings. The Framers used as a model New York's lieutenant governor, as set forth in the New York Constitution of 1777. Just as the lieutenant governor was elected with the governor, so too would the vice president be elected with the president; just as the lieutenant governor filled the governor's office in the event of incapacity to serve or vacancy, so too would the vice president succeed the president; and just as the New York Constitution made the lieutenant governor the presiding officer of the Senate, so too would the Framers of the Constitution make the vice president the president of the Senate. (See Richard Albert, "The Evolving Vice Presidency," *Temple Law Review* [Winter 2005], 811.) For the nation's first 150 years, and until President Truman gave his vice president some responsibilities, the only duty of the vice president was to preside over the Senate and break ties. Vice President John Adams actually did preside, but by the time Thomas Jefferson became vice president during the Adams presidency, he seldom attended Senate sessions. Jefferson established what the norm became for vice presidents, who only showed up for special occasions and to break tie votes. Presidents all but ignored their vice president until Truman became president, for he appreciated the problem. President Franklin Roosevelt never told his vice president of the existence of the Manhattan Project during World War II, yet four months after FDR died in office,

Truman would have to decide to drop the bomb. (See David McCullough, *Truman* [New York: Touchstone Books, 1992], 378–79, 391–95. See also, Albert, "The Evolving Vice Presidency," 384 n. 125.) Truman kept his vice president, Alben Barkley, well informed. Truman, when asking Congress to enact a new national security law, requested and Congress agreed that the vice president should be an ex officio member of the National Security Council, giving the vice president statutory responsibility. President Dwight Eisenhower added to the role of his vice president, promising Richard Nixon he would make it "a real job," which he did by sending Nixon around the world on high-level diplomatic missions. (Albert, "The Evolving Vice Presidency," 384, citing Julie Nixon Eisenhower.) Nixon, on the other hand, gave his vice president, Spiro Agnew, virtually nothing to do.

19 Paul Light, "Vice-Presidential Influence under Rockefeller and Mondale," *Political Science Quarterly*, vol. 98 (Winter 1983–1984), 617–40. (Professor Light established Mondale's actual influence on Carter and the Carter presidency by interviewing the staff of both the Ford and Carter White Houses, and over 80 percent of Carter's believed that Mondale was an influence while only 14 percent of Ford's staff thought Rockefeller had any influence.)

20 Lou Dubose and Jake Bernstein, *Vice: Dick Cheney and the Hijacking of the American Presidency* (New York: Random House, 2006), 136–41.

21 The White House, "Vice President Dick Cheney" at http://www.whitehouse.gov/vicepresident/.

22 Schlesinger's portrayal in *The Imperial Presidency* (1973) was not pretty: "Through a diversity of means—through the mystique of the mandate, through the secrecy system, through executive privilege and impoundment, through political and electronic surveillance in the name of national security, through the use of the White House itself as a base for espionage and sabotage against the political opposition—the imperial Presidency has threatened to become the revolutionary Presidency. In our own times ... an extraordinary attempt has gone forward to transform the Presidency of the Constitution, accountable every day to Congress, the courts and the people, into a plebiscitary Presidency, accountable once every four years at the ballot box." Arthur M. Schlesinger, Jr., *The Imperial Presidency* (New York: Houghton Mifflin Company, 1973), quoting from the book's jacket.

23 Joan Didion, "Cheney—The Fatal Touch," *The New York Review of Books* (Oct. 5, 2006).

24 Dick Cheney, "Vice President's Remarks to the Traveling Press,"

The White House (Dec. 20, 2005) at http://www.whitehouse.gov/news/ releases/2005/12/20051220-9.html.

25 Paul Starobin, "In Cheney's Shadow," *The New York Review of Books* (Nov. 2, 2006) at http://www.nybooks.com/articles/19530. (Joan Didion, in her earlier article "Cheney—The Fatal Touch," had written that David Addington has written this document. Like Didion, I have little doubt that Addington had direct or indirect influence on the congressional report, because he worked for Cheney on the Iran-Contra committee at this time.)

26 Jane Mayer, "The Hidden Power; Letter from Washington," *The New Yorker* (July 3, 2006), 44.

27 The joint committee was created by the House, titled the Select Committee to Investigate Covert Arms Transactions with Iran, which was chaired by Lee H. Hamilton (D-IN) with Dante B. Fascell (D-FL) as vice chairman; the Democratic members were Thomas S. Foley (WA), Peter W. Rodino, Jr. (NJ), Jack Brooks (TX), Louis Stokes (OH), Les Aspin (WI), Edward P. Boland (MA), and Ed Jenkins (GA). Republican members included Dick Cheney, the ranking Republican, and William S. Broomfield (MI), Henry J. Hyde (IL), Jim Courter (NJ), Bill McCollum (FL), and Michael DeWine (OH). The Senate committee was called the Select Committee on Secret Military Assistance to Iran and the Nicaraguan Opposition, and it was chaired by Daniel K. Inouye (D-HI) with vice chair Warren Rudman (R-NH). Democratic senators on the panel were George J. Mitchell (ME), Sam Nunn (GA), Paul S. Sarbanes (MD), Howell T. Heflin (AL), and David L. Boren (OK). Republican senators were James A. McClure (ID), Orrin G. Hatch (UT), William Cohen (ME), and Paul S. Trible, Jr. (VA). It has always been clear to me as I am sure it was to Dick Cheney that "joint committees" are highly ineffective, for they are too large, the staff cannot service the members, and everyone wants part of the action. This, of course, was to the benefit of the Reagan administration, which could have been more embarrassed had the committee been less cumbersome.

28 Editorial, "Trivializing the Iran-Contra Affair," *New York Times* (Nov. 18, 1987), A-34.

29 Congress had enacted, and President Reagan had approved (wrongly in Cheney's view), a series of amendments to appropriations measures that became known as the Boland Amendments (they were introduced by Representative Edward Boland [D-MA]). The amendments were enacted because the majority of Congress did not believe the United States should get bogged down in another situation like Vietnam and they did not believe that the left-leaning and

Communist-supported government of Nicaragua was a threat to the national
interest of the United States.

30 Take, for example, the opening chapter, "The Foreign Affairs Powers
and the Framers' Intentions," where it draws on the Constitution—ignoring
the text—and relies on secondary material like *The Federalist Papers.* When
one checks the sources they cite, however, they do not support the claims they
make. After I found a half dozen such fundamental errors in the sections, I
stopped looking. The example set forth below is typical. I have first stated what
is found in the minority report, followed by my comments.

Minority Report:

In making its case for a preeminent role in foreign affairs, Cheney's minority
report quotes or cites the following Federalist Papers: Nos. 2 through 5, regarding the dangers of foreign wars or invasions; and Nos. 23, 37, 48, 70, 72, and
75. Not one of these essays, however, states or suggests that the president has
a preeminent role in foreign affairs. Nonetheless, the minority report, drawing
on these documents, claims that each branch has a core function for which it
"was supposed to be best suited to perform." "If deliberation was the key word
for designing the legislature, energy, the ability to act, was the central concept
for the Presidency." "The need for an effective foreign policy, it turned out, was
one of the main reasons the country needs an 'energetic government,' according to Alexander Hamilton in Federalist Nos. 22 and 23." "Madison made the
same point in No. 37: 'Energy in government is essential to that security against
external and internal danger, and to that prompt and salutary execution of the
laws which enter into the very definition of good government.' The relevance
of these observations about the government's power is that the Framers saw energy as being primarily an executive branch characteristic." The minority report
closes this section by relying on Alexander Hamilton's assertion in Federalist
No. 70 that "energy in the executive is a leading character in the definition of
good government" and other quotes about the benefits of "energy," such as being "essential to the protection of the community against foreign attacks."

Comment:

The minority report has completely distorted the historical record. The claims
they made based on *The Federalist Papers* make it understandable why the Senate committee's vice chairman, Warren Rudman, called the minority's work "pa-
thetic." (Paul A. Gigot, "GOP Backbench Blowup," *Wall Street Journal* [Nov.
25, 1987], A-1.) Their claims here were distorted when not mendacious. For
example, they quote and cite Hamilton's Federalist Papers Nos. 22 and 23 re-

garding the need for "energetic government." But neither No. 22 nor No. 23 contains the words "energetic government." They have completely mischaracterized the arguments in these essays. The contention that Madison made "the same point in No. 37" is incorrect for two reasons. First, Hamilton does not make the point they claim in Nos. 22 and 23. Second, in No. 37 Madison is only obliquely addressing foreign policy.

The minority report relies heavily on Hamilton's Federalist Paper No. 70, in which he argues for a "single" executive rather than plural or a council, as had been employed in many of the States; it is not an argument for presidential preeminence in foreign policy. Also, it must be noted that Hamilton's view of the presidency was rejected by the Convention, and scholars have warned us all about the dangers of *The Federalist Papers,* particularly Hamilton's. "I want to admonish you not to cite the explanation given in the Federalist Papers," says Robert A. Dahl, Sterling Professor Emeritus of Political Science at Yale University and past president of the American Political Science Association. "These were very far from critical, objective analyses of the constitution," he warns. In fact, he says they are "propaganda ... written post hoc by partisans.... [T]hey render the work of the Convention more coherent, rational, and compelling than it really was. Ironically, by the way, the task of explaining and defending the Framers' design for the presidency was assigned to Hamilton, who had somewhat injudiciously remarked in the Convention that as the executive, 'The English model was the only good one on this subject,' because 'the hereditary interest of the king was so interwoven with that of the nation ... and at the same time was both sufficiently independent and sufficiently controuled [sic], to answer the purpose.' He then proposed that the executive and one branch of the legislature 'hold their places for life, or at least during good behavior.' Perhaps as a result of these remarks, Hamilton seems to have had only a modest influence in the Convention on that matter or any other." (Robert A. Dahl, *How Democratic Is the American Constitution?* [New Haven, Conn.: Yale University Press, 2001], 63–64.) Conspicuously absent from the minority report are Federalist Papers Nos. 47 through 51, where Madison explained the operations of the "separations of powers" and "checks and balances" of the system. Similarly, they have omitted Hamilton's essays (Nos. 76 and 77) that explained the president's relationship with the Senate regarding selection of ambassadors or ratification of treaties.

31 Louis Fisher, "Exercising Congress's Constitutional Power to End a War," Senate Committee on the Judiciary (Jan. 30, 2007) at http://judiciary.senate.gov/testimony.cfm?id=2504&wit_id=432.

32 Dick Cheney, "The Dark Side: Cheney In His Own Words," *Frontline* (posted June 20, 2006) at http://www.pbs.org/wgbh/pages/frontline/darkside/themes/ownwords.html. Cheney's American Enterprise Institute essay is found in full in Robert A. Goldwin and Robert A. Licht, eds., *Foreign Policy and the Constitution* (Washington, D.C.: American Enterprise Institute, 1990).

33 James Mann, *Rise of the Vulcans: The History of Bush's War Cabinet* (New York: Viking, 2004), 189.

34 Congressional leaders had given the president strong bipartisan support for the use of sanctions against Iraq in response to Saddam's action, with both House and Senate passing resolutions of support, while urging continued efforts to find a diplomatic solution. The Constitution clearly gives Congress the power to declare war, not the commander in chief. President Bush I was inclined to seek a resolution authorizing the use of force should he need to go to war with Saddam, so he "requested his White House Counsel Boyden Gray review the Tonkin Gulf resolution." Historian Gary R. Hess reports that White House counsel Gray provided President Bush a distorted "historical record, making it appear that Johnson had encouraged careful congressional consideration and ignored his pressure to rush the resolution through Congress [before they got the facts straight]." Operating on the information his counsel had provided, Bush was prepared to go the route Johnson had taken with the Gulf of Tonkin Resolution on August 7, 1964, which had passed the Senate with a vote of 88–2, and the House by a vote of 414–0, the last occasion the Congress had authorized a president to go to war. (Adam Clymer, "Congress Acts to Authorize War in Gulf; Margins Are 5 Vote in Senate, 67 in House," *New York Times* [Jan. 13, 1991], A-1.) Bush Senior soon learned, however, that he did not have widespread support on the Hill, it was a Democratic Congress, and many were not certain war was necessary. Others were not sure the Kuwaitis were worth it. For example, former Nixon White House staffer, then New York's Democratic senator, Daniel Patrick Moynihan, who spoke with authority because he had served as the United States chief delegate to the United Nations, did not believe the United States should be concerned about defending Kuwait. "I remember the Kuwaitis as a particularly poisonous adversary of the U.S.," Moynihan told his Senate colleagues, "and their anti-Semitic attitude was at the level of being personally loathsome." (Adam Clymer, "Confrontation in the Gulf; Legislators Take Sides for Combat or for Reliance on the Sanctions," *New York Times* [Jan. 10, 1991], A-1.)

35 Mann, *Rise of the Vulcans*, 188.

36 Gary R. Hess, *Presidential Decisions for War: Korea, Vietnam, and the*

Persian Gulf (Baltimore and London: Johns Hopkins University Press, 2001), 177.

37 Cheney, "The Dark Side."

38 Michael Ross, "Senate Opens Gulf Debate, Warns Bush Not to Overstep His Powers," *Los Angeles Times* (Jan. 5, 1991), A-15.

39 Helen Dewar and Tom Kenworthy, "Canceling Recess, Lawmakers Prepare to Debate War," *Washington Post* (Jan. 4, 1991), A-19.

40 Anonymous, "ACLU, 51 Groups Urge Congress to Deny Bush Power to Start War," *Los Angeles Times* (Jan. 2, 1991), A-12.

41 Sara Fritz and James Gerstenzang, "President Asks Congress to OK War with Iraq," *Los Angeles Times* (Jan. 9, 1991), A-1.

42 Clymer, "Congress Acts to Authorize War in Gulf," A-1.

43 Ibid.

44 Ibid.

45 See, for example, Terry Eastland, *Energy in the Executive: The Case for a Strong President* (New York: Free Press, 1992).

46 Richard Nixon, *RN: The Memoirs of Richard Nixon* (New York: Grosset & Dunlap, 1978), 805.

47 Andrew Rudalevige, *The New Imperial Presidency: Reviewing Presidential Power After Watergate* (Ann Arbor: University of Michigan Press, 2005), 101–2, 138.

48 See, for example, the material found in Gordon S. Jones and John A. Marini, eds., *The Imperial Congress: Crisis in the Separation of Powers* (New York: Pharos Books, 1988), and "The American Congress," *The Public Interest,* vol. 100 (Summer 1990) (the entire issue addresses excessive congressional power from a conservative point of view). Throughout the 1980s, when the House was controlled by Democrats, the GOP mantra accused Congress of being the "imperial" institution, not the Reagan and then Bush I presidency—which, in fact, were doing their best to exercise imperial powers. Charging Congress with "imperial" status was name-calling, not reality. See, for example, William M Leogrande, "Tug of War: How Real Is the Rivalry Between Congress and the President Over Foreign Policy?" *Congress & the Presidency* (Autumn 2002), 113 (this entire issue addresses the balance between the branches, and notes that by 1990 scholars were "questioning whether the Imperial Congress was really all that it was cracked up to be").

49 Rudalevige, The *New Imperial Presidency*, 139.

50 Ibid., 183–84.

51 See, for example, Elizabeth Holtzman and Cynthia L. Cooper, *The*

Impeachment of George W. Bush: A Practical Guide for Concerned Citizens (New York: Nation Books, 2006); David Lindoff and Barbara Olshansky, *The Case for Impeachment: The Legal Argument for Removing President George W. Bush from Office* (New York: Thomas Dune Books, 2006); Anita Miller, ed., *George W. Bush versus the U.S. Constitution: The Downing Street Memos and Deception, Manipulation, Torture, Retribution, and Coverups in the Iraq War and Illegal Domestic Spying* (Chicago: Academy, 2006); and John W. Dean, *Worse Than Watergate: The Secret Presidency of George W. Bush* (New York: Warner, 2005), 154–55.

52 Rudalevige, *The New Imperial Presidency*, 208–9.

53 George Will, "GOP See Bush as Commanding Leader," Cincinatti .com (Oct. 25, 1999) at http://www.cincypost.com/opinion/1999/will102599.html.

54 Moe Richards, "White House Dos and Don'ts," *Wall Street Journal* (Dec. 29, 1992), A-8.

55 Cynthia R. Farina, "Undoing the New Deal Through the New Presidentialism," *Harvard Journal of Law and Public Policy* (Fall 1988), 227.

56 This so-called theory, in fact, was invented by a group of collegial conservative legal scholars. "The crucible in which the unitary executive theory was forged was the Reagan-era Office of Legal Counsel (OLC) at the Justice Department," writes legal reporter Jeffery Rosen in tracing its origins. Steven Calabresi, who served as special assistant to Attorney General Edward Meese before he turned to teaching law, told Rosen, the phrase "unitary executive" was "commonplace around the Justice Department" when he worked there. Calabresi said, "The inspiration for the phrase was Alexander Hamilton's call for 'unity' in the executive." (Jeffrey Rosen, "Bush's Leviathan State," *The New Republic* [July 24, 2006], 8.) Rosen reports, "The initial purpose of the unitary executive theory was to strike a blow at the heart of the regulatory state," the array of administrative and regulatory agencies created by Congress during the New Deal era like the Securities and Exchange Commission, the Federal Trade Commission, the Federal Communications Commission, and later, such bodies as the Environmental Protection Agency. "The idea was that the president needed complete control over the executive branch," Rosen continues, "therefore, he needed the power to fire executive officials—including the independent counsel and the heads of independent agencies like the Securities and Exchange Commission—who didn't share his vision."

57 Beth Nolan, "Statement on Supreme Court nominee Judge Samuel Alito," *U.S. Senate Committee on the Judiciary* (Jan. 12, 2006) at http://judiciary.senate.gov/testimony.cfm?id=1725&wit_id=4905.

58 Edward Kennedy, "Sen. Kennedy Speaks on the Nomination of Samuel Alito," *CQ Transcriptions* (Jan. 19, 2006) at http://www.washingtonpost.com/wp-dyn/content/article/2006/01/19/AR2006011902515.html.

59 Karl Manheim and Allan Ides, "The Unitary Executive," *Legal Studies Paper No. 2006-39, Loyola Law School* (Nov. 2006) at http://ssrn.com/abstract=943046.

60 Ibid. The law journal articles to which I refer include Steven G. Calabresi and Kevin H. Rhodes, "The Structural Constitution: Unitary Executive, Plural Judiciary," *Harvard Law Review*, vol. 105 (1992), 153; Steven G. Calabresi and Saikrishna B. Prakash, "Presidential Power to Execute the Laws," *Yale Law Review*, vol. 104 (1994), 541; Steven G. Calabresi, "Some Normative Arguments for the Unitary Executive," *Arkansas Law Review*, vol. 48 (1995), 23; Steven G. Calabresi and Christopher S. Yoo, "The Unitary Executive During the First Half-Century," *Case Western Reserve Law Review*, vol. 47 (1997), 1451; John Yoo, "Laws as Treaties?: The Constitutionality of Congressional-Executive Agreements," *Michigan Law Review*, vol. 99 (2001), 757; Christopher S. Yoo, Steven G. Calabresi, and Anthony Colangelo, "The Unitary Executive in the Modern Era, 1945–2001," *Vanderbilt Law Review* (2002); Christopher S. Yoo, Steven G. Calabresi, and Anthony Colangelo, "The Unitary Executive in the Modern Era, 1945–2004," *Iowa Law Review*, vol. 90, no. 2 (2005), 601.

61 Louis Fisher, "Lost Constitutional Moorings: Recovering the War Powers," *Indiana University School of Law–Bloomington Journal*, vol. 81 (Fall 2006), 1199, 1234.

62 Herman Schwartz, *Right Wing Justice: The Conservative Campaign to Take Over the Courts* (New York: Nation Books, 2004), 5.

63 Charlie Savage, "Bush Challenges Hundreds of Laws," *Boston Globe* (April 30, 2006) at http://www.boston.com/news/nation/articles/2006/04/30/bush_challenges_hundreds_of_laws/.

64 See Christopher S. Kelley, "A Comparative Look at the Constitutional Signing Statement: The Case of Bush and Clinton," paper presented at the 61st Annual Meeting of the Midwest Political Science Association (April 2003) at http://mpsa.indiana.edu/conf2003papers/1031858822.pdf.

65 Chitra Ragavan, "Cheney's Guy: Barely Known Outside Washington's Corridors of Power, David Addington Is the Most Powerful Man You've Never Heard Of," *U.S. News & World Report* (May 2006) at http://www.usnews.com/usnews/news/articles/060529/29addington.htm.

66 Charlie Savage, "Cheney Aide Is Screening Legislation: Adviser Seeks to Protect Bush Power," *Boston Globe* (May 28, 2006) at http://www.boston

.com/news/nation/washington/articles/2006/05/28/cheney_aide_is_
screening_legislation/.

67 Ms. Green's policing for information on signing statements took her to
the Senate Judiciary Committee's confirmation hearing for former Ken Starr
aide Brett Kavanaugh, who went to work in the Bush White House. During
their informal pre-hearing conversation, Kavanaugh had informed Senator
Charles Schumer (D-NY) that as White House staff secretary he had been involved in signing statements. (Hearings at 6.) The staff secretary at the White
House is like a traffic cop for papers in and out of the Oval Office; he or she
makes certain papers are seen by all appropriate staff, and all those whose input
the president might wish will have given that information to the White House
before a matter is taken to the president. Kavanaugh explained this to Chairman
Specter. (Hearings at 21.) While he received a number of questions, he provided
little new information. As staff secretary, he claimed he was not responsible
for signing statements. See "Confirmation Hearing on Brett Kavanaugh to Be
Circuit Judge for the District of Columbia," Hearings Before the Senate Committee on the Judiciary (May 9, 2006) at http://www.coherentbabble.com/sign-
ingstatements/Congress/SenHrgJudComm050906.pdf.

68 Phillip J. Cooper, "George W. Bush, Edgar Allan Poe, and the Use and
Abuse of Presidential Signing Statements," *Presidential Studies Quarterly* (2005),
515, 522, as cited and quoted in the report of the American Bar Association's
Task Force on Presidential Signing Statements and the Separation of Powers
Doctrine at http://www.abanet.org/op/signingstatements/aba_final_signing_
statements_recommendation-report_7-24-06.pdf (hereafter ABA Task Force
Report).

69 In fact, such advice dates back to President Buchanan in 1860 and to
President Wilson in 1919. "This advice is, we believe, consistent with the views
of the Framers," Dellinger added, citing for his source what many legal scholars
have argued was an errant remark by James Wilson, one of the Framers who later
was appointed to the Supreme Court by President Washington. (James Wilson
told the Pennsylvania ratifying convention that if Congress "transgresses the
bounds assigned to it, and an act may pass, in the usual mode, notwithstanding
that transgression; but when it comes to be discussed before the judges ... it is
their duty to pronounce it void.... In the same manner, the President of the
United States could shield himself, and refuse to carry into effect an act that violates the Constitution." Quoted in "17 Opinions of the Office of Legal Counsel
of the United States Department of Justice" [1993] at http://www.usdoj.gov/
olc/signing.htm.) "Moreover, four sitting Justices of the Supreme Court have

joined in the opinion that the President may resist laws that encroach upon his powers by 'disregard[ing] them when they are unconstitutional.'... (Scalia, joined by O'Connor, Kennedy and Souter, concurring in part and concurring in judgment)," Dellinger added. In a later opinion, and in an informal briefing, Dellinger refined his advice.

By 1994 Dellinger had reflected further on this difficult (and at times complex) question. He repeated his earlier advice that the president "may properly *announce* to Congress and to the public that he will not enforce a provision of an enactment he is signing. If so, then a signing statement that challenges what the President determines to be an unconstitutional encroachment on his power, or that announces the President's unwillingness to enforce (or willingness to litigate) such a provision, can be a valid and reasonable exercise of Presidential authority." (Emphasis in original.) Having found further authority, he added, "The Supreme Court recognized this practice in *INS v. Chadha,* 462 U.S. 919 (1983): the Court stated that 'it is not uncommon for Presidents to approve legislation containing parts which are objectionable on constitutional grounds' and then cited the example of President Franklin Roosevelt's memorandum to Attorney General Jackson, in which he indicated his intention not to implement an unconstitutional provision in a statute that he had just signed." Dellinger observed that "These sources suggest that the President's signing of a bill does not affect his authority to decline to enforce constitutionally objectionable provisions thereof."

And in an effort to give President Clinton guidelines, Dellinger advised: When a law conflicts with the Constitution, a president's oath requires he defer to the Constitution; the president should notify Congress when considering legislation if he thinks it unconstitutional; a president should presume an act of Congress is constitutional and seek to read the law in a manner that avoids a constitutional conflict; "if the President believes that the Court would sustain a particular provision as constitutional, the President should execute the statute, notwithstanding his own beliefs" to the contrary; if the president believes the bill unconstitutional, and he concludes that the Supreme Court would find it unconstitutional, he must make a decision whether to enforce the law—and relevant to that decision "is the likelihood that compliance or noncompliance will permit judicial resolution of the issue," thus "the President may base his decision to comply (or decline to comply) in part on a desire to afford the Supreme Court an opportunity to review the constitutional judgment of the legislative branch." Finally, Dellinger noted that a president has "enhanced responsibility to resist unconstitutional provisions that encroach upon the constitutional powers of the Presidency," and to protect the office of the president. Dellinger's conclusion:

> We do not believe that a President is limited to choosing between vetoing, for example, the Defense Appropriations Act and executing an unconstitutional provision in it. In our view, the President has the authority to sign legislation containing desirable elements while refusing to execute a constitutionally defective provision. We recognize that these issues are difficult ones. When the President's obligation to act in accord with the Constitution appears to be in tension with his duty to execute laws enacted by Congress, questions are raised that go to the heart of our constitutional structure. In these circumstances, a President should proceed with caution and with respect for the obligation that each of the branches shares for the maintenance of constitutional government ("18 Opinions of the Office of Legal Counsel of the United States Department of Justice" [1994] at http://www.usdoj .gov/olc/nonexeut.htm).

For Clinton these hypothetical situations became real when Congress passed the 1996 Defense Authorization Act over his veto with a provision requiring that any members of the armed forces who were HIV positive be discharged—an amendment tagged onto the bill by right-wing California Republican representative Robert Dornan. When signing the law, Clinton issued a signing statement that read "I have concluded that this discriminatory provision is unconstitutional. Specifically, it violates equal protection by requiring the discharge of qualified service members living with HIV who are medically able to serve, without furthering any legitimate governmental purpose.... In accordance with my constitutional determination, the Attorney General will decline to defend this provision. Instead, the Attorney General will inform the House and Senate of this determination so that they may, if they wish, present to the courts their argument that the provision should be sustained." (William Jefferson Clinton, "Statement on Signing the National Defense Authorization Act for Fiscal Year 1996," Public Papers of the Presidents at http://frwebgate2. access.gpo.gov/cgi-bin/wasigate.cgi?WAISdocID=676593281666+1+0+0&W AISaction=retrieve.) Before the statement was issued, White House counsel Jack Quinn and assistant attorney general Walter Dellinger appeared at the regular morning White House press briefing, where they explained what the president intended to do, and in the early afternoon they held a special press

briefing. In the morning Q & A it came out that the Dornan Amendment affected about a thousand men and women in the armed services who were HIV
positive, and that the Justice Department anticipated that a lawsuit would be
filed almost immediately—which the government would not defend. In addition, it was explained that to implement the signing statement the president was
issuing an executive order to instruct the executive branch on how to deal with
this offensive provision. (Transcript, "White House Regular Daily News Briefing," FDCHeMedia, Inc. [Feb. 9, 1996].) In the special briefing reporter Helen
Thomas asked if the secretary of defense had been instructed not to enforce
the law. According to the White House transcript both Quinn and Dellinger
explained that the president was not flatly refusing enforcement, but that the
situation was a bit more nuanced:

> MR. QUINN: There are ample reasons why we're not in a position to
> direct the secretary of defense not to enforce it. What it boils down to,
> frankly, is that we don't have the benefit of a prior judicial determination
> to the effect that this provision is unconstitutional, and in circumstances
> where you don't have the benefit of such a prior judicial holding, it's ap-
> propriate and necessary to enforce it, among other things, by setting in
> motion enforcement of this policy. That is how we will get a case mov-
> ing, the ultimate result of which, of course, we believe firmly, will be for
> the courts to strike this down as unconstitutional....
>
> MR. DELLINGER: Let me add one point to that, Ms. Thomas. When
> the president's obligation to execute laws enacted by Congress is in tension
> with his responsibility to act in accordance to the Constitution, questions
> arise that really go to the very heart of the system, and *the president can
> decline to comply with the law, in our view, only where there is a judgment
> that the Supreme Court has resolved the issue.* And here, the courts have not
> had an opportunity to resolve it; and the action the president is taking, if
> the leadership of the House and Senate chooses to defend this provision,
> will ensure that the courts are presented with a full range of arguments in
> making their determination. [Emphasis added.]

Congress eventually backed down, repealing the Dornan Amendment before it could even be challenged in court. Clinton's actions were, in my view,
a responsible exercise of presidential power. What are we to make of Bush's
avalanche of signing statements, about which the public, the Congress, and the
courts remain largely in the dark?

70 The follow members served on the ABA Task Force: Neal R. Sonnett, a Miami criminal lawyer, chaired; William S. Sessions, a former director of the Federal Bureau of Investigation, chief U.S. district court judge for the Western District of Texas, U.S. Attorney for the Western District of Texas, and chief of the Government Operations Section of the U.S. Department of Justice; Patricia M. Wald, a former chief judge of the U.S. Court of Appeals for the District of Columbia Circuit and an assistant attorney general for legislative affairs in the Carter Administration; former representative Mickey Edwards, a lecturer at Princeton University's Woodrow Wilson School of Public and International Affairs and director of the Aspen Institute–Rodel Fellowships in Public Leadership, served in the House Republican Leadership as a member of Congress from 1977 to 1992, was a founding trustee of the Heritage Foundation, former national chair of the American Conservative Union, and director of the policy advisory task force for the Reagan presidential campaign; Bruce Fein, a constitutional lawyer and international consultant with The Lichfield Group, was associate deputy attorney general and assistant director of the Office of Legal Policy of the Department of Justice under President Reagan, once an adjunct scholar with the American Enterprise Institute and a resident scholar at the Heritage Foundation; dean and professor Harold Hongju Koh, a former assistant secretary of state, advised former secretary of state Madeleine K. Albright on U.S. policy on democracy, human rights, and the rule of law, and also served as an attorney in the Office of Legal Counsel of the Department of Justice; Charles Ogletree, the Harvard Law School Jesse Climenko Professor of Law, and founding and executive director of the Charles Hamilton Houston Institute for Race and Justice; professor Stephen A. Saltzburg of George Washington University Law School, a former associate independent counsel in the Iran-Contra investigation and deputy assistant attorney general in the Criminal Division of the U. S. Department of Justice; professor Kathleen M. Sullivan of Stanford Law School, a former dean of the school, heads Stanford's Constitutional Law Center, has taught at Harvard and University of Southern California law schools, and is a visiting scholar at the National Constitution Center; Mark Agrast, a senior fellow at the Center for American Progress in Washington, D.C., formerly served as counsel and legislative director to Rep. William D. Delahunt (D-MA) and aide to Rep. Gerry E. Studds (D-MA); Tom Susman, a partner in a Washington, D.C., law firm, has served as general counsel to the U.S. Senate Judiciary Committee and several of its subcommittees, and in the Office of Legal Counsel of the U.S. Department of Justice; Alan Rothstein

serves as adviser to the task force and is general counsel to the Association of the Bar of the City of New York.

Signing statements have been examined by Phillip J. Cooper, a professor of public administration at Portland State University, who has written widely, including *By Order of the President: The Use and Abuse of Executive Direct Action* (2002) (http://web.pdx.edu/~pcooper/); Christopher S. Kelley, an assistant professor of political science at Miami University in Ohio, who was very timely in selecting signing statements as the topic for his Ph.D. dissertation (http://www.users.muohio.edu/kelleycs/); and Neil Kinkopf, an associate professor of law at Georgia State University College of Law, who has extensive Washington experience and study of signing statements (http://law.gsu.edu/directory/view.php?id=35). The study drew heavily from the Opinions of the Attorneys General (see U.S. Department of Justice, Office of Legal Counsel, Memoranda and Opinions at http://www.usdoj.gov/olc/opinionspage.htm).

71 Examples of signing statements examined by the ABA Task Force in which President Bush stated he would not follow the law provide a good cross section of the issues involved:

> bills banning the use of U.S. troops in combat against rebels in Colombia; bills requiring reports to Congress when money from regular appropriations is diverted to secret operations; two bills forbidding the use in military intelligence of materials "not lawfully collected" in violation of the Fourth Amendment; a post–Abu Ghraib bill mandating new regulations for military prisons in which military lawyers were permitted to advise commanders on the legality of certain kinds of treatment even if the Department of Justice lawyers did not agree; bills requiring the retraining of prison guards in humane treatment under the Geneva Conventions, requiring background checks for civilian contractors in Iraq and banning contractors from performing security, law enforcement, intelligence, and criminal justice functions.

In addition, the ABA included in its discussion Bush's statements that he would refuse to honor the requirement in the USA Patriot Act to report to Congress regarding secret searches of homes or the seizing of private papers; his refusal to honor Senator John McCain's amendment that forbids any U.S. official from using torture or cruel, inhumane, or degrading treatment of prisoners; his insistence that the requirement of the Intelligence Authorization Act of

2002 requiring regular reports to Congress would be treated as "advisory" only, and he would construe the law "in a manner consistent with the President's constitutional authority to withhold information, the disclosure of which could impair foreign relations, the national security, the deliberative processes of the Executive or the performance of the Executive's constitutional duties." (See ABA Task Force Report cited in note 68.) There is also the remarkable signing statement in which Bush objects to Congress passing a law requiring that the attorney general report to Congress when a law is not being enforced because the president believes it to be unconstitutional. (See 28 U.S.C. § 530D Report on enforcement of law.)

72 Charlie Savage, "House Panel Probing Bush's Record on Signing Statements," *Boston Globe* (Feb. 1, 2007) at http://www.boston.com/news/nation/washington/articles/2007/02/01/house_panel_probing_bushs_record_on_signing_statements/?rss_id=Boston+Globe+--+National+News.

73 Laurence Tribe, "On the ABA Signing Statements Report," Balkinization (Aug. 6, 2006) at http://balkin.blogspot.com/2006/08/larry-tribe-on-aba-signing-statements.html.

74 Joyce A. Green, "Are Signing Statements the Whole Paper Trail of the Expanding and Advancing Unitary Executive Theory?" Frequently Asked Questions at http://www.coherentbabble.com/signingstatements/FAQs.htm.

75 See Paul 't Hart, *Groupthink in Government: A Study of Small Groups and Policy Failure* (Baltimore, Md.: Johns Hopkins University Press, 1990).

Chapter Three: Third Branch: Toward the Breaking Point

1 Alliance for Justice, a Washington-based organization with offices throughout the country, brings together "environmental, civil rights, mental health, women's, children's, and consumer advocacy organizations" with the aim of advancing "the cause of justice for all Americans, strengthening the public interest community's ability to influence public policy, and fostering the next generation of advocates." One of AFJ's overriding goals is to keep our federal courts fair and independent. See Alliance for Justice (AFJ) mission statement at http://www.afj.org/about_AFJ/index.html. Quotation from AFJ's Frequently Asked Questions at http://www.allianceforjustice.org/judicial/about/frequently.html.

2 Jeffery M. Shaman, *Constitutional Interpretation* (Westport, CT: Greenwood Press, 2000), xiv.

3 Ibid., xiv–xv (citing from Holmes's classic *The Common Law*).

4 Ibid., xiv. (Quotation from *U.S. v. Butler,* 297 U.S. 62-63 [1936]).

5 Ibid.

6 Martin Garbus, *Courting Disaster: The Supreme Court and the Unmaking of American Law* (New York: Times Books, 2002), 10–11. (Garbus also quotes Chief Justice Hughes on his blog at HuffingtonPost.com.)

7 Cass R. Sunstein, *Radicals in Robes: Why Extreme Right-Wing Courts Are Wrong for America* (New York: Basic Books, 2005), xi–xiv.

8 Ibid., xiv–xv.

9 Stephen E. Ambrose, *Nixon: The Triumph of a Politician—1962–1972* (New York: Touchstone, 1989), 159. Ambrose writes, "By 1968 [referring to the 1968 presidential campaign], Nixon had become almost as critical of the Warren Court as he was of the Johnson Administration. He was promising, as President, to appoint judges who would reverse some of the basic decisions of the past fifteen years."

10 Henry J. Abraham, a leading scholar on the history of U.S. Supreme Court nominations and confirmation proceedings, has written a definitive work on the Supreme Court. See Henry J. Abraham, *Justices, Presidents, and Senators: A History of the U.S. Supreme Court Appointments from Washington to Clinton* (Lanham, Md: Rowman & Littlefield, 1999). Paraphrasing and quoting from this work (unless otherwise indicated), the following history emerges, which confirms my own observations that Presidents Ford and Clinton looked for the most qualified candidates with centrist legal philosophies, for neither wanted unnecessary political fights over their selections.

President Ford's attorney general, Edward Levi, and White House counsel Phillip Buchen developed two lists for Ford when William O. Douglas announced his retirement. The first list included two Republican members of Congress, Senator Robert P. Griffin (R-MI) and Representative Charles E. Wiggins (R-CA), Solicitor General Robert H. Bork, and five sitting judges on the U.S. Circuit Courts of Appeals (Arlin M. Adams, Paul H. Rooney, John P. Stevens, William H. Webster, and J. Clifford Wallace); the second list included several women, with Betty Ford pushing for the selection of the first woman to the Court: Carla A. Hills (Secretary of House and Urban Development), Ruth Bader Ginsburg (a litigator for the ACLU), Shirley Hufstedler (a federal judge on the 9th circuit), Cornelia Kennedy (a federal district court judge in Michigan), Sandra Day O'Connor (GOP leader of the Arizona State Senate), Dorothy Wright Nelson (law professor at UCLA), and Constance Baker Montley (a federal district court judge in New York). It was clear from Ford's lists that political affiliation was not one of his criteria. The lists, largely under the influence of Levi and Buchen, were winnowed down to John Paul Stevens and Arlin M. Adams, and after reading all their written opinions, they recommended Stevens—first in his undergraduate class at the University of Chicago and first in his class at Northwestern University Law School—as the name they favored, and Ford agreed.

As the attorney general of Arkansas, Bill Clinton testified against former solicitor general Bork's nomination to the Supreme Court. When campaigning for the presidency in 1992, Clinton criticized both Reagan and Bush I's politicalization of the federal judiciary. "For the past 12 years, Presidents Reagan and Bush have pursued a single-minded effort to remake the federal judiciary by selecting judges who shared their restricive views of constitutional rights," he told the American Bar Association. "Mr. Reagan and Mr. Bush have had a profound, and negative, impact on the federal judiciary. If elected, I would strive to bring the federal courts back toward their traditional role as guardians of constitutional rights." Candidate Clinton also felt that because of Reagan and Bush's efforts "to move the federal judiciary toward a restrictive view of the Constitution," it had "on occasion delayed the confirmation process because of serious reservations about the nominees chosen," a clear reference to the highly contentious and divisive nominations of ultraconservatives Robert Bork, who was rejected by the Senate, and Clarence Thomas, who squeaked through. (Anonymous, "Bush v. Clinton: The Candidates on Legal Issues," *American Bar Association Journal* [Oct. 1992], 57; see also Abraham, *Justices, Presidents, and Senators*, 316–17.)

In March 1993, Justice Byron "Whizzer" White announced his retirement after thirty-one years on the Court, giving Clinton his first appointment. Clinton instructed his White House counsel Bernard Nussbaum to prepare a list of candidates, and directed Nussbaum to use his 1987 testimony opposing the Bork nomination as his criteria. Abraham reports Clinton stated during his testimony opposing Robert Bork: "During my public career, I have tried to bridge the gap of race, philosophy, and party to work on an agenda of unity that will take us into the 21st century.... We cannot afford to spend the next 25 years fighting the battles of the last 25.... I would appoint to the federal bench only men and women of unquestioned intellect, judicial temperament, broad experience.... I believe that public confidence in our federal judiciary is furthered by the presence of more women lawyers and more minority lawyers on the bench, and the judicial system and the country benefit from having judges who are ex-

cellent lawyers with diverse experience." To which Clinton did add he wanted a
"pro-choice" nominee, and a person "with a big heart and political experience"
rather than selecting the type of legal technicians that Reagan and Bush had
chosen by focusing on sitting judges.

White House counsel Nussbaum developed a list of forty-two possible candidates. Clinton's first choice was New York governor Mario Cuomo, but he
declined. Clinton then narrowed Nussbaum's list to three candidates: Bruce
Babbitt, the former attorney general and later governor of Arizona, who was
serving as Clinton's secretary of the interior; Judge Stephen G. Breyer, who
Carter had appointed to the First Circuit Court of Appeals, and Judge Ruth
Bader Ginsburg, a Carter appointee to the District of Columbia Circuit Court
of Appeals. Clinton says he met with both Babbitt and Breyer. He decided he
did not want to lose Babbitt from his cabinet, and Breyer had a minor "nanny"
problem (an illegal alien who cared for his children, for whom social security
had not been deducted; a similar situation had resulted in Zoë Baird—Clinton's
initial selection to be attorney general—withdrawing herself from consideration). In his memoir, Clinton explains his decision: "Like everything else that
happened in the White House in the early months, my interviews with both
men leaked, so I decided to see Ginsburg in my private office in the residence
of the White House on a Sunday night. I was tremendously impressed with
her. I thought that she had the potential to become a great justice, and that, at
the least, she could do the three things I felt a new justice needed to do on the
Rehnquist Court, which was closely divided between moderates and conservatives: decide cases on the merits, not on ideology or the identities of the parties;
work with the conservative Republican justices to reach consensus when possible; and stand up to them when necessary." Clinton says he was particularly
impressed with what she had written in one of her articles: "The greatest figures
of the American judiciary have been independent thinking individuals with
open but not empty minds; individuals willing to listen and to learn. They have
exhibited a readiness to reexamine their own premises, liberal or conservative, as
thoroughly as those of others." When Justice Harry Blackmun retired in 1994,
after twenty-four years on the Supreme Court, Clinton was again turned down
by his first choice, Senator George Mitchell (D-ME), majority leader and a
former federal district court judge, who had announced his retirement from the
Senate. Clinton seriously considered his friend Richard Arnold, widely considered one of the best minds in the federal judiciary as Circuit Court of Appeals
judge, but his earlier bout with cancer, which he had beaten, was a problem.
Clinton says, "I probably would have appointed him, except for the fact that

he had been treated for cancer and his prognosis was not clear. My Republican predecessors had filled the federal courts with young conservatives who would be around a long time, and I didn't want to risk giving them another position," so he passed on Judge Arnold and selected Judge Stephen Breyer, with whom he had been impressed in their earlier meeting (and who had resolved his minor nanny problem).

11 The Southern strategy was a soft racist appeal to white Southern Democrats to split their ticket and vote for him. Nixon was too smart to be a racist and too savvy to play the race card in the South, knowing it would reverberate nationally. Instead, he said often when speaking in the South that he was opposed to racial segregation and that he supported civil rights laws. But he also used coded speech, where he made clear he was for "states' rights" and did not believe Washington should "dictate" to the South. Nixon figured out how to have it both ways: to not have northern liberals attacking him, while Southern conservatives accepted what he said but did not believe he was talking to them, rather that he was talking to those Northern liberals. Nixon biographer Stephen Ambrose noted how it worked, quoting a typical southerner from Atlanta: "This fellow [George Romney, who had been lecturing southerners about civil rights] really means it. Dick Nixon comes down South and talks hard on civil rights, but you know he has to say what he does, for the Northern press." (Ambrose, *Nixon*, 89.) Ambrose, who had spent a lot of years in the South and understood it, felt that "Nixon's appeal to the South was not based on racism. Southerners liked him for his general conservatism, for his denunciation of crime in the streets and of riots (which his critics said was a code for racism), for his outspoken patriotism, and most of all for his insistence on victory in Vietnam." (Ibid., 90.) Nixon discovered, as other conservatives did later, a rhetorical means to have it both ways, and when in office, how to give Southern racists just enough of what they wanted that they felt they were better off voting for him. (Reagan would deal in a similar fashion with the religious right.) Nixon's most repeated promise to southerners had been to appoint an attorney general who would given them "law and order," and to nominate justices to the Supreme Court who were "strict constructionist" (a term that Reagan, Bush I, and Bush II would use in their presidential campaigns). Since no one knew exactly what a strict constructionist was, the White House sent an inquiry to the assistant attorney general in charge of the Office of Legal Counsel at the Justice Department, William Rehnquist. He sent back a report indicating that a "strict constructionist" was a judge who liked prosecutors and disliked criminal defendants, and favored civil rights defendants over plaintiffs. Rehnquist's

explanation was not exactly something any president dare say, however. But it was an accurate description.

12 Broadly viewed, the federal judiciary consists of courts, judges, and justices, all who have been created by acts of Congress under both Articles I and III of the Constitution, to wit: the U.S. Supreme Court (with 9 justices), thirteen circuit courts of appeal (with 179 judges), ninety-four district courts (with 661 judges, including 10 temporary judgeships), bankruptcy courts (whose judges are appointed by circuit court judges), territorial courts (with 4 judges), the court of federal claims (with 16 judges), the court of international trade (with 9 judges), the tax court (with 19 judges), and courts of appeal for veterans claims (with 7 judges). During his two terms in office, Ronald Reagan appointed 3 Supreme Court justices, 82 circuit court judges, and 293 district court judges for a total of 378—most all of them rock-ribbed conservatives. No modern president (beginning with FDR) has selected as many federal judges as Reagan. (By way of comparison, the total judges and justices of his predecessors and successors are: FDR—198, Truman—133, Eisenhower—177, Kennedy—124, Johnson—168, Nixon—228, Ford—65, Carter—258, Bush I—66, Clinton—373, Bush II [as of March 2007]—266). David M. O'Brien, "Federal Judgeships in Retrospect," in W. Elliot Brownlee and Hugh Davis Graham, *The Reagan Presidency: Pragmatic Conservatism and Its Legacies* (Lawrence: University Press of Kansas, 2003), 328, Table 14.1 (which I have updated for presidents after Reagan. See Alliance for Justice, Judicial Selection Data Base, Federal Judiciary by President at http://www.afj.org/judicial/judicial_selection_resources/selection_database/byCourtAndAppPres.asp). Since the number of judgeships continues to grow, equally telling is Reagan's comparative percentage. University of Virginia professor David M. O'Brien, who specializes in judicial politics, reports that no Republican president, other than Eisenhower, "filled a greater percentage of the federal bench" since FDR than Reagan. Professor O'Brien notes, "even the [Reagan] administration's critics agree that Reagan's judicial appointees had a profound impact on the composition of the federal judiciary with major consequences for the direction of the federal courts." (O'Brien, "Federal Judgeships in Retrospect," in Brownlee and Graham, 327.)

Sheldon Goldman, a professor of political science at the University of Massachusetts at Amherst, has examined the judicial selection process below the Supreme Court from Franklin Roosevelt through Ronald Reagan in *Picking Federal Judges: Lower Court Selection from Roosevelt through Reagan* (1997). He entitles his lengthy chapter on Reagan's selections as "Reorganizing the Judiciary," which is a scholarly way to describe how Reagan turned the federal judiciary upside down (or as they viewed it, right side up). Reagan's influence on the judiciary has been described as the flip side of FDR's, who turned it to the left during his four terms in office, but close examination reveals there is a significant difference: There was wide diversity of views among FDR's appointees while Reagan's selections were single-minded conservatives. Professor O'Brien say that Reagan perfected the "Republican ideological judicial selection" process that was "inspired" by Richard Nixon. (O'Brien, "Federal Judgeships in Retrospect," in Brownlee and Graham, 330.)

13 Lou Cannon, *President Reagan: The Role of a Lifetime* (New York: Public Affairs, 1991), 722.

14 According to Henry J. Abraham's account, this search occurred a few notches above the Office of Legal Policy with Attorney General Smith, White House counselor Meese, and Deputy Secretary of State William P. Clark, a close friend of Reagan's whom he had placed on the California Supreme Court, running the search for Supreme Court candidates. From an initial list of twenty-five candidates, roughly half of them women, the list was further winnowed to five candidates: Arizona Court of Appeals judge Sandra Day O'Connor, U.S. Court of Appeals judge Cornelia Kennedy, and three men: Dallin H. Oaks, a judge on the Utah Supreme Court and former president of Brigham Young University; J. Clifford Wallace, a judge on the U.S. Court of Appeals for the Ninth Circuit; and Robert H. Bork, former U.S. solicitor general in Nixon's Justice Department and a law professor at Yale School of Law. On paper, all were solid conservatives. (Abraham, *Justices, Presidents, and Senators*, 283–85; Cannon, *President Reagan*, 722–23.)

15 Ibid.

16 Abraham, *Justices, Presidents, and Senators*, 283–85.

17 I asked Pulitzer Prize–winning historian and Madison biographer Garry Wills if Eastland's point was legitimate. Wills said it was not.

E-mail question to Garry Wills:
Per chance do you know what the expression used by Madison in Federalist No. 47 referring to judges as "shoots of the executive stock" means? Here it is in fuller context, and No. 47 is attached should you want it handy: "The judges can exercise no executive prerogative, though <u>they are shoots from the executive stock</u>; nor any legislative function, though they may be advised with by the legislative councils." I assume given his use of the word "stock" with "shoots" that it is a botanical reference, as with a plant used for cuttings. Not that this helps me understand Madison's use of the expression. I am reading Terry Eastland's

"Energy in the Executive: The Case for the Strong Presidency" (1992) in which he uses this phrase repeatedly—out of context and without citation—to ratchet up presidential powers ever so small a notch by just tossing it into the mix. I read the phrase as nothing more than a rhetorical flourish. But I was curious, and you were the only living American I could think of who just might know, not to mention an esteemed historian and student of historical speech that I might cite on or off the record.

His response:
You've got it. The meaning is to say that the judges are mainly part of the judiciary function, though their appointment is from the executive (the botanical reference). This is clear from the immediately preceding and following denials, that the judges have "<u>no</u> executive prerogative ... nor <u>any</u> legislative function." Two departments eliminated, only one remains—the judiciary. The fact that the executive appoints them (with legislative approval) only makes the general point of this Number, that the separation is not absolute. He says that the separation is to prevent "the accumulation of <u>all</u> powers ... in the <u>same</u> hands." He is answering opponents of the Constitution who note that there is cooperation of the three departments (as there had to be). But the cooperation of the executive and legislative in the appointment of judges is like the cooperation in the nomination and confirmation of the judges <u>to have a separate and independent function</u>. You might dwell on the word "prerogative," which is not always a benign one. By the way, where did the term "at the pleasure of the president" come from? The confirmation and impeachment powers do not give the president a free hand in the Constitution.

18 Terry Eastland, *Energy in the Executive: The Case for the Strong Presidency* (New York: Free Press, 1992), 268–69.

19 Ibid., 239.

20 Ibid., 239–40.

21 Henry J. Abraham, in his comprehensive history of Supreme Court selections, summarized Scalia's credentials: "Even ideological foes were hardpressed to challenge Scalia's demonstrably meritorious credentials. An only child, he was the son of a college professor and a grade and high school teacher, both devout Roman Catholics. By all accounts, devotion to his religious faith and academic pursuits had guided the future justice's youth. A product of New York public schools at the primary level, Scalia was graduated, tied for first in his class from Xavier High School, a Jesuit institution in Manhattan. A former classmate offered the following description of the young Scalia: 'This kid was

a conservative when he was 17 years old. An arch-conservative Catholic. He could have been a member of the Curia. He was the top student in his class. He was brilliant, way above everybody else.' Scalia continued his pattern of academic excellence at Georgetown University, from which he was graduated as valedictorian and summa cum laude. He earned his law degree magna cum laude at Harvard, where he served as "Notes" editor of the law review and as a postgraduate fellow. On leaving Harvard, Scalia began a six-year stint as an associate at [Jones, Day, Reavis & Pogue] a Cleveland law firm. He left the firm to join the law faculty at the University of Virginia and never returned to private practice. Instead, he alternated between government positions: 1971–72, general counsel, White House Office of Telecommunications Policy; 1974–77, assistant attorney general in the Office of Legal Counsel at the Justice Department; and academic appointments at the Georgetown Law Center, the American Enterprise Institute, Stanford Law School, and the University of Chicago Law School. He had been a University of Chicago law professor for five years (and chairman of the ABA's Administrative Law Section from 1981 to 1982) when in 1982 President Reagan nominated him for a seat on the U.S. Court of Appeals for the District of Columbia." (Abraham, *Justices, Presidents, and Senators*, 293–94.)

22 Abraham also discovered that most every press account of Scalia's nomination noted his Italian American heritage. Politicians of Italian descent from the left and right were delighted to embrace the nomination. For example, Senator Peter Domenici (R-NM) called the nomination a "magnificent tribute to Italian Americans," and Congressman Mario Biaggi (D-NY) expressed his "special pride." By the time of the Scalia confirmation hearing the Senate Judiciary Committee was drained from their struggle with Rehnquist, along with his supporters and detractors. No member of the Senate with a significant Italian American population was anxious to attack this son of Italy, regardless of his views. Italian Americans are a potent force in the electorate. For example, Answers.com (based on the *Encyclopedia of American History*) reports the following strongholds: "The most heavily Italian American states are New Jersey (1.5 million, 18.5 percent), Connecticut (653,000, 19.8 percent), and Rhode Island (202,735, about 20 percent). The Italian American population of New York is about 2.7 million, or 14.8 percent; Pennsylvania, 1.4 million or 13 percent; Nevada, 142,658 or 7.3 percent; California, 1.4 million or 4.3 percent; and Massachusetts, 890,000 or 14.5 percent. Other states with significant Italian American populations are Illinois (706,000, 5.8 percent), Florida (1 million, 6.5 percent), Ohio (713,015, 6.7 percent), and Louisiana (360,333, 5.2

percent)." The fact that the states with heavy Italian American populations had Democratic senators made it much easier for Scalia.

23 Ibid., 294.

24 Garbus, *Courting Disaster*, 10.

25 Cited in John W. Dean, *The Rehnquist Choice: The Untold Story of the Nixon Appointment That Redefined the Supreme Court* (New York: Free Press, 2001), 318n. 57–60.

26 Former governor of Massachusetts William Weld served as the assistant attorney general in charge of the Justice Department's criminal division. On March 19, 1988, Weld, along with the deputy attorney general Arnold Burns, resigned over attorney general Ed Meese's improper involvement with a friend's oil business. Meese is the only known attorney general to remain in office after the head of the criminal division had advised the president that his attorney general should be prosecuted and sent to jail. When not prosecuted, Meese would claim he had been "completely vindicated." See Cannon, *President Reagan*, 720.

27 Eastland's account makes it appear that the efforts outside the Senate by interest groups against Bork were unchallenged, and that Bork had no similar operation. Eastland writes about how this campaign against Bork "was largely unopposed" before the hearings and during the hearings there was "no comparable effort on Bork's behalf." (Eastland, *Energy in the Executive*, 248–49.)

28 For example, the media's long failure to challenge conservative misrepresentation of what had transpired during the Bork confirmation process has resulted in claims like those of conservative legal activist Jay Sekulow that the Bork proceedings took place at "a time when the right was not mobilized at all," and Bork himself claiming he had "no groups in my support" has prompted Fairness & Accuracy In Reporting (FAIR) to look down the memory hole to correct the record. FAIR found the public record shows there was wide special-interest support for Bork from groups such as Knights of Columbus, the Fraternal Order of Police, the National Federation of Republican Women, the Southern Baptist Convention Public Affairs Committee, the Coalitions for America, Concerned Women for America, and countless other organizations. Estimates of fund-raising were reported as high as $10 million. See Media Advisory, " 'Borking' History:1987 Supreme Court Fight Often Misremembered," Fairness & Accuracy In Reporting (7/21/05) at http://www.fair.org/index.php?page=2592.

"When the nomination was announced, Bork supporters went to work," Herman Schwartz writes. "Bill Roberts," an experienced campaign strategist, "who had led the successful recall campaign against California Chief Justice Rose Bird in California in 1986 and … a former Reagan campaign manager, was brought in to raise $2.5 million for an advertising campaign, and to target some twelve senators who seemed important," Schwartz reports. In addition, "Jerry Falwell's Moral Majority delivered 22,200 postcards to the Senate Judiciary Committee on Bork's behalf, and senators were continually bombarded with orchestrated pro-Bork mail and phone calls." (Herman Schwartz, *Right Wing Justice: The Conservative Campaign to Take Over the Courts*, [New York: Nation Books, 2004], 87–88.)

29 Eastland, *Energy in the Executive*, 48–49.

30 Ibid., 246–50.

31 Jeffrey A. Segal and Harold J. Spaeth, *The Supreme Court and the Attitudinal Model Revisited* (New York: Cambridge University Press, 2002), 194.

32 Ronald Reagan, "Remarks at a Campaign Rally for Senator James T. Broyhill in Charlotte, North Carolina" (Oct. 28, 1986) at http://www.reagan. utexas.edu/archives/speeches/1986/102886g.htm.

33 Lena Williams, "Blacks Cast Pivotal Ballots in Four Key Senate Races, Data Show," *New York Times* (Nov. 6, 1986), A-33.

34 Schwartz, *Right Wing Justice*, 86-88.

35 Gerald M. Boyd, "Move to Right Seen: Opposition Focusing on Abortion Position and Role in Watergate," *New York Times* (July 2, 1987), A-1.

36 Special to the *New York Times*, "Baker Sees Tough Fight Over Bork but Says He Didn't Oppose Choice," *New York Times* (July 3, 1987), A-9.

37 Eastland, *Energy in the Executive*, 248.

38 Those who voted against Robert Bork included Southern conservative Democrats like John Breaux of Louisiana, Howell Heflin of Alabama, and even conservative stalwarts like John Stennis of Mississippi and John Warner of Virginia. To win confirmation in a Senate that was 55 Democrats to 45 Republicans, Bork needed the votes of Southern conservatives; not only did he not get those votes, he lost moderate Republicans like John Chafee of Rhode Island and Bob Packwood of Washington. (For the vote by the Senate on Judge Bork's nomination to the Supreme Court see *Congressional Record* [Oct. 23, 1987] at http://www.senate.gov/reference/resources/pdf/348_1987.pdf.)

39 Although Reagan and Bush I went about systematically selecting conservatives for these judgeships, Bush II has sought out even more radical conservatives than his predecessors, regularly selecting authoritarian conserva-

tives for the lower federal courts. Bush II has not only given conservatives a majority in many circuits, he has placed radical conservatives in control of the D.C. Circuit and the Fourth Circuit, courts which have the greatest dealings with issues relating to the operations of the federal government. Today, virtually every Republican on the federal bench is a conservative. See the chart of presidential appointees at page 174.

40 Tinsley E. Yarbrough, *David Hackett Souter: Traditional Republican on the Rehnquist Court* (New York: Oxford University Press, 2005), 104.

41 Richard Thornburgh, *Where the Evidence Leads: An Autobiography* (Pittsburgh: University of Pittsburgh Press, 2003); reviewed by J. Mark Alcorn at http://www.bsos.umd.edu/gvpt/lpbr/subpages/reviews/Thornburgh1203.htm.

42 Ibid.

43 Abraham, *Justices, Presidents, and Senators*, 305.

44 David Brock, *Blinded by the Right: The Conscience of an Ex-Conservative* (New York: Crown, 2002), 89.

45 Neil Lewis, "Bar Association Splits on Fitness of Thomas for the Supreme Court," *New York Times* (Aug. 22, 1991), A-1.

46 Eleanor Cutri Smeal, Testimony, "Nomination of Judge Clarence Thomas to Be Associate Justice of the Supreme Court of the United States," Hearings Before the Committee on the Judiciary, United States Senate, 102nd Congress, First Session (September 17 and 19, 1991), 1095–1096.

47 See, for example, cases like *Cross Sound Ferry Services v. ICC*, 934 F.2d 327 (1991), where Thomas dissented, and *Citizens Against Burlington v. Busby*, 938 F.2d 190 (1991). (In *Citizens*, Thomas wrote, "Interestingly enough, birds and deer show no signs of being affected by the noise or exhaust fumes at the Toledo Express Airport, and officials of the Ohio Department of Natural Resources have also seen there some endangered animals, such as the spotted turtle [*Clemmys guttata*]. State officials report that endangered plants, such as the cross-leaved milkwort [*Polygala cruciata*] and twisted yellow-eyed grass [*Xyris torta*], are even thriving right beside the main runways." Today, I am told by a Toledo local, the birds and deer have gone, as have the spotted turtle, cross-leaved milkwort, and twisted yellow-eyed grass. The animals simply left and the plants died.)

48 Leahy pressed Thomas as to whether he had ever discussed or debated *Roe v. Wade* when he was a law student at Yale, or anytime. Thomas dodged and evaded. Finally, Leahy asked, "Have you ever discussed *Roe v. Wade*, other than in this room, in the 17 or 18 years it has been there?" Thomas answered, "Only,

I guess, Senator, in the fact in the most general sense that other individuals express concerns one way or the other, and you listen and you try to be thoughtful. *If you are asking me whether or not I have ever <u>debated</u> the contents of it, that answer to that is no, Senator.*" (Emphasis added.) Thomas's biographer Andrew Peyton Thomas takes the position that his earlier discussions of *Roe,* which are reported in the biography, were not "debates" and Thomas had been "careful to say he had never 'debated' the case—in other words, discussed it with a person of opposing viewpoint." This was a facetious claim, as anyone who read the biography realized. (See Timothy Noah's analysis below.)

49 For example, Timothy Noah of *Slate* lined up the earlier "discussions" and found that they were, in fact, "debates" under the common definition of that word:

> [Thomas] discussed abortion a good deal with [his fellow lawyer in the Missouri attorney general's office] Mike Boicourt, who was working on several cases in which the state was defending statutes restricting the right to an abortion (and he would go on to be the lead counsel in the landmark abortion case *Webster v. Reproductive Health Services,* handed down by the Supreme Court in 1989). Because of his views, Boicourt was "ambivalent" about his work on these cases. Thomas, on the other hand, made it clear that he was anti-abortion. As part of these conversations, Boicourt and Thomas discussed *Roe.* Boicourt said years later that he could not remember what Thomas's views were. (APT) at 165.
>
> Thomas also strongly endorsed a right to life for the unborn, a view which [Reagan assistant attorney General William Bradford] Reynolds shared. The two discussed *Roe v. Wade,* the landmark abortion rights case. Reynolds said, "I know we discussed it. I think that he thought little of *Roe v. Wade.* . . . [F]rom a scholarly standpoint, we were talking about constitutional law, constitutional issues, and Supreme Court decisions. It was clear he didn't think much of it." (APT) at 246.
>
> Thomas limned a similar philosophy in his talks with Armstrong Williams. They discussed *Roe v. Wade,* which both of them opposed. "He would also talk about where the Supreme Court would've erred on some of these decisions," said Williams. "He thought they weren't interpreting the Constitution but trying to make law. And that's not the proper role for a judge." (APT) at 247.

Noah made Andrew Peyton Thomas's claim his "Whopper of the Week," observing, "Surely one can 'debate' an issue even with someone one agrees with. Otherwise your half of the conversation will consist only of saying 'I absolutely agree' over and over again." See Timothy Noah, "Whopper of the Week: Clarence Thomas," *Slate* (Oct. 12, 2001) at http://www.slate.com/id/1008424/.

In fact, contrary to Andrew Peyton Thomas's position, it does not take two to debate, or even an opposing view. The *American Heritage Dictionary* defines debate: (1) To deliberate; consider. (2) To engage in argument by discussing opposing points. (3) To engage in a formal discussion or argument. It is clear that Clarence Thomas did "debate" the matter on several occasions, and even his understanding of the word—based on Senator Leahy's question about whether he had *discussed Roe*—was to use Leahy's term interchangeably with debate.

50 Andrew Peyton Thomas, *Clarence Thomas: A Biography* (San Francisco: Encounter Books, 2001), 376.

51 That Clarence Thomas was untruthful to the Senate Judiciary Committee became fully apparent not long after he took his seat on the Supreme Court. Two months after he arrived at the Court, they agreed to hear a case from Pennsylvania, *Planned Parenthood vs. Casey*, that challenged a newly adopted set of abortion regulations that tightened the restrictions in *Roe* by requiring that pregnant teens obtain the consent of their parents or, if married, that they inform their husband before having an abortion, and wait twenty-four hours before undergoing the procedure. The justice who had no opinion on *Roe* sixty days earlier, and who had many options on how to deal with the case, took the most extreme position by dissenting with Chief Justice Rehnquist and Justice Scalia, who called for overturning *Roe,* with Scalia comparing *Roe* with the infamous pro-slavery ruling in the *Dred Scott* ruling. (505 U.S. 833 [1992]; for the timing of Thomas's action, see David Savage, "Lone Justice," *Los Angeles Times Magazine* [Nov. 1994].) David Savage quotes University of Virginia law professor Pamela S. Karlan: "[Thomas] clearly lied to them (his confirmation committee) about legal issues," adding, "I think he perjured himself about *Roe.*"

52 Segal and Spaeth, *The Supreme Court*, 198.

53 Thomas, *Clarence Thomas*, 428.

54 Transcript, "Hearing of the Senate Judiciary Committee on the Nomination of Clarence Thomas to the Supreme Court" (Oct. 11, 1991), Electronic Text Center, University of Virginia Library at http://etext.lib.virginia.edu/etcbin/toccer-new-yitna?id=UsaThom&images=images/modeng&data=/lv6/workspace/yitna&tag=public&part=24.

55 Dianne Rucinski, "Rush to Judgment? Fast Reaction Polls in the Anita Hill–Clarence Thomas Controversy," *The Public Opinion Quarterly* (Winter 1993), 575–92. More carefully conducted national polls showed opinion had shifted from supporting Thomas's version of the truth to supporting Hill's. What happened? Ms. Rucinski explains that fast reaction polls can affect the response rate, and because the polling organizations are under pressure to get a response, and provide public reaction to breaking news, polling organizations often design "questioning strategies that suppress public ignorance or indecision." Ms. Rucinski notes that news organizations are not interested in "the ambiguity inherent in an event such as the Hill-Thomas dispute." She cautions that there is need for better safeguards when the information will impact such major decisions, for there are "dangers inherent in collecting the information under conditions that threaten its validity." (Ibid.)

56 When writing her account of these events, *Speaking Truth to Power,* some six years after the events, Anita Hill provided the transcript of the questions asked her by Paul Minor, a former FBI polygraph program coordinator, an expert with impeccable credentials. After discussing her charges against Thomas with Minor, the following exchange occurred when she was hooked up to the machine to measure her blood pressure, heart rate, and respiration:

> PAUL MINOR: Have you deliberately lied to me about Clarence Thomas?
>
> ANITA HILL: No.
>
> PAUL MINOR: Are you fabricating the allegations that Clarence Thomas discussed pornographic material with you?
>
> ANITA HILL: No.
>
> PAUL MINOR: Are you lying to me about the various topics that Clarence Thomas mentioned to you regarding specific sexual acts?
>
> ANITA HILL: No.
>
> PAUL MINOR: Are you lying to me about Clarence Thomas making reference to you about the size of his penis?
>
> ANITA HILL: No.

(Anita Hill, *Speaking Truth to Power* [New York: Doubleday, 1997], 223–24.)

57 Edward Lazarus, "John Roberts as the Anti–Robert Bork: How Roberts's Nomination, and Conservatives' Senate Hearings Strategies, Reflect Lessons Learned from the Bork Debacle," FindLaw (Aug. 5, 2005) at http://writ .lp.findlaw.com/lazarus/20050805.html.

58 A breakdown of the Senate vote confirming Chief Justice John Roberts is found at http://www.c-span.org/congress/roberts_senate.asp.

59 See American Bar Association ranks at http://www.abanet.org/scfedjud/ratings/ratings110.pdf.

60 Edward Kennedy, "Sen. Kennedy Speaks On Restoring Rule of Law and Repairing Supreme Court Nomination Process," US Fed News Service (March 29, 2007).

61 Edward M. Kennedy, "Roberts and Alito Misled Us," The Huffington Post at http://www.huffingtonpost.com/sen-edward-m-kennedy-/roberts-and-alito-misled-_b_26095.html.

62 Senator Kennedy provides a number of specific examples. I have summarized one relating to each nominee. Kennedy reports that during the Roberts confirmation hearings, he "asked him about his [earlier] statement that a key part of the Voting Rights Act constitutes one of 'the most intrusive interferences imaginable by federal courts into state and local processes.' In response, he suggested that his words were nothing more than an 'effort to articulate the views of the administration ... for which I worked 23 years ago.'" Yet Kennedy points out that once on the Court, in his first Voting Rights Act case that related to Tom DeLay's shenanigans in redistricting Texas, Roberts (joined by Alito) dissented, stating that the Supreme Court should not be involved in this "sordid business, this divvying us up by race"—which was the view of the administration for which he worked 23 years earlier and from which he had distanced himself. (Edward M. Kennedy, "Roberts and Alito Misled Us," *Washington Post* [July 30, 2006], B-1.) During the Alito hearings, Senator Kennedy asked the nominee about a statement he had written in his 1985 job application to move to the solicitor general's office, stating that he believed "very strongly in the supremacy of the elective branches of government." Kennedy explains that during the hearings, Alito "backpedaled, claiming: 'I certainly didn't mean that literally at the time, and I wouldn't say that today.'" Nonetheless, Kennedy notes Alito joined Justice Clarence Thomas in a dissent claiming a judicial "duty to accept the Executive's judgment in matters of military operations and foreign affairs" regarding the Bush administration's use of military commissions to try detainees at Guantánamo. (Ibid.)

63 Cass R. Sunstein, "The Minimalist," *Los Angeles Times* (May 25, 2006), B-11.

64 Jennifer Barrette, "Q&A: Judge Alito's 'Pattern of Conservatism': How Samuel Alito Could Tilt the Balance in the Supreme Court," *Newsweek* (Nov. 1, 2005) at http://www.msnbc.msn.com/id/9880810/site/newsweek/.

65 Cass R. Sunstein, *Washingtonpost.com* (Nov. 1, 2005).

66 E-mail exchange with the author, May 3, 2007.

67 To appreciate how close we are to a radical change in the federal judiciary, look at the present composition of the Supreme Court as of the summer of 2007. It is currently composed of seven Republican justices and two Democrats. More specifically, in chronological order of their selection (and noting the president who appointed each along with the date of birth of each), the Court consists of the following justices: John Paul Stevens (Ford, born 1920), Antonin Scalia (Reagan, born 1936), Anthony M. Kennedy (Reagan, born 1936), David H. Souter (Bush I, born 1939), Clarence Thomas (Bush I, born 1948), Ruth B. Ginsburg (Clinton, born 1933), Stephen G. Breyer (Clinton, born 1938), John G. Roberts, Jr. (Bush II, born 1955), and Samuel A. Alito, Jr. (Bush II, born 1950). The two oldest members of the Court, Justices Stevens and Ginsburg, are both considered to be "liberals" by conservatives. In fact, there are no true liberals on the current Court; rather, those who are centrists, given the far right thinking of Scalia, Thomas, Alito, and Roberts, are considered liberal. Should Stevens or Ginsburg leave the Court for any reason while Bush II is in office, it would dramatically change the dynamics of the Court. The question is not merely whether the court will have a solid conservative majority; for when Justice Kennedy votes with the Chief Justice and Justices Scalia, Thomas, and Alito, they have a conservative majority, as has become evident with a number of rulings. A rather dramatic shift will come when there is a solid fundamentalist bloc on the Court.

68 Martin Garbus, *The Next 25 Years: The New Supreme Court and What It Means for Americans* (New York: Seven Stories Press, 2007), 207.

69 Ibid., 151–52.

70 Thomas M. Keck, *The Most Activist Supreme Court in History: The Road to Modern Judicial Conservatism* (Chicago: University of Chicago Press, 2004), 2.

71 Garbus, *The Next 25 Years*, 202.

72 Sunstein, *Radicals in Robes*, 229.

73 Ibid., 230.

74 See *The Slaughterhouse Cases*, 83 U.S. 36 (1873).

75 Garbus, *The Next 25 Years*, 68.

76 Sunstein, *Radicals in Robes*, 63–64.

77 *Kansas v. Marsh*, 548 U.S. ____; 126 S. Ct. 2516 (2006).

78 Sunstein, *Radicals in Robes*, 65.

79 *Lawrence v. Texas*, 539 U.S. 558 (2003).

80 Earl M. Maltz, ed., *Rehnquist Justice: Understanding the Court Dynamic* (Lawrence: University Press of Kansas, 2003), 78.

81 *Warth v. Seldin*, 422 U.S. 490, 498 (1975).

82 See *Baker v. Carr*, 369 U.S. 186 (1962), *Westbury v. Sanders* 376 U.S. 1 (1964), and *Reynolds v. Sims* 377 U.S. 533 (1964).

83 Robert H. Bork, *The Tempting of America* (New York: Touchstone, 1990), 89.

84 Mark A. Graber, "Clarence Thomas," in Maltz, ed., *Rehnquist Justice*, 78–79.

85 Sunstein, *Radicals in Robes*, 244–45.

Chapter Four: Repairing Government: Restoring the Proper Processes

1 Pew Research Center, "Democrats Fail to Impress in First 100 Days," (March 29, 2007) at http://people-press.org/reports/display.php3?ReportID= 315.

2 Pew Research Center, "Trends in Political Values and Core Attitudes: 1987–2007" (March 22, 2007) at http://people-press.org/reports/display.php3? ReportID=312.

3 Pew Research Center, "Public Knowledge of Current Affairs Little Changed by News and Information Revolutions" (April 15, 2007) at http:// people-press.org/reports/display.php3?ReportID=319.

4 Calculation based on data from ABC News/*Washington Post* Poll of congressional job approval/disapproval at PollingReport.com.

5 *Newsweek* Poll of Presidential job approval/disapproval at Polling Report.com.

6 See Supreme Court job approval/disapproval at PollingReport.com.

7 See John R. Hibbing and Elizabeth Theiss-Morse Morse, *Congress as Public Enemy: Public Attitudes Toward American Political Institutions* (New York: Cambridge University Press, 1995).

8 Lt. Col. Paul Yingling, "A Failure in Generalship," *Armed Forces Journal* (May 2007) at http://www.armedforcesjournal.com/2007/05/2635198.

9 Hibbing and Theiss-Morse, *Congress as Public Enemy*, 127.

10 Ibid, 130. In Table 7.1—Characteristics of propensity groups— Hibbing and Morse break down the categories into which their 1,433 respondents

fell: persons (143), party (66), policy (359—a number they discovered had been artificially inflated), and process (195). I have converted those numbers to percentages.

11 Ibid.

12 To determine who were the experts within their 1,433 respondents, as opposed to "novices" who have little knowledge about government and politics, Hibbing and Theiss-Morse asked four general knowledge questions: (1) Can you recall who is head of the new Russian republic? (2) Do you happen to recall who is the secretary of state? (3) Who is the secretary of defense? (4) Is the current federal deficit larger or smaller than it was when Ronald Regan first took office in 1991? (Hibbing and Morse state: "At the time of the survey, Boris Yeltsin was head of the Russian Republic, James Baker or Lawrence Eagleburger was secretary of state [President Bush reshuffled his cabinet during the time our survey was being administered], Richard Cheney was secretary of defense, and the budget deficit was larger than when President Reagan took office." Hibbing and Theiss-Morse, *Congress as Public Enemy,* 139.) A correct answer was given a 1 and an incorrect a 0, which resulted in their creating three levels of expertise (or lack thereof): "novices"—those who got none or one correct (32 percent of the respondents); "mid-level"—those who gave two or three correct answers (49 percent of the respondents); and "experts"—those who got all four questions correct (20 percent percent of the respondents). When matching political expertise with propensities, Hibbing and Theiss-Morse discovered more telling traits about those who view public affairs through the lenses of process. "Experts are more than twice as likely as novices to rely on a process propensity (38 percent of experts and 15 percent of novices). In fact, experts are more likely to hold a process propensity than any other propensity." Everyone is to some extent attuned to process, Hibbing and Theiss-Morse note, but "emphasizing process concerns to the point that they become a propensity demands that a person think about a variety of issues: how government works; the interrelationship among government institutions and among the people in them; the competing forces that influence government decision making; and the processes that best allow politicians to do their jobs." It is not surprising, therefore, that the highest number of experts is found among those who view government and politics as process.

13 John R. Hibbing and Elizabeth Theiss-Morse, *Stealth Democracy: Americans Beliefs About How Government Should Work* (New York: Cambridge University Press, 2002), 236.

14 Ibid., 13.

15 Ibid., 236–37.

16 Described slightly differently, the way most Americans see and judge the political processes is by whether there has been "procedural justice" in the process. What is procedural justice? It means that central features of the process are "neutrality, lack of bias, honesty, efforts to be fair, politeness, and respect for citizen's rights," Hibbing and Theiss-Morse state, quoting a leading authority, Tom R. Tyler, researcher and professor of psychology at New York University, as establishing these central features of procedural justice. (Tyler's lab Web page outlines his work and prolific writing. See http://www.psych.nyu.edu/tyler/lab/.) It is not necessary for my purposes to delve into this fascinating research, but a brief word is in order, albeit a gross oversimplification. Procedural justice research commenced in the mid-1970s; it initially was undertaken in the context of litigation and dispute resolution. This research revealed that litigants were satisfied—win or lose—if they perceived the process that they had been through was fair. Later research found the procedural justice concepts relevant and explanatory of other processes as well, expanding its application beyond the legal realm to the political and managerial areas. Although Hibbing and Theiss-Morse did not employ procedural justice testing directly to their work, others have done so, and confirmed their reliance on this standard in their analysis. See Amy Gangl, "Procedural Justice Theory and Evaluations of the Lawmaking Process," *Political Behavior*, vol. 25 (June, 2003), 119–49. In addition, Hibbing and Theiss-Morse advocate a different approach than Tyler for making processes more attractive to people, for they do not find that personal involvement in the political process is a source of satisfaction to most people.

17 Hibbing and Theiss-Morse, *Stealth Democracy*, 237–38.

18 Hibbing and Theiss-Morse, *Congress as Public Enemy*, 15.

19 Ibid.

20 I have not seen the sign, unfortunately. It is quoted and cited in Mark Green, *Losing Our Democracy: How Bush, the Far Right, and Big Business Are Betraying Americans for Power and Profit* (Naperville, IL: Sourcebooks, 2006), 1.

21 Ilya Somin, "When Ignorance Isn't Bliss: How Political Ignorance Threatens Democracy," *Cato Institute Policy Analysis* (Sept. 22, 2004), 2, 4, 5. (Report available online.)

22 Ibid.

23 See "Voter Turnout-Global Survey" (as of March 7, 2005) at http://www.idea.int/vt/survey/voter_turnout_pop2.cfm. For the highest French election turnout, John Ward Anderson and Molly Moore, "Sarkozy Wins, Vows to Restore Pride in France," *Washington Post* (May 7, 2007) at http://www.

washingtonpost.com/wp-dyn/content/article/2007/05/06/AR20070506
00216.html?hpid=topnews.

24 U.S. Census Bureau, "Voting and Registration in the Election of November 2004" (March 2006) at http://www.census.gov/prod/2006pubs/p20
-556.pdf .

25 Studies do establish why other countries have higher voting turnout,
which prompted me to write a column a few years ago suggesting one or more
states try mandatory voting as is done in Australia (and a number of democracies). See John W. Dean, "Is It Time to Consider Mandatory Voting Laws?
Worsening Voting Statistics Make a Strong Case," FindLaw (Feb. 28, 2003) at
http://writ.news.findlaw.com/dean/20030228.html.

26 Hibbing and Theiss-Morse, *Stealth Democracy*, 224–25.

27 Here, in a nutshell, are the rather startling findings that emerged from
Hibbing and Theiss-Morse's fascinating work:

> We show that [a substantial number of] people want to distance them-
> selves from government not because of a system defect but because many
> people are simply averse to political conflict and many others believe po-
> litical conflict is unnecessary and an indication that something is wrong
> with government procedures. People believe that Americans all have the
> same basic goals, and they are consequently turned off by political de-
> bate and deal making that presupposes an absence of consensus. People
> believe that these activities would be unnecessary if decision makers
> were in tune with the (consensual) public interest rather than with the
> cacophonous special interests. Add to this the perceived lack of impor-
> tance of most policies and people tend to view political procedures as a
> complete waste of time. The processes [these] people really want would
> not be provided by the populist reform agenda they often embrace; it
> would be provided by a stealth democratic arrangement in which deci-
> sions are made by neutral decision makers who do not require sustained
> input from the people in order to function.

Ibid., 7.

28 Ibid., 143. ("Thus, for our purposes, stealth democratic tendencies are
indicated if a respondent (1) agreed that 'elected officials would help the country more if they would stop talking and just take action on important problems,' (2) agree that 'what people call compromise in politics is really just selling
out on one's principles,' and (3) agreed either that 'our government would run

better if decisions were left up to non-elected, independent experts rather than politicians or the people' *or* that 'our government would run better if decisions were left up to successful business people.' ") The authors acknowledge these are an imperfect measure, but they are certainly suggestive of a "stealth attitude." Based on responses to their survey: Only 7 percent of the respondents had no inclinations toward such stealth democracy, 24 percent had one trait, 42 percent had two traits, and 27 percent had all three traits. Ibid., 144.

29 E-mail exchange with the author, May 3, 2007.

30 Susan Davis, "Weight of Speaker Post Off Hastert," *Roll Call* (March 8, 2007).

31 Jennifer Yachnin, "TriCaucus Says Staff Diversity Increasing," *Roll Call* (April 12, 2007).

32 Louise M. Slaughter (Rules Committee Chairwoman-Designate), "Summary of House Rules Package Opening Day of the 110th Congress," House Rules Committee at http://www.rules.house.gov/110/text/110_Hres6_secbysec.pdf (hereafter Summary of House Rules).

33 Ibid.

34 Thomas E. Mann, Molly Reynolds, and Peter Hoey, "OpChart: Is Congress on the Mend?" *New York Times* (April 28, 2007), A-27.

35 "[Senator John] McCain became the first Republican presidential contender to urge Gonzales to resign, and the fourth Republican senator to do so, joining Tom Coburn of Oklahoma, Gordon Smith of Oregon and John Sununu of New Hampshire. Several others have stopped short of demanding Gonzales's resignation but have harshly criticized his leadership." Associated Press, "McCain Latest Republican to Call for Gonzales Resignation," *Boston.com* (April 28, 2007) at http://www.boston.com/news/nation/articles/2007/04/26/mccain_latest_republican_to_call_for_gonzales_resignation/.

36 Terry Eastland, *Energy in the Executive: The Case for the Strong Presidency* (New York: Free Press, 1992), 306.

37 Harvey C. Mansfield, "The Case for the Strong Executive," *Wall Street Journal* (May 2, 2007) at http://www.opinionjournal.com/federation/feature/?id=110010014.

38 Louis Fisher, "Invoking Inherent Powers: A Primer," *Presidential Studies Quarterly* (March 2007), 10.

39 Jules Lobel, "The Commander in Chief and the Courts," *Presidential Studies Quarterly* (March 2007), 52.

40 See, for example, Cass R. Sunstein, *Why Societies Need Dissent* (Cambridge, Mass.: Harvard University Press, 2005) and Irving L. Janis, *Groupthink:*

Psychological Studies of Policy Decisions and Fiascoes (New York: Houghton Mifflin Company, 1982).

41 R.S.K. [author identification], "Ignoring Evidence to the Contrary, *USA
Today* editorial asserted 1994 'Contract with America' was 'effective ... in bringing Republicans to power,'" Media Matters (Oct. 20, 2006) at http://media
matters.org/items/200610210001?show=1. (Media Matters reported that "only
a small percentage of voters said they were influenced by the Contract" during
1994 exit polls. A NBC/*Wall Street Journal* poll found some 90 percent of voters
had never heard of the House GOP's Contract with America. Other polls fell in
the same 30 percent knowledge range, and all the major polling organizations
made inquiry. To claim that the Contract had any significant impact on the
1994 elections is not supported by the solid evidence to the contrary.)

42 John W. Dean, "Attorney General Alberto Gonzales's 'Reconfirmation
Hearings': Why, in the End, They Will Change Nothing," FindLaw (April 20,
2007) at http://writ.news.findlaw.com/dean/20070420.html.

43 John W. Dean, *Conservatives Without Conscience* (New York: Viking,
2006), 184.

Appendix A: Separation of Powers

1 Jay M. Shafritz, *American Government & Politics* (New York: Harper
Collins, 1993), 418.

2 See Robert V. Remini, *The House: The History of the House of Representatives* (Washington, D.C.: Smithsonian Books, 2006). (Remini's work was relied
upon for background and thoughts in this material.)

3 Alexander Hamilton, James Madison, and John Jay, *The Federalist Papers*, edited and with an introduction by Garry Wills (New York: Bantam Classic, 1982), 63.

4 Remini, *The House*, 24.

5 Bruce Ackerman, *The Failure of the Founding Fathers: Jefferson, Marshall,
and the Rise of Presidential Democracy* (Cambridge, Mass.: Belknap Press of Harvard University Press, 2005), 12–13.

6 Forrest McDonald, *The American Presidency: An Intellectual History*
(Lawrence: University Press of Kansas, 1994), 218.

7 Samuel Eliot Morison, *The Oxford History of the America People, Volume
Two: 1789 Through Reconstruction* (New York: Meridian, 1994), 34.

8 Daryl J. Levinson and Richard H. Pildes, "Separation of Parties, Not

Powers," *Harvard Law Journal* (June 2006), 2311. (This article can be found online at http://www.harvardlawreview.org/issues/119/june06/levinson_pildes .shtml.)

9 Levinson and Pildes, "Separation of Parties," 2329.

10 To the contrary, in footnoting that "(at least) two," they state: "If we took into account every factor that bears on intragovernmental political competition at least as heavily as branch affiliation, the number of 'systems' might hit double digits"—thus acknowledging that branch affiliation can provide checks and balances. Their other factors beyond unified or divided government can include "the coherence of the two major parties" and "different patterns of party division: House and Senate versus President, House and President versus Senate, and so on." (Levinson and Pildes, "Separation of Parties," 2329 n. 63.)

Appendix B: Republican Appropriations Process Abuses

1 This summary of the federal fiscal process is based on materials prepared by the Congressional Reference Service (CRS), the General Accountability Office (GAO), and personal knowledge. See, e.g., Sandy Streeter, "The Congressional Appropriation Process: An Introduction," *CRS Report for Congress* (Dec. 8, 2006), and Office of the General Counsel, "Principles of Federal Appropriations Law"(Nov. 2006) at http://www.gao.gov/special.pubs/redbook1 .html. (This encyclopedic source is commonly known as "The Red Book," and is written for the general reader. However, a page-turner it is not.)

2 David Baumann, "Why Government by CR Matters," *National Journal* (Nov. 1, 2003), 3345.

3 John W. Dean, *Warren G. Harding* (New York: Times Books, 2004), 105.

4 Lee Lescaze, "Federal Shutdown Ends as Reagan, Hill Agree," *Washington Post* (Nov. 24, 1981), A-1.

5 Streeter, "The Congressional Appropriation Process," 1.

6 David Hoffman and Keith B. Richburg, "President Shuts Down Government," *Washington Post* (Oct. 5, 1984), A-1.

7 In December 1981, Reagan had authorized the CIA to covertly support the Contra rebel movement in Nicaragua, which sought to overthrow the dictatorial Sandinista government with ties to the Soviet Union. President Carter had cut off aid to Nicaragua shortly before leaving office. Congress was divided on the question of support for the Contras, but fear of involving the United

States in another Vietnam, and public opinion polls showing Americans opposing such action, caused support on Capitol Hill to shrink. "Congress prohibited Contra aid for the purpose of overthrowing the Sandinista Government in fiscal year 1983, and limited all aid to the Contras in fiscal year 1984 to $24 million," the "Report of the Congressional Committees Investigating the Iran-Contra Affair" noted. ("Report of the Congressional Committees Investigating the Iran-Contra Affair with Supplemental, Minority, and Additional Views": H. Rept. No. 100-433 and S. Rept. No. 100-216 [Nov. 17, 1987], 3. Hereafter "Joint Committee Iran-Contra Report.") When it became public that the CIA had mined Nicaraguan harbors without informing Congress, which resulted in increased public criticism, Congress clamped down even further. Chairman of the Senate Intelligence Committee, Senator Barry Goldwater (R-AZ), correctly believed that the Reagan administration was lying to Congress, so he refused to back a foreign policy "when we don't even know what is going on." (Ibid.) Accordingly, "Congress exercised its Constitutional power over appropriations and cut off all funds for the Contras' military and paramilitary operations. The statutory provision cutting off funds, known as the Boland Amendment, was part of the fiscal year 1985 omnibus appropriations bill, and was signed into law by the President on October 12, 1984," the Joint Committee Iran-Contra Report explains. The Boland Amendment, which had been offered by Representative Richard Boland (D-MO), in the relevant part stated: "During fiscal year 1985, no funds available to the Central Intelligence Agency, the Department of Defense, or any other agency or entity involved in intelligence activities may be obligated or expended for the purpose or which would have the effect of supporting, directly or indirectly, military or paramilitary operations in Nicaragua by any nation, group, organization, movement, or individual." (Dick Cheney, who was the ranking Republican member of the House Committee in the joint House and Senate investigation of the Iran-Contra affair, claimed that this prohibition did not apply to the President's National Security Council. This reading makes clear why Cheney might have had difficulty with the Law School Aptitude Test.)

Before Reagan signed the bill, however, a desperate effort was made to prevent the Democratic House from cutting off Contra funds and to obtain further appropriations. By the spring of 1984 the $24 million had virtually run out. Many conservatives believed—and none more strongly than Reagan—that supporting the Contras was protecting the free world from the spread of communism. Thus, when the funds ran out, Reagan instructed his national security adviser, Robert McFarlane, to keep the Contras together "body and soul." He wanted support to continue. McFarlane assigned this task to National Security Council staffer Lt. Col. Oliver North, who had been the liaison with the CIA on the support operation. McFarlane and North, in turn, began their "tin cup" diplomacy efforts with foreign nations to get them to underwrite the Contra efforts.

After the House had passed the spending bill with the cutoff of funds and the Boland Amendment, the Reagan White House put on a full-court press with the Republican Senate, and by a vote of 57 to 42 the Senate rejected the House's halt of assistance to the Contra and the Boland Amendment, and while unwilling to give the Administration the money they wanted, the Senate did agree to $6 million in "phase-out" funds for the Contras. (Helen Dewar, "Federal Shutdown Readied as Senate Works on Funding," *Washington Post* [Oct. 4, 1984], A-1.) Clearly, the "phase-out" money did not do the job. It is difficult to believe that the White House did not tell the Senate to keep squeezing the House, so when the legislation went to conference to sort out the difference in the House and Senate version, more money could be added for the Contras, because the White House had convinced the Senate Intelligence Committee to provide $28 million for fiscal year 1985. But GOP Senate leader Howard Baker was unable to complete work on the spending bill, so Reagan announced he would shut down the government—again—rather than sign a continuing resolution. This again looked like a squeeze play on the House. For in doing so, despite the fact it was the Senate that had failed to complete its work, Reagan blamed the Democrats, saying, "You can lay this right on the majority party of the House of Representatives." (David Hoffman and Keith B. Richburg, "President Shuts Down Government," *Washington Post* [Oct. 5, 1984], A-1.) Broadly speaking, that was true. They had cut off funds for the Contras, but given the lack of public support for this cause, Reagan dared not say so.

The shutdown lasted only a half day. Reading between the lines of what was reported at the time, and the information that later surfaced in the Iran-Contra investigations, it is possible to reconstruct what actually occurred during the House-Senate conference. Rather than sign an extended continuing resolution, Reagan signed several very brief continuing resolutions to keep government going, while keeping pressure on the Democrats. Democrats, it appears, figured out what was occurring and refused to buckle by eliminating the Contra fund cutoff, not to mention the $28 million in additional funding for the Contras. Here is how the House Democrats outfoxed the Senate Republicans on this issue. As with all omnibus appropriations bills, this spending package was loaded with pork: $18 billion in earmarks for water projects throughout the country, which had been added by the House. The Senate had rejected these water projects, but they were using them as leverage to get what they (and the Reagan White House) wanted for the Contras. But the House Democrats said they would eliminate all $18 billion of the water projects, even though a number of Republican senators had wanted them as well for their political benefit—the rugs were pulled out from under the Senate. No longer did they have any leverage over the House whatsoever. The *Washington Post* reported, "The agreement on Nicaragua dealt a serious blow to administration hopes for continuation of once-covert aid to the contras. It permits the president, however, if reelected with a strong mandate, to deal from a position of greater strength on the issue next year." (Helen Dewar, "Conferees Approve '85 Funds; 5-Month Ban Voted on Further Aid to Nicaraguan Rebels," *Washington Post* [October 11, 1984], A-1.)

8 Lawrence E. Walsh, *Firewall: The Iran-Contra Conspiracy and Cover-up* (New York: W. W. Norton, 1997), 19.

9 No one took Reagan's 1986 shutdown seriously. "IRS auditors, Justice Department lawyers and Census Bureau statisticians obediently locked up their desks. Guards closed the Washington Monument to tourists. At the White House, the gardeners hung up their rakes. At the State Department, the passport processors turned away lines of people," the *Washington Post* reported on October 18, 1986, about the third Reagan shutdown. (Sharon La Franiere and Peter Perl, "Federal Workers Create Noon Stampede; Most of 350,000 Employes [*sic*] Here Sent Home in Spending Bill Crisis," *Washington Post* [October 18, 1986], B-1.) Federal employees shrugged and went shopping, got haircuts, went to bars, or headed home with no concern because on the two prior occasions Reagan pulled this stunt—November 23, 1981, and October 4, 1984—Congress later paid them for the day off. A House subcommittee on civil service estimated the half day off would cost tax payers $61 million in lost work, but later revised the estimate of what the press called "The Great Government Shutdown of 1986" as costing only $33 million. (Marjorie Williams, "Showdown Price Tag: About $33 Million," *Washington Post* [Oct. 29, 1986], A-17.) Reagan's OMB, however, contested this number, claiming, "There has never been an accurate figure for the costs of these things and there never will be." Reason: "Because they are trying to put a value on the price of work lost. It's not a cash cost," and OMB also contested the incidental costs relating to the work stoppage (like turning off computer system, stopping printing presses, distributing layoff notices, etc.).

10 Dan Balz and John E. Yang, "Bush Closes Most Government Operations," *Washington Post* (Oct. 6, 1990), A-1.

11 John E. Yang, "House Democrats Join Revolt on Budget Deal; Vote Counts Show Both Parties Falling Short," *Washington Post* (Oct. 4, 1990), A-1.

12 Balz and Yang, "Bush Closes Most Government Operations."

13 John E. Yang and Steven Mufson, "Bush, Hill Agree to End Government Shutdown; Stopgap Funds, Deficit-Cut Outline Approved," *Washington Post* (Oct. 9, 1990), A-1.

14 John H. Aldrich and David W. Rohde, "The Republican Revolution and the House Appropriations Committee," *The Journal of Politics*, vol. 62 (Feb. 2000), 14-15.

15 Eric Pianin and John E. Yang, "GOP Budget Plan Advances; Clinton Threatens to Veto Bill Assembled by House Panel," *Washington Post* (Oct. 13, 1995), A-1.

16 David Maraniss and Michael Weisskopf, *"Tell Newt to Shut Up!"* (New York: Touchstone, 1996), 149.

17 Ibid.

18 Bill Clinton, *My Life* (New York: Alfred A. Knopf, 2004), 683.

19 Peter Morton, "November U.S. Government Shutdown Cost Us $1.4B," *Financial Post* (Jan. 13, 1996), 5.

20 When the Pew poll asked (during the period of Jan. 11–14, 1996, when the shutdown was ending) what was the "most important news event that happened in the nation or in the world in the past few weeks," only 10 percent ranked the government shutdown. And with regard to public attentiveness to the shutdown story, 42 percent of respondents said they followed it very or fairly closely. By way of comparison, the same number said they followed the Firestone tire recall, but only 2 percent said they followed the split between Tom Cruise and Nicole Kidman. See http://people-press.org/nii.

21 Adam Clymer, "G.O.P. Revolution Hits Speed Bump," *New York Times* (Jan. 15, 1996), A-1 ("Polls suggest that shutting down the Government was a net loss for Republicans"). See also Kevin Phillips, "Why This Congress Must Be Considered the Worst in a Half-Century," *Los Angeles Times* (Feb. 4, 1996), M-1.

Appendix C: Bush and Cheney's Radical Lawyer

1 See "The President's Constitutional Authority to Conduct Military Operations Against Terrorists and Nations Supporting Them," U.S. Department of Justice at http://www.usdoj.gov/olc/warpowers925.htm. Yoo's opinion gives the president far broader powers than those adopted by Congress on September 14, 2001, in its "Authorization to Use Military Force," a fact noted by Yoo's opinion. It is quite remarkable that Yoo, a deputy, would be issuing this opinion, rather than the assistant attorney general who heads the Office of Legal Counsel, if not the attorney general himself.

2 I am certainly not alone in reaching this conclusion, although I may be blunter in stating it. For example, in the special issue of the *Presidential Studies Quarterly* (March 2007), which I have drawn from in this appendix, the following well-credential scholars take exception to Yoo's scholarship in different ways: Louis Fisher explains that Yoo can use law journals to publish much of his questionable work because they are not peer reviewed, so he can publish flat-out wrong information since student editors do not tell law professors they are wrong. Bruce Fein politely calls Yoo's thinking "misconceived" and "naïve." Richard Pious bluntly corrected Yoo when he wrote, "It is clear that the Constitution ...," by explaining the opposite to, in fact, be clear. Jack Rakove simply dismisses the "weaknesses of the arguments made by Professor John Yoo" in a footnote.

3 See David Luban, "The Defense of Torture," *New York Review of Books* (March 15, 2007), 39.

4 John Yoo, *War by Other Means* (New York: Atlantic Monthly Press, 2006), 2 (Citing Philip B. Heymann, *Terrorism, Freedom, and Security: Winning Without War* [Cambridge, Mass.: MIT Press, 2003], 20.)

5 Ibid. (Citing Gary Hart and Joyce Appleby, "Bush Power Grab Must Be Stopped by U.S. Citizenry," *San Jose Mercury News* [March 29, 2006].)

6 Ibid. (Citing Bruce Ackerman, *Before the Next Attack: Preserving Civil Liberties in an Age of Terrorism* [New Haven, Conn.: Yale University Press, 2007], 13.)

7 Ackerman, *Before the Next Attack*, 13–22.

8 United States Commission on National Security/21st Century, "New World Coming: American Security in the 21st Century—Major Themes and Implications (Sept. 15, 1999), 4.

9 Ibid., 8.

10 See Phillip B. Heymann, *Terrorism, Freedom and Security: Winning Without War* (Cambridge, Mass.: MIT Press, 2003), 3–35.

11 Briefly stated, the section says, "The first phases of our post-9/11 efforts rightly included military action to topple the Taliban and pursue al Qaeda. This work continues. But long-term success demands the use of all elements of national power: diplomacy, intelligence, covert actions, law enforcement, economic foreign policy, foreign aid, public diplomacy, and homeland defense. If we favor one tool while neglecting others, we leave ourselves vulnerable and weaken our national efforts." *The 9/11 Commission Report: Final Report of the National Commission on Terrorist Attacks Upon the United States* (New York: W. W. Norton) 363.

12 Yoo, *War by Other Means*, 246 n.15.

13 See Center for the Study of the Presidency at http://www.thepresidency .org/index.html.

14 Louis Fisher, "Invoking Inherent Powers: A Primer," *Presidential Studies Quarterly*, vol. 37 (Mar. 2007), 1. (Hereafter *Special Issue PSQ.*)

15 Ibid.

16 Ibid.

17 Bruce Fein, "Presidential Authority to Gather Foreign Intelligence," *Special Issue PSQ*, 23.

18 Neil Kinkopf, "Inherent Presidential Power and Constitutional Structure," *Special Issue PSQ*, 37–40.

19 Ibid., 41.

20 Ibid., 52.

21 See John W. Dean, "Thoughts on the Bringing Terrorists to Justice Act of 2006," FindLaw (Sept. 22, 2006) at http://writ.news.findlaw.com/ dean/20060922.html; and Michael Dorf, "Why the Military Commissions Act Is No Moderate Compromise," FindLaw (Oct. 11, 2006) at http://writ.news. findlaw.com/dorf/20061011.html.

22 Richard M. Pious, "Inherent War and Executive Powers and Prerogative Politics," *Special Issue PSQ*, 66. (The scholarship he cites and relies upon includes: David Gray Adler, "The Constitution and Presidential Warmaking: The Enduring Debate," *Political Science Quarterly*, vol. 103 [1988], 1–36; Michael Glennon, *Constitutional Diplomacy* [Princeton, N.J.: Princeton University Press, 1990]; Louis Henkin, *Foreign Affairs and the U.S. Constitution*, 2d ed. [Oxford, UK: Clarendon Press, 1996]; Harold Koh, *The National Security Constitution* [New Haven, Conn.: Yale University Press, 1990]; and Abraham Sofaer, *War, Foreign Affairs and Constitutional Power* [Cambridge, Mass.: Ballinger, 1976]. He also refers to "among others," setting forth two dozen scholars in his bibliography.)

23 Ibid., 75.

24 Ibid., 81-82.

25 Jack N. Rakove, "Taking the Prerogative out of the Presidency: An Originalist Perspective," *Special Issue PSQ*, 85. (Quote from essay summary.)

26 Ibid., 98–99.

27 Jonathan Elliot, *The Debates in the Several State Conventions of the Adoption of the Federal Constitution, As Recommended by the General Convention at Philadelphia, in 1787* (Washington, D.C.: U.S. Congress, 1839), vol. 4, 114. (Hereafter Elliot, *Debates,* which can be found online at http://memory.loc .gov/ammem/amlaw/lwed.html.) There are literally thousands of professional journal articles, and hundreds of books, that address questions that relate to presidential powers relating foreign policy and national security. Over the years I have read hundreds of articles and have at least a dozen books on my shelf addressing the subject. If I had to select one article as recommended reading, and one book, it would be those that I have relied on in refreshing my recollections and constructing the arguments in this section: "The Constitution and Presidential Warmaking: The Enduring Debate," an article written by Idaho State University political science professor David Gray Adles for the *Political Science Quarterly* (Spring 1988), which is available online at JSTOR (Journal Storage), an archive of scholarly journals that unfortunately requires a subscription for access; the one book would be Louis Fisher's *Presidential War Power* (2d edition), published by the University Press of Kansas. Fisher, also a political scientist, served for several decades as a specialist in separation of powers at the Congressional Research Service of the Library of Congress, and he is currently a specialist with the Law Library of the Library of Congress.

28 Elliot, *Debates*, vol. 4, 108.

29 Edward S. Corwin (5th rev. ed.), edited by Randall W. Bland, Theodore T. Hindsen, and Jack W. Peltason, *The President: Office and Powers, 1787–1984* (New York: New York University Press, 1984), 264.

30 Fisher, *Presidential War Power*, 49.

31 See, e.g., Clinton Rossiter, *Constitutional Dictatorship: Crisis Government in the Modern Democracies* (Princeton, N.J.: Princeton University Press, 1948), and John W. Dean, "Presidential Powers in Times of Emergency: Could Terrorism Result in a Constitutional Dictator," FindLaw (June 7, 2002) at http://writ.news.findlaw.com/dean/20020607.html.

32 Fisher, *Presidential War Power*, 49.

33 Victor Lasky, *It Didn't Start with Watergate* (New York: The Dial Press, 1977), 1.

34 See, e.g., Bernard Schwartz, *Decisions: How the Supreme Court Decides Cases* (New York: Oxford University Press, 1996), 239–40. (Professor Schwartz discusses how even the highest court in the land, recognizing that it has made wrong decisions, stays with the rulings under the doctrine of *stare decisis*, to "ensure that the law will not merely change erratically, but will develop in a principled and intelligible fashion," unless the precedent is so outdated or un-founded as to demand departure from the doctrine.)

35 See Lasky, *It Didn't Start with Watergate*, index.

36 According to the *Report in Foreign Relations of the United States* (FRUS), an official State Department publication that gathers and reports official his-tory, President Truman met regularly with congressional leaders, who reported complete support in Congress for his actions. At a meeting with Senate leaders on the afternoon of July 3, 1950, the president presented a proposed "Joint Resolution expressing approval of the action taken in Korea." The report con-tinues: "It was not proposed that the President should ask for such a resolution but that the initiative for this should come from the members of Congress," Secretary of state Dean Acheson explained, adding that "various Senators and Congressmen" had suggested such action. When Truman asked Senate majority leader Lucas for "his personal opinion," Lucas responded "that he frankly ques-tioned the desirability of this. He said that things were now going along well.... He said that the President had very properly done what he had to without con-sulting Congress. He said the resolution itself was satisfactory and that it could pass." After Truman said he had made no decision, Lucas added "that to go up and give such a message to Congress might sound as if the President were ask-ing for a declaration of war." Lucas thought the president should give a "fireside chat." After listening to the advice of others in the meeting, including the State and Defense Departments, with no suggestion he go to Congress, Truman said, "it was necessary to be very careful that he would not appear to be trying to get around Congress and use extra-Constitutional powers." Truman later added, "it was up to Congress whether such a resolution should be introduced, that he would not suggest it." FRUS, 1950, vol. VII, 286. On July 19, 1950, Truman sent a message to Congress explaining what he was doing, but Congress never introduced a resolution, nor did Truman request congressional action.

37 This statement is based on a private exchange I had via e-mail with Mr. Fisher on March 13, 2007.

38 John C. Yoo, "The President's Constitutional Authority to Conduct Military Operations Against Terrorists and Nations Supporting Them," *Memorandum Opinion for the Deputy Counsel to the President*, U.S. Department of Justice (Sept. 25, 2001) at http://www.usdoj.gov/olc/warpowers925.htm

39 Louis Fisher, "Lost Constitutional Moorings: Recovering the War Power," *Indiana Law Journal* (Fall 2005), 1199.

40 Rakove, "Taking the Prerogative out of the Presidency," 94.

41 Editorial, "The President's War Powers," *Time* (June 1, 1970) at http://www.time.com/time/printout/0,8816,878290,00.html.

42 John C. Yoo, *The Powers of War and Peace: The Constitution and Foreign Affairs After 9/11* (Chicago: University of Chicago Press, 2005), 99–100.

43 Stephen Holmes, "John Yoo's Tortured Logic," *The Nation* (May 1, 2006) at http://www.thenation.com/doc/20060501/holmes.

INDEX

Abortion: judicial fundamentalism, impact on, 166; and polarization, 65; Supreme Court nominees on, 134

Abraham, Henry, 146, 285, 290, 291–92

Abramoff, Jack, 11, 43, 46, 190

Abramson, Jill, 153

Abu Ghraib, 41, 283

Ackerman, Bruce, 210, 230–32, 231n

Adams, Arlin M., 286

Adams, John, 79, 269

Addington, David, 84, 112–13, 271

Adles, David Gray, 314

Affirmative action, judicial fundamentalism, impact on, 166

Afghanistan invasion, 231

African Americans, voter discrimination, Thomas (Clarence) on, 172–73

Alito, Samuel: as minimalist, 159–60; Supreme Court appointment, 155–61; unitary executive, support of, 103–6, 299

Alliance for Justice, 119, 284

Ambrose, Stephen, 288

American Bar Association: signing statements task force study, 114, 282–84; on Thomas (Clarence) nomination, 146–47

American Enterprise Institute, 81, 88, 274

American public: attitude structures of, 258; on broken government, 12–15, 59–60, 257; on Bush/Cheney administration, 12–14, 73, 176; on governance and political party, 176–77; government/politics, lack of knowledge, 1n, 185–86, 302–3; on government shutdowns, 56; invisible government, preference for, 187–88, 304; political propensities of, 16–17, 182, 258, 302; politics, basic view of, 187; presidential candidates, information needs, 254; on procedural justice, 303; process, attitude toward, 3, 7, 15–17, 258; process, mental approach to, 180–84; trust in government, 12, 12n–13n; voter ignorance/apathy, 185–89

Americans for Tax Reform, 48

Antideficiency Act (1870), 216n

Apathy, American voters, 187–88

Appleby, Joyce, 230

Appropriations bills, lack of, Republican Congress, 55–58

Appropriations Committee, partisanship, 222n–23n

Appropriations process: and annual budget, 218–19; authorizing legislation, 217; Congress, activities of, 215–19; Constitution

Appropriations process (*cont.*)
on, 215; continuing resolutions
(CRs), 218, 220; Republican
governement shutdowns, 220–25
Armey, Dick, 223
Arnold, Richard, 287–88
Articles of Confederation, 207–8
Authoritarian conservatives: groups
representing, 101; judicial approach,
131, 137, 155, 161–62, 296–97;
Republican Party takeover by, 199;
versus traditional conservatives, 101,
199; 2008 presidential candidates, 137
Authorizing legislation, 217

Babbitt, Bruce, 287
Baird, Zoë, 287
Baker, Howard, 141–42, 311
Baker, James, 131
Baker, Peter, 141
Barkley, Alben, 270
Barnes, Fred, 5–6
Barone, Michael, 5
Beinart, Peter, 266
Bicameralism: founder's development of,
53–54, 208–9; Republican disregard
for, 49–51
Biden, Joe, 153, 155
Bill of Rights, judicial fundamentalism,
impact on, 166–67
Bipartisanship: as Democratic Party
goal, 49; and Iraq War, 274;
Republican destruction of, 31, 38,
48, 222
Blackmun, Harry: retirement of, 287;
Supreme Court appointment, 127,
129
Blogs/bloggers: on CNN "Broken
Government" report, 14, 257; news
media sources for, 7; process, attitude
toward, 8, 255
Boicourt, Mike, 296
Boland Amendment, 221, 271, 308
Bork, Robert: Clinton opposition to,
286–87; judicial appointment defeat,
137–43, 294; Kennedy description
of, 138–39; special-interest support
for, 293–94
Bork, use of term, 138*n*

Bowsher v. Synar, 113
Brandeis, Louis, 69
Breaux, John, 294
Breyer, Stephen, Supreme Court
appointment, 126*n*, 287
Bribes. *See* Corruption/bribes
Brock, David, 151–52
Broder, David, 63
Broken government: American public
on, 12–15, 257; and Congress, 25–
70; journalistic consensus about, 12–
15, 27–30; and judiciary, 119–74;
and presidency, 71–117; as process
issue, 3
"Broken Government," report, 12–15,
257
Brooks, Jack, 212
Brown, Jerry, 3
Brownback, Sam, 181*n*
Brownell, Herbert, 127
Brown v. Board of Education, 136
Broyhill, James T., 140
Buchanan, James, 74, 75, 76, 278
Buchanan, Patrick: on Bush presidency,
72; and wedge issues, 63–64
Buchen, Phillip, 285
Buckley, William F., Jr., 72
Budget, annual: and appropriations
process, 218–19; Clinton surplus, 43;
Republicans, lack of, 56–58
Bureau of the Budget, 218
Burger, Warren: as judicial minimalist,
128; Supreme Court appointment,
127–29
Burnham, James, 101
Burns, Arnold, 293
Burns, Conrad, 46
Burton, Dan, 97*n*
Bush, George H. W.: Cheney as defense
secretary, 88–91; and Congress, 96;
government shutdowns, 221–22;
judicial appointments, 144–53, 294;
Kuwait invasion, 89–91, 235; and
presidential power, 90–92, 95–96;
and wedge issues, 64
Bush, George W.: governance, ignorance
of, 81; negative traits of, 73, 76, 114;
See also Bush/Cheney administration;
Bush/Cheney presidency

Bush/Cheney administration: American
  public disapproval, 12–14, 73, 176;
  Cabinet posts, allowing abuses, 197;
  corruption/bribes, 46–49; executive
  branch, impact on. *See* Bush/Cheney
  presidency; failures of, 11, 74, 76–77;
  government shutdowns, 221–22;
  impeachment, reasons for, 98, 111,
  114–15, 276; Iraq invasion. *See* Iraq
  War; judicial appointments, 153–62;
  legal council. *See* Yoo, John Choon; as
  partnership, 8*n*–9*n*; and polarization
  problem, 61–62, 64, 69; Republican
  disapproval of, 54, 72–73, 200–201;
  secrecy in, 5–6, 8, 25–26, 71*n*, 95,
  268, 270; *See also* individual
  branches of government; Republican
  Congress
Bush/Cheney presidency, 71–117;
  Cheney's dominance in, 77–78, 99–
  100; inherent presidential powers
  concept, 236–43; negative impact on
  office, 71–73, 78; oversight, lack of,
  38–43; presidential power, Cheney's
  view of, 75, 83–84, 89, 92–93, 99–
  100, 103, 110–13, 116, 192; signing
  statements, abuse of, 110–16; unitary
  executive theory, 102–10; wartime
  powers abuse, 75, 235–41; worst in
  history, 73–77, 263–66; *See also*
  Cheney, Dick
Bush v. Gore, 163, 176
Byrd, Robert, 213

Cafferty, Jack, 12
Calabresi, Steven, 106–8, 276
Campaign finance reform: judicial
  fundamentalist view, 164; as process
  issue, 6
Campbell, Carroll, 63
Cannon, Joseph G., 33
Cannon, Lou, 131
Carney, David, 6
Carswell, G. Harrold, 128–29, 142
Carter, Jimmy: Mondale vice presidency,
  79–80, 270
Carville, James, 39*n*, 64
Case-Zablocki Act (1972), 94*n*
Celler, Emanuel, 212

Center for the Study of the Presidency,
  236
Centrists, on Supreme Court, 300
Chaffee, John, 294
Checks and balances. *See* Separation of
  powers
Cheney, Dick: as Bush foreign-policy
  tutor, 79, 100; Bush running mate,
  acceptance of, 79–81; Congress,
  negative view of, 88–89;
  Constitution, disregard for, 78, 81–
  82, 89–90; Deficit Reduction Act
  vote, 51; energy bill, 43; at
  Halliburton, 79, 81; health issues, 78,
  80, 268; historical legacy of, 81; and
  Iran-Contra affair, 41; Iran-Contra
  committee minority report, 85–87,
  271–73; judgment, impaired, 78,
  268; Kuwait invasion, role in, 89–91;
  and Libby indictment, 98; as neo-
  Nixonian, 85, 92, 98–99; political
  career, 81–82, 268–69; presidential
  power, view of, 75, 83–84, 89, 92–
  93, 99–100, 103, 110–13, 116, 192;
  secrecy, 5–6, 26, 71*n*, 268–69; and
  surveillance, illegal, 92, 269;
  Watergate, view of, 82–83, 93; *See
  also* Bush/Cheney administration;
  Bush/Cheney presidency
Cheney, Lynne, 14, 85
Church, Frank, 41
Church and state separation, judicial
  fundamentalism, impact on,
  170–71
Citizens Against Burlington v. Busby, 295
Civil rights: judicial fundamentalism,
  impact on, 167–68; Thomas
  (Clarence) position, 147
Clark, William P., 290
Clark Amendment (1976), 94*n*
Clausewitz, Carl von, 176
Clawson, Rosalee, 7
Clinton, Bill: budget surplus, 43;
  government shutdowns, 224–25;
  judicial appointments, 126*n*,
  286–88; oversight subpoenas by
  Republicans, 39, 41; presidency,
  status of, 98–99, 99*n*–100*n*; and
  signing statements, 113–14, 279–81;

Clinton, Bill (*cont.*)
  Starr investigations, 96–97; and
  unitary executive theory, 102–3
Clinton, Hillary: McCain relationship,
  32*n*; Whitewater, 96
Closed rules, 10, 37–38
CNN, "Broken Government" report,
  12–15, 257
Coburn, Tom, 305
Colangelo, Anthony, 108, 277
Cole, Tom, 67–68
Commander in chief, Constitution on,
  87*n*, 88, 243–46
Commercial speech, 165
Congress, 25–70: appropriations
  process, 215–19; bicameralism, 49–
  51, 53–54, 208–9; budget resolution,
  annual, 56; Cheney's view of, 88–89;
  congressional oath, 50*n*; continuing
  resolutions (CRs), 58*n*; democratic
  process, 4, 25; filibuster, 4–5;
  founder's development of, 53–54,
  208–9; judicial fundamentalism,
  impact on, 165; majorities, number
  needed, 25*n*; national security,
  power of, 87–88, 87*n*–88*n*, 91, 91*n*;
  public approval ratings, 177–78;
  Rules Committee, role of, 37;
  unitary executive theory, impact on,
  104, 107; Watergate, impact on,
  93–99; *See also* Democratic
  Congress; Republican
  Congress
Congressional Budget Act, 99
Congressional Budget and
  Impoundment Control Act (1974),
  56, 83, 94*n*, 261
Conservatives/conservatism:
  authoritarian. *See* Authoritarian
  conservatives; disapproval of Bush/
  Cheney, 72–73; fiscal spending,
  approach to, 45–46; governance,
  guiding principles, 18–22; judicial
  activism, use of, 123, 123*n*; judicial
  philosophies of, 124–25; legal
  scholars, radical. *See* Yoo, John
  Choon; oversight, view of, 42;
  presidency, use and abuse of, 100–
  102; on presidential powers, 102,
  193–94; taxation, view of, 45, 221;
  and unitary executive theory, 102; *See
  also* Republican Party
Conservatives Without Conscience (Dean),
  xi–xiv, xvii, 9, 21, 59*n*, 78, 181, 256,
  270, 308
Constitution of the United States: on
  appropriations, 215; bicameralism,
  49–51, 53–54; Bush/Cheney legal
  council distortions. *See* Yoo, John
  Choon; on commander-in-chief, 87*n*,
  88, 243–46; Congress, national
  security powers, 87*n*; operation of
  government, 194–95; Republican
  disregard for, 49–61, 213–14, 227;
  separation of powers, 49, 49*n*–50*n*,
  69, 207–14; Supreme Court, impact
  on, 122–23
Continuing resolutions (CRs), 58*n*,
  218, 220
Contract with America, 196, 223,
  306
Conyers, John, Jr., 42, 115, 213
Cooper, Philip, 113
Corn, David, 4–5
Corporate interests, judicial
  fundamentalism, impact on, 165
Corruption/bribes, 46–49; Abramoff
  schemes, 46, 48–49; and
  Cunningham, 46–47; and DeLay, 22,
  48, 299; K Street Project, 48–49;
  redistricting, 34, 48; and Republican
  Congress, 11, 46–49; and Republican
  machinery, 48–49
Corwin, Edward S., 245
Cost of Living Council, 82
Coulter, Ann, 189
Covert operations, presidential
  authority, 104
Cross Sound Ferry Services v. ICC, 295
Crowley, Candy, 2
Cruel and unusual punishment, judicial
  fundamentalism, impact on, 168
Cunningham, Randy "Duke," 46–47,
  216
Cuomo, Mario, 287

Dahl, Robert A., 273
Danforth, John, 148

Dean, Howard, process issues in campaign, 5–6

Death penalty, judicial fundamentalist support, 168

Deaver, Michael, 19, 131

Defense Authorization Act (1996), 280

Deficit Reduction Act (2005): changed after House vote, 51–54; testing legality, lawsuits, 53–54, 260–61

DeLay, Tom: on legislation drafted by lobbyists, 22–23; redistricting scheme, 34, 48, 299

Dellinger, Walter, 113–14, 279–81

Democratic Congress: Congress, restoration of institution, 190–92; earmarks, reform of, 59; Iraq War, ending possibilities, 178; oversight role, 42–43, 192; Pelosi efforts, 190, 191, 212; process abuses, reversal of, 190–91; 2006 control, 2, 17, 25; 2008 control scenario, 34–35; work ethic of, 4, 191–92

Democratic Party: governance, public opinion of, 176–77; oversight, historical view, 40–41; post-government service affiliations, 21; process issues, neglect of, 2–3, 8–11; public service as power motive, 23, 201; Republican Congress abuse of, 10–11; wealthy and support of, 18n

Democratic process: essence of, 3–4; See also Process; Process issues

Department of Justice, politicalization of, 197–98

Dewey, Thomas, 127

Didion, Joan, 82

Dingell, John, 40, 42, 212, 213

Dorf, Michael, 53

Dornan Amendment, 280–81

Douglas, William O., 285

Dowd, Matt, 61–62, 62n

Dred Scott v. Sandford, 163

Due process clause, 167

Durbin, Richard, 155

Earmarks: Democratic reform, 59, 191; Republican use of, 43–44, 58–59, 59n

Eastland, James, 135

Eastland, Terry, 100–101, 132–33, 138–40, 142, 290–91, 293

Edsall, Thomas, 61–62

Edwards, Mickey, 68–69

Ehrlichman, John, 246–47, 247n

Eighth Amendment, 168

Eilperin, Juliet, 28, 31–33, 37, 48, 60

Elections: Republican tactics, 17–18, 23; See also Presidential elections

Elliot, Jonathan, 314

Ellis, Susan, 65n

Emancipation Proclamation, 237

Emerson, Jo Ann, 58

Enemy combatants: Cheney on, 92; extraordinary rendition, 235, 237; McCain amendment, 283–84; See also Torture

Energy bill, 43

Enron, 107

Environmental protection: judicial fundamentalism, impact on, 168–69, 295; Thomas (Clarence) position, 148

Environmental Protection Agency, 168

Ethics in Government Act (1978), 95n

Executive branch, Bush/Cheney impact on. See Bush/Cheney presidency

Executive privilege: Bush, G. H. W. use of, 96; Nixon misuse, 96; post-Watergate presidency, 98–99

Extraordinary rendition, 235, 237

Fallows, James, 253

Falwell, Jerry, 131

Farina, Cynthia, 102

Federal Advisory Committee Act, 94n

Federal government: energetic, necessity of, 100, 272–73; limiting, as Republican goal, 18–22, 34, 45–46, 55; process, defined, 3, 3n

Federalist Papers: on appropriations, 216; on commander-in-chief clause, 244; democracy versus republic, 208; on energetic government, 100, 272–73; minority report distortions of, 272–73

Federalist Society, 103, 106, 110, 146, 151

Fein, Bruce, 237

Feinstein, Diane, 155
Feulner, Edwin J., 20
Fifth Amendment, 168
Filegate, 96
Filibuster, 4–5, 56
First Amendment, judicial fundamentalism, impact on, 164–65, 169
Fiscal activities: appropriations, 55–58, 216–19; budget resolutions, absence of, 56–58; conservative approach, 45–46; continuing resolutions (CRs), 58n; Deficit Reduction Act (2005), 51–54; Democratic cleanup (2007), 59, 191; earmarks, 43–44, 58–59, 59n, 191; pork-barrel spending, 43–44; Republican Party abuses, 36, 43–46, 55–58, 218–25; tax cuts, 45
Fisher, Louis, 87–88, 108–9, 194, 236, 248–50, 314
Fiske, Robert, 96
Fitzgerald, Patrick, 97, 198
Floor debate, Republican Congress, lack of, 10–11, 31, 33, 35–37
Foley, Mark, 11
Foley, Thomas, 89–90
Ford, Gerald, 82: judicial appointments, 126n, 285–86
Foreign Intelligence Surveillance Act (1978), 94n, 235
Foreign travel, Republicans, absence of, 31–32
Fortas, Abe, 127–28
Foster, Vince, 96
Fostergate, 96
Fourteenth Amendment, 167–68
Frank, Barney, 213
Frankfurt, Harry G., 236, 236n
Frankfurter, Felix, as judicial minimalist, 125
Freedom of Information Act Amendments (1974), 94n
Free speech, judicial fundamentalism, impact on, 169
Frist, Bill, 58
Fulbright, William, 41, 212
Fundamentalism, judicial. See Judicial fundamentalism

Garbus, Martin, 162, 162n, 167
Garner, John Nance, 79
Gay rights, judicial fundamentalism, impact on, 169
General Accounting Office Amendments (1980), 95n
Geographic area, and polarization, 65
Gerhardt, Michael, 53
Gerson, Mike, 100
Gilmore, Jim, 181n
Gingrich, Newt: and Bush (G. H. W.) tax package, 221–22; and Clinton government shutdown, 223–25; Congress, dismantling of, 28, 31–34, 55–56; 2008 presidential candidate, 181n
Ginsburg, Douglas Howard, 143
Ginsburg, Ruth Bader: Ginsburg, Ruth Bader, Supreme Court appointment, 126n, 285–87
Giuliani, Rudy, 181n
Goeas, Ed, 59–60
Goldman, Sheldon, 289–90
Goldwater, Barry, 131, 262, 308
Gonzales, Alberto: abuses of, 197; on presidential war powers, 75; resignation, Republican requests for, 305
Gorbachev, Mikhail, 221
Gore, Al, on Republican "assault on reason," 199
Government in the Sunshine Act (1976), 94n
Government shutdowns, 219–25; cost of, 220, 225; and Iran-Contra affair, 309–10; under Republicans, 55–56, 220–25
Governors, as presidential candidates, 181
Gray, C. Boyden, 145, 146, 274
Gray, L. Patrick, 247
Green, Joyce, 112, 112n, 116, 278
Greenberg, David, 265–66
Griffin, Robert P., 285
Gun control, judicial fundamentalism, impact on, 169–70

Habeas corpus, judicial fundamentalism, impact on, 170

Hagel, Chuck, 20, 181*n*

Halliburton, 79, 81, 268

Hamdan v. Rumsfeld, 241*n*

Hamdi v. Rumsfeld, 104–5

Hamilton, Alexander: on commander in chief clause, 244; on energetic president, 100, 272; on presidential power, 242, 273; and unitary executive theory, 276

Hannity, Sean, 189

Harman, Jane, 85

Harris, Katherine, 20

Hart, Gary, 230, 232

Hart, Jeffrey, 73

Hart-Rudman commission, 232

Hastert, Dennis, 33, 190; and Deficit Reduction Act changes, 52–53

Hatch, Orrin, 20, 152

Haynsworth, Clement, 128, 142

Heflin, Howell, 294

Heritage Foundation, 110

Hess, Gary R., 274

Heymann, Philip, 230, 232–34

Hibbing, John R., 15–17, 68, 180–84, 187–88, 258, 302–4

Hill, Alfred, 55–56

Hill, Anita: Hill-Thomas hearings, 16, 149–53, 298; polygraph, excerpt, 298

Hills, Carla A., 285

Hoffman, Nicholas von, 76–77

Holmes, Oliver Wendell, Jr., 122: as judicial majoritarian, 124

Holmes, Stephen, 251–52

Homeland Security, 6

Hoover, Herbert, 74

Hoover, J. Edgar, and Supreme Court appointments, 129

House of Representatives: founder's development of, 208–9; polarization of, 60–61; *See also* Congress

Hruska, Roman, 129

Huckabee, Mike, 181*n*

Hufstedler, Shirley, 285

Hughes, Charles Evans, 123

Hughes-Ryan Amendment (1974), 94*n*

Hunter, Duncan, 91, 181*n*

Hurricane Katrina, 11

Hussein, Saddam, Kuwait invasion, 89–91

Ides, Allan, 108

Imperial presidency: and Clinton, 99*n*–100*n*; creation, elements of, 270; and Nixon, 77, 82, 93

Incorporation doctrine, 167

Independent council: absence, benefits to Republicans, 97–98; Starr investigations, 96–97

Independent Council Act, expiration of, 97, 99

Independents: in Congress, 25*n*; voters, view of Republicans, 200

Inherent presidential powers, 236–43; defined, 237; founder's rejection of, 238–39, 242; *Hamden v. Rumsfeld*, 241*n*; *Presidential Studies Quarterly (PSQ)* on, 236–42; as unconstitutional, 237–39, 246–47

Inouye, Daniel, 213

"Inside-baseball approach," 7

Inspector General Act (1978), 94*n*

INS v. Chadha, 113, 279

Intelligence Authorization Act (2002), 283

Intelligence Oversight Act (1980), 95*n*

International Emergency Economic Powers Act (1977), 94*n*

Iran-Contra affair, 83–87, 308–10; Boland Amendment, 221, 308; events of, 83*n*–84*n*, 308–9; minority report, 85–87, 271; presidential power abuse, 104, 308; Reagan fiscal tactic, 220–21, 308–9

Iraq War: American public opposition, 12; Bush/Cheney deception, 26, 99, 178, 240–41, 269; ending, by Democrats, 178; Tonkin Gulf resolution, Bush use of, 91, 274

Iredell, James, 210, 244

Italian Americans: Scalia, support of, 292; voter strongholds, 292–93

Internment camps, 231

Jackson, Andrew, 75
Jackson, Robert, 136
Jackson-Vanik Amendment (1974),
    94*n*
Jefferson, Thomas, 75, 210, 269
Johnson, Andrew, 75
Johnson, Lyndon, 40, 79, 265, 266;
    Supreme Court nominees, 127;
    Tonkin Gulf resolution, 91, 274
Jones, Edith, 144–45
Jones, Gordon S., 275
Judges, federal. *See* Judicial
    appointments
Judicial activism, conservatives, use of,
    123, 123*n*
Judicial appointments: Alito
    confirmation hearing, 103–6; Bork
    defeat, 137–43; Breyer, 126*n*, 287–
    88; of Bush, G. H. W., 144–53; of
    Bush, G. W., 153–62; of Clinton,
    126*n*, 285–88; confirmation, Bush's
    corruption of, 156–57; conservative,
    dangers of, 119–20, 125–26, 162–63;
    Democratic versus Republican
    (2007), 174; diversity, necessity of,
    195; of Ford, 126*n*, 285–86; in
    future, cautions about, 161–62, 299–
    300; Ginsburg, 126*n*, 287; Kennedy,
    144; of Nixon, 126–30, 285;
    O'Connor, 131–32, 134;
    politicalization of, 126–30; Powell,
    127, 129; process issues, 4–5; of
    Reagan, 130–32, 289–90; Rehnquist,
    127, 129–30; Roberts, Chief Justice,
    153–54; Scalia, 132–34; Souter, 144–
    46; Stevens, 126*n*, 286; Thomas,
    146–53; and unitary executive theory,
    104–5
Judicial approaches: centrism, 300;
    fundamentalists. *See* Judicial
    fundamentalism; majoritarianists,
    124; minimalists, 124–25, 128–29,
    132, 134, 144, 158–60;
    perfectionists, 124
Judicial fundamentalism, 134–37; on
    abortion, 166; on affirmative action,
    166; approach of, 125, 163–64;
    authoritarian conservatives, 131, 155,

161–62, 294–95; on Bill of Rights,
    166–67; on campaign finance,
    unregulated, 164; on church and
    state separation, 170–71; on civil
    rights, 167–68; Congress,
    dismantling of, 165; corporate
    interests, 165; on cruel and unusual
    punishment, 168; dangers of, 125; on
    environmental protection, 168–69,
    295; on free speech, 169; on gay
    rights, 169; on gun control, 169–70;
    on habeas corpus, 170; philosophy of,
    125–26; and Rehnquist, 129–30,
    134–37; and Scalia, 132–34; on
    sex-related activities, 171; on
    standing to sue, 171–72; and
    Thomas, 153, 165, 167, 170; and
    unitary executive theory, 164; on
    voting, 172–73
Judiciary: courts/judges, number of,
    289; federal judges, functions of,
    121–22, 290–91; founder's concept
    of, 209; *See also* Judicial
    appointments; Supreme
    Court

Kavanaugh, Brett, 278
Keck, Thomas M., 123*n*
Kennedy, Anthony M.: as judicial
    minimalist, 144; Supreme Court
    appointment, 144
Kennedy, Cornelia, 285, 290
Kennedy, Edward: and Alito
    confirmation, 299; on Bork, 138–39;
    on Kuwait invasion, 90; O'Connor
    (Sandra), support of, 131; and
    Roberts confirmation, 155, 299; on
    Supreme Court confirmation
    hearings, 156–57; terms in Congress,
    213; on unitary executive theory,
    106–7
Kennedy, John F., 79
Kerry, John, process issues, neglect of,
    8–9
Kingston, Jack, 58
Kinkopf, Neil, 237–38, 237*n*–38*n*
Klein, Joe, 5
Koppel, Ted, 5

Korean War, 248–50, 249n
Kosovo, 41
Krauthammer, Charles, 101
K Street Project, 48–49, 190
Kuttner, Robert, 9
Kuwait invasion: Bagdad ignored, 235; Cheney's role in, 89–91

Lantos, Tom, 213
Lasky, Victor, 247–48
Lawrence v. Texas, 169
Lazarus, Edward, 154
Leahy, Pat, 35, 42, 148, 213
Leogrande, William M., 275
Levi, Edward, 285
Levin, Carl, 213
Levinson, Daryl, 62, 69, 211–12
Lewinsky, Monica, 96
Lewis, Jerry, 58
Libby, I. Lewis "Scooter," indictment/conviction of, 84, 98, 198–99
Liberals/liberalism: judicial philosophies of, 124–25; oversight, view of, 42; Republican negativity toward, 18, 23; See also Democratic Party
Lieberman, Joe, 25n
Lieberman, Lee, 146
Limbaugh, Rush, 189
Lincoln, Abraham, 231: extraordinary wartime measures, 231, 237, 243, 245–46, 248; on presidential duty, 50; ranking among presidents, 75–76, 264, 266
Line item veto, 99
Lobbyists: K Street Project, 48–49; legislation drafted by, 22–23; power, given by Republicans, 22, 49
Lobel, Jules, 194, 239
Locke, John, on executive power, 193–94, 239
Lott, Trent, 19, 262
Luban, David, 229
Lucas, Scott W., 249

McCain, John: conservatism, degree of, 181n; enemy combatants, amendment on treatment, 283–84;

on Gonzales resignation, 305; and Hillary Clinton, 32n
McCain-Feingold, campaign finance reform contested, 6
McCarthy, Joseph, 40
McConnell, Mitch, 6
McCullough, David, 40
McDonald, Forrest, 210
McElvaine, Robert S., 73n
McFarlane, Robert, 308–09
Madison, James: on appropriations, 216; on energetic government, 272–73; on inherent presidential powers, 242; republic, concept of, 207–8; on role of federal judges, 290–91; separation of powers concept, 207–11
Majoritarianism: approach of, 124; Supreme Court justice, 124
Malbin, Michael J., 84–85, 88
Manheim, Karl, 108
Mann, James, 89
Mann, Thomas E., 27, 30–31, 34, 36, 39, 41, 44, 47, 191, 258–59
Mansfield, Harvey C., 193–94
Maraniss, David, 223
Marbury v. Madison, 210, 238
Marini, John A., 275
Marshall, John, 195, 210, 238
Marshall, Thurgood, 146
Martin, Susan Taylor, 265
Mayer, Jane, 84–85, 153
Medicare: Deficit Reduction Act provisions, 51–52; prescription drug bill, 38
Meese, Edwin: conservatism, view of, 19; investigation of, 137; and judicial appointments, 131, 133; oil-company involvement, 293; on post-Watergate Congress, 95, 98
Meyerson Harold, 265
Miers, Harriet, 155
Military Commissions Act (2006), 35–36, 106, 239–40
Mills, Wilbur, 212
Minimalism: approach of, 124–25; Supreme Court justices, 124–25, 128–29, 132, 134, 144, 158–60
Minor, Paul, 298

Minority report: and Cheney, 85–87;
    fundamental errors in, 272–73
Mitchell, George, 287
Mitchell, John, 128–29
Mondale, Walter, vice presidency,
    expansion of, 79–80, 270
Monroe, James, signing statements,
    110n
Montley, Constance Baker, 285
Moral Majority, 131
Morison, Samuel Eliot, 210
Morris, Jonathan, 7
Moss, John, 42
Movement conservatives. See
    Authoritarian conservatives
Moynihan, Daniel Patrick, 274
Mueller, John, 235, 235n
Myers v. United States, 69

National Defense Authorization Act for
    Fiscal Year 2006, 111
National Emergencies Act (1974), 94n
National Humanities Council, 85
National security, 87n; congressional
    powers, 87–88, 87n–88n, 91, 91n;
    Hamdi v. Rumsfeld, 104–5; See also
    War powers, presidential
National Security Act, 104
National Security Agency, 41
National Security Council, and vice
    president, 270
Nelson, Dorothy Wright, 285
New Deal, and unitary executive theory,
    276
New Jersey Plan, 208
News media: inside baseball stories, 7;
    political journalists on government,
    6n, 14n; process issues, presentation
    of, 4–8, 253; right-wing
    spokespersons, 189
Ney, Bob, 46
9/11 Commission, law enforcement
    approach, 234, 313
Nixon, Richard: abuses of office, 82;
    appropriations, refusal to spend, 56,
    261; imperial presidency, 77, 82, 93;
    judicial appointments, 126–30,
    285; neo-Nixonians, 21–22, 85;
    Southern strategy, 62–63, 262, 288;

as vice president, 270;
    war powers, justification for,
    246–48, 250–51; Watergate, 82–83,
    93–98
No Child Left Behind, 58n
Noden, Merrell, 68n
Nolan, Beth, 103
Norquist, Grover, 19–20
North, Oliver, 86, 309
Novak, Robert D., 19
Nussbaum, Bernard, 286–87
Nussle, Jim, 28

Oaks, Dallin H., 290
O'Brien, David M., 289
Obscenity, judicial fundamentalism,
    impact on, 171
O'Connor, Sandra Day: as judicial
    minimalist, 125, 132, 134; retirement
    of, 153; Supreme Court appointment,
    131–32, 134
Office of Management and Budget
    (OMB), 218–19, 310
Omnibus bill, 36
O'Neill, Tip, 220
One-vote victory, 37
Ornstein, Norman J., 27, 27n, 30–31,
    34, 36, 39n, 41, 44, 47, 258–59
Oversight: Clinton administration, 39,
    41; and Democratic Congress, 42–
    43, 192; foreign affairs, historical
    examples, 40–41; liberal versus
    conservative views of, 42; Republican
    Congress, absence of, 26, 38–43

Packwood, Bob, 294
Page, Susan, 265
Partisanship: Appropriations
    Committee, 222n–23n; Republican
    Party, 11, 28, 33, 42, 60, 68, 96, 190,
    224; See also Bipartisanship;
    Polarization; Politicalization
Patriot Act, Bush's abuse of, 283–84
Paterson, William, 208
Pelosi, Nancy: on amending rules of
    Congress, 28–29; on Bush
    impeachment, 98, 114; as
    institutional-minded, 212; on lack of
    appropriations bills, 58; on

polarization problem, 11, 62; and restoration of Congress, 190–91

Perfectionism: approach of, 124; Supreme Court justices, 124

Phelps, Timothy, 149

Pildes, Richard, 62, 69, 211–12

Pious, Richard M., 240–41, 313

Planned Parenthood v. Casey, 297

Plessy v. Ferguson, 136

Polarization, 60–70; and abortion issue, 65; and Bush/Cheney administration, 61–62; destructive impact of, 33–34, 60–61, 64–65, 68–69; extreme and Republicans, 67–70; and geographic area, 65; historical view, 62–64, 66; myth or reality, Princeton conference on, 64–69, 263; neoconservatives on, 65*n*; and redistricting, 60, 67; separation of powers, negative impact, 68–69, 211–12; and wedge issues, 63–64; *See also* Politicalization

Policy, relationship to process, 4, 60, 179–80

Politicalization: Department of Justice, 197–98; of lobbying, 48–49; Supreme Court, 120–21, 130; *See also* Polarization

Political process. *See* Process; Process issues

Pork-barrel spending, 43–44

Pound, Roscoe, 122

Powell, Adam Clayton, 212

Powell, Lewis: as judicial minimalist, 129; retirement of, 137; Supreme Court appointment, 127, 129

Prakash, Saikrishna B., 277

Presidency: Bush/Cheney impact on. *See* Bush/Cheney presidency; Cheney's view of, 75, 83–84, 89, 92–93, 99–100, 103, 110–13, 116, 192; commander in chief, 87*n*, 88, 243–46; congressional investigation, laws related to, 94–95, 94*n*–95*n*; conservatives use and abuse of, 100–102; Constitutional Convention, 267, 273; executive privilege, 96; greatest president rankings, 263–64, 266–67; great presidents, traits of, 75–76; imperial presidency, 77, 82,

93, 99*n*–100*n*, 270; inherent powers, 236–43; post-Clinton status, 98–99, 99*n*–100*n*; presidential oath, 50*n*; Starr investigations, effects of, 96–97; unitary executive theory, 102–10; war powers, 243–52; Watergate, impact on, 93–98

Presidential elections: candidate information, needs of public, 254; past (1960–2004), process issues in platform, 9–10, 256; process issues, neglect of, 4–5, 8–11; 2008, Republican candidates, 181, 181*n*, 199–200

Presidential Records Act (1978), 81, 94*n*

Presidential Studies Quarterly (PSQ), on inherent presidential powers, 236–42

Price, David E., 28–29, 28*n*–29*n*, 33, 38, 41, 44–45, 48

Princeton conference, polarization, myth or reality, 64–69, 263

Procedural justice, American public on, 303

Process: American public, view of, 3, 7, 15–17, 258; defined, 3, 3*n*; mental processing of, 180–84; relationship to policy, 4, 60, 179–80; process propensity of individuals, 182–84, 302–3; proper, ways of knowing, 184–85

Process issues: CNN "Broken Government" report, 12–15; Democrats neglect of, 2–3, 8–11; media presentation of, 4–8, 253; in past presidential election platforms, 9–10; secrecy as, 9

Project for Excellence in Journalism (PEJ), 7–8, 255

Public Citizen, 54, 260

Public opinion. *See* American public

Quayle, Dan, 145

Quinn, Jack, 280–81

Rakove, Jack N., 241–42, 241*n*

Randolph, Edmund, 207

Rangel, Charles, 78, 212

Ray, Laura, 136

Reagan, Ronald: approval ratings, 101;
Boland Amendments, 221, 271,
308–9; Bork defeat, 137–43; and
Congress, 95–96; government
shutdowns, 220–21, 309–10;
impeachment threat, 141n–42n; Iran-
Contra affair, 41, 83–87, 83n–84n,
95–96, 104, 220–21, 307–9; judicial
appointments, 130–32, 144, 289–90;
on limited government, 18–19, 55;
and presidential power, 95; Reagan
Revolution, 262; signing statements,
113; and unitary executive theory,
102–4
Redistricting: DeLay scheme, 34, 48,
299; and polarization, 60, 67
Reed, Thomas B., 33
Reeves, Richard, 73–74
Regulation: judicial fundamentalism,
impact of, 163–65, 168, 172; and
unitary executive theory, 102–3, 276
Rehnquist, William: on commander in
chief clause, 243–44; death of, 153;
false statements of, 135–37, 137n;
and judicial fundamentalism, 129–
30, 134–37, 165; Supreme Court
appointment, 127, 129–30
Reid, Harry, 191
Rehnquist Choice: The Untold Story of the
Nixon Appointment That Redefined the
Supreme Court, The (Dean), 137n,
154n, 293
Republic, Madison's concept of, 207–8
Republican Congress: American public
disapproval, 12–13, 59–60; Anti-
Federalist approach of, 34;
appropriations process abuses, 55–58,
218–25; bipartisanship, destruction
of, 31–32, 32n, 38, 48, 222; budget
resolutions, absence of, 56–58; closed
rules, 10, 37–38; conference
deliberations, Democrats shut-out,
38, 51; constitutional principles,
disregard for, 49–61; corruption/
bribes, 46–49; Deficit Reduction Act
(2005), changed after vote, 51–54;
earmarks, 43–44, 58–59, 59n; failure,
journalistic consensus on, 12–15, 27–
30; fiscal abuses, 36, 43–46, 55–58;

floor debate, lack of, 10–11, 31, 33,
35–37; Gingrich dismantling of, 28,
31–34, 55–56; government
shutdowns, 55–56, 220–25;
investigative activity abuses, 97;
legislation, muscle-through methods,
37–38; overseas travel cutback, 31–
32; oversight, lack of, 26, 38–43;
political polarization, 33–34, 60–70;
process abuses, 10–11, 25–26; rule by
cabal, 30–35; secrecy condoned by,
25–26; spending abuses, 36, 43–46;
2006, loss of control, 17, 25; work
time, limited, 4, 31, 35–36, 191–92
Republican Party: authoritarian
conservatives' takeover, 199;
conservative position, historical view,
262–63; Constitution of the U. S.,
disregard for, 49–61, 213–14, 227;
disapproval of Bush/Cheney, 54, 72–
73, 200–201; evangelical link, 34;
expatriated members, 2, 196; fiscal
policy, basis of, 45–46; governance,
public opinion of, 176–77; liberalism,
negativity toward, 18, 23; limited
government as goal, 18–22, 34, 45–
46; and lobbyist power, 22; neo-
Nixonian aspirations, 21–22; 1994
Congress, winning tactics, 196;
partisanship, 11, 28, 33, 42, 60, 68,
96, 190, 224; post-government
service affiliations, 21; process issues,
2–24, 30–31; rule versus govern, 2,
23–24, 70; self-interest as power
motive, 21–23, 29, 30, 116–17, 200–
201; Supreme Court, transformation
of, 125–26, 130, 144, 153, 161, 163,
173–74, 195–96, 285–86, 289–90;
2008 Congress, plans for, 34–35, 49,
196; 2008 presidential candidates,
181, 181n, 199–200; wealthy and
support of, 17n–18n; winning
elections, tactics, 17–18, 23
Reverse discrimination, 166
Reynolds, Molly, 191
Reynolds, William Bradford, 133, 296
Ricks, Thomas, 6n
Ridge, Tom, 6
Risen, James, 6n

Roberts, John: chief justice, appointment as, 153–54; Kennedy questioning, 299; as minimalist, 158–60; presidential power, view of, 105
Roberts, Owen, 122
Robinson, Michael, 65n
Roe v. Wade: Alito position, 156; judicial fundamentalism, impact on, 166; Thomas (Clarence) position, 148, 295–96; See also Abortion
Romney, George, 288
Romney, Mitt, 181n
Rooney, Paul H., 285
Roosevelt, Franklin D.: extraordinary wartime measures, 212; and oversight, 40; on presidential powers, 269, 279; ranking among presidents, 75, 264; Truman investigation of, 76
Roosevelt, Theodore, 75, 267
Rose, Jonathan C., 131
Rosen, Jeffrey, 276
Rove, Karl: on 2008 Congress, 34; Bush presidential campaign, 81; and polarization problem, 61–62
Rucinski, Dianne, 298
Rudalevige, Andrew, 93–99, 267
Rudman, Warren, 145, 272
Rules Committee, role of, 37
Rumsfeld, Donald: in Ford administration, 82; incompetence of, 197; and Iraq War decision, 269

Safire, William, 3, 7, 63–64
Samuels, Dorothy, 9
Santorum, Rick, 39n
Saunders, Bernie, 25n
Savage, Charlie, 111–12, 115
Savage, David, 297
Scalia, Antonin: background information, 291–92; Italian Americans, appeal to, 292–93; as judicial fundamentalist, 125, 132–34, 167; presidential power, view of, 105; on Roe v. Wade, 297; Supreme Court appointment, 132–34
Schakowsky, Jan, 10–11
Schecter, Cliff, 262
Schiavo, Terri, 11

Schlesinger, Arthur, 82, 270
Schumer, Charles, 155
Schwartz, Bernard, 136, 316
Schwartz, Herman, 110, 141, 162n, 293–94
Scowcroft, Brent, 78
Secrecy: Cheney's health, 80, 268; Cheney's role in, 5–6, 26, 71n, 268–69; condoned by Republican Congress, 25–26; functions for executive, 71, 71n; and imperial presidency, 270–71; and Nixon, 8, 82, 94; as process issue, 9
Securities and Exchange Commission, 55
Segal, Jeffrey, 140
Sekulow, Jay, 293
Select Committee to Investigate Covert Arms Transactions with Iran, members, 271
Senate: founder's development of, 208–9; vice president's role, 26, 269–70; See also Congress
Sensenbrenner, James Jr., 31
Separation of powers, 207–14; and Constitution, development of, 207–10; inherent versus mandated, 213–14; polarization, negative impact of, 68–69, 211–12; Republican disregard for, 49, 49n–50n, 60, 117
September 11 attacks: 9/11 Commission Report, 234, 313; presidential powers increased after, 227–28; war on terror, basis of, 228–35
Sex-related activities, judicial fundamentalism, impact on, 171
Shaman, Jeffrey, 121–22
Shenkman, Richard, 73n
Shutdowns, government, 55–56
Signing statements, 110–16; ABA task force study, 114, 282–84; Bush administration abuse, 111–16, 283–84; and Clinton, 113–14, 279–81; compared to veto, 110n; elements of, 110n; examples of, 111–12, 283; House Judiciary Committee investigation (2007), 115; Kavanaugh involvement, 278; number by Bush, 112; Supreme Court on, 278–79; and

Signing statements (*cont.*)
   unitary executive theory, 116; Web
   site information source on, 112*n*
Silberman, Lawrence, 144
Simpson, Alan, 152
Slaughterhouse Cases, 167
Smeal, Eleanor Cutri, 148, 295
Smith, Gordon, 305
Smith, William French, 131
Sofaer, Abraham, 242
Souter, David, Supreme Court
   appointment, 144–46
Spaeth, Harold, 140
Spaight, Richard, 244
Specter, Arlen, 39, 39*n*, 152: on unitary
   executive theory, 105–6
Spencer, Stu, 130
Standing to sue, judicial
   fundamentalism, impact on, 171–72
Stare decisis, 247, 315
Starr, Kenneth: Clinton investigation,
   96–97; Nixon administration role,
   132, 134; as Solicitor, 144
Steiger, William, 82
Stennis, John, 294
Stevens, John Paul: as judicial
   perfectionist, 124; Supreme Court
   appointment, 126*n*, 285
Stevens, Ted, 35–36, 44
Stewart, Potter, 131
Sundquist, James L., 94
Sunstein, Cass, 123, 125, 132, 165, 173
Sununu, John, 145, 305
Supreme Court: appointments. *See*
   Judicial appointments; Judicial
   approaches; and *Bush v. Gore*, 176;
   confirmation hearings, Bush's abuse
   of, 156–57, 156*n*; Constitution,
   impact on, 122–23; diversity,
   necessity of, 195; future
   appointments, cautions about, 161–
   62, 300; judicial activism, 123;
   judicial review, 195; politicization of,
   120–21, 130; public approval ratings,
   177–78; swing votes, 144, 146;
   transformation, Republican efforts,
   125–26, 130, 144, 153, 161, 163,
   173–74, 176, 195–96, 285–86,
   289–90

Surveillance, illegal: and Cheney, 92,
   269; as impeachment issue, 98, 197;
   and imperial presidency, 270; and
   inherent presidential powers, 237;
   Nixon administration, 256; as
   oversight abuse, 41, 283–84; Yoo
   on, 235
Suskind, Ron, 6*n*
Swing votes, Supreme Court, 144, 146

Taft, William Howard, 267–68
Taibbi, Matt, 29–32, 35–36, 38–39,
   39*n*, 43–44, 47, 58*n*
Tax cuts, as conservative ideal, 45, 221
Thatcher, Margaret, 193
Theiss-Morse, Elizabeth, 15–17, 68,
   180–84, 187–88, 258, 302–3
Thomas, Andrew Peyton, 148, 296
Thomas, Bill, 38
Thomas, Clarence: false statements of,
   148–49, 151, 296–97; judicial
   fundamentalism of, 153, 165, 167,
   170; on presidential powers, 104–5;
   on *Roe v. Wade*, 148, 295–97;
   Supreme Court appointment, 146–
   53; Thomas-Hill hearings, 16, 149–
   53, 298
Thompson, Fred, 181*n*
Thornberry, Homer, 127
Thornburgh, Richard, 145
Tonkin Gulf resolution, Iraq War, Bush's
   use of, 91, 274
Torture: Abu Ghraib, 41, 283; as
   Cheney's policy, 92, 268–69;
   condoned by Republican Congress,
   26; as criminal act, 26, 98, 106, 197;
   fundamentalist view, 168; McCain
   amendment prohibiting, 283; torture
   bill, 35, 106, 239–40; Yoo torture
   memos, 228–29, 235
Totenberg, Nina, 149
Tribe, Laurence, 107, 115
Truman, Harry: armed forces,
   desegregation, 262; Bush's self-
   comparison to, 265–66; investigation
   of FDR, 212; oversight, example of,
   40; ranking among presidents, 75;
   steel mill seizure, 237; on vice
   presidency, 79; as vice president,

269–70; war powers, misuse of, 248–50, 249n, 315
Tuesday to Thursday Club, 31
Turley, Jonathan, 53
Tyler, Tom R., 303

Udall, Morris, 131
Ullman, Harlan, 14
Unitary executive theory, 102–10; and Alito confirmation hearing, 103–6; Clinton use of, 102–3; defined, 102–3; development of, 276; *Hamdi v. Rumsfeld*, 104–5; impact on Congress, 104, 107; judicial fundamentalist view, 164; legal scholarship on, 106, 108–10, 276–77; national security under, 102, 104–5; and signing statements, 116
United States v. Curtiss-Wright Export Corp., 238
U.S. v. Butler, 122

Veto: compared to signing statements, 110n; line item veto, 99
Vice president: historical development of, 79, 269–70; Mondale expansion of, 79–80; removal from office, 80; Senate, role in, 26, 269–70
Violence Against Women Act, 167–68
Virginia Plan, 208
Vladeck, David, 53
Voters/voting: independent, view of Republicans, 200; judicial fundamentalism, impact on, 172–73; voter ignorance/apathy, 185–89; voter turnout statistics, 187
Voting Rights Act (1965), 62

Wallace, George, 201
Wallace, J. Clifford, 285, 290
Walsh, Lawrence, 220–21
Walton, Reggie, 199
War: Iraq invasion. *See* Iraq war; presidential powers. *See* War powers, presidential; terrorism-based. *See* War on terror
Warner, John, 294

War on terror: abuses. *See* Enemy combatants; Surveillance, electronic; Torture; label, danger of, 230–31; law enforcement approach, 232–34, 234n; 9/11 Commission Report recommendations, 313; use of term, 230, 232–33; Yoo justification for, 229–34
War powers, presidential, 243–52; Bush's abuses, 75, 235–41; Bush's safety measure (torture bill), 35, 239–40; commander in chief, 87n, 88, 243–46; defensive powers issue, 250–52; extraordinary measures, examples of, 231, 237, 243, 245–46, 248; inherent presidential powers, false basis, 236–42; and Kuwait invasion, 89–91; radical Republican interpretation, 235; Truman violations, 248–50, 249n, 315; and unitary executive, 102, 104–5
War Powers Act, Cheney on, 83
War Powers Resolution (1973), 94n, 99
Warren, Earl: as judicial perfectionist, 124; retirement of, 127
Washington, George: and presidential power, 242, 267; ranking among presidents, 75, 266
Watergate: Cheney's view of, 82–83; impact on presidency/Congress, 93–98
Watson, Robert, 75–76
Waxman, Henry, 42, 53, 213
Webster, William H., 285
Webster v. Reproductive Health Services, 296
Wedge issues: defined, 64; and polarization, 63–64
Weisskopf, Michael, 223
Weld, William, 293
Weyrich, Paul, 148
White, Byron, 286
Whitewater, 96
Wiggins, Charles E., 285
Wilentz, Sean, 74–75, 77
Wilkinson, Laurence, 269
Will, George, 100–101
Wills, Garry, 291
Wilson, James, 53–54, 278

Wilson, Joe, 198
Wilson, Valerie Plame, 97, 198
Wiretapping: past presidents, 247–48,
    256; *See also* Electronic surveillance
Wolfe, Alan, 23, 23*n*, 29, 33–34, 42,
    45, 49, 60
Women's rights: judicial
    fundamentalism, impact on, 167–68;
    Thomas (Clarence) position, 147
Woodward, Bob, 6*n*
*Worse Than Watergate: The Secret
    Presidency of George W. Bush* (Dean),
    xi–xii, xiv, 8–9, 71, 270
Wright, Jim, 28

Yingling, Paul, 178
Yoo, Christoper, 108, 277
Yoo, John Choon, 228–36; background
    information, 228; misleading
    information by, 229–34, 251–52,
    312; presidential power, view of,
    108, 193, 235, 312; torture memos,
    228; war, justifications for, 229–34;
    on war powers, presidential, 92, 243,
    251–52
Young, Bill, 218

Zeigler, Jim, 54
Zernike, Kate, 265